JAMES THOMSON
1700–1748

A Life

JAMES SAMBROOK

CLARENDON PRESS · OXFORD
1991

Oxford University Press, Walton Street, Oxford OX2 6DP

Oxford New York Toronto
Delhi Bombay Calcutta Madras Karachi
Petaling Jaya Singapore Hong Kong Tokyo
Nairobi Dar es Salaam Cape Town
Melbourne Auckland

and associated companies in
Berlin Ibadan

Oxford is a trade mark of Oxford University Press

Published in the United States
by Oxford University Press, New York

British Library Cataloguing in Publication Data
(data available)

Library of Congress Cataloging in Publication Data
Sambrook, James.
James Thomson (1700–1748): a life/James Sambrook.
Includes bibliographical references and index.
1. Thomson, James, 1700–1748—Biography. 2. Authors,
Scottish—18th century—Biography. I. Title.
PR3733.S26 1991 821'.5—dc20 91-4380
ISBN 0-19-811788-4

Typeset by Best-set Typesetter Ltd. Co.

Printed and bound in
Great Britain by Biddles Ltd.
Guildford and King's Lynn

Contents

List of Illustrations   vi

Acknowledgements   viii

1. Scotland, 1700–1725   1
2. London and *Winter*, 1725–1726   24
3. A Rising Poet: *Summer, Newton, Spring, Britannia*; 1726–1729   47
4. Recognition: *Sophonisba* and *The Seasons*, 1730   81
5. The Grand Tour and an Establishment, 1730–1733   106
6. The Poet of Liberty, 1734–1736   128
7. His Highness' Man at Kew: *Talbot* and *Agamemnon*, 1737–1738   157
8. Censored: *Edward and Eleonora* and *Alfred*, 1738–1742   188
9. Courtship: Revised *Seasons* and *Tancred and Sigismunda*, 1742–1745   214
10. Last Years: *The Castle of Indolence* and *Coriolanus*, 1746–1748   248

Appendix: Portraits of Thomson   285

Abbreviations   288

Notes   289

Bibliography   318

Index   323

List of Illustrations

(see Appendix: Portraits of Thomson)

Between pages 32 and 33

1. James Thomson, engraving by Basire, 1761, after William Aikman, *c.*1725
   (Printed in Thomson's *Works*, 1762)

2. James Thomson(?), attributed to William Aikman, 1720(?)
   (Reproduced by permission of the Scottish National Portrait Gallery)

3. James Thomson, after William Aikman
   (Reproduced by permission of the Huntington Library)

4. James Thomson(?), by John Vanderbank, 1726
   (Reproduced by permission of the Scottish National Portrait Gallery)

Between pages 148 and 149

5. James Thomson with the Figure of Liberty, by Stephen Slaughter, *c.*1736
   (Reproduced by permission of the Yale Center for British Art, Paul Mellon Collection)

6. James Thomson(?), by Stephen Slaughter
   (Reproduced by permission of the Art Gallery, Leicester)

Between pages 162 and 163

7. Charles Talbot, 1st Baron Talbot of Hensol, by Jonathan Richardson
   (Reproduced by permission of the National Portrait Gallery)

8. James Quin, by William Hogarth
   (Reproduced by permission of the Tate Gallery)

Between pages 170 and 171

9. George Lyttelton, 1st Baron Lyttelton; artist unknown
   (Reproduced by permission of the National Portrait Gallery)

10. Frederick Louis, Prince of Wales, by Philip Mercier
    (Reproduced by permission of the National Portrait Gallery)

Between pages 250 and 251

11. James Thomson, engraving by Basire, 1761, after John Patoun, 1746
    (Printed in Thomson's *Works*, 1762)

12. James Thomson, after John Patoun
    (Reproduced by permission of the Scottish National Gallery)

Acknowledgements

My first debt is to the two notable Thomson scholars of the 1940s and 50s: Alan Dugald McKillop and Douglas Grant. McKillop's exhaustively annotated edition of Thomson's *Letters and Documents* (1958) has been a constant and reliable guide while Grant's *James Thomson, Poet of 'The Seasons'* (1951) has been a challenging model: I have been able to supplement Grant's information, but not match his vitality and humanity. Like Grant, I am also indebted to the earlier biographers, from Shiels, Murdoch, and Johnson, down to the prodigiously industrious Leon Morel (*James Thomson, sa Vie et ses Œuvres*, 1895). Recent scholars whose work I have found particularly valuable include Hilbert Campbell, Ralph Cohen, John C. Greene, Mary-Jane Scott, and Arthur H. Scouten. I have drawn upon the patient and courteous services of librarians at the Bodleian Library, the British Library, Edinburgh University, the National Library of Scotland, the Scottish Record Office, Southampton University, the Victoria and Albert Museum, the Beinecke Rare Book and Manuscript Library at Yale University, the Pierpont Morgan Library, New York, the New York Public Library, the Australian National Library, and the Library of the Australian National University. In addition, I have been helped by the following individuals: Dr Iain G. Brown, Professor Graeme Clark, Ms Jacqueline Duras, Dr Stephen Goss, Mr James Holloway, Dr Bill Hutchings, Dr Nicholas Muellner, Mrs Barbara Ward, Dr R. R. Wark, and the Revd Peter Wright. Finally, I acknowledge with gratitude the visiting fellowships I enjoyed at Magdalen College, Oxford, St John's College, Oxford, the Hawthornden Castle International Retreat for Writers, and the Humanities Research Centre of the Australian National University. These awards enabled me to write in agreeable surroundings and congenial company. I hope that what follows will not disgrace them.

I

Scotland, 1700–1725

THE future poet of the *Seasons* was a child of the manse. His father was Thomas Thomson, minister of Ednam; this is a village on the River Eden in Roxburghshire, two miles north of Kelso, close to the border with England. Thomas Thomson, born about 1666 at Ednam, was the son of a gardener, educated at the College in Edinburgh, licensed to preach by the presbytery of Kelso in 1691, and ordained minister of his native parish the following year.[1] The only contemporary account of his character is a brief, bland statement by Patrick Murdoch, the poet's college friend and biographer: he 'was but little known beyond the narrow circle of his co-presbyters, and to a few gentlemen in the neighbourhood; but highly respected by them, for his piety, and his diligence in the pastoral duty: as appeared afterwards in their kind offices to his widow and orphan family'.[2]

Thomas Thomson married Beatrix Trotter, of Fogo in Berwickshire, in October 1693: she brought some property to the marriage, for she was co-heiress of Widehope, or Wideopen, on the Kale Water, which flows into the Teviot between Kelso and Jedburgh; she brought aristocratic connections too, for she was a distant cousin of Lady Grizel Baillie, daughter of Patrick Hume, Earl of Marchmont. Lady Grizel wrote poetry, her social links proved useful to the poet Thomson when he first went to London, and she was a family link with an exciting and honourable Scottish Whig tradition. As a girl, she carried secret letters between her own father and the father of her future husband, both of whom were prosecuted for involvement in the Rye House Plot. The latter became known as 'the Scottish Algernon Sidney' and was hanged in 1684; the former lived to serve William III (as did Grizel's husband) and became a strenuous supporter of the Union and the Hanoverian cause (as Grizel's brother was also).[3]

James Thomson's Whiggism was bred in the bone; so, too, was his religious spirit, where the mother was as influential as the father. She is described by Murdoch as

a person of uncommon natural endowments; possessed of every social and domestic virtue; with an imagination, for vivacity and warmth, scarce inferior to her son's, and which raised her devotional exercises to pitch bordering on enthusiasm. But whatever advantages Mr *Thomson* might derive from the complexion of his parent, it is certain he owed much to a religious education; and that his early acquaintance with the sacred writings contributed greatly to that *sublime*, by which his works will be for ever distinguished.[4]

Four children were born to the Thomsons at Ednam: Andrew, baptized 7 May 1695, Alexander, baptized 7 March 1697, Isobel, baptized 4 January 1699, and James, the future poet, baptized 15 September 1700; he was probably born on 11 September, which is the date of birth given in Murdoch's biography. On 6 November 1700 Thomas Thomson was admitted minister of Southdean, a parish south-west of Jedburgh, at the foot of Carter Fell; his manse was a small thatched cottage. Here five more children were born: Margaret, Mary, Elizabeth, Jean, and John.[5]

Southdean, pronounced Sou'den, was the place where images of nature first impressed themselves upon the poet of the *Seasons*. It was a hamlet on the upper reaches of the Jed Water in Roxburghshire, about eight hundred feet above sea level on the northern slopes of the wide, bare, rounded Cheviot Hills, which carry their caps of snow into April. To the north the landscape assumed a pastoral softness as it fell away towards the ancient market town of Jedburgh and the rich dales of Teviot and Tweed, but everywhere the views were, and are, wide and airy. Douglas Grant's description of the special character of this Border region cannot be bettered:

Green and brown, and their various tones, are the dominant colours; the others are submerged and must be sought out; but to compensate for this uniformity, the effects of light and shade are more vivid and impressive than those of any other district. From the heights the volatile interchange of sunlight and shadow can be followed across the plain; the clouds massing on the horizon before they extend throughout the wide air, and the rain scud which strikes before their advance, can be watched as though they were an army manoeuvring; and the unstained clarity of a winter's day, when the air seems as solid but as lucent as crystal, can almost be touched. Each change of wind or weather is finely and immediately recorded in the variations of light. This landscape trained Thomson to observe and describe nature in a particular way, and it will be found that its peculiarity is exactly reflected in his poetry.[6]

Through Southdean ran a drover's track up to Carter Bar and the crossing into England some five miles to the south, though the exact whereabouts of some of the border was uncertain: land hereabouts was still termed 'disputed ground' as late as Armstrong's map of 1769. The hills were dotted all around with the ruins of sixteenth-century peel towers, fortifications for the defence of men and cattle. The Battle of Otterburn was fought in 1388 on the strategically important track through Southdean; the Scottish chieftains met in Southdean church on the evening before the battle. The 'massy Mound' of a Celtic Iron-

Age fort on Southdean Law appears in Thomson's *Spring* as a monument to the long history of border warfare now happily ended by the Union.[7]

This was a harsh landscape. The minister of Southdean wrote of his parish in 1794: 'The principal disadvantage is want of shelter, defence from the scorching sun in summer, and protection in winter from the piercing winds, frequent and violent rains, and destroying blasts of snow.'[8] The thin soil supported sheep and a little arable, but at the opening of the eighteenth century the system of holding and managing the land was poor: Daniel Defoe travelled in this region and commented upon the backwardness of agriculture compared with other parts of Britain.[9] Times were especially hard in Thomson's boyhood. An eighteenth-century Roxburghshire minister said that in Scotland 'from 1697 to 1705 the crops were inadequate to the maintenance of the population, that several thousands of the poor had actually perished of starvation, that as many had emigrated, and that multitudes were compelled to have recourse to unnatural food, as wild spinage, snails, etc.'[10] A modern historian adds: 'The land had not recovered from its troubles when the terrible famine of 1709 came to bring ruin on farmers and starvation to the people—the crops and cattle destroyed by continuous disastrous weather.'[11]

A population so subject to the vagaries of climate turned to religion. We may glimpse its temper in Defoe's description of a great field meeting of the old Covenanting sort, which he came upon when travelling in the Borders:

an old Cameronian, preach'd to an Auditory of near 7,000 People, all sitting in Rows on the steep Side of a green Hill, and the Preacher in a little Pulpit made under a Tent at the Foot of the Hill; he held his Auditory, with not above an Intermission of half an Hour, almost seven Hours; and many of the poor People had come fifteen or sixteen Miles to hear him, and had all the Way to go home again on Foot.[12]

By the time he had become a Londoner and a sort of court playwright and poet to the Prince of Wales Thomson had travelled a long way from such a place as Sou'den and such a folk as the Scottish Borderers, but his religious enthusiasm, imbibed from his parents, remained strong, albeit redirected; he was always sympathetic to human suffering, and he was always the poet of nature (especially of wide prospects and skyscapes) and of solitude in nature.

The Cheviot Hills gave him material for descriptions of nature's harshness and dangerousness in *Winter*; the 'sylvan Jed' provided, for instance, the salmon-fishing episode added to *Spring* nearly twenty years after he left Scotland and such incidental details as the Scottish red elder.[13] The whole wide landscape impressed upon Thomson's alert eye all those weather signs in the air and in the activity of birds and animals that bulk so large in the *Seasons*. *Winter*, the first published of the *Seasons*, opens with a reference to the poet's wandering through the 'rough Domains' of nature in his youth, observing signs of the brewing tempest, and treading the virgin snows: in all this 'nurs'd by careless *Solitude*'.[14] Most of his extended first-hand nature descriptions are explicitly or implicitly those of a solitary walker. Southdean was sparsely populated; though Thomson had brothers and sisters he seems to have been happy in solitude. John Moir, apparently drawing on first-hand testimony, wrote in 1777,

His attachment to rural simplicity and romantic solitude, was early and singular. Scenes, where nature wantons in the wildest irregularity, were homogeneous to his mind. While yet a child he has been known to steal away from his little companions, who sometimes found him strolling all alone among the brakes, thickets, the banks of streams, and the sides of hills; which even then seemed possessed of some secret enchantment, which corresponded to the soft inexplicable movements of his rising genius. From this sauntering and pensive habit he acquired an aukwardness of manner which never forsook him.[15]

Thomson may have received his early education at a parish school in Southdean, but about 1712 he was sent to the grammar school in Jedburgh, about eight miles away. Jedburgh was an ancient royal borough, a market town, with a castle and substantial town houses. The grammar school was a pre-Reformation foundation of some repute, but, as the old buildings were ruinous, the boys had their lessons in the south transept of the abbey church. Its picturesque, roofless Norman and Early Decorated nave and tower dominated the view as Thomson approached from Southdean, having passed through the relics of the ancient forest of Jedwood. The church was beside the market place and the abbey gate was the hub of busy town life. This environment was markedly more sophisticated than Southdean, but not without its simple superstitions, to judge by the story told locally about a Mr Brown, who was master of the school when Thomson was a pupil. It was popularly believed that Brown was drowned one night in the River Jed by a coven of witches, led by his wife:

Some of the Jedburgh folk who had been awakened by the noise heard him singing the twenty-third Psalm as they were leading him with a rope about his neck down to the water, and at the same time a company of fairies were observed to be dancing on the top of the steeple of Jedburgh Abbey.[16]

It does not appear that Thomson distinguished himself at school. Robert Shiels, the earliest biographer, writing in 1753, decares that the poet 'in the early part of his life, so far from appearing to possess a sprightly genius, was considered by his schoolmaster, and those which directed his education, as being really without a common share of parts'.[17] Thomas Somerville, who was minister at Jedburgh in the 1770s and spoke to former schoolfellows of the poet, collected the following anecdote of his schooldays: 'Being one day overheard to exclaim "Confound the Tower of Babel!" he was asked by the teacher what he meant; when he replied, "If it were not for the Tower of Babel there would be no languages to learn!" He was then studying Latin and Greek.'[18] For all that, his Latin was good enough to earn him exemption from the first-year course at the College of Edinburgh; Jedburgh was a 'Latin school', where Latin only was used during lessons.

Thomson had begun to write poetry before he left school. The Earl of Buchan, eager to link his beloved poet with his own country seat, declared in 1792 that it was believed that Thomson 'first tuned his Doric reed' at Dryburgh, 'with Mr Haliburton, of New-mains, a friend of his father's',[19] but this belief is not found in any other biographical source. The two first biographers agree that Thomson's early poetry was written with the encouragement of the scholar and poet Robert Riccaltoun, born 1691, who lived in Hobkirk, a neighbouring parish to Southdean. He was educated at Jedburgh grammar school and the College in Edinburgh; eventually he was licensed to preach in 1717 and at last presented to a living in 1725, but when Thomson first met him he was cultivating a small farm. Shiels describes him as 'a man of such amazing powers, that many persons of genius, as well as Mr Thomson, who conversed with him, have been astonished, that such great merit should be buried in an obscure part of the country'.[20] Riccaltoun published theological works, but published none of his poems over his own name. Thomson acknowledged that the design of his own *Winter* was suggested by 'some masterly strokes' in a poem by Riccaltoun; this poem may perhaps be 'A Winter's Day', printed as by Mallet in 1726 and as by 'a Scotch Clergyman' in 1740.[21] Riccaltoun undertook the direction of Thomson's studies out of school hours, 'furnished him with the proper books, corrected his performances; and was daily rewarded with the pleasure of seeing his labour so happily employed'.[22] He also criticized Thomson's early poetic efforts: it is reported that when he was asked to read the work of another young poet years later he replied: 'I would treat him as I did Mr Thomson, and still do all my friends in that way, viz.: to discourage to the uttermost of power indulging that humour, where it requires more judgement than everybody is master of to keep imagination and fancy to their proper province.'[23] The poet himself evidently believed in practical criticism, for, every New Year's Day, says Murdoch, Thomson destroyed the previous year's poetical compositions: 'committing his little pieces to the flames, in their due order; and crowning the solemnity with a copy of verses, in which were humorously recited the several grounds of their condemnation.'[24] The annual ritual could not, however, have resulted in a perfect holocaust, because more than thirty poems written by Thomson before the age of 20 survive.[25]

A clergyman better placed than Riccaltoun to advance Thomson's worldly career was William Gusthart, a friend to the whole Thomson family. Shiels tells us that Gusthart was 'Thomson's patron in the early part of his life, and contributed from his own purse (Mr Thomson's father not being in very affluent circumstances) to enable him to prosecute his studies'. After the death of Thomas Thomson, Gusthart 'was no less serviceable to Mrs *Thomson* in the management of her little affairs; which . . . required the prudent counsels and assistance of that faithful and generous friend'.[26] At this time Gusthart was minister of Crailing and Nisbet, close to Jedburgh, but was marked out for higher preferment, already having been deputed to congratulate George I on his accession. Recognized as a pillar of the Hanoverian establishment, he was translated to the Tolbooth Kirk in Edinburgh in 1721, going on to become a Royal Chaplain and Dean of the Edinburgh Chapel Royal in 1726,[27] advancement that he owed to those great Whig managers, the Duke of Argyll and his brother the Earl of Islay. In Edinburgh, Gusthart helped James's widowed mother when she moved to the city and after her death acted as a second father to the daughters.[28]

Gusthart's predecessor at Crailing and Nisbet was John Cranstoun,[29] who, from 1704, was minister at Ancrum, a beautifully situated village, or, rather, decayed burgh, on the Ale Water, which flows into the Teviot a little north of Jedburgh. Thomson was a visitor to the manse and must have shown his juvenile poems there, for the minister's signature appears on a manuscript collection of them.[30] Beyond the manse the Ale Water flows beneath a high red sandstone cliff containing a number of caves, one of which acquired locally the name of 'Thomson's Cave', because it was said that the young poet there 'frequently indulged his reveries'.[31] Whatever the truth of that literary association, it is probable that the 'well-known Cleugh', with its embowering trees and moss-grown cascades, recalled by Thomson when he was writing *Winter*,[32] was near Ancrum. The poet was friendly with two of the minister's sons; John Cranstoun, five years younger than Thomson, followed him in the Divinity course at the College of Edinburgh and for a while shared lodgings with him, but Thomson was on closer terms of intimacy with the older brother William Cranstoun, MD. Their closeness is apparent in the free and familiar letters written by Thomson around the great turning-point in his life, his leaving Scotland for London. William was sufficiently well-connected to provide letters of introduction when Thomson went to London and sufficiently wealthy for Thomson to ask for a loan after six months there.

Allan Cunningham claimed in 1841 that the merits of young Thomson were recognized by that notable Border family, the Elliots of Minto, 'at whose seat he passed some of his school vacations'; Sir Harris Nicolas in 1847 conjectured further that the Mr Elliot of London, to whom Thomson was given a letter of introduction by William Cranstoun in 1725, was probably a brother of

Sir Gilbert Elliot, later Lord Minto (1693–1766).[33] The circumstance of
Thomson's cousin and uncle being employed as gardeners on the Elliot estate
gave rise to a story told by the Earl of Buchan in 1792:

Thomson sent [Sir Gilbert Elliot] a copy of the first edition of his Seasons, which Sir
Gilbert showing to a relation of the poet's who was gardener at Minto, he took the book,
which was finely bound, into his hands, and having turned it round and round, and gazed
on it for some time, Sir Gilbert said to him, 'Well, David, what do you think of James
Thomson now? There's a book that will make him famous all over the world, and his
name immortal!' 'Indeed, Sir,' said David, 'that is a grand book! I did not think the lad
had ingenuity enough to have done such a neat piece of handicraft.'[34]

This is highly circumstantial, but Sir Gilbert is not named among the subscribers to the first edition of *The Seasons*, the 1730 quarto. Beyond these late
assertions and the Buchan anecdote there is no positive evidence that the Elliots
of Minto were directly associated with the poet.

There is, however, no doubt that the young Thomson enjoyed the patronage
of another local baronet. He was Sir William Bennet of Grubbat, who, as
Murdoch informs us, 'was highly delighted with our young poet, and used to
invite him to pass the summer vacation at his country seat: a scene of life which
Mr *Thomson* always remembered with particular pleasure'.[35] A letter from
Thomson to Sir William expresses such pleasure with a reference to 'your
charming retreat, whence I drew the first ideas of Beauty'; another letter
acknowledges that 'it was you who first distinguish'd my Genius, and stamp'd
all the value it has upon it'.[36] The country seat was Marlfield, on the Kale
Water, a tributary of the Tweed south of Kelso: it was close to Thomson's
mother's property at Wideopen, so perhaps the budding poet was brought to Sir
William's attention through Mrs Thomson's well-connected family. Bennet
was one of the leading Whigs in Roxburghshire; he sat in the Scottish
parliament from 1693 until the Union in 1707, and thereafter in the first
session of the United Kingdom parliament; he was the patron of several
Edinburgh poets, the most notable of whom was Allan Ramsay; he wrote verse
himself. According to John Ramsay of Ochtertyre (1736–1814), he 'bore a high
character for wit and genius, being regarded by the poets as a minor Maecenas.
But he was too lazy, and too fond of his bottle, to submit to the toil of
composition; his effusions, therefore, were mostly extempore.'[37]

Sir William Bennet supplied Thomson with a secular, Anglicized cultural
pattern very different, one imagines, from anything he could have found in the
manse. The surviving juvenile poems which commemorate their relationship
show Thomson in the uncomfortable and unlikely posture of a rustic, maladroit
Alexander Pope, addressing the Scottish equivalent of Sir William Trumbull or
Lord Lansdowne. They include a short 'Poetical Epistle to Sir William Bennet'

in which the addressee is hopefully likened to Augustus, some lines 'Upon Marle-feild', which constitute a rather scrappy contribution to the genre of the 'local poem', and a hundred lines 'Upon Mrs Elizabeth Bennet', full of awkward, indeed somewhat presumptuous, gallantry addressed to the patron's daughter, who was just a year older than the poet.[38] One would like to think that it was for poems other than these, poems now lost, that Sir William valued Thomson's genius. Thomson's English verse imitation of a Latin epistle to Bennet by William Scott is now lost, except for two lines in one of his letters to Bennet.[39] It is not clear whether Sir William's patronage of Thomson began during his school or his university days, but it continued until the patron's death in 1729.

Thomson was intended for the Presbyterian ministry, in preparation for which he entered the College of Edinburgh in the autumn of 1715 and spent the greater part of ten years there, but in this period from adolescence to early manhood a minister was unmade and a poet was created. It is said that the 15-year-old Thomson rode to Edinburgh seated behind his father's servant on horseback and was so appalled by the city that he returned on foot more quickly than the servant did on horse, declaring that he could study as well on the braes of Sou'den as at Edinburgh.[40] The story first appears in the nineteenth century; if it is true (as seems unlikely) Thomson was nevertheless back at College in time to matriculate at the beginning of the academic year.

Whether at home or at College in October 1715, he would have experienced the alarms of the Jacobite rising. An Anglo-Scottish Jacobite force under Viscount Kenmure passed through Jedburgh in mid-October on its way to defeat at Preston on 14 November. Sir William Bennet, charged with the defence of Kelso, prudently withdrew his militia when a superior force of Jacobites arrived, occupied the town, and proclaimed King James the Eighth. Jacobite raiding parties hovered outside Edinburgh, but the place was well fortified and perfectly safe once the Whigs had frustrated an attempt by traitors within to seize the Castle. The Lord Provost of the City was Sir George Warrender of Lochend, a prosperous merchant, a zealous Hanoverian, Member for Edinburgh in the United Kingdom Parliament: altogether the copybook Whig. Thomson would later become a close friend of Sir George's son Hugh.

The southern Jacobite forces in Kelso and around Edinburgh were scanty and ill-armed, and lacked any strategic direction, but further north the situation was different: until the Battle of Sheriffmuir was fought on 13 November there was a real threat that the rebellion would succeed. The Hanoverian army, under John Campbell, Duke of Argyll, was outnumbered four to one by the main Jacobite force, which would have swept into England had it not been commanded by 'a self-centred, monstrously incompetent poltroon',[41] as a modern historian has justly characterized the Earl of Mar. As it was, the Jacobite army, abandoned by its discredited general and the Pretender, melted away before its pursuers throughout the bitterly cold winter, while the Whigs in Edinburgh and London secured their hold upon government and patronage even more strongly than before.

The Earl of Mar's initial success in raising so widespread and potentially dangerous a rebellion was in large part owing to the Pretender's promise to repeal the Act of Union of 1707, which was still repugnant to many Scotsmen. The Duke of Argyll, though, embodied the idea of the Union. He was a leading Scottish promoter of the Act; a year later, testifying to the strength and unity of the new Protestant state created by the Union, he commanded the British infantry in the thick of the fighting at Oudenarde, with Marlborough as his commander-in-chief and the future George II playing a courageous part with the German cavalry; after his success at Sheriffmuir he became, with his brother the Earl of Islay, the chief manager of Scottish affairs for successive Whig administrations in London. Thomson had a Presbyterian upbringing, his first aristocratic patron, Sir William Bennet, was the leading Whig in a predominantly Whig area, so the events of 1715 and 1716 probably did no more than confirm the young poet's existing political inclinations. Among the consistently Whiggish political statements in the earliest versions of the *Seasons* may be found praise of the Union in *Spring* (1728) and of Argyll in *Autumn* (1730).[42]

The political climate of Edinburgh was predominantly Whiggish, but in every other respect Thomson's surroundings could not have been more different from the rural solitude of Southdean. The place he had migrated to was a walled city huddled upon a narrow mile-long ridge: it consisted of little more than one long street, running from the Castle to Holyroodhouse, with some sixty lateral, and in some cases precipitous, wynds or alleys forming a street plan resembling the skeleton of a fish. The city's growth in the previous two centuries had not been outwards so much as upwards in high, cramped 'lands' or tenements. When Defoe was there in the first decade of the eighteenth century, it could be said 'with Truth, that in no City in the World so many people live in so little Room as at *Edinburgh*'. Defoe further notes that the circumstances of 'a rocky and mountainous Situation, throng'd Buildings, from seven to ten or twelve Story high, a Scarcity of Water, and that little they have difficult to be had, and to the uppermost Lodgings, far to fetch', created acute problems of hygiene.[43] Every day the streets were as crowded as in other cities they would be at a market, a fair, a whipping, or even a hanging.

The cramped and unwholesome tenements provided accommodation for all ranks of society. Even after Thomson's death, when tastes and expectations were changing, the occupants of one 'first-class' Edinburgh 'land' or tenement are listed as: 'First floor, Mrs Stirling, fishmonger; second Mrs Urquhart, lodging-house keeper; third-floor, the Countess Dowager of Balcarres; fourth Mrs Buchan of Kelloe; fifth the Misses Elliot, milliners and mantua-makers; garrets, a variety of tailors and other tradesmen'.[44] Such a social mixture in the new circumstances of the Union generated its own excitement:

In the first decade or so after the Union a passion for literary and debating societies sprang up, and in these dark howffs [inns] in the High Street was engendered something of the spirit that was to give Scotland a brief period of international renown. It is not too fanciful to discern the impact of Edinburgh's peculiar society upon the Scottish Enlightenment of the eighteenth century. Its tall lands housed a cross-section of the entire society, nobles, judges and caddies [errand-boys and odd-job men] rubbing shoulders with each other on the common stair.[45]

They were rubbing shoulders with undergraduates also. John Macky observes in 1723: 'The Scholars are not in Commons and kept to strict Rules as in the Colleges in *England*, nor wear Gowns; they lodge and diet in the Town, as at the Colleges in Holland, and are required to attend at their several Classes from eight in the Morning till twelve, and from two to four.'[46] Thomson may conceivably have lodged between a dowager countess and a fishmonger, but one anecdote reported by Henry Mackenzie to illustrate his superstitious fears refers in passing to the cheapness of his lodgings: 'his circumstances obliged him to have a sharer of his humble apartment whom Thomson's late sitting up, reading or writing, much incommoded; but his chum contrived to force Thomson into bed by blowing out the candle and working on his terror for ghosts.'[47]

The influence of the College and the friends he made there may be seen throughout Thomson's later life and writings, but the thronging streets of Edinburgh town are reflected in only one or two early poems. 'Upon the Hoop' defends the hoop petticoat and tartan plaid against Puritan strictures. The plaid was used by a woman to cover her head and muffle her face in the street; so eighteenth-century council records 'abound in edicts against the use of this piece of dress, which, they said, confounded decent women with those who were the contrary'. Hoops achieved a less ambiguously immodest effect: 'In going down a close or a turnpike stair, ladies tilted them up and carried them under their arms. In case of this happening, there was a *show petticoat* below; and such care was taken of appearances that even the *garters* were worn fine, being either embroidered or having gold and silver fringes and tassels.'[48] Thomson's fascinated delight in the spectacle of hooped women sweeping along the streets of Edinburgh emerges also in the lines 'Upon Beauty', and the hoop is one of the attractions described in 'Upon Mrs Elizabeth Bennet'. A very different and more literally striking excitement of Edinburgh street life is the subject of 'Description of ten a-clock of night in the town'. This would-be

Swiftian poem refers to the common Edinburgh practice of emptying chamber pots into the streets from upper windows; it ends with the customary alarm call of pedestrians: 'For God's sake hold your hand till I be by.'[49] The crudely gallant adolescent author of 'Upon the Hoop' is perhaps discernible in an anecdote surviving from the 1770s in different versions, none of firm authority, which tells of Thomson making a hole in the floor of his room above the chamber where a young lady was to undress for bed, falling asleep while he lay in wait for her to appear, disclosing his presence by loud snores, and having his nose burned by a candle held up to the hole by the lady or her waiting-woman.[50]

A rather differently sensational anecdote is first told in the 1840s, with the claim that it originated with Thomson's contemporary, John Cranstoun (died 1790), and was transmitted by Thomas Somerville, minister of Jedburgh in the 1770s. According to this story, the poet's father was prevailed upon to attempt laying an evil spirit at Woolie in the parish of Southdean; but

beheld, when he had just begun to pray, a ball of fire strike him upon the head. Overwhelmed with consternation, he could not utter another word, or make a second attempt to pray. He was carried home to his house, where he languished under the oppression of diabolical malignity, and at length expired.[51]

This story is not found in other, independent accounts of the poet which draw upon local traditions, and there is no reference to ghosts or exorcism in a letter written on the very day of Thomas Thomson's death (9 February 1716) by a fellow minister who was with him when he died.[52] Whether the death was brought about by the devil or more natural causes, the event was so sudden that James was unable to return from Edinburgh quickly enough to receive his father's last blessing. Murdoch observes, 'This affected him to an uncommon degree; and his relations still [in 1762] remember some extraordinary instances of his grief and filial duty on that occasion.'[53]

Thomson duly came back to Edinburgh, where life was returning to normal after the alarms of the rebellion: the gates were unwalled, the new trenches levelled, the barricades removed, and, in December 1716, Sergeant Ainslie was hanged over the walls of Edinburgh Castle for having plotted to betray the castle to the Pretender. A more memorable event was the brilliant aurora borealis of 6 March 1716, described in Thomson's *Summer* (1727).[54] The dead father's manse was required for another incumbent, so Mrs Thomson 'consulted her friend Mr *Gusthart*', mortgaged her share of the Widehope property, and came with her younger children to Edinburgh, 'where she lived in a decent frugal manner, till her favourite son had not only finished his academical course, but was even distinguished and patronized as a man of genius'.[55] Whether or not James now came to live in the same apartment as his mother, younger brother, and sisters, the family circle must have been to some extent closed up again. A sense of close familial ties and big-brotherly affection speaks clearly through the lines on 'Lisy's parting with her Cat', which James wrote when his younger sister Elizabeth went away to boarding school.[56] This is probably Thomson's earliest surviving poem in blank verse; it is the freshest and liveliest of all the Edinburgh poems.

The College of Edinburgh had a far more liberal intellectual atmosphere than was found in Scotland generally and its political cast was Whiggish. This was the cultural inheritance left by William Carstares, Principal of the College from 1703 to his death in 1715. He had been William III's right-hand man in Scottish affairs and the architect of the Revolution settlement by which the Scottish Presbyterian Church was established; he was a zealous Whig and a proponent of religious tolerance, who did much to prise Scottish university education free from the grip of the fanatical clergy who once dominated the Kirk. In his time the Arts curriculum of the College was drastically reformed, so that, instead of 'regents', who took one class through all the compulsory subjects of a four-year course before beginning again with another class, there were specialized professors on the model of the Dutch universities.

When Thomson matriculated in 1715 he entered directly into the second-year Arts class, that is the Greek class taught by Professor William Scott, his schooling at Jedburgh being found on examination to have been sufficiently thorough for him to pass over the first-year class in Latin. College laws laid down in 1704 enjoined that:

The students are obliged to discourse always in Latin; as also, to speak modestly, chastely, courteously, and in no manner uncivilly or quarrelsome, but to entertain good, profitable, and pious conferences. Those who transgress, especially such as speak English within the college, are liable the first time in a penny, the next in twopence.[57]

Here might be a ready explanation of the Latinisms in Thomson's poetry, for this collegiate rule of Latin discourse was superimposed upon a vernacular that was itself already far more Latinate than the English spoken in England. Whatever the state of his Latin, it seems that Thomson fell behind his class, probably because of his return home at the time of his father's death. He was obliged to repeat his Greek course in the academic year 1716–17, before proceeding in the usual way to third-year Logic and Metaphysics under Professor Colin Drummond and fourth-year Natural Philosophy and Ethics under Professor Robert Stewart, which completed his studies for the degree of MA.

First impressions are important, so the two years in Scott's Greek class could hardly have failed to have some effect on young Thomson. Perhaps it was Scott who taught him to respect that Greek cultural ideal that was to dominate his work for the theatre and to colour many of his other mature writings; it is equally possible that Scott played a part in undermining Thomson's intention to enter the Presbyterian ministry. Certainly Scott proclaimed religious views far more liberal than anything Thomson is likely to have heard in his father's manse. The diaries of Robert Wodrow, an orthodox Calvinist preacher of the old school, contain some revealing observations on Scott and his colleagues, recorded less than ten years after Thomson passed out of the Greek class. Both Drummond and Stewart are praised for their 'gravity' and for 'recommending religion' to their pupils:

But I am well informed Mr Scot is quite otherwise, and turning intollerable. He stands not openly to tell his scholars that, next to the Neu Testament, Homer is the most religiouse book he knoues of in the world! When he comes to such places of the Neu Testament, in his Greek lessons, as relate to Christ's Divinity, he is sure to give them the most lax and loose sense.

Wodrow goes on to recount tales about Scott mocking the doctrines of the Trinity and of election:

He falls foul upon justification by Christ's righteousness; he tells his scholars, there is no justification but by obeying the commands of God, and any other justification than this is nonsense . . . Alas! what can be expected after such nurture as the boyes have when at their language and philosophy?[58]

Of Colin Drummond's teaching little is known beyond Wodrow's testimonial concerning its gravity and religious orthodoxy. A nineteenth-century historian of the College says it is probable that he

taught Logic and Metaphysics according to the old tradition of the College of Edinburgh, tempering Scholasticism with Ramism. How far any of the modern spirit, which was beginning to move in Edinburgh, was caught by Drummond we know not. But he belonged to the Rankenian Club, founded in 1717, among the members of which that spirit was fostered.

It was said 'that the Rankenians were highly instrumental in disseminating through Scotland freedom of thought, boldness of disquisition, liberality of sentiment, accuracy of reasoning, correctness of taste, and attention to composition'.[59]

There is little doubt that the modern spirit was afoot in the fourth-year class. Soon after the great curriculum reform in 1708 Robert Stewart 'dropped the Ethics and Aristotelianism in general, and became a Natural Philosopher in the school of Newton. It was a mighty change',[60] a change assisted by the fact that the new system had already been expounded for some years in optional arts lectures. This was first done by David Gregory; according to the *DNB*, he was 'the first professor who publicly lectured on the Newtonian philosophy', and later by his brother James, who succeeded him as Professor of Mathematics in 1692. A transcript of Stewart's lectures in 1724 survives, giving clear evidence that he taught astronomy according to Newton's system and taught it in such a way as to demonstrate religious truths.[61] This was the doctrine of Thomson's *Seasons*. Equally Thomsonian is the superstitious side of Stewart's intellectual character, revealed by his relating a story about witches to Robert Wodrow, that avid collector of dreams, portents, bewitchings, premonitions, and other remarkable providences.[62]

Thomson completed the Arts course, but, following the example of many Edinburgh students at that period, did not choose to graduate. Lack of a degree did not prevent him from continuing his studies; it was the practice of William Hamilton, Professor of Divinity, to admit students to his course without the formality of graduation, despite understandable protests by Professor Stewart.[63] So, in 1719, Thomson 'was entered in the Divinity Hall, as one of the candidates for the ministry, where, the students, before they are permitted to enter on their probation, must yield six years attendance'.[64] Another Jacobite rising in that year, with a Spanish invasion of the west coast of Scotland which ended in fiasco, brought short-lived alarm to Edinburgh, but can hardly have affected Thomson's studies.

In the Divinity School the old system of 'regenting', abolished in Arts in 1708, still continued; so it fell out that Thomson was taken through his entire course by Professor William Hamilton, a man of some importance in the Presbyterian Church of his day. Between 1712 and 1730 he was five times elected Moderator of the General Assembly of the Church of Scotland, twice during Thomson's college career; as adviser successively to the Earl of Roxburgh, the Duke of Argyll, and the Earl of Islay in the management of Scottish ecclesiastical patronage he was a key figure in the Edinburgh Whig establishment. Robert Wodrow, always a foe to new-fangledness, complained that Hamilton, having 'sett up to manage all things in this Church, so as to keep fair with England, and the Court, and the Dissenters at London, seems to have fallen in with every thing that tends to depart from the usages and principles of this church'. So, 'it's thought he is departed from the Calvinisticall doctrine, and the ordinary doctrine taught in this Church, though he hath the wisdom to keep himself in the clouds'.[65] For the orthodox Wodrow there was much in Hamilton's lectures that was unsound:

One of his scholars had occasion, in a discourse, to insist upon the absolute necessity of believing the doctrine of the Trinity, and its being a foundation point. This subject he handled with some zeal. The Professor commended the discourse, but cautioned against too much positiveness in that matter, since good and great men could not satisfy themselves in that matter, as to its fundamentality.

Wodrow adds: 'This is resented, and the hazard insisted upon, that when the necessity of a truth is quitt, the next step is to quitt the point itself.' As a result, says Wodrow, Hamilton's pupils 'are, generally speaking, full of latitude and loosnes in point of principle'.[66] Whatever allowances one makes for Wodrow's prejudices, it is clear that Hamilton was theologically liberal, perhaps as close as one could come to being a latitudinarian in the Scottish church.

Thomson always spoke of Hamilton with respect, and Thomson's Divinity classmate and lifelong friend Patrick Murdoch describes their teacher as 'a gentleman universally respected and beloved; and who had particularly endeared himself to the young divines under his care, by his kind offices, his candor, and affability'.[67] It is difficult to believe that Hamilton did not play some part in shaping the religious tempers of Thomson, who became theologically liberal to the point of deism, and of Murdoch, who made his clerical career in the broad Church of England.

Important as it may have been in his intellectual development, Thomson's study of Greek, natural philosophy, and liberal theology in the classroom was less significant than his informal education in the literary clubs which sprang up immediately after the Union and were devoted to the discussion and imitation of modern English authors. Referring to Thomson's student days, Murdoch writes,

About this time the study of poetry was become general in *Scotland*, the best *English* authors being universally read, and imitations of them attempted. Addison had lately displayed the beauties of *Milton*'s immortal work; and his remarks on it, together with Mr *Pope*'s celebrated *Essay* [*on Criticism*], had opened the way to an acquaintance with the best poets and critics.[68]

The biographer of Lord Kames, writing in 1807, dates the Scottish

taste for polite literature from the time that the *Tatler, Spectator*, and *Guardian* were published; the result was that [in Scotland] the attention of our youth, fresh from their academical studies, which yet retained a strong tincture of the antient school dialectics, was insensibly attracted to the more pleasing topics of criticism and the belles lettres.[69]

Needless to say, Robert Wodrow looked upon such developments with alarm:

the latitude and loosenes in many of the younger sort may be ascribed to the unhappy clubbs and meetings which, for many years, have been at Edinburgh, very much to the corrupting of the youth. From whatever this floues, it's certain that there are many sad tokens of wrath among many that are students of Divinity . . . there is nothing like meetings for prayer, conference on cases of conscience, or practicall subjects, nou for many years . . . and many meet in other clubs, and for drinking . . . and I am told severall of them go openly to the dancing school at Edinburgh, and are very nice and exact as to that. The Lord appear, and help, and pity this poor Church in the time to come![70]

John Ramsay of Ochtertyre, who was born in 1736, indicates a more insidious threat to Scottishness than mere secularization and moral laxity when he discusses the revolution in Scottish literary taste brought about by the diffusion of English books in Scotland after the Union. His remarks on the emergence of new writers after 1715 apply to Thomson:

These juvenile adventurers and their counsellors would soon see the impossibility of making a distinguished figure in the republic of letters without a proper attention to the graces of composition. Latin was by that time out of fashion, except in colleges. And for more than a century nothing of character had appeared in the dialect usually called 'broad Scots'. To render it polished and correct would have been a Herculean labour, not likely to procure them much renown. Nothing, therefore, remained but to write classical English, which, though exceedingly difficult to men who spoke their mother tongue without disguise, was greatly facilitated by the enthusiastic ardour with which they studied the best English authors.[71]

Thomson spoke broad Scots all his life; his written English was an acquired language which retained to the end a slight strangeness; so, for instance, Johnson's *Dictionary* definitions repeatedly indicate words in the *Seasons* which are not current English.[72]

One of the Edinburgh literary clubs of which Thomson is known to have been a member was the Grotesque Club, but nothing is now known of this society beyond Aaron Hill's reference to it in his *The Plain-Dealer*, number 46 (28 August 1724), when introducing what is probably the first of Thomson's poems to be printed in England. Retailing information from an unidentified Scots correspondent, Hill describes the club as

A Society of Young Gentlemen, most, if not all of them, Students in the University of *Edinburgh*, who from a Sympathy of Affections, founded on a Similitude of *Parts*, and *Genius*, have united themselves into a Body . . . Their Business, to express it in the Words of one of their own Members, is, *A Friendship that knows no Strife, but that of a generous Emulation, to excell, in Virtue, Learning, and Politeness*.

Of the other literary aspirants in the Grotesque Club, the most important for Thomson's later fortunes was David Malloch (or Mallet, in the later, better-known, Anglicized alias, which so aroused Johnson's scorn). Malloch was two years younger than Thomson, but more precocious. By 1717 he was a janitor in the Edinburgh High School, by 1720 he was resident tutor to the unruly sons of a middling gentleman in return for 'heating, clothes, and diet, but no fixed salary',[73] at the same time as he was studying at the college and making his mark in the Grotesque Club. Attracted by the noble prospect of tutoring the sons of the Duke of Montrose, at thirty pounds a year, he gave up his tutoring post in Scotland and, in the summer of 1723, took the high road that led him to England. At that time Malloch was inclined to agree with others that Thomson was a 'dull fellow' and 'the jest of our club', but he quickly and generously changed his opinion as soon as he saw what Thomson was capable of writing once he arrived in England; he then regretted 'the injustice I did him' in Edinburgh, by 'joining with my companions to ridicule the first, imperfect essays of an excellent genius'.[74] Malloch is permanently transfixed by Johnson's jibe that he was 'the only Scot whom Scotchmen did not commend',[75] but he became a good friend of Thomson, who always spoke of him with respect. Though Shiels wrote his *Life* of Thomson under Johnson's eye and perhaps under Johnson's roof, he attests that the intimacy between the two Scotsmen 'improved with their years, nor was it ever once disturbed by any casual mistake, envy, or jealousy on either side: a proof that two writers of merit may agree, in spite of the common observation to the contrary'.[76]

The same could not be said in the case of Joseph Mitchell; he seems to have been the chief arbiter of taste among Thomson's immediate acquaintance and had published poems in both Edinburgh and London before embarking, about 1720, upon a search for literary fame and fortune in England. Golden reports of his early success came back to Edinburgh; Malloch retailed such a report in September 1721: 'Mitchell is, I am informed, in a very fair character at London, and is valued by several of the greatest wits, as Mr Pope, Mr Watts, Mr Hill &c.'[77] It is possible that news of this sort encouraged Malloch and Thomson to take their chance south of the border. After Thomson had achieved some celebrity with *Winter*, Mitchell made a self-important public claim upon his friendship, implying that he had encouraged him in Edinburgh:

> I prophesy'd of Thee; nor blush to own
> The joy I feel, in making THOMSON known.
> Thy first Attempts, to me, a Promise made:
> That Promise is, by this Performance paid.[78]

This claim was published in 1729, by which date Mitchell was in his mid-forties, having gained a literary reputation only as Sir Robert Walpole's absurd laureate. Thomson was unimpressed: by now he recognized Mitchell for the dunce he was.

Younger fellow-poets at the College of Edinburgh included William Paterson and Robert Symmer, with both of whom Thomson maintained a friendship to his death. Paterson was about Thomson's age, Symmer five years younger: he is described by Malloch in 1720 as 'a boy of fifteen, and very sprightly'.[79] Paterson, like Thomson, was later a political playwright in London and shared Thomson's last government sinecure; Symmer contributed poems to the *Edinburgh Miscellany* and later made his career as a tutor in England. Another college contemporary whose lifelong friendship would be of even more significance for Thomson was Patrick Murdoch, who was a distinguished student of mathematics and entered Divinity Hall in 1721, two years after Thomson. He lived in England as tutor and clergyman, compiled and edited mathematical works, and wrote the most authoritative of the early 'Lives' of Thomson. There is no clear evidence that Thomson ever met the leading Edinburgh poet of his college years, Allan Ramsay (though Malloch knew Ramsay), or that he met the future author of *The Grave*, Robert Blair, who was his contemporary at the College and a fellow-contributor to the *Edinburgh Miscellany*.

As we have seen, Thomson was regarded by some as 'the jest of our club'. Murdoch suggests reasons why Thomson's earliest work was not appreciated by 'certain learned gentlemen' among his contemporaries at Edinburgh: 'Some inaccuracies of stile, and those luxuriances which a young writer can hardly avoid, lay open to their cavils and censure; so far indeed they might be competent judges: but the fire and enthusiasm of the poet had entirely escaped their notice.'[80] However, most of the poems and fragments which survive from Thomson's teenage writings display so little promise that it is hard to understand how they came to escape their author's annual burnings of his juvenilia. The longest, 'Upon Happiness', is a disjointed moral vision, to a large extent a paraphrase of John Norris of Bemerton, but it provides a glimpse of the orthodox Calvinism in which, one supposes, Thomson was brought up, and which he shed easily before he came of age as a poet:

> Here you'll behold upon the fatal Tree
> The GOD of Nature bleed, expire and die
> For such as 'gainst his holy Laws rebel,
> And such as bid Defiance to his Hell . . .
> Behold the GOD-HEAD just, as well as good,
> And Vengeance pour'd on Tramplers on his Blood.[81]

The shorter poems include sentimental amorous pieces, one of which, 'The yeilding Maid', totters timidly on the borders of lubricity; there are also versified fables, biblical paraphrases, and other moral and devotional poems; there are some formal pastorals and much conventional pastoral twittering in other descriptive pieces. The reader's impression of stock exercises on set themes is confirmed when it is discovered that an Aesopian fable versified by Thomson was versified also by a fellow-student.[82] Only now and then does it appear that Thomson is writing about what he has seen, as when, in 'The Morning in the Country', the shepherd throws his plaid around his shoulders, calls his dog, and then

> Around the fold he walks with carefull pace
> And fallen clods sett[s] in their wonted place.[83]

Three poems by Thomson, four by Malloch, and one by Symmer were printed in *The Edinburgh Miscellany: consisting of Original Poems, Translations, etc.*

By various hands, published in Edinburgh on 4 January 1720. In a letter of 5 October 1720 Malloch explains to a friend that the *Edinburgh Miscellany* 'was undertaken by an Athenian Society here, who received the poems, and published all they thought worthy of seeing the light'.[84] Perhaps 'Athenian' is to be understood in terms of general approval, rather than as the proper name of a society, for the Preface to the *Miscellany* itself makes it clear that the poems come from a variety of sources, printed and manuscript, and that some of the contributors are strangers to the compiler of the collection; this was conceivably a bookseller: 'We don't pretend to know every one whose Productions we have judg'd tolerable, and worthy of a Place in this Collection. But, if we guess right, the best of 'em are done by young People, at School or College.'[85] The only poem of Thomson's three which is of much interest in the light of his later development is 'Of a Country Life', a short georgic distantly modelled on Gay's *Rural Sports*. About a hundred lines long, in heroic couplets, it briefly reviews the scenes of the four seasons, anticipates some episodes of the *Seasons* in descriptions of a snowstorm and fishing, and provides the occasional anticipation of Thomson's distinctive vocabulary, when, for instance, the struck pike 'rages, storms and flounces thro' the Stream'.[86]

Meanwhile Thomson continued his Divinity course. That his intention to enter the ministry was taken seriously by others as well as himself is indicated by his being elected to a bursary by the Presbytery of Jedburgh on 2 November 1720 and being annually re-elected for four years, during which period he performed the homilies, lectures, and other required public exercises that would help to train him for the pulpit.[87] One of these exercises was remarked upon by both early biographers, for it seems to mark an epoch in Thomson's transition from future minister to future poet. Murdoch recalls that Professor Hamilton called upon Thomson to paraphrase and illustrate a psalm 'in which the power and majesty of God are celebrated'. He delivered this exercise 'in a stile so highly poetical as surprized the whole audience. Mr *Hamilton*, as his custom was, complimented the orator ... but ... told him, smiling, that if he thought of being useful in the ministry, he must keep a stricter rein upon his imagination, and express himself in language more intelligible to an ordinary congregation.' Shiels adds that this 'sublimely elevated' discourse was written in blank verse.[88]

Later biographers have speculated that the paraphrase was of Psalm 98, or part of 119, or 104.[89] Shiels writes of a paraphrase of Psalm 104, not in connection with the college exercise, and such a paraphrase survives in manuscript.[90] As it is in heroic couplets it is probably not the exercise itself; it is based upon the metrical version by Tate and Brady and it announces some of the physico-theological themes that would be developed in the *Seasons*. According to Shiels, this paraphrase was submitted to Riccaltoun for his approval, after which Thomson's friends were allowed to make copies. One of these fell into the hands of William Benson, the critic, who,

expressing his admiration of it, said, that he doubted not if the author was in London, but he would meet with encouragement equal to his merit. This observaton of Benson's was communicated to Thomson by a letter, and, no doubt, had its natural influence in inflaming his heart, and hastening his journey to the metropolis.[91]

He would have had further reason to hasten his journey if he had known that a poem of his had been printed and praised in London in 1724. However, the poem was not attributed to him until 1841, and there is some doubt as to it being his.[92] This poem is a blank-verse physico-theological meditation upon 'The Works and Wonders of Almighty Power', and is much indebted to Shaftesbury's *The Moralists* (1709).[93] It proclaims a complacent natural religion, where theological questions are wholly rhetorical:

> Can I *see* those *Stars*,
> And *think* of others, far beyond my Ken,
> Yet want Conviction of creating Power?
> What, but a Being, of immense Perfection,
> Cou'd, through unbounded Spaces, thus, dispose
> Such num'rous Bodies, All, presumptive *Worlds*?[94]

This poem was printed anonymously in Aaron Hill's *The Plain-Dealer* on 28 August 1724, as an example of the work of Edinburgh students. Hill writes:

To how surprizing a Degree these fine Spirits have succeeded in their noble *End*, let the following Sentiments declare; conceiv'd, and express'd, with all the Clearness, Depth, and Strength of an *experienc'd Philosopher*, by a Member of this *Grotesque Club*, who was in his *Fourteenth Year only*, when he compos'd, in Blank Verse, a Poem, now in my Hands; and founded on a Supposition of the Author's sitting, a whole Summer Night, in a Garden, looking upwards, and quite losing himself, in contemplation on *the Works, and Wonders, of Almighty Power.*—If this was a subject, naturally above the Capacity of so very a Boy, to what a Degree does it increase our Wonder, when we find it treated, in this Masterly Manner!

If the poem is Thomson's it may have been communicated to Hill by Malloch, whose much-admired ballad 'William and Margaret' was printed anonymously in *The Plain-Dealer* five weeks earlier. If Thomson wrote his age on the manuscript it is quite possible that he wrote '19' and that this was misread as '14', for it is very difficult to distinguish the two digits from one another in Thomson's hand.

Thomson's earliest surviving letter is dated 11 December 1724,[95] from Edinburgh, and is addressed to his old friend at Ancrum, William Cranstoun, who was now a physician. This letter shows the erstwhile son of the manse taking on something of the character of an Anglicized, sophisticated man-about-town, while asserting that he is too humble to be conversant with the beau monde:

had I been taught to cut a caper to hum a tune to take a pinch and lisp Nonsence with all the grace of fashionable stupidity then I could—what could I have done?—hardly write. but however I might have made a shift to fill up an half sheet with ratt me demme &c interspers'd with broken Charrecters of ladies gliding o'er my fancy like a passing Image o'er a Mirror.

Nature, though, has not made him 'a Shapely or a Sir Fopling Flutter'. He apostrophizes foolish women who are susceptible to the flattery of 'the flutter-ing generation' of fops: 'is it not witt that immortalizes beauty, that heightens it, and preserves it in a fresh eternal bloom? and did ever a Fop either justly praise or admire you?' He then reflects,

perhaps what I am railing at is well-order'd and if ther was such a familiar intercourse betwixt witt and beauty as I would have, witt would degenerate into softness and luxury and lose all its edge and keeness 'twould dissolve in sighs or burst in nonsense. Witt and beauty thus join'd would be as Shakespear has it making honey a sauce to sugar.

One may infer that Thomson was awkward with women and serious about poetry.

This letter was intended to begin a series that would provide a commentary on the Edinburgh scene: Thomson looks forward to 'a frequent correspondence this winter' and asks Cranstoun to 'settle our correspondence into some order and acquaint me on what subject you would have me write to you'; so it is surprising to find that his next letters,[96] only two months later, are to thank Cranstoun for letters of introduction to friends and relations in London as he waits for his ship to sail. Thomson finds the introductions from Cranstoun himself to be all that he desires. He is not overjoyed, however, on receiving nothing more than a recommendation to God from Alexander Colden, the elderly minister in whose Border parish lay the ancestral seat of the titled and influential branch of the Cranstoun family: 'I wish he had exerted something more of the layman on this occasion.' More recommendations are promised from other well-wishers, says Thomson, 'when I'm fixed on any particular view, which would make them more pointed and effectual'. It seems that the decision to go to England has been taken, or announced at least, rather suddenly, and that either he does not know or he is not prepared to state clearly the reason for this decision.

Murdoch, described by Thomson at this time (February 1725) as 'a treasure of a good comerade',[97] was in a better position than most to know what was in Thomson's mind. In the poet's biography he states that Thomson was 'conscious of his own strength' as a poet during his student days and 'began to turn his views towards *London*; where works of genius may always expect a candid reception and due encouragement'. Shiels, the earliest biographer, speculates that Thomson perhaps imagined the ministry 'a way of life too severe for the freedom of his disposition: probably he declined becoming a presbyterian minister, from a consciousness of his own genius, which gave him a right to entertain more ambitious views'.[98]

Whatever the lingering disapproval of secular poetry in the stricter reaches of the Scottish Kirk, the professions of minister and poet were not necessarily incompatible with one another in England, but Thomson's last letter to Cranstoun before leaving Edinburgh hints, through its agitated uncertainty, that his ambitions are not to be fully satisfied in the Presbyterian ministry: 'I have gotten severall recommendations, and am promis'd more afterwards, when I'm fix'd on any particular view, which would make them more pointed and effectual. I shall do all that's in my powr; act, hope, and so either make something out or be bury'd in obscurity.'[99]

Murdoch tells us that when Thomson went to England he 'received some encouragement from a lady of quality, a friend of his mother's, then in *London* ... And although this encouragement ended in nothing beneficial, it served for the present as a good pretext, to cover the imprudence of committing himself to the wide world, unfriended and unpatronized, and with the slender stock of money he was then possessed of.'[100] It has been conjectured[101] that this 'friend' of Thomson's mother was in fact a distant relation, Lady Grizel Baillie, even though it is likely that Lady Grizel did in fact confer a benefit on Thomson by obtaining a tutorship for him in the family of her son-in-law. Thomson obtained all-important patronage fairly quickly in London and was not without friends there. Indeed, it is possible that one of his brothers, perhaps the younger brother John, accompanied him on the voyage to England or was already there when he arrived. Certainly a brother returned to Scotland in June 1725, with a letter of recommendation, dated 31 May, saying that he had 'been improving himself a little' in London.[102] He was only one of the many Scotsmen who thronged to London in the wake of the Union in order to improve themselves and their prospects. In December 1725, David Malloch (who by now had improved his surname to Mallet, because, he said, 'there is not one Englishman that can pronounce it') wrote in comic exasperation,

Our country pours forth her annual swarms, increasing, inexhaustible. Good Lord! what strange, unseemly creatures they are too! I have seen three and twenty of my own acquaintances, who, I believe, will not be provided for these three and twenty years. But all the poor service I can do shall never be wanting.[103]

Mallet, though, was able to serve Thomson well with introductions; also he set an example of a young poet using the aristocratic connections available through his tutorship in a ducal household in order to further a literary career—a career launched on a new kind of poem. (In Mallet's case the new poem was 'William and Margaret', which would be as significant in the eighteenth-century romantic ballad revival as *Winter* would be in the rise of the romantic nature-descriptive poem.) Whatever were Thomson's precise intentions when he withdrew from Divinity Hall and sailed from Leith to London in February 1725, his career in England would follow a course not dissimilar to Mallet's, and more glittering.

London and *Winter*, 1725–1726

LONDON was immensely larger than Edinburgh. When Thomson arrived there in February 1725 it was far and away the largest city and port in Britain and the largest centre for shipping and international trade in Europe. The only Continental city of comparable size was Paris, but whereas Paris contained only about one fortieth of the inhabitants of France, London held one tenth of the population of England. Daniel Defoe, in his *Tour thro' the Whole Island of Great Britain* and other writings, never tires of expressing his delight and wonder at the pull of the London market on other parts of the United Kingdom. London was a magnet for people too: a modern demographer has calculated that one adult in every six in mid-eighteenth-century England was either living in London or had spent part of his or her life there, a calculation that leaves out of account large numbers of fleeting visitors.[1] The thronged, bustling, exciting, changing, and bewildering city of the *Tatler* and *Spectator*, Ned Ward's *London Spy* and Gay's *Trivia*, and of *Moll Flanders* and the *Dunciad*, was, for better or worse, a powerful engine of social change.

In the 1720s a great tide of building, which had begun to flow after the Peace of Utrecht, was still in full flood. Defoe notes in his *Tour* that

the vast Extent of Ground taken in, and now become Streets and Noble Squares of Houses, by which the Mass, or Body of the whole, is become so infinitely great, has been generally made in our Time, not only within our Memory, but even within a few Years.

So the face of London is now spread out 'in a most straggling, confus'd Manner, out of all Shape, uncompact, and unequal'.[2] Defoe devotes several pages to the new building on the east, north, and west of the old City of London, and to the growth in Westminster, to the north of St James's Park and Charing Cross. There the most fashionable new houses were being built in terraces and squares of the sort that would not be seen in Edinburgh until Thomson's nephew James Craig designed the New Town. One of the newest building developments was Hanover Square, the most prominent residents of which were wealthy, titled Whigs, among them the Duke of Montrose, Mallet's employer. Unlike Edinburgh, where a single tenement could hold a complete cross-section of social ranks, different areas of London had very different social characters. A speaker in Steele's *The Tender Husband* (1705) refers to 'the very different Nations of *Cheapside, Covent-Garden*, and *St James's*';[3] it so happens that in the space of less than two years from his arrival in London Thomson would live among all three nations.

It is likely that when Thomson first came to London he lived in furnished lodgings, probably above a tradesman's shop, in the area of what is now Trafalgar Square, because, in a letter of 22 April, he asks for letters to be directed to him at Forest's Coffee-House, which was a well-known resort for Scotsmen on the south-west side of Charing Cross.[4] Standing before Forest's door one could see the gate of the Royal Mews, the ducal palace of Northumberland House, the bronze equestrian statue of Charles I looking down Whitehall, and perhaps the spire of the almost-completed new church of St Martin-in-the-Fields; one could also see, as Johnson remarked, 'the full tide of human existence',[5] for Charing Cross was one of the busiest focal centres in a busy, crowded city. Here, at the western end of the Strand, Thomson was not too far from the fashionable quarter of St James's and was safely remote from the insalubrious haunts of the dunces. (Dulness, in Pope's *Dunciad* a few years later would sit in state at the *eastern* end of the Strand to preside over the heroic games of her devotees.)

Presumably Thomson's social life, like that of many of his contemporaries, was centred upon the coffee-houses. Steele observed in 1711: 'The Coffeehouse is the Place of Rendezvous to all that live near it.' Johnson was told just before he came to London in 1737: 'A man might live in a garret at eighteen pence a week ... few people would enquire where he lodged and if they did it was easy to say, "Sir, I am to be found at such a place"', giving the address of a coffee-house or tavern.[6] In the coffee-houses pamphlets and newspapers could be bought, borrowed, or read on the spot for a small fee. The anonymous author of *A Trip through London* provides a vivid glimpse of a coffee-house near Charing Cross about the time of Thomson's arrival in London:

I entered this *Three-half-Penny-Library*, amidst various kinds of Politicians, who were exercising their Chaps and Spectacles over the several *Papers*; in one Corner stood a Poet, and in another a Parson, who, I observ'd, went forth edify'd, without paying the usual Fee; being (as I was afterwards inform'd) admitted like a poor Whore at a Play, or an Author at a Nobleman's Table, *in Forma Pauperis*.[7]

Thomson's first call after he landed at Billingsgate was to wait upon Mallet in the Duke of Montrose's fine new West End house in Hanover Square. Shiels reports what happened on the way:

He had received letters of recommendation from a gentleman of rank in Scotland, to some persons of distinction in London, which he had carefully tied up in his pocket-handkerchief. As he sauntered along the streets, he could not withhold his admiration of the magnitude, opulence, and various objects this great metropolis continually presented to his view. These must naturally have diverted the imagination of a man of less reflexion, and it is not greatly to be wondered at, if Mr Thomson's mind was so ingrossed by these new presented scenes, as to be absent to the busy crowds around him. He often stopped to gratify his curiosity, the consequences of which he afterwards experienced. With an honest simplicity of heart, unsuspecting, as unknowing of guilt, he was ten times longer in reaching Hanover-Square, than one less sensible and curious would have been. When he arrived, he found he had paid for his curiosity; his pocket was picked of his handkerchief, and all the letters that were wrapped up in it. This accident would have proved very mortifying to a man less philosophical than Thomson; but he was of a temper never to be agitated; he then smiled at it, and frequently made his companions laugh at the relation.[8]

The truth of Shiels's story is confirmed in Thomson's earliest surviving letter from London, dated 3 April 1725, in which he thanks William Cranstoun for having obtained on his behalf a second letter of introduction to 'Mr Elliot'.[9] He then describes his reception by Elliot: 'he receiv'd me affably enough and promish'd me his assistance tho att the same time he told me (which ev'ry one tells me) that 'twill be prodigiously difficult to succeed in the business you know I design'.[10] A little later, on 22 April, Thomson wrote to his patron Sir William Bennet: 'I'm sorry to say I've had no success in my designs hitherto, and find that 'twill be very difficult to have any att all. But since I'm now engag'd, I shall make a thorough tryal; and fortune must either favour me or give me a flat denial.'[11] Thomson is no more explicit about his design here than he was in the February letter to Cranstoun, but it clearly has nothing to do with training for the ministry, because when he mentions such training in the early letters from London it is as an alternative to the 'design': it is a fall-back position. Thus, on 3 April to Cranstoun:

succeed or not I firmly resolve to pursue divinity as the only thing now I am fitt for. now if I can't accomplish the design on which I came up I think, I had best make interest and pass my tryalls here so that if I be oblidg'd soon to return to Scotland again I may not return no better than I came away. and to be deeply serious with you the more I see of the vanity and wickedness of the world I'm more inclin'd to that sacred office. I was going to bid you suppress that rising laugh but I check myself . . .

The 'trials' are the examinations and catechisms required for qualification in the Presbyterian ministry.[12]

Three months later, in July, having found employment as a tutor, he writes again to William Cranstoun:

I hope I shall not pass my time here without improvement, the great design of my coming hither, and then in due time, I resolve thro' God's assistance, to consumate my original

Study of Divinity; for, you know the business of a Tutor is only precarious, and for the present.

Thomson now regrets his mood of 'giddy discontent' at Edinburgh, when he had spoken slightingly to William's brother John about the study of divinity. The 'design' is here equated vaguely with 'improvement', something not incompatible with divinity, one would have thought, but the earlier references imply a more precise design: perhaps a tutorship, perhaps even the romantic ambition to have an independent writing career. We could perhaps be more certain if an important section of this letter were not fragmentary. It reads: '. . . contemptible notions of things at home and romantic ones of things abroad; perhaps I was too much infected that way, but I hope in the issue it shan't be the worse for me . . . ';[13] the words immediately before and after this passage are missing from both the transcripts in which the letter survives. Nevertheless the general impression is that Thomson's doubts about his design have grown to the extent that he sees it as romantic; he no longer thinks it necessary to defend himself against his friend's rising laugh at the thought of his studying divinity after all. He is resolved.

The resolution does not last. After July 1725 there is no further reference in Thomson's correspondence to the possibility of his preparing for the ministry, and there is no evidence that he tried to 'make interest' or carry out any other moves towards consummating the study of divinity. Some ten years after leaving his father's manse to go to college, and after a deal of vacillation, Thomson rejected the humble certainties of the manse for himself and threw himself into the life of a literary adventurer. Murdoch informs us that Mallet made him acquainted with 'several of the wits of that time; an exact information of their characters, personal and poetical, and how they stood affected to each other'.[14] In the April letter to Sir William Bennet Thomson duly adopts the posture of man-about-the-literary-scene, and reveals that he has already been introduced to Richard Savage:

I might say witt's at a very low ebb here, and being distributed among so many, not a grain falls to the share of every particular. Pope indeed subsists on Homer's stock or else he might come to be as destitute as his neighbours. — The scribbling riming generation (lord deliver us!) buzz and swarm here like insects on a summer's day, and are as noxious: so that every coffee-house shop and stall in town crawl with their maggots. one vengefull hornet (savage, if you'll indulge me a pun as his name) so plague'd and stung me yesterday, with everlasting repetition, as provokes me to this rude, perhaps, complaint to you. for my part I renounce the tunefull starving trade.[15]

Savage would continue to be vexatious, as a half-amused letter from Thomson to Mallet in the following year testifies, but evidently relations improved on further acquaintance and Thomson became more tolerant than most men with respect to this proud, unhappy, dissipated, difficult, and highly-gifted Bohemian. Johnson writes: 'Savage, who lived much with Thomson ... always spoke with the most eager praise of his social qualities, his warmth and constancy of friendship, and his adherence to his first acquaintance when the advancement of his reputation had left them behind him.'[16]

Savage may have provided Johnson with the story that, on Thomson's arrival in London, 'His first want was a pair of shoes';[17] but Thomson's earliest surviving letters from England make it clear that he was not penniless. The letter to Cranstoun on 3 April reveals that he had visited the theatre, by no means an inexpensive entertainment, no fewer than five times in the space of a fortnight, though he admits ruefully: 'my purse will not keep pace with my inclinations in that matter.'[18] Theatrical entertainments in Edinburgh at that time 'were violently opposed by the magistrates and ministers ... who prosecuted the players as rogues and vagabonds':[19] Thomson evidently revelled in the free atmosphere of London; he was drawn to the bright lights of the theatre as a moth to the candle. He writes to Cranstoun about seeing Barton Booth play Addison's Cato, the part he had created fourteen years earlier and that had made him famous: 'Mr Booth has a very majestic appearance a full harmonious voice and vastly exceeds them all in acting tragedy. The last act in Cato he does to perfection and you'd think he expir'd with the oh! that ends it.' He saw the 60-year-old Robert Wilks play Hamlet and play Sir Harry Wildair in Farquhar's *The Constant Couple*, a role *he* had created in 1699: 'Mr Wilks I belive has been a very fine actor for the fine Gentleman and the young Hero but his face now is wrinkle'd his voice broken and age forbids the youthfull cheat.' Thomson's 'risible faculty' was exercised by Theophilus Cibber as Daniel in Thomas Southerne's *Oroonoko*; but he was most excited by the actresses:

Mrs Oldfeild has a smiling jolly face acts very well in comedy but best of all, I suppose, in bed. She twines her body and leers with her eyes most bewicthingly Mrs Porter excells in tragedy has a sharp peircing voice and enters most into her charrecter. and if she did not act well she could not be endur'd being more disagreeable in her appearance than any of them. Mrs Booth acts some things very well and particularly Ophelia's madness in Hamlet inimitably but then she dances so deliciously has such melting lascivious motions airs and postures as indeed according to what you suspect almost throws the material part of me into action too indeed the women are generally the handsomest in the house and better actors than the men but perhaps their sex prejudices me in their favours.[20]

A rather more idealized conception of womanhood and an awareness of the power of great actresses would be combined with the themes and setting of *Cato* in the conception of Thomson's first play: his Sophonisba, played by Anne Oldfield, was in some respects a female Cato. Among the players he saw on stage within three weeks of his landing in London, Wilks, John Mills, Colley

Cibber and his son Theophilus, Anne Oldfield, and Mary Porter would all at some time act in plays written by Thomson.

Life could not be all play; the improvement which Thomson designed in coming up to London required financial support. So, like Mallet before him and his other Edinburgh friends Murdoch and Symmer after him, he became a tutor in a noble family. In a letter to Sir William Bennet on 31 May 1725 he announced that he had 'had the good fortune to fall into Jerviswood's Family as Tutor to Lord Binning's Eldest son. Whatever my encouragement, which I don't know yet, shall be, I'll have the opportunity of improving my self here in the meantime, which was what I cheifly propos'd in coming up.' (By 'encouragement' is meant stipend.)[21] Joseph Spence claimed, from conversation with Mallet, that it was the ever-helpful Mallet himself who obtained this employment for Thomson,[22] but it is likely that Lady Grizel Baillie was involved too, in view of the facts that the child being tutored was her grandson and that Thomson refers to the family by the Baillies' title Jerviswood, instead of by Lord Binning's family title, which was Haddington.

Lord Binning's son was at this time four years old and Thomson was teaching him to read, an employment which took him to live with the family, sometimes at Great Marlborough Street, close to Hanover Square in the fashionable West End, and sometimes at East Barnet in Hertfordshire, where they had a country property. From East Barnet on 20 July Thomson gave a somewhat disenchanted view of his tutorship to William Cranstoun: 'Now I'm pretty much at ease, in the country, ten miles from London, teaching Lord Binning's son to read, a low task you know not so suitable to my temper, but I must learn that necessary Lesson of suiting my mind and temper to my state.'[23] His state is such that, as we have seen, he seriously (but for the last time) considers adjusting his mind and temper to the renewed study of divinity.

Thomson's employment gave him leisure to write verse. At the end of a letter to Mallet on 10 July, probably from East Barnet, he writes, 'to fill up this letter I shall give you a few loose lines I compos'd in my last evening walk they may be once worth the reading but no more'. Such offhandedness is disingenuous, because what follows is the substantial first version of 'Hymn on Solitude'. Written in octosyllabic couplets and modelled upon Milton's *Il Penseroso*, it is an invocation to the protean personification of Solitude, as philosopher, hermit, shepherd, huntress, and lover, in whose train come the personified virtues of the 'sage and swain', innocence, contemplation, and religion, also the Muses. Solitude perceives, creates, and embodies the scenes of nature:

> Now o'er the meads and groves you fly
> And now you sweep the vaulted sky
> And nature dances in your eye . . .

> Your's is the fragrant morning blush
> And your's the silent evening hush
> Your's the refulgent noonday gleam
> And your's ah then! the gelid stream.

These lines are unpolished and unpruned ('silent hush' is, indeed, enough to make a poet blush), but the poem is not as casual as 'loose lines' would imply; Thomson is beginning to feel his way towards that special kind of perception in the *Seasons*, where subject and object interpenetrate: 'nature dances in your eye'. One might add that he thought the poem was worth more than one reading because he revised and enlarged it (from the 43 lines here) at least three times and authorized the publication of at least two variant versions.[24]

The 'ease' to which Thomson refers in the July letter to Cranstoun is the restoration of his composure after the shocking news of his mother's death on 12 May. He mourned her in a poem written, like most of his verse before 1726, in heroic couplets, and never published in his lifetime. Through its conventional praise of the 'mother and the saint' seeps a hint of guilt about his leaving home:

> When on the margin of the briny flood
> Chill'd with a sad presaging damp I stood
> Took the last look ne'er to behold her more
> And mix'd our murmurs with the wavy roar.[25]

The timing of brother John's return to Scotland, to set up a business in Kelso, may have been affected by their mother's death, for Thomson's letter recommending him to the notice of Sir William Bennet is dated 31 May.

The patrons Thomson was seeking for himself and finding in London were men of Bennet's type, that is, Scottish Whigs who dabbled in literature. Lady Grizel Baillie wrote Scotch songs; her husband, George Baillie of Jerviswood, was a Member of Parliament, a staunch Hanoverian, and a Lord of the Admiralty under George I. Their son-in-law, Charles Hamilton, Lord Binning, who was Thomson's employer, wrote songs, which, like those of Lady Grizel, found their way into printed anthologies; he and his father, the Earl of Haddington, were loyal Hanoverians, who fought under the Duke of Argyll at Sherrifmuir in 1715; by 1722 both were sitting in Parliament.[26] They were among the seven Hamiltons, probably not all kinsmen, who subscribed to the 1730 quarto edition of the *Seasons*.

Thomson's Scottish Whig connections in London soon brought him other introductions. Murdoch tells us that Duncan Forbes, the great Scots lawyer and minor poet, 'having seen a specimen of Mr *Thomson*'s poetry in *Scotland*, received him very kindly, and recommended him to some of his friends'.[27]

Duncan Forbes' daughter added more detail in a letter to the Earl of Buchan in 1791:

my Father having been Mr Thomson's first acquaintance & patron on his coming to London and the former having a numerous acquaintance amongst people of the first rank, and also amongst the Literati folk; he did not fail to bring Thomson forward as much as lay in his power, his first Introductions were to the D. of Argyle, the Earl of Burlington, and Sir Robert Walpole, to Dr Arbuthnot, Mr Pope, & Mr Gay.[28]

All these men, except Gay, were among the subscribers to the 1730 quarto *Seasons*; Argyll's example might have encouraged some of the ten other Campbells (not all of them kinsmen) who also subscribed; but it was only the introduction to Pope that would lead to a long and fruitful friendship.

Duncan Forbes was a protégé of the Duke of Argyll and an impeccable Whig. In the 1715 rebellion he and his brother, the Laird of Culloden, recaptured Inverness for the Hanoverians after the main body of Jacobites had gone south; as a Member of Parliament from 1721 he generally supported Walpole; his patriotism is praised in *Autumn* (1730); and in 1745 he ruined his estate in defence of the Hanoverian cause in Scotland.[29] His son John (the 'joyous Youth' in *The Castle of Indolence*) became a friend of Thomson's, as too did Duncan Forbes' clerk and confidential agent George Ross.[30] Murdoch says that Duncan Forbes introduced Thomson to the fashionable Scottish portrait painter William Aikman, 'who lived in great intimacy with many persons of distinguished rank and worth'. James Anderson, in a short Life of Aikman published in 1793, gives Aikman, not Forbes, the credit of introducing Thomson to the society of 'Sir Robert Walpole, who wished to be the patroniser of genius, Arbuthnot, Swift, Pope, Gay, and the other *beaux esprits*'.[31] Both Aikman and John Vanderbank painted portraits of Thomson in the late 1720s; at this time Aikman was living elegantly at the wealthy end of town, in Leicester Fields.[32]

Whoever made what introductions, it is clear that introductions to men of power and wit were made. Thomson's early acquisition of a well-placed patron may be inferred from the fact that by 3 April 1725 his mother had been supplied with a frank, so that letters from family and friends in Scotland could be sent to Thomson free;[33] this was most probably by arrangement with a Scottish Member of the United Kingdom Parliament. Aikman, Mallet, and Thomson were the first prominent group of Scots artists to prosper in England after the Union by assimilating themselves to English ways without losing their Scottish connections; their patrons were Scots Hanoverian gentry; they supported one another. When, in June 1726, Mallet wrote to a friend in Scotland about Thomson's newly-revealed genius, he reveals how a system of mutual help was intended to function; he writes that Thomson 'is now settled in a very good place, and will be able to requite all the services his friends have done him, in time'.[34]

Thomson was gaining admission to quite high social circles, but his closest ally in 1725 was still Mallet. When he sent the 'Hymn on Solitude' to his friend in July he referred to another poem, evidently already in Mallet's hands: 'you may take what liberties you please with my poem, and I'll thank you for it.' This may be a reference to one of the detached descriptive pieces which, according to Spence, were shown to Mallet and eventually combined to make *Winter*;[35] but the earliest certain reference to *Winter* is in a letter from Thomson to William Cranstoun about the end of September or beginning of October:[36]

Now, I imagine you seized with a fine romantic kind of a melancholy, on the fading of the Year. Now I figure you wandering philosophical, and pensive, amidst the brown, wither'd groves: while the leaves rustle under your feet. the sun gives a farewell parting gleam and the birds

> Stir the faint note, and but attempt to sing.

then again, when the heavns wear a more gloomy aspect, the winds whistle and the waters spout, I see you in the well known Cleugh, beneath the solemn Arch of tall, thick embowring trees, listning to the amusing lull of the many steep, moss grown Cascades; while deep, divine Contemplation, the genius of the place, prompts each swelling awfull thought . . .

Nature delights me in every form, I am just now painting her in her most lugubrious dress; for my own amusement, describing winter as it presents it self. after my first proposal of the subject,

> I sing of winter and his gelid reign;
> Nor let a riming insect of the spring
> Deem it a barren theme. to me tis full
> Of manly charms; to me, who court the shade
> Whom the gay seasons suit not, and who shun
> The glare of summer. Welcom! kindred Glooms
> Drear awfull wintry horrors, welcome all, &c

After this introduction, I say, which insists for a few lines further I prosecute the purport of the following ones

> Nor can I, o departing Summer! choose
> But consecrate one pitying line to you;
> Sing your last temper'd days, and sunny calms,
> That chear the spirits, and serene the soul

Then terrible floods, and high winds, that usually happen about this time of year, and have already happen'd here (I wish you have not felt them too dreadfully) the first produced the enclosed lines, the last are not completed.

None of the lines quoted here is repeated in quite the same form in the printed poem, but prose and verse phrases anticipate the invocation to philo-

1. James Thomson, engraving by Basire, 1761, after William Aikman, *c.* 1725.

2. James Thomson(?), attributed to William Aikman, 1720(?).

3. James Thomson, after William Aikman.

4. James Thomson(?), by John Vanderbank, 1726.

sophic melancholy in *Winter*, lending support to the conjecture that the germ of that poem was description and reflection in the 'Penseroso' mood; there are accounts of 'terrible floods and high winds' in *Winter*; finally, the longer verse passage in the letter anticipates the opening of *Winter*, not so much in its verbal parallels as in the confident tone of a poet stepping forward to take possession of new literary territory.[37] Thomson is probably writing from East Barnet, for he says: 'this country, I am in, is not very entertaining. no variety but that of woods, and them we have in abundance. but where is the living stream? the airy mountain? and the hanging rock?' He walks in spirit in the woods of Ancrum; he is word-painting the Scottish autumn and winter from well-known scenes of his youth.

Descriptions of the harshness of winter were not as uncommon in Scots poetry as in English. Such pieces are found as early as the beginning of the sixteenth century, but Thomson tells Cranstoun that Robert Riccaltoun's 'poem on winter, which I still have, first put the design into my head. in it are some masterly strokes that awaken'd me.' This poem has never been satisfactorily identified; the copy 'which I still have' was presumably a manuscript. A tradition recorded by John Richmond, then minister of Southdean, for the Earl of Buchan's Thomson celebrations in 1812, states that Riccaltoun's poem was 'on the Storm gathering around Rubberslaw, a hill in the neighbourhood';[38] this tradition is confirmed by Thomas Somerville, reporting, in 1814, his own conversations with Riccaltoun fifty years earlier. When Somerville's account was printed in 1853, Peter Cunningham added the claim that Riccaltoun's poem was the brief heroic-couplet piece entitled *A Winter's Day*, printed over Mallet's name in *Savage's Miscellany*, that is, *Miscellaneous Poems and Translations* (1726), and reprinted as 'Written by a *Scotch* Clergyman. Corrected by an eminent Hand' in *Gentleman's Magazine* 10 (1740), page 256.[39]

The letter to Cranstoun reveals that Thomson had resumed his playgoing, because he reports on a performance of Colley Cibber in *Love Makes a Man* at Drury Lane on 28 September. There is perhaps a certain ingenuousness in his mentioning so recent a theatre visit, in view of the fact that the primary object of this letter is a request to borrow twelve pounds to pay his debts in London; he expects to repay the money when his late mother's property at Widehope is sold. We do not know the fate of this appeal, because Thomson's next surviving letter to Cranstoun is dated nearly ten years later,[40] but it seems likely that Thomson was able to satisfy at least his more pressing creditors, for, within about a fortnight of his request for a loan from Cranstoun, we find him arranging to leave Lord Binning's employment and travel down to Hampshire to stay for a while with Mallet at Shawford House, a country seat of the Duke of Montrose.

Writing from East Barnet on 12 October, he tells Mallet that he has had enough of small children: 'Flesh and blood cannot endure, to be expos'd here, as in the Deil-house of a steeple, to the raging elements.' He would rather be a soldier, 'but above all, with an erected mind, I fly to improvement, I'm certain of, in your company: and which I, in a good part, want: particularly, as to Greek, and French. You're, as it were, my refuge: and I know the real pleasure, the being so will give you.' He is parting on good terms from his patron and patroness: 'they are very well satisfy'd I go, just now; if I imagine it more for my advantage', 'though', he adds: 'I'm affraid of little money from them.' He is evidently on good terms with the Baillies of Jerviswood too, because he asks Mallet to direct letters for him to their house in Great Marlborough Street; though the Baillies are out of Town, their man is arranging a stage-coach place for Thomson's journey to Hampshire in the following week. There is no indication in the letter as to what Thomson's position in the Duke of Montrose's house would be. He implies that he will be staying with Mallet for 'this season', indicating perhaps the whole of autumn or even winter; his remarks about improving his Greek and French, and Mallet's statement to Spence that he wrote 'winter pieces' at Shawford, also indicate something more than a brief visit.

The letter of 12 October ends with what is probably a reference to the writing of 'A Paraphrase on the latter Part of the Sixth Chapter of St Matthew':

'Tis a charming portion of Scripture you recommend; and worthy of the saviour of the world, the Mercifull Jesus. I dispatched mine on sunday night. perhaps if I had waited a little longer, 'till my mind was more disengag'd, 'twould have been better done–but while I mus'd, the fire burn'd within me. I shall show you it att meeting att which time, I expect some beautifull lines from you, on the same subject, according to your proposal.[41]

The 'Paraphrase' first printed in 1729 is an extended version of Matthew 6: 25–30, introducing references to the varied seasons in its elaboration of the gospel reference to birds ('the light Tenants of the barren Air'). Mallet was also making recommendations upon a more important literary work. Shiels says: 'Winter was first wrote in detached pieces, or occasional descriptions; it was by the advice of Mr Mallet they were collected and made into one connected piece.' This is also what Mallet told Spence.[42]

Thomson's *Winter*, in its first version of 405 lines, published in April 1726, is a more connected piece than the later *Seasons* would be. The natural descriptions form a regular sequence, as, for the most part, do the passages of moral reflection which arise, usually logically, from them. The poet proceeds from the 'last, temper'd, Days, and sunny Calms' of autumn, through that season's mists, when every branch has morning dewdrops, which,

> quivering, seem to fall away, yet cling,
> And sparkle in the Sun, whose rising Eye,
> With Fogs bedim'd, portends a beauteous Day,

on into winter, with storms, on land and sea, of rain and snow, all with increasing severity; the first bringing a flood,

> From the chapt Mountain, and the mossy Wild,
> Tumbling thro' Rocks abrupt, and sounding far;

the last, a 'whitening Shower' through 'the hush'd Air',

> At first, thin-wavering; till, at last, the Flakes
> Fall broad, and wide, and fast, dimming the Day;

finally, hard frost, breathed from the dark-red eastern sky, and a thaw. In these paintings from external nature, which constitute about two-thirds of his poem, Thomson 'gives back', in Hazlitt's phrase, 'the impression which the things themselves make upon us in nature'. Nature description of such particularity and exactness, and as the prime matter of a poem was new in English verse; its novelty and familiarity are noted by Johnson when he remarks that the reader 'wonders that he never saw before what Thomson shews him, and that he never yet has felt what Thomson impresses'.[43]

These autumnal and wintry scenes are vividly realized, and, though they are not localized beyond the poet's opening reference to the 'rough Domain' where he spent his youth, it is evident that all but the last are drawn from first-hand observation. *Winter* is the most Scottish poem that Thomson wrote in England. Allan Ramsay claimed in the Preface to his anthology of early Scottish verse, *The Ever-Green* (1724), that the work of Scots poets 'is the Product of their own Country ... Their *Images* are native, and their *Landskips* domestick ... the *Rivers* flow from our own Fountains, and the *Winds* blow upon our own Hills.'[44] Thomson would have known Ramsay's *Ever-Green*, published in Edinburgh the year before he left that city, and he had an immediate Scottish model in Riccaltoun's poem. John Armstrong's blank-verse 'Imitation of Shakespeare', first published in his *Miscellanies* (1770), is a long, mostly unlocalized description of winter, which, according to the publisher's note, was written at the same time, but independently of Thomson's poem.

The one descriptive passage in *Winter* not drawn from Scotland and direct observation is the thaw in the Arctic Ocean, when ice-fields break up with an awesome noise, bringing danger and fear to the weary, hungry crew of a ship, 'lost amid the floating Fragments ... While Night o'erwhelms the Sea'. Details of this episode of mental travel are drawn from accounts by Frobisher, Barents, and other explorers, whose deeds would increasingly fire Thomson's imagination, though an unwieldy Leviathan splashes into the description from the Book of Job, the scriptural text which contributes most to the religious-sublime rhetoric of other parts of the poem. Indeed, the overall tone and intention of the Arctic thaw passage itself owe more to Job than to Frobisher, for Thomson's chief concern is to assert that '*Providence*, that ever-waking *Eye*', watches over men even where nature wears its cruellest aspect.[45]

None of the interspersed passages of moral reflection has a Scottish cast. In the first of them, scenes of autumnal decay inspire a state of 'Philosophic Melancholy', akin to the contemplative-creative mood of Milton's *Il Penseroso*, which, in Thomson, bears the poet's swelling thought aloft to Heaven and prompts the spirit of social benevolence. Later reflective passages successively invoke 'Nature, great Parent', and 'Father of Light, and Life! Thou *Good Supreme*'. In his conclusion the poet directly addresses the reader, comparing the seasons from spring to winter with the passage of human life, but reminding him that winter will not finally shut his scene, because his prospect is the Last Judgement and eternal life. The moral reflections thus make a rising scale of devotion from approval of good deeds to the contemplation of eternity; but this pattern, if it is a pattern, is broken by a passage of forty lines in the middle of the poem, praising Virgil, Homer, and Milton, along with three ancient Roman and seven ancient Greek heroes who embodied the ideal of selfless public virtue. This pantheon foreshadows Thomson's later concern with political issues, but *Winter* as a whole is mostly in keeping with its devotional conclusion. Its logic is summed up in one of its invocations:

> Nature! great Parent! whose directing Hand
> Rolls round the Seasons of the changeful Year,
> How mighty! how majestick are thy Works!
> With what a pleasing Dread they swell the Soul,
> That sees, astonish'd! and, astonish'd sings![46]

It was clear to Thomson's first readers that *Winter* was a would-be Miltonic poem; the very choice of blank verse in the 1720s was almost enough to enrol one in the school of Milton. Johnson is correct, though, when he says that Thomson's 'blank verse is no more the blank verse of Milton or of any other poet than the rhymes of Prior are the rhymes of Cowley. His numbers, his pauses, his diction, are of his own growth, without transcription, without imitation.'[47] Certainly his pauses are of his own growth. He does not give himself the opportunity to emulate Milton's famous enjambement and caesura because he inserts a punctuation mark for every three words on average throughout the poem. Subordinate clauses of every kind are set off by commas, according to eighteenth-century usage, but single adjectives and adverbs are frequently placed between commas, giving a jerky, parenthetic effect. The reader moves through *Winter* slowly against a driving mingled hail of commas, semi-colons, colons, dashes, stops, and exclamation marks, so that punctuation helps to define a syntax which, in Geoffrey Tillotson's words, 'fittingly con-tributes to rendering the external world in all its multitudiousness and turbulence'.[48] Heavy punctuation can be combined with metrical irregularity and a sort of buffeting alliteration to enact the roughness of a storm, and then, with a succession of sibilants, a calm:

> Wild Uproar lords it wide: the Clouds commixt,
> With Stars, swift-gliding, sweep along the Sky.
> All Nature reels.—But hark! the *Almighty* speaks:
> Instant, the chidden Storm begins to pant,
> And dies, at once, into a noiseless Calm.[49]

This is the ending of a paragraph, where Thomson's pauses are again his own; for, as Saintsbury pointed out, he has a mannerism by which he frequently ends his paragraphs with 'curious end catchlines more or less identical in form'.[50] The next paragraph ending, only seven lines on from the passage just quoted, is 'And lay the medling Senses all aside'. The same formula concludes no fewer than four paragraphs earlier in the poem;[51] it may have been suggested by the famous last line of the first paragraph of *Paradise Lost*, but Thomson employs it twice as often in two hundred lines of *Winter* as Milton does in the first three books of his epic poem.

The diction of *Winter* has something of the Latin feel that one might expect to find in a poet with Thomson's Scottish education writing a Miltonic poem, for instance in the use of 'abrupt' and 'dissipated' in their primary concrete senses[52] (both defined in Johnson's *Dictionary* with citations from *Winter*).[53] The poem is mostly written in an elevated language, but has a lower register represented by such words as 'drizzly' and 'chidden'.[54] Significantly, though, both of these examples were refined away before 1728 in the very first stages of that long process of revisal whose effect is nicely summed up by Johnson: 'They are, I think, improved in general; yet I know not whether they have not lost part of what Temple calls their *race*, a word which, applied to wines, in its primitive sense, means the flavour of the soil.'[55] The only word apparently coined by Thomson in *Winter* is 'dimply', the product of a common eighteenth-century method of word formation.[56]

It is not known when Thomson's poem was ready for the printer, but Benjamin Victor, the theatrical historian, recalled that Mallet and he 'walked one November day to all the Booksellers in the Strand, and Fleet-street, to sell the copy'.[57] Eventually John Millan, a Scotsman who had Anglicized his name from MacMillan and recently set up in business, accepted it, and, according to Victor, gave three pounds for the copy; but if this was so he had bought only very limited rights in view of the fact that Thomson was able to sell the copyright of a revised *Winter* in 1729. Victor was writing fifty years later; some details in other parts of his narrative are manifestly incorrect, so he may be wrong about 'November' too; in any event, the publication date of the poem was

8 April 1726. Victor is not mentioned in Shiels's account, though Shiels agrees that *Winter* was offered to several booksellers before Mallet induced Millan to publish it. Mallet, as reported by Spence, confirmed this.[58] The bookseller Park Egerton, who succeeded to Millan's business, claimed in 1790 that Thomson actually finished *Winter* in the apartment over Millan's shop, next to the Horse Guards in Whitehall.[59] This is close to where we know Thomson lodged during his early days in London; so too is Lancaster Court, at the west end of the Strand, where Thomson was living 'in the year 1726, when he published his poem of winter', according to the reliable testimony of a neighbour and friend, the expatriate Scots surgeon William Robertson.[60]

At the time that Mallet was advising Thomson on the composition of *Winter* and arranging for its publication, he was advancing his own literary prospects by cultivating the acquaintance of Aaron Hill, a poet and playwright of middling talent, but a generous friend to poets and the centre of a well-connected coterie of writers. During 1725 Mallet wrote several letters to Hill 'under a feign'd name'; he also celebrated the leading woman member of Hill's circle, Martha Fowke Sansom, in an adulatory poem, part of which he showed to Thomson in July 1725. The poem was published in *Savage's Miscellany* in February 1726, under the title 'To Mira from the Country. By the Author of the celebrated Ballad of William and Margaret', along with 'A Winter's Day', said to be by the same author. This may have been the cue for Mallet's entry to the charmed circle, for, on 21 February he announces proudly, 'I had a message from Mr Hill to meet him'; Mallet reveals too that he has been 'made acquainted with Dr Young'.[61] 'William and Margaret', like 'The Works and Wonders of Almighty Power', was printed in Hill's periodical *The Plain-Dealer* nearly two years earlier, but neither Mallet nor Thomson seems to have thought this a sufficient pretext for an introduction to Hill immediately upon their arrival in London.

Mallet's introduction, once it was effected, was to lead to important literary relationships for him and Thomson, because Mallet sent a pre-publication copy of *Winter* to Hill, who replied on 2 April with effusive and well-turned compliments. As Hill intended, the letter was shown to Thomson, who promptly on 5 April addressed a letter to him in terms of what Johnson not unfairly describes as 'servile adulation'.[62] The letter opens:

Having seen a Letter you wrote to my Friend Mr Mallet, on Saturday last, tho' I cannot boast the Honour and Happiness of your Acquaintance, and ought with the utmost Deference and Veneration to approach so supreme a Genius; yet my full Heart is not to be repress'd by Formalities; and you must allow me the Pleasure of pouring forth by best Acknowledgments.

It continues in the same vein, and ends

If I wrote all that my Admiration of your Perfections, and my Gratitude, dictate, I should never have done; but, lest I tire you, I'll for the present rather put a Violence on myself: Only let me cherish one Hope further—of being, some time or other, admitted into the most instructive and entertaining Company in the World.

Hill gave an encouraging reply; so Thomson opens his next letter, on 18 April:

I receiv'd yours with a Soul awaken'd all to Joy, Gratitude, and Ambition. There is such a noble Excellence of Mind, so much uncommon Goodness, and Generosity of Heart, in every thing you say, as at once charms and astonishes me ...

   While I meditate your encouraging Lines, for a while, I forget the Selfishness, Degeneracy, and Cruelty of Men, and seem to be associated with better and more exalted Beings.

He ends 'ravish'd with the Hope, you give me, of your nearer Acquaintance'.

   The two men first met on 26 April; on the following day Thomson continues, in the same style, to thank his host:

There is, in your Conversation, such a Beauty, Truth, Force, and Elegance of Thought, and Expression; such animated, fine Sense, and chastis'd Fancy; so much Dignity and Condescension, Sublimity and Sweetness ... to descend from your Company, and mingle with the Herd of Mankind, is like Nebuchadnezzar's descending from a Throne, to graze with the Beasts of the Field.[63]

Perhaps we have no occasion to regret that Hill's side of this correspondence has not survived.

   Thomson thus gained his place in the literary circle surrounding Aaron Hill. Richard Savage was already of the circle; he was present at Thomson's first meeting with Hill,[64] an occasion which apparently gave pleasure to all three men. Hill had provided publicity and support in *The Plain-Dealer* two years earlier to Savage's claim to be the illegitimate son of Lady Macclesfield (a claim vehemently denied by the putative mother), and was still providing generous and frequent assistance in the shape of money, hospitality, solicited subscriptions, and corrections to his writings—this last form of help being altogether less welcome than the others. The other notable poet in the group before the accession of Mallet and Thomson was the Welshman John Dyer, who at this date had ambitions to be a painter. His 'Grongar Hill' had by now been printed:[65] its descriptive-meditative vein and Miltonic octosyllabic couplets are not unlike Thomson's 'Hymn on Solitude', though the two poems were written quite independently of one another.

   Whereas many groups of writers met at coffee-houses, Hill's generally met at his house or the house of Mrs Sansom, where they drank tea and engaged in platonic flirtations. When Thomson joined the circle Martha Fowke Sansom was in her mid-thirties and the object of much gossip, some of it self-generated. Her amatory correspondence with William Bond, an older member of the Hill group and joint editor with him of *The Plain-Dealer*, was printed by Curll in 1720 as *The Epistles of Clio and Strephon*. She herself was possibly the author of a romantic autobiography, *Clio, or a Secret History of the Life and Amours of the late celebrated Mrs S–n—m*; it is full of affectionate reference to Hill, written in 1723, but not printed until 1752, after the deaths of both parties. Dyer painted Mrs Sansom's portrait, and, along with Hill, Savage, and Mallet, wrote complimentary verses to her. She was generally addressed as Clio, though Mallet, in the passport-verses already referred to, called her 'Mira'. It was tartly noted in the *British Journal* on 24 September 1726 that the name of Clio 'has of late been so abused and scandalized, that I am informed she has lately changed it for that of Myra; and that a dapper Scotch gentleman . . . was the first that new-christened her'.[66] Benjamin Victor, who was of the circle too, recalled nearly twenty years later in a letter to Dyer, 'How many delightful hours have we enjoyed with that elegant lover [Hill] and his charming Clio! how like those scenes we read in our youthful days in Sir Philip Sidney's pastoral romance!'[67]

Thomson was no more likely an Arcadian than Savage; he was, as it happens, the only poet in the group who did not publish sentimental verse-addresses to Clio/Mira;[68] but his letters to Hill indicate that he was studying hard to acquire the flattering rhetoric of the Sansom–Hill salon. This was probably not the most congenial social setting for him (certainly not if we judge by his later well-known tastes, or by his references to Edinburgh alehouses in the first letter to Cranstoun), but there is no reason to suppose that Thomson was drawn to Hill's company merely by the hope that the older, well-connected man would further his literary career as he had furthered Savage's. Behind the pompous mutual adulation, there was evidently something amiable in the character and impressive in the conversation of this widely-travelled, versatile man of the world which attracted talented young men and made them warm to his company.

Thomson should certainly have warmed to Hill's considerable and un-qualified praise of *Winter*, particularly as it was his first poem of ambitious length and the first with his name on a title-page. As it happens, his name is there given as 'James Thomson, A. M.', but, as he had never taken his degree, he was not entitled to use these letters after his name, and never did in subsequent editions of any of his poems. According to some early accounts, *Winter* was very slow to obtain notice until drawn to public attention by a gentleman of taste, variously identified as 'Mr Whatley', Thomas Rundle, Joseph Spence, and Joseph Mitchell;[69] but the rapidity with which a Dublin piracy and a second London edition were published implies that Murdoch was nearer the mark when he wrote that the poem

was no sooner read than universally admired: those only excepted who had not been
used to feel, or to look for, any thing in poetry, beyond a *point* of satirical or
epigrammatic wit, a smart *antithesis* richly trimmed with rhime, or the softness of an
elegiac complaint . . . But, in a short time, the applause became unanimous; every one
wondering how so many pictures, and pictures so familiar, should have moved them but
faintly to what they felt in his descriptions . . . From that time Mr *Thomson's* acquaintance was courted by all men of taste; and several ladies of high rank and distinction
became his declared patronesses.[70]

Winter was dedicated to Sir Spencer Compton, who was in his early fifties
and had been Speaker of the House of Commons since 1715; he was, needless
to say, a loyal Whig. It is not known at whose suggestion he was singled out by
Thomson, for, as is admitted in the prose Dedication, written, as Spence says,
by Mallet, the poem's author was 'Unknown Himself, and only introduced by
the *Muse*'.[71] It may just conceivably have seemed in 1726 that he was in fact the
patriot that Mallet calls him in the Dedication, and that he was marked out for
greatness; indeed, greatness was thrust upon him when George II ascended the
throne in 1727 and asked him to be Prime Minister, but Compton, after some
delay, confessed his incapacity to undertake so arduous a task and allowed it to
be handed over to Walpole. He was created Baron Wilmington in 1728 and
Earl of Wilmington in 1730; on Walpole's fall in 1742 he became an ineffectual
and little more than nominal Prime Minister. He died in 1743, when his
achievement was mordantly summed up by Pope in a letter:

Three hundred thousand pound the sum total of his life! without one worthy Deed,
public or private! he had just sence enough to *see* the bad measures we were ingag'd in,
without the heart to *feel* for his Country or spirit to oppose what he condemn'd; as long as
a Title, or a Riband, or a little lucrative employment, could be got, by his tame
submission, & Concurrence. He lov'd no body, for (they say) he has not left a Legacy,
not ev'n to his flatterers: he had no ambition, with a vast deal of Pride, and no Dignity,
with great Stateliness. His Titles only must be his Epitaph; & there can be nothing on
his monument remarkable, except his nose, which I hope the Statuary will do justice
to.[72]

It seems that Compton's permission had not been sought before the dedication was made; certainly he did not make the accustomed recognition as
quickly as Thomson and his friends had hoped, so it was hastily determined
that ungrateful patrons should be satirized in commendatory poems that Hill
and Mallet were writing to preface the enlarged, revised, second edition of
Winter that Millan was preparing to publish only weeks after the first edition.
Thomson saw Hill's commendatory verses before 24 May and Hill's on 3 June;
Johnson states that Hill's verses were printed in a newspaper, but I have been
unable to trace such a printing.[73] A puff contributed to the *London Journal* of
4 June in praise of *Winter* dwelt upon the question of patronage, named

Compton, and delicately alluded to 'Want of Encouragement'; but on that very morning the patron had done his duty. Thomson wrote to Hill on 7 June:

I hinted to you in my last, that, on Saturday Morning, I was with Sir Spencer Compton. A certain Gentleman, without my Desire, spoke to him concerning me; his Answer was, that I had never come near him: Then the Gentleman put the Question, if he desir'd that I should wait on him; he return'd, he did: On this, the Gentleman gave me an introductory Letter to him. He receiv'd me in what they commonly call a civil Manner, ask'd me some Commonplace Questions, and made me a Present of Twenty Guineas.

Now he asks Hill to tone down his verses: 'As the case now is, one of your infinite Delicacy will be the best Judge, whether it will be proper to print these two inimitable Copies of Verses I have from you, and Mr Mallet, without such little Alterations as shall clear Sir Spencer of that best Satire I ever read.' Thomson's embarrassment is all too plain: he wants to keep Hill's friendship and he wants to publish Hill's praise of himself, 'the Applause of the great Genius of the Age, my Charter of Fame';[74] but to print the satire would be to bite the hand that, perhaps grudgingly, had just fed him.

Thomson had already written to Mallet, who was in the country, probably at Shawford with his employer; but it appears that when Mallet replied it was to the effect that he would not or could not revise his lines: they should stand, or be removed entirely from the forthcoming volume. In his letter to Mallet on 13 June Thomson exclaims,

Twenty Guineas—twenty Curses on them! if They serve me that Trick—I expected that our Names should have lived together, there, when Money, and all it's Lovers, shall perish—All the first Page might, still, stand intire, and the others fill'd out a thousand Ways—If you will have Satire; a Remedy the Age much wants, and which may be executed with a good Design, a public Spirit, and Success, I need not mention to You the Avarice, Littleness, Luxury, and Stupidity of our Men of Fortune; the general, barbarous, Contempt of Poetry, that noblest Gift of Heaven! Our venal Bards, as you have lash'd them already—our lewd, low, spiteful, Writers: Hornets of Parnassus— Operas, Maskerades, Fopperies, and a thousand Things. You might make a glorious Apostrophe to the drooping Genius of Brittain—have Shakespear, and Milton, in your Eye, and invite to the Pursuit of genuine Poetry—I have written to Mr Hill after such a Manner, as he cannot refuse me; so that I am almost certain of receiving another Copy of Verses from Him every Day.

Under this persuasion Mallet promised to alter his verses, but then, as Thomson explains to Hill about two weeks later, 'after several Attempts, he found it absolutely out of his Power; and, rather than lose them, I resolv'd to print them, as they at first were'.[75] When eventually printed in the second edition of *Winter*, Hill's revised poem proved no less severe than Mallet's in its satire upon ungrateful patrons in general, though neither is an attack upon Compton in person.

All this time the printer was waiting. The second edition of *Winter* was in the press by 13 June, when its author was still negotiating with Hill and Mallet; its imminent publication was advertised by Millan on 13 and 17 June; but in the event publication was not till 16 July. During the month or more that copy was at the printers there was some press correction which removed a compliment to Sir Spencer Compton from Thomson's new Preface to his poem, so that it harmonizes a little more with Hill's and Mallet's poems, but correspondingly less with Mallet's adulatory prose Dedication, which is reprinted unaltered from the first edition. The irregular collation of all surviving copies of the second edition indicates that the printer allowed for more commendatory poems than those eventually printed.[76] It is known that John Dyer was asked to contribute prefatory satirical verses, but, before 13 June, 'very luckily' he 'very handsomely excus'd himself'.[77] Three preliminary poems were actually printed in the volume: Hill's, Mallet's, and a non-satirical piece written by Martha Sansom at Mallet's request under her sobriquet 'Mira'. Thomson's Edinburgh acquaintance Joseph Mitchell printed a partly self-congratulatory address 'To Mr Thomson, the Author of Winter' in his *Poems on Several Occasions* (1729), but there is no evidence to suggest that Thomson wanted to include it in his own volume. By August 1726, and probably earlier, the two men were on bad terms with one another.

The text of the second edition of *Winter* is revised in many details and is lengthened from 405 to 463 lines, chiefly by additional foreign excursions where the reader is invited to view the Russian winter and shudder at the grave-digging wolves of the Alps and Apennines, 'Burning for Blood! bony, and ghaunt, and grim!' Also, by contrast, there is an added homely scene, probably recollected from Thomson's own youth, in which a hungry robin enters the house, and

> Eyes all the smiling *Family*, askance,
> And pecks, and starts, and wonders where he is:
> Till, more familiar grown, the Table-Crumbs
> Attract his slender Feet.[78]

The most considerable addition in the volume, though, is an ambitious Preface, nearly half as long as the poem itself, in which Thomson calls for serious poetry on lofty topics:

let POETRY, once more, be restored to her antient Truth, and Purity; let Her be inspired from Heaven, and, in Return, her Incense ascend thither; let Her exchange Her low, venal, trifling, Subjects for such as are fair, useful, and magnificent; and, let Her execute these so as, at once, to please, instruct, surprize, and astonish . . .

Nothing can have a better Influence towards the Revival of POETRY than the chusing of great, and serious, Subjects; such as, at once, amuse the Fancy, enlighten the Head, and warm the Heart. These give a Weight, and Dignity, to the Poem ...

I know no Subject more elevating, more amusing; more ready to awake the poetical Enthusiasm, the philosophical Reflection, and the moral Sentiment, than the *Works of Nature*. Where can we meet with such Variety, such Beauty, such Magnificence? All that enlarges, and transports, the Soul? What more inspiring than a calm, wide, Survey of Them?

In his exalted claims for the divine inspiration of great poetry, 'the DIVINE ART' that has 'charmed the listening World from *Moses* down to *Milton*', Thomson aligns himself with John Dennis, the most prominent contemporary advocate of the sublime; he also echoes the Preface to Aaron Hill's *The Creation* (1720).[79]

Thomson ends his Preface by declaring that he intends to write poems on the other seasons. It was probably this intention that prompted Millan to issue the second edition of *Winter* in octavo, rather than the folio format used for the first edition. All the individual Seasons that were separately issued in Thomson's lifetime by his two authorized publishers were in octavo too, so that they could be variously bound together to make a copy of *The Seasons* complete. Knowing that there were Seasons to come, Millan further arranged for the printing of three press-variant title pages for *Winter*, reading 'Second', 'Third', and 'Fourth' editions respectively.[80] This was a common booksellers' device to prolong the sale of a work of uncertain popularity, but in this case it also provided a stock of 'latest edition' copies of *Winter* to be advertised whenever another individual Season was first published.

We do not know what payment, if any, Millan made for the revised text of *Winter* and its long Preface, or how much Thomson derived from the sale of his late mother's property, or how he supported himself in the six months after he gave up his tutorship in Lord Binning's household. A week before Compton presented the accursed, but useful, twenty guineas the poet had returned to regular paid employment. On 28 May he went 'to reside at Mr Watts's Academy in Little Tower-street, in Quality of Tutor to a young Gentleman there'.[81] Mallet described it as 'a very good place', adding that Thomson's acquisition of it would enable him 'to requite all the services his friends have done him, in time'.[82] Presumably the goodness of the place was determined as much by the gentility of Thomson's (unidentified) pupil as by the high quality of the education offered at Watts's Academy. Thomson's position was in the academy rather than of it; he was, apparently, a private tutor engaged to superintend the education of a particular boarding pupil at school, under an arrangement similar to the one that took Jacob Jolter to Winchester College alongside Peregrine Pickle. One can only hope that Thomson had a more biddable charge. Thomson's new tutorship brought him eastward into another of the 'nations' of London; it provided him with an unexpectedly stimulating intellectual environment too.

Little Tower Street was the eastward extension of Eastcheap towards Tower Street proper. It is described by John Strype in 1720 as 'a spacious Street, well built and inhabited by able Tradesman', and 'having fair houses for Merchants'.[83] The whole area had been rebuilt in brick since the Great Fire; the slum-dwellers had for the most part moved to those suburban areas so graphically charted by Pat Rogers.[84] The wealthy families connected with court and government had moved west, so the 'City' was becoming almost wholly commercial in character. This place could not offer the social mixture of the Charing Cross area, where Thomson probably spent most of his first year in England, but it was extremely busy. The half-mile between Billingsgate and the Tower was the port of the world's greatest trading empire; all the wharves licensed for overseas trade lay between London Bridge and Tower Dock and much coastal trade came to land there too. The huddled sheds and cranes were edged by a forest of ships' masts and the streets were thronged with carts, tradesfolk, and seamen. Like other parts of London, this area was flavoured by a stench and filth that could be allayed only slightly by the tidal scourings of the river, but the commercial power embodied in its crowded bustle excited Thomson. In *Summer* (1727) and at greater length in *Autumn* (1730) he enthuses over the port's activity, where the 'loaded street' is choked with 'foreign plenty', where 'groves of masts' are like 'a long wintry forest'; he applauds even the 'sooty hulk' of a Newcastle collier coming in slowly to dock at Billingsgate coal wharf.[85] Commerce was always an important constituent in Thomson's patriotism; he spent nearly all his writing career in or very near London and London is the heart of his idea of Britannia.

Some idea of the curriculum and clientele of Watts's Academy may be gleaned from the advertisement regularly printed in newspapers during Thomson's time there:

At the Academy in Little Tower-street is to be learned every Qualification necessary for Business or Accomplishment, after a peculiar and approved Method; there being retain'd several Professors, capable to answer for their respective Trusts, to teach Writing, Arithmetick, and Merchants Accounts; all Parts of Mathematicks; and to give Courses of Experimental Philosophy, also the Classicks and Modern Languages; and to Foreigners and others, not well inform'd therein, the English Language, Drawing, Dancing, &c. There are also proper Accomodations for Boarding; and those that do not Board, may be taught either in Publick or Private, the Pupils being under proper Regulations, and the whole Education so calculated, as to answer the Ends of those whose Fortunes are not abounding, as well as of the Rich, the Charge increasing only with the Number of Qualifications to be attain'd; as may be seen at large in the Account of the Conditions and Terms, to be had at the said Academy. Letters are directed to

Messieurs Tho. and W. Watts: And from this Academy Noblemen, Gentlemen, and Merchants, may be always likely to be supply'd with Stewards, Clerks, or Book-Keepers, duly qualify'd, and capable to give Security for their Fidelity.[86]

What this prospectus does not reveal is that Thomson's colleagues included men of some intellectual distinction, such as John Bland, the calligrapher, Bernard Lens, the painter, and, more notably, James Stirling, friend and associate of Bernoulli and Newton, and one of the leading Scottish mathematicians of his time.[87] Watts's Academy was one of the many places where Newtonian science was being popularized in the 1720s. Lectures given by Stirling and William Watts included courses on 'the *Galilean* and *Newtonian* Philosophy; . . . 'Opticks, Explaining the Nature of Vision, of Reflecting and Refracting Glasses, and of Light and Colours, according to Sir *Isaac Newton*'s Theory', and 'Geography and Astronomy [in which] will be explain'd the System of the Universe in General, and the Terraqueous Globe in Particular; from whence will be given a distinct Idea of those Sciences, and their Application to History, Chronology, Navigation, Dyalling, &c. The Whole illustrated from Globes, Maps, Sphere, Orrery, and several other Instruments.'[88] Thomson's interest in Newtonian optics and astronomy, first awakened in Edinburgh, was deepened at Watts's Academy; so too was his interest in geography. The first fruit of these quickened interests was *Summer*.

3

A Rising Poet: *Summer, Newton, Spring, Britannia*, 1726–1729

THOMSON had probably begun to write *Summer* before he went to live in Little Tower Street, for he refers in a letter of 13 June to Mallet's reception of the opening lines: 'If my Beginning of Summer please You, I am sure it is Good. I have writ more which I'll send you in due Time.'[1] He writes of Mallet's poem-in-the-making, *The Excursion*, the idea of which strikes him 'vehemently', and he modestly compares his own efforts with his friend's: 'How wild you sing, while I, here, warble like a City-Linnet, in a Cage.' In a letter to Hill accompanying the newly published second edition of *Winter* Thomson transcribed a draft of what would become lines 393–402 of the first edition of *Summer*;[2] then in a series of letters to Mallet in August he discussed his own new poem and *The Excursion* as the two friends exchanged draft passages. A draft of lines 183–306 probably accompanied Thomson's letter of 2 August:

In the enclosed Sheets of Summer, I raise the Sun to nine, or ten, a-clock; touch lightly on his withering of Flowers: give a Groupe of rural Images: make an Excursion into the Insect Kingdom; and conclude with some suitable Reflections—I have written a good Deal more.

In the same letter he thanked Mallet for the 'Hints of the Saphire, Emerauld, Ruby, &c', which would be worked up into lines 132–44, and proposed some sublime scenes and amazing prospects for inclusion in Mallet's poem.[3]

From the next letter on 11 August it appears that Mallet had now questioned the original plan 'to contract the Season into a Day'; but Thomson declares it is now too late to change it, because 'I am so far advanced, having writ three Parts of Four'. He continues,

We intirely agree from the Noon-Day Retreat to the Evening. I have already writen of Shade, and Gloom, and Woodland Spirits, &c exactly as You hint more than a Week ago. Verdure, and Flowers, belong to the Spring; and Fruits to the Autumn; and therfor not to be anticipated. I design towards the End of my Poem to take one short Glance of Corn-Fields ripe for the Sickle, as the Limit of my Performance I thank you heartily for your Hint about personizing of Inspiration. It strikes me—Next Post I will send you a Sheet, or two more.[4]

In the printed text of the first edition personized inspiration is mentioned at line 15, and passages on the noon-day retreat, shade, gloom, and woodland spirits are found between lines 345 and 450.

Sending more drafts to Mallet towards the end of August, Thomson writes,

They contain a Panegyric on Brittain, which may perhaps contribute to make my Poem popular. The English People are not a little vain of Themselves, and their Country. Brittania too includes our native Country, Scotland. After this I make an Excursion into Africa, which I intersperse, and conclude with some Reflections—What remains of my Poem is a Description of Thunder, and the Evening. Thunder I have writ, and am just now agreeably engag'd with the Evening. The Beginning of the Sheets I have sent You, at this Time, connects with the Cataract.[5]

The description of the cataract begins at line 456 of the printed text, the description of thunder at 736, and the description of evening at 939. With the lengthy panegyric on Britain (lines 498–609) and the longer excursion into Africa (610–735) *Summer* becomes expansive in more senses than one; with this growth Mallet's objections to the framework of the single summer's day appear more and more justifiable. Though Thomson tells Mallet he has already written of thunder he makes no specific mention of Celadon and Amelia (lines 827–76), so perhaps this, the first of the interpolated stories in the *Seasons*, was an afterthought designed to supply human drama and narrative interest, hitherto lacking.

Whether or not this story is an afterthought, the letters to Mallet indicate that Thomson is working quickly and to a plan; on 2 August he writes: 'I am resolved not to correct till I have first rough-writ the whole.' He is full of self-confidence; although he flatters his friends, he does not allow them to dictate the way he writes. So, when he tells Mallet on 11 August about a convivial evening with William Aikman, he observes that Aikman's 'Reflections on my Writings are very good; but He does not, in Them, regard the Turn of my Genius enough. Should I alter my Way, I would write poorly. I must chuse, what appears to me the most significant Epithet or I cannot, with any Heart, proceed.'[6]

After due allowance has been made for flattery, Thomson's comments on *The Excursion* throw some light on his own poetic ambitions.

My Idea of your Poem is a Description of the grand Works of Nature, raised, and animated by moral, and sublime, Reflections. Therfor, befor You quit this Earth, You ought to leave no great Scene unvisited: Eruptions, Earthquakes, the Sea wrought into a horrible Tempest, the Alps amidst whose amazing Prospects, how pleasing must that be of a deep Valley, covered with all the tender Profusion of the Spring. Here if You could insert a Sketch of the Deluge, what more affecting, and noble? Sublimity must be the Characteristic of your Peice . . . .

There is an inimitable Mixture of animated Simplicity, and chastised Sublimity in what You write. It strikes one forcibly, at first, and yet still unfolds brighter, penetrates to the Heart, and yet still mixes deeper. As you write, in your former agreeable Letter, You every Day converse with the Sages, and the Heroes, of Antiquity. You think like Them too, your Bosom swells with the same divine Ambition, and would, if in the same Circumstances display the same heroic Vertues, that lye all glowing at your Heart. This I venture to affirm on the truest Knowledge, and let Me add Sympathy of Nature. Trust me, my Freind! I could run with You the Race of Glory, if Heaven would permit.

He quotes 'The rough Rock rises bleak, and chills the Sight' and adds, 'This is a very full, natural, dismal, Picture. It rises even abrupt in the Poem, and that too with some surprize. I am not only chill'd, but shiver at the Sight.'[7]

The ideal of sublimity underlying these comments and implicit, too, in Thomson's Preface to *Winter* could almost be regarded as the critical property of John Dennis at this time, so it is not surprizing to find Thomson attempting to cultivate Dennis's acquaintance. On 15 August Savage told Mallet that he had recently enjoyed a three-day visit by Dennis; this may have prompted Thomson to act. At the end of that month he reported to Mallet, 'I writ to Dennis a Letter on Journals, but have not received an Answer. He bid Millan last Day give his Service to Me, and thank Me for my Letter.'[8]

Thomson's position as a rising poet was recognized by his being singled out for attack in the first of a series of satirical essays on the 'false-Sublime', printed in the *British Journal* on 20 August 1726. Its author ironically praises the 'Inventors of a Style, which, without fettering Words with Sense or Meaning, makes a sonorous rumbling Noise' and proposes for the post of Secretary to the Brotherhood of these 'sublime Penners':

my very good Friend the Author of *Winter*, whom I think every Way qualified for so important a Trust; but if the Brotherhood should imagine, upon reading his Poem, that his Excellence in the Sublime-obscure is not sufficient, I can assure them that the Author of the *Preface* is able to atone for that Want by a Mastery in the Flat-unintelligible.

Thomson told Mallet that he suspected this essay to be the work of 'that Planet-blasted Fool' (as he calls him), Joseph Mitchell, who elsewhere in this same letter is referred to as 'our present Blockhead Laureat, or Laureat blockhead'. The 'Laureat' jibe alludes to the the fact that a year earlier Mitchell had published a ridiculous verse-petition addressed to Walpole, asking to be elevated to the dignity of Poet-Laureate in Scotland. Mitchell's name also heads Thomson's list of dunces, when he refers to 'the lowest Depth of the poetical Tophet, prepared, of Old, for Mitchel, Morrice, Rook, Cook,

Beckingham, and a long &c'. [9] The poets' quarrel was sufficiently well known to be the subject of an anecdote by Shiels many years later. Shiels reports that Mitchell responded to Thomson's gift of a copy of *Winter* with the couplet:

> Beauties and faults so thick lye scattered here,
> Those I could read, if these were not so near.

Thomson answered extempore:

> Why not all faults, injurious Mitchell; why
> Appears one beauty to thy blasted eye;
> Damnation worse than thine, if worse can be,
> Is all I ask, and all I want from thee.

Shiels continues, 'Upon a friend remonstrating to Mr Thomson, that the expression of blasted eye would look like a personal reflexion, as Mr Mitchell had really that misfortune, he changed the epithet blasted into blasting.'[10] The echo of 'blasted' in Thomson's letter to Mallet gives some warrant for the probability of this story.

The August letters to Mallet contain one teasing reference to Thomson's private life: 'What you write about——is very diverting. She can make You sigh for all that, when You think upon Her. Perhaps I may tell You in my next whether or not we design to consummate our unfinisht Loves, and transmit You a Letter I received yesterday.'[11] Léon Morel detects here an echo of Buckingham's *The Rehearsal*:

> Boar beckons sow to trot in chestnut groves,
> And there consummate their unfinished loves.

He comments, 'ce souvenir indique suffisament que les amours dont parle ici Thomson n'ont rien de platonique'.[12] The lady has not been identified and nothing is known about her relationships with Thomson and Mallet.

Thomson's correspondence with Aaron Hill continued in the accustomed adulatory vein. In August Hill set out on a journey to Scotland, leaving London in great style in his own coach and six. Having arrived at Inverness, he wrote to Savage, making favourable mention of Thomson; Savage duly showed the letter to Thomson, who wrote to Hill on 20 October,

Every Muse, every Virtue, here, languishes for your Return: To me your Absence would be much severer, if my partial Sympathy in the Happiness of my native Country did not alleviate the Misfortune. I congratulate her on the Presence of such a kind Inspirer, and candid Observer: *There*, you may chance to find, in that neglected Corner of the World, depress'd Merit, uninform'd Beauty, and good Sense cloath'd in the Rags of Language.[13]

Perhaps Thomson's desire to ingratiate himself with an English patron induces him to depreciate the language of his own countrymen, but it does seem that he believed Scots was not a suitable language for serious poetry. Although he spoke with a Scots accent to the end of his life, the diction of his poetry is Scottish for the most part only to the extent that it is Latinate. *Winter* is virtually free of Scotticisms; so is the much longer poem of *Summer*, which Thomson finished before the end of 1726.

The language of *Summer* is more conspicuously Latinate than that of *Winter*. To take only the beginning and ending of the poem, such words as 'impregn'd', 'fluctuating', 'erroneous', 'conglob'd', and 'contagious' occur. They are part of the language of science which is Thomson's new interest in this poem; they occur also in *Paradise Lost*. Thomson introduces his own Latinisms, such as 'relucent', for which Johnson's *Dictionary* cites only *Summer*, and 'elucent', which is not in Johnson's *Dictionary* or the *NED*, or, indeed, later editions of *Summer*. There is more of what an eighteenth-century reader would have recognized as Miltonic in the obsolete diction, inversion, dropping of prepositions, and transposition of parts of speech in such passages as:

> *th'Effulgence* tremulous, I drink,
> With fix'd Peruse,

and

> He stands,
> Gazing th'inverted Landskip, half afraid
> To meditate the blue Profound below.

Some of Thomson's un-Miltonic liberties with language prompted disapproving comments in Johnson's *Dictionary* definitions, for instance: 'Savag'd'—'A word not well authorized'; 'dissembled'—'This is not the true signification'; 'broadens'[14]—'I know not whether this word occurs, but in the following passage.'

Like *Winter*, *Summer* is essentially a devotional poem, singing the works and wonders of Almighty Power. Thomson proclaims that Nature is the book where, 'in each exalted Line | And all the full, harmonic Universe', the Almighty Poet displays his power and goodness: 'The Cause, the Glory, and the End of All!' God is present in every link of the 'mighty Chain of Beings', from microscopic creatures to angelic spirits. In *Summer*, as in *Winter*, he is most evident in storms. Thomson's developing scientific interests now impel him to introduce some touches of chemistry into a long and prominent description of a thunderstorm, so that, for instance, 'Nitre, Sulphur, Vitriol' ferment in 'wrathful Vapour', but 'wrathful' is not a metaphorical flourish: the thunder is 'by the powerful Breath of GOD inflate'. The climax of the storm section is a story illustrating the incomprehensibility of God's actions. It tells of two virtuous lovers, Celadon and Amelia, caught in a thunderstorm. The fearful Amelia is assured by Celadon that her virtue protects her from danger, that 'HE, who enwraps yon Skies | In Frowns of Darkness, ever smiles on Thee', but at that very moment she is killed by lightning. The poet exclaims 'Mysterious Heaven!', but makes no attempt to speculate upon the meaning of the event: the mysterious ways of Divine Providence remain mysterious. He rounds off his story indeed with the nicely-turned, but unoriginal conceit of a mourner transformed by grief to the marble of a tomb:

> But who can paint the Lover, as He stood,
> Struck by severe Amazement, hating Life,
> Speechless, and fixt in all the Death of Woe!
> So, faint Resemblance! on the Marble-Tomb
> The well-dissembl'd Mourner, stooping, stands,
> For ever silent, and for ever sad.[15]

Quite apart from its concluding lines, Thomson's narrative has a rococo sentimentality that appealed to generations of illustrators of the *Seasons*; but the religious belief underlying the episode owes something to the Book of Job, one of the texts cited in the Preface to *Winter* and echoed in the poem itself.

Rather more of *Summer* than of *Winter*, though, is concerned with natural phenomena that can be comprehended, not by faith only, but by the '*Philosophic Eye*'[16] of scientific intelligence. *Summer*, even more obviously than *Winter*, is a physico-theological argument in which the discoveries and conjectures of scientists are used to demonstrate the existence and benevolent attributes of God on the evidence of the created universe. In this poem Thomson shows himself to be 'the first Scottish Newtonian poet', as a modern historian of Scottish literature has called him.[17] His opening account of the place of the sun in the planetary system brings in not only Newtonian gravitation but Newton's demonstration that if the planets were projected with the correct initial velocities their present orbits would follow as a matter of course:

> With what a perfect, World-revolving Power
> Were first th'unweildy Planets launch'd along
> Th'illimitable Void! thus to remain.

Newton's discoveries underly Thomson's delighted proclamation that sunlight is the source of all colour; Thomson's account of precious stones is organized around Newton's demonstration that the colours of the spectrum blend into white light; even the reference to a 'few erroneous Rays' of light at nightfall employs the scientific vocabulary of Newton's *Opticks*. The major architects of the English scientific revolution, Bacon, Boyle, and 'comprehensive' Newton, are included in a small pantheon of philosophical and poetical heroes.[18]

Newton was in 1726 the only living member of this pantheon, the other members of which are Sir Thomas More, Locke, Shakespeare, Milton, and the theologians Isaac Barrow and John Tillotson. Milton, who receives the longest applause of these *Summer* heroes, is appearing for the second time in the *Seasons*; his importance for Thomson is indicated by the fact that he is praised also in *Winter*, as the equal of Homer and Virgil. All these British poets and philosophers are celebrated in the course of an extended apostrophe to

> HAPPY BRITANNIA! where the Queen of Arts,
> Inspiring Vigour, LIBERTY, abroad,
> Walks thro' the Land of Heroes, unconfin'd,
> And scatters Plenty with unsparing Hand.

In what he frankly admits is a digression, because he is 'transported by my Country's Love', Thomson offers an unreflective and optimistic vision of social and commercial progress, already evident in England and potential in Scotland. He is a child of the Union and perhaps the first important poet to write with a British, as distinct from a Scottish or English, outlook. He briefly touches upon what would become his darling theme of 'Rule Britannia' when he observes that Britain's subjection of the seas ensures that her 'naval Arm' can shake distant nations, whereas she is not to be shaken: 'all Assaults | Baffling, like thy hoar Cliffs the loud Sea-Wave'. Finally he prays that God will send forth upon Britain appropriate virtues, the foremost of which is *'public Zeal'*. Public virtue would, for better or worse, become a major preoccupation of Thomson's verse from about 1730 onwards, but in *Summer* its celebration is acknowledged, half-apologetically, half-boastfully, to be 'Nobly digressive from my Theme'.[19]

The theme to which he returns at this mid-point in his poem is not, however, the British summer, but 'various Summer-Horrors', mostly culled from popular travel accounts of North Africa. Thomson retells an old traveller's tale about a rich merchant and a poor carrier who both died of thirst in the Sahara desert, the merchant having given the carrier ten thousand ducats for one cruse of water. He draws upon Defoe and Lucretius for his descriptions of plague and upon Virgil's *Georgics* for his forest fire, but where Virgil tells of an Italian olive grove set alight by a careless shepherd Thomson has Africa's 'aromatic Groves' more exotically being fired by the noonday sun. Various travel books contribute the savage beasts whose roars resound through the wilderness 'From *Atlas* eastward to the frighted *Nile*' and terrify a mysterious unhappy solitary, perhaps a shipwrecked sailor or escaped slave. Lucan's *Pharsalia* provides a sandstorm and the fearsome serpent which forbids access to a spring; Lucan also supplies the heroic Cato, who withstands the monstrous terrors of the desert in his struggle to preserve Roman liberty against Caesarism. Here for the first time political history shapes Thomson's handling of foreign scenes. At one point Thomson ventures briefly south of the Sahara to sketch a region of great wealth and romantic beauty, rich in gold and gems, where cooling fruits grow on the

'balmy Banks' of the River Niger or in 'Spicy *Abyssinian* Vales', where a
multitude of exotic creatures play in the shade of the peaceful elephant, 'And
Birds, of bolder Note, rejoice around'. By contrast, its human denizens, 'of
gloomy Hue | And Features gross', are given 'to ruthless Deeds, | Wan
Jealousy, red Rage, and fell Revenge'.[20] Thomson's entire African excursion
emphasizes the bizarre or repellant aspects of that continent, in striking and
deliberate contrast with the condition of 'Happy Britannia'.

The two hundred lines on Britannia and Africa in the middle of the poem
signal two of the directions in which this and the other *Seasons* would grow
under Thomson's revising hand, but *Summer* consists substanially of natural
description, which, by virtue of Thomson's new subject, is more sensuous than
that of *Winter*. Thomson delights in 'all that chears the Eye and charms the
Heart'; he is attentive to the 'Blush of clustering Roses', the 'Willows grey,
close-crowding o'er the Brook', the mower resting under 'tedded Hay, with
Flowers perfum'd', the 'woolly Shower' of thistledown in the 'fickle Air',[21] and
countless other common phenomena, now freshly seen. Extended descriptions
in *Summer*, unlike *Winter*, are sometimes organized pictorially, the result
possibly, it has been suggested, of Thomson's association with the painter John
Dyer.[22] Joseph Warton observed in 1756 that the word-painting of cattle
cooling themselves in a stream with a sleeping cowherd on the bank was
'A groupe worthy the pencil of Giacomo da Bassano'.[23] There is a picturesque
quality at times in the grand apostrophe to sunlight with which *Summer* opens:

> Rude Ruins glitter; and the briny Deep,
> Seen from some pointed Promontory's Top,
> Reflects, from every fluctuating Wave,
> A Glance, extensive as the Day.

The tale of Celadon and Amelia ends not with a moral but the description of a
statue. Thomson's prayer for public virtues to be sent down on Britain is
conceived as an allegorical painting or statuary group, with, for instance,
Charity 'shedding Tears thro' Smiles' and every other personified virtue in
some appropriate attitude.[24]

Allegorical figures slip into the most naturalistic descriptions too, for instance
at the beginning of the summer's day which provides the narrative framework of
the poem:

> Young *Day* pours in a-pace,
> And opens all the lawny Prospect wide.
> The dripping Rock, the Mountain's misty Top
> Swell on the Eye, and brighten with the Dawn.
> Blue, thro' the Dusk, the smoaking Currents shine;
> And, from the bladed Field, th' unhunted Hare

Limps aukward: while, along the Forest-Glade,
The wild Deer trip, and, often turning, gaze
At early Passenger.

Also at the end of the day:

    CONFESS'D, from yonder slow-extinguish'd Clouds,
The Sky begreying, sober *Evening* takes
Her wonted Station in the middle Air,
A thousand *Shadows* at her Beck. First *This*
She sends on Earth; then *That* of deeper Die
Steals soft behind; and then a *Deeper* still,
In well-adjusted Circles, gathers round,
To close the Face of Things. Th'expected Breeze
Begins to wave the Wood, and stir the Stream,
Sweeping with shadowy Gust the Fields of Corn,
While the Quail clamours for his running Mate.[25]

The personified Evening is a member of what Collins would call 'the shadowy tribes of mind'. She is blended so fully with the natural scene that we are only half-aware of her as an allegorical being at all, and her movement carries forward into the more natural but, in a sense, more mysterious animation of the 'shadowy Gust'.

The poem does not end with summer nightfall, though, for Thomson concludes with an invocation to natural and moral philosophy, which develops into a celebration of the intellectual and imaginative powers of the poet himself. Nature is

    To *Reason*'s, and to *Fancy*'s Eye display'd;
The First up-tracing, from *the vast Inane*,
The Chain of Causes, and Effects to HIM,
WHO, absolutely, in HIMSELF, alone,
Possesses *Being*; While the *Last* receives
The whole Magnificence of Heaven, and Earth,
And every Beauty, delicate or bold,
Obvious or more remote, with livelier Sense,
A World swift-painted, on th'attentive Mind![26]

God has set limits upon the extent of human knowledge, but the very last lines of the poem proclaim Thomson's faith that the future life will be an infinite ascent of mind from stage to stage; immortality will be the endless extension of knowledge:

    Enough for Us we know, that this dark State,
In wayward Passions lost, and vain Pursuits,
This Infancy of Being! cannot prove

The final Issue of the Works of GOD,
By *Love*, and *Wisdom*, inexpressive, form'd,
And ever rising with the rising Mind.[27]

This conclusion parallels in some respects the vision of the Last Day with which *Winter* ends, and it performs a similarly apocalyptic function, but it has less to do with orthodox Christianity and more to do with the intellect and sensibility of the poet himself. In this, as much as in the frankly-admitted digression and the discursiveness that extended *Summer* to 1,146 lines or nearly three times the length of the first *Winter*, Thomson displays his newly-won confidence as a poet.

Summer was published on 16 February 1727 by John Millan, who was apparently not over-generous when paying for the copy of this quite substantial poem. Joseph Warton, confirming what Victor says of *Winter*, writes, 'It may be of use to inform young adventurers, that Thomson sold his *Winter* to Millan for only three guineas. He gained but little more for his *Summer*.'[28] If this is true, Thomson certainly earned more by his dedication of the poem to George Bubb Dodington (1691–1762), one of the most generous of patrons. There are two accounts of how this dedication came about. Joseph Spence, informed by Mallet three years after the event, writes that, after the publication of *Winter*, 'Dodington gave his services to him by Dr Young and desired to see him. That was thought hint enough for another dedication to him, and this was his first entrance to that acquaintance.'[29] Johnson, taking his information much later (by way of Lord Hailes) from Lady Murray, a near relative of Lord Binning, says that Thomson intended to dedicate *Summer* to Binning, 'but the same kindness which had first disposed lord Binning to encourage him determined him to refuse the dedication, which was by his advice addressed to Mr Doddington; a man who had more power to advance the reputation and fortune of a poet.'[30] These two accounts are not contradictory. As Whig members of the Commons and fellow diners at George Baillie's table, Binning and Dodington were acquainted with one another; Dodington was a well-practised patron who had mastered the art of conferring favours in a tactfully obliging manner. Like Compton, he was a prominent and influential politician. He had carried out diplomatic missions in Spain; on his appointment as a Lord of the Treasury in 1724 he became one of Walpole's ablest lieutenants in financial affairs. Unlike Compton, he would take a continuing interest in Thomson's career. His first token of interest was a gift of fifty pounds for the dedication.[31]

Dodington was one of the more important of a number of patrons acquired as a result of the success of *Winter*. Murdoch mentions 'the Countess of *Hertford*, Miss *Drelincourt*, afterwards the Viscountess *Primrose*, Mrs. *Stanley*, and others', and adds that 'the chief happiness which his *Winter* procured him was, that it brought him acquainted with Dr *Rundle*, afterwards Lord Bishop of *Derry*', who 'introduced him to his great friend the Lord Chancellor *Talbot*'.[32] The Countess of Hertford and Mrs Stanley both appear in the *Seasons*, Thomas Rundle and Lord Chancellor Talbot in *Liberty*; all four are referred to in other poems too; but this statement by Murdoch, together with the subscription list for the quarto *Seasons* in 1730, is the only contemporary evidence we have of Thomson's link with the future Viscountess Primrose. It is unfortunate that we know so little, because, unlike all Thomson's other aristocratic patrons, Lady Primrose was a lifelong Jacobite. In her later years she housed and raised money for Flora MacDonald, and she entertained the Pretender himself on his stealthy visit to England in 1750.[33]

Mrs Sarah Stanley belonged to a prominent Whig family, being the daughter of Sir Hans Sloane, President of the Royal Society from 1727 and Royal Physician. Frances, Countess of Hertford and later Duchess of Somerset, a great heiress, was close to the throne in her position as Lady of the Bedchamber to Caroline, Princess of Wales, who became queen in 1727. Lady Hertford wrote verses and was the patroness of other poets in Thomson's circle. Thomas Rundle, who was a chaplain to William Talbot, Bishop of Durham, was a useful patron in himself and by virtue of his intimacy with the Talbot family. He was a close friend and adviser of the bishop's lawyer son Charles Talbot, who was a political associate of Compton and Walpole in Parliament and was appointed Solicitor-General in 1726. Rundle was a man of wit, charm, and learning; he won the admiration of Pope and Swift as well as Thomson.[34]

On 4 March 1727 Mallet and Thomson welcomed Aaron Hill on his safe return from Scotland. Thomson's note of greetings to his friend and patron is dated from Old Man's Coffee-House in his old haunt at Charing Cross, but it does not necessarily follow that he had left Watts's Academy by this date: Charing Cross was a convenient place from which to go and wait upon Hill in Westminster.[35] By now Thomson had probably begun to write *Spring*, but the death of Sir Isaac Newton on 20 March at the age of 84, diverted his attention to a new poem. He worked so quickly that his 212-lines long *Poem to the Memory of Sir Isaac Newton* was published on 8 May.

Before he began to write he already had a layman's understanding of Newton's achievements. He was exposed to Newtonian ideas at Edinburgh and Watts's Academy, as we have seen; but Murdoch tells us that composition of the new poem was also assisted by 'his friend Mr *Gray*, a gentleman well versed in the *Newtonian Philosophy*, who on that occasion, gave him a very exact, though general, abstract of its principles'. John Gray would later collaborate with a fellow Scotsman, Andrew Reid, to edit an abridgement of the *Philosophical Transactions* of the Royal Society from 1720 to 1732.[36]

Long before his death Newton had become a legend. To Addison he was 'the

Miracle of the Present Age', the man of godlike mind who strengthened men's religious beliefs as he enlarged their understandings, drawing from the system of the universe scientific 'Demonstrations of infinite Power and Wisdom'.[37] The effect of his discoveries was to deepen a religious awareness of the wonders of the created world. Religious hope and comfort were to be gained both from the increase in scientific knowledge and from the evident limitations upon such knowledge. Newton and his followers agreed that natural philosophy led men's minds by a chain of cause and effect towards a First Cause, but as earthly life is so short and man's view so limited it appears 'that our present state would be very imperfect without a subsequent one; wherein our views of nature, and of its great Author may be more clear and satisfactory'.[38] So Thomson's *Poem to Newton* is appropriately a kind of hymn on the works and wonders of almighty power, in which the imagination follows Newton on a great celestial voyage into a future life which is envisaged as the infinite ascent of mind. The poem thus makes a natural sequel to the conclusion of *Summer*.

Thomson's narrative device of a journey through the heavens towards the source of all light (physical, intellectual, spiritual) conveys the idea of Newton's apotheosis, while enabling the poet to enumerate the great scientist's discoveries in astronomy and optics. The response to each of those discoveries is an intermingled intellectual excitement and aesthetic delight:

> He also fix'd the wandering *Queen of Night*,
> Whether she wanes into a scanty Orb,
> Or waxing broad with her pale shadowy Light
> In a soft Deluge overflows the Sky.
> Her every Motion clear-discerning, He
> Adjusted to th'obsequious Main, and taught
> Why now the mighty Mass of Waters swells
> Resistless, heaving on the broken Rocks,
> And the full River turning; till again
> The Tide revertive, unattracted, leaves
> A yellow Waste of idle Sands behind.

The wonder embraces the natural phenomena and their rational explanation. So, too, with Newton's investigation into the spectrum, where he 'Untwisted all the shining Robe of Day'. Thomson exclaims:

> Did ever Poet image ought so fair,
> Dreaming in whispering Groves, by the hoarse Brook!
> Or Prophet, to whose Rapture Heaven descends!
> Even now the setting Sun and liveri'd Clouds,
> Seen, *Greenwich*, from thy lovely Heights, declare
> How just, how beauteous the refractive Law.[39]

The terms of science are not bathetic for this poet.

Taken separately Newton's discoveries are wonderful, but what is more wonderful is the comprehensive simplicity of a universe governed by his simple, ll-inclusive laws of motion:

> O unprofuse Magnificence divine!
> O Wisdom truly perfect! thus to call
> From a few Causes such a Scheme of Things,
> Effects so various, beautiful and great,
> An Universe compleat!

The magnificence is God's of course, but it is Newton's also. The Englishman had 'rescu'd Heaven and Earth' from 'the wild Domain|of the *French Dreamer*',[40] as Thomson scathingly and chauvinistically calls Descartes, whose system was more complicated and less comprehensive than Newton's.

In the concluding lines Thomson takes up the patriotic thread again; he addresses the glorified Newton as '*Britain's* Boast' and prays to him to be the Genius to 'Assuage the Madness of a jarring World', and to correct the manners, steer the councils, and inspire the youth of his own country, 'guilty as she is'.[41] This striking reversal of the 'Happy Britannia' sentiments of the previous August may perhaps be explained by reference to Thomson's dedication of the poem to Sir Robert Walpole (no less), who is addressed as Britain's 'most illustrious *Patriot*', a man engaged in 'balancing the Power of *Europe*, watching over our common Welfare, informing the whole Body of Society and Commerce, and even like Heaven dispensing Happiness to the Discontented and Ungrateful'.[42] At the time the *Poem to Newton* was published Walpole was seriously ill and the country faced uncertainty and seeming danger. For some months the great European powers had been on the brink of war; there was no formal declaration of hostilities, but the Spaniards, who had entered a treaty to put the Pretender on the British throne, were preparing to besiege Britain's outpost in Gibraltar, and a British force under Admiral Hosier was in the Caribbean, blockading the Spanish treasure fleet. At home, the regular attacks upon Walpole by his political opponents were raised to new heights of virulence and wit by the weekly periodical *The Craftsman*, which first appeared in December 1726. To Walpole it may have seemed that one of his most conspicuously ungrateful countrymen was Bolingbroke, once a convicted traitor, pardoned by Walpole's consent, and now seeking to destroy him by means of backstairs court intrigue and a brilliantly virulent satirical pen. 'People are very warm and very angry', wrote Pope on 17 February; 'The Dispute about a War or no War still continues', wrote Swift on 13 May.[43]

Though Walpole later obtained the well-deserved reputation of being an enemy to the wits and though Thomson was to attack government policy only

two years later in *Britannia*, there is nothing inherently strange in the patriotic
dedication of the *Poem to Newton* to him. Soon after the appearance of *Winter*,
dedicated to Speaker Compton, Thomson was invited by the pro-Walpole
London Journal (4 June 1726) to dedicate some future work to the Great Man
himself:

For it must be own'd, that Encouragement is necessary to animate every Endeavour to
excel; especially in Works of Genius. And this gives an Opportunity to the Great to share
in the Honour of the Poet. It was to a POLLIO and a MECAENAS, that the *Romans* owed
their VIRGIL; it was to a SOMERS and a HALLIFAX, that the present Age ow'd its
ADDISON; and I hope, *future Ages* will have reason to say, *It was to a* W—POLE *or a*
C——TON, *that we owe a* THOMSON.[44]

In private letters of August 1726 Thomson disparages verse panegyrics of
Walpole by Young and Mitchell, but he condemns the poetry, rather than its
recipient. Of Young he says, 'The Dr's very Buckram has run short on this
Occasion.' As for Mitchell and others, including Savage, who have had their
'Fling' at Sir Robert, 'He had better bribe Them to Silence. Posterity will
call Him, if Posterity hear any Thing of the Matter the Maevius-Baevius-
Maecenas, the discelebrated Knight.'[45] Thomson was of course not obliged to
grab at the bait dangled by the *London Journal* (for the next work after that
invitation was *Summer*, dedicated to Dodington), nor did he need to show that
good poets as well as bad could have a fling at Walpole, but his dedication of the
Poem to Newton was not necessarily based on a mercenary calculation. One
might venture to suggest that, in the eyes of a responsible, patriotic Whig during
the apparently dangerous early months of 1727, Britain would have seemed
safer under the leadership of Walpole, for all his electoral and administrative corruption, than under the erratic Bolingbroke, tainted as he was with
Jacobitism, or indeed under the disaffected Whig Pulteney to the extent that he
was compromised by his opportunistic alliance with Bolingbroke. With *Winter*
and *Summer*, Thomson's new poem completed a trio of impeccably Whig
dedications, declaring his political affiliations. There is a kind of progression
similar to that by which, just a year earlier in 1725–6, Young dedicated the last
three satires of his *Universal Passion* to Dodington, Compton, and Walpole.
Thomson's case is very like that of other then and future opposition wits, Swift,
Pope, Gay, and Fielding, all of whom made some kind of bid for government
patronage in the years of Walpole's power. Walpole gave Pope a grant of £200
from the Treasury on 29 April 1725 for his translation of the *Odyssey*. In the
Free-Briton of 13 August 1730, when Thomson was accused of ingratitude
towards Walpole, it was said, probably on good authority, that the poet had
received £50 from the Prime Minister for the dedication of the *Poem to
Newton*.[46]

The *Poem to Newton* was published by Millan on 8 May and entered to him in the Stationers' Register on the same day. As with the first edition of *Winter*, the format was folio; as with the second edition of *Winter*, the single print run included press-variant title-pages which indicated, not three, but five serially numbered 'editions'; as with *Winter*, copies of the same text gathered under different press-variant titles were put on sale at decent and plausible intervals, from the first edition in May 1727 to the 'fifth edition' in June 1730.[47] Millan was again employing this old booksellers' device to encourage sales by making a book appear to be more in demand than it was, but Thomson would soon have no need for such expedients.

His growing reputation is unexpectedly attested to in the memoranda of that crusty old ecclesiastical historian Robert Wodrow, who records in July 1727 that Walter Stewart, formerly a college acquaintance of Thomson's, had visited him in his parish near Glasgow and spoken of 'Mr James Thomson, so famed at London for his poems, Winter and Summer, and some others ... His genius led him to poetry when at Professor Hamilton's lessons, and his reputation was good.' Stewart further reported that Thomson had been a private tutor, had received twenty guineas from Compton and fifty pounds from Dodington for his dedications, that he had gone into the country to write a poem on Newton, and that 'he is well-liked at London'.[48] Stewart must have received his news of Thomson in March or April; by 30 April the poet was back in London, where, with Mallet, he met Sir John Clerk of Penicuik. Sir John, a Midlothian landowner, landscape gardener, judge, antiquary, patron of Allan Ramsay, and dabbler in poetry himself, was cousin to William Aikman, who may well have introduced his two young poet friends to him. Reading his memorandum of the meeting, some allowance should perhaps be made for national prejudice: 'at night on my return I met with Mr Maloch & Mr Thomsone two young Lads of my Country & justly esteam'd at present the best poets in Britain.'[49]

Mallet refers to this meeting in a letter of 25 May, when he writes about progress on his poem *The Excursion*, which, having passed Thomson's scrutiny, was being read by other friends and acquaintances: 'by Mr Molineaux the prince's Secretary, by Mr Hill, Dr Young, and Sir John Clerk, whose acquaintance I had the good fortune to obtain while he was in London. It is now in the hands of Mr Dennis ... I will try the town with this before I venture out a tragedy that I have been long meditating.'[50] As Mallet had come to the notice of the Prince of Wales's Secretary, Samuel Molyneux, so Thomson was now acquainted with the Princess's Lady of the Bedchamber, the Countess of Hertford.

As it fell out, Lady Hertford would do much more for Thomson than Molyneux for Mallet;[51] she proved to be his most valuable woman patron. Her attention was drawn to him by her friend Elizabeth Rowe, an admired poet and devotional writer, who recommended *Winter* to her by transcribing a meditative passage on 'Philosophic Melancholy', 'forming Fancy', and 'the pitying Tear', verses calculated to appeal to the refined sensibilities and kind heart of the Countess.[52] In the summer of 1727 Thomson stayed at Marlborough Castle in Wiltshire as the guest of the Countess and her husband, a colonel in the Horse Guards, who had served under the Duke of Marlborough in Flanders. It was probably while Thomson was staying with the Earl and Countess that he received the verse epistle from his friend, and hers, John Dyer, which is preserved in Lady Hertford's commonplace book of about this date. Dyer, ill and depressed in Wales, laments his present separation from Thomson and recalls happy hours with him 'at Field in Amicable parle'; he fears he will die without seeing his friend on this earth, but expects to meet him in Heaven, along with their heroes, Socrates, Cicero, Homer, Virgil, Milton, and Newton.[53] This was perhaps a not inappropriate poem to send to a house often visited by Mrs Rowe at a time when she was writing what was to be her most famous work, *Friendship in Death*, but Dyer was to survive for another thirty years and outlive Thomson.

Johnson writes that it was the Countess's practice

to invite every summer some poet into the country to hear her verses and assist her studies. This honour was one summer conferred on Thomson, who took more delight in carousing with lord Hertford and his friends than assisting her ladyship's poetical operations, and therefore never received another summons.[54]

Bishop Thomas Percy (of the *Reliques*) gave another reason for the alleged breach between Thomson and his patron, for, in a note written later than 1780 to accompany the manuscript of a love song by Thomson, he repeats Johnson's story, and adds, 'If there be any Truth in this anecdote, the presumption of the inclosed may best account for the Discontinuance of the Invitations.' The song in question is the utterance of a lover who can speak his love only to the trees and flowers, who are asked to communicate with the lady:

> Hard is the Fate of Him who loves,
>   Yet dares not tell his trembling Pain,
> But to the sympathetic Groves,
>   But to the lonely listning Plain . . .
>
> Oh tell Her what She cannot blame,
>   Tho Fear my Tongue must ever bind,
> Oh tell Her that my heavenly Flame
>   Is as her sacred Soul refin'd.

These verses cannot be dated; in tone and subject they resemble other 'bashful lover' poems and fragments by Thomson, written perhaps in the 1730s, some of which were transcribed by the Countess.[55] The existence of these transcripts implies that Lady Hertford was not offended by the poet's 'presumption', if that is what it was. She was a young woman, only a year older than Thomson; he, like many other men, then and now, could be coarse in the company of his own sex, but was a sentimentalist where women were concerned. The patron-client relationship, tempered perhaps by a genuine mutual esteem and fostered by a common delight in sentimental poetry, could have brought about a well-bred, platonic, indeed conventional, literary-salon flirtation. Johnson was certainly misinformed over the lack of future summons, whatever may have been his accuracy in the matter of carousing: Thomson's visits to Lord and Lady Hertford continued in the 1730s and it appears that the Countess retained an interest in the poet's career down to his death.

One poem of Thomson's that was certainly transcribed by Lady Hertford during or very soon after Thomson's visit in 1727 was the 'Hymn on Solitude', now extensively revised from the version sent to Mallet two years earlier. Eight lines are deleted, fourteen are added, and the whole poem is made more polished: for instance, the following lines:

> Your's is the fragrant morning blush
> And your's the silent evening hush
> Your's the refulgent noonday gleam
> And your's ah then! the gelid stream,

now become:

> Thine is th'unbounded Breath of Morn,
> Just as the dew-bent Rose is born;
> And while *Meridian* Fervors beat,
> Thine is the Woodland dumb Retreat;
> But chief, when Evening Scenes decay,
> And the faint Landskip swims away,
> Thine is the doubtful dear Decline,
> And that best Hour of Musing thine.

Other additions include a compliment to the 'gentle-looking' Lady Hertford and a reference to her companion, 'Philomela', the pen-name of Elizabeth Rowe.[56] These revisions are not inconsiderable, but Thomson's major poetic undertaking while at Marlborough Castle was to continue writing *Spring*. When this poem was published in 1728 it was dedicated to Lady Hertford in terms that recall the rural retirement of poet and patron together:

Happy! if I have hit any of those Images, and correspondent Sentiments, your calm Evening Walks, in the most delightful Retirement, have oft inspired. I could add too, that as this Poem grew up under your Encouragement, it has therefore a natural Claim to your Patronage.

In the poem itself there is a verse dedication to the countess, who is pictured
walking 'With Innocence and Meditation join'd'.[57] These are the virtues
personified in the 'Hymn on Solitude': Thomson is hinting that Lady Hertford
is a kind of genius of the place, even a muse.

Later in the year of his first visit to Marlborough Castle Thomson was
lodging in grander surroundings, at Eastbury, Dodington's great house in
Dorset. Begun shortly before 1720 to the designs of Vanbrugh and still only
half completed by 1727, Eastbury was inferior in size and splendour only to
Blenheim Palace and Castle Howard among the heavy loads that Vanbrugh laid
upon earth. Dodington was as flamboyant as he was wealthy; his style of living at
Eastbury when Thomson visited him was probably very similar to what it was in
the 1750s, as described by Richard Cumberland: 'he was not to be approached
but through a suite of apartments, and rarely seated but under painted ceilings
and gilt entablatures'; but he 'was excelled by no man in doing the honours of
his house and table; to the ladies he had all the courtly and profound devotion
of a Spaniard, with the ease and gaiety of a Frenchman towards the men'.
However his enemies might deride his overdressed, corpulent figure and his
appetite for praise, it is clear that he was a generous, attentive, and amusing
patron. Cumberland observes, 'as the trivial amusement of cards was never
resorted to in Mr Dodington's house, it was his custom in the evenings to
entertain his company with reading, and in this art he excelled'.[58] Thomson, by
contrast, was a poor reader, even of his own verse. Dodington once 'was so
much provoked by his odd utterance, that he snatched the paper from his hand,
and told him that he did not understand his own verses'.[59]

A fellow guest of Thomson's at Eastbury was Edward Young, already friendly
with Mallet and Savage, not highly regarded as a poet by Thomson, but
personally known to him, if only as Dodington's intermediary over the dedication of *Summer*. It was probably at Eastbury that Young saw the manuscript of
Thomson's *Spring*, which he mentions in a letter to Thomas Tickell on
17 November 1727,[60] and, as Young speaks in the same breath about his own
acquaintance with Voltaire, it may have been at Eastbury that Thomson and
Voltaire met one another. Voltaire certainly visited Dodington's country mansion during his stay in England between May 1726 and March 1729 and it has
been shown that this visit must have been in the second half of 1727. In 1764 he
wrote 'Tomson; je l'ai connu il y a quelque quarante années', and in 1750,
thanking George Lyttelton for a copy of Thomson's *Works*, he remarks:

You was beneficient to Mr Thompson, when he Liv'd, and you is so to me in favouring
me with his works. J was acquainted with the author when j stay'd in England. J
discovered in him a great genius and a great simplicity, j lik'd in him the poet and the
true philosfer, j mean the Lover of mankind. J think that without a good stock of such a
philosofy a poet is just above a fidler, who amuses our ears and can not go to our soul.[61]

Voltaire quite closely imitated Thomson's *Poem to the Memory of Newton* in his *Epître à la Marquise du Châtelet*, prefixed to his *Eléments de la Philosophie de Newton* (1738).[62] Most of his recorded comments on Thomson's writing refer to plays, including Voltaire's own *Socrate* which he fathered on Thomson (see Chapter 9 below).

Mallet was also at Eastbury, at least for the later part of Thomson's stay, which did not come to an end until the beginning of December. One assumes that Thomson engineered the invitation, as Mallet had engineered invitations to Shawford House for Thomson; thus, as Mallet had prophesied, Thomson was beginning to requite the services his friend had done him. The two poets were therefore out of town when Aikman received the manuscript of a long poem, 'in Milton's way', on the subject of landscape architecture and gardening, written by Sir John Clerk of Penicuik and now sent to London by its author to be shown to Thomson and Mallet for their criticisms and corrections.[63] The two friends were also out of London when, on 20 November, Richard Savage stabbed a man in a drunken brawl at Robinson's Coffee-House in Charing Cross.

No doubt the most important public happening of 1727 was the accession of George II on the death of his father in June and Walpole's retention of his Prime-Ministerial office because the new King's favourite, Sir Spencer Compton, was incapable of taking the post when it was offered to him. However, the event that probably impressed itself most deeply upon Thomson's circle of friends was Savage's trial for murder in December and the sentence of death passed upon him. That he was not hanged was owing to the intercession of the Countess of Hertford, 'who engaged in his Support with all the Tenderness that is excited by Pity, and all the Zeal which is kindled by Generosity', and persuaded the new Queen, her mistress, to obtain the grant of a Royal Pardon.[64] Perhaps Thomson or Dyer, or both men, used their interest with the Countess on Savage's behalf.

It would appear that in the first half of 1727 Thomson earned a hundred pounds by his dedications to Dodington and Walpole, and was paid some smaller sum by Millan for the copyrights of *Summer* and the *Poem to Newton*. He made protracted visits to Marlborough Castle and Eastbury between summer and the end of November, so one may conjecture that he had given up his tutorship at Watts's Academy by the middle of that year and was attempting to make his living by his pen. To this end he published in January 1728 *Proposals* to print *The Seasons* by subscription. He announces that the work,

which is in great Forwardness, and will be published with all possible speed', will contain 'The Four Seasons, with a Hymn on their Succession. To which will be added a Poem sacred to the Memory of Sir Isaac Newton. And an Essay on Descriptive Poetry will be prefixed to the whole . . . N.B. The Pieces already published, viz. Winter, Summer, and a Poem on the Death of Sir Isaac Newton, will be corrected and enlarged in several places.

The entire price of the book in sheets, one guinea, was to be paid at the time of subscribing; subscriptions would be taken in Edinburgh by the poet-bookseller Allan Ramsay and in London by the author and by three Scots booksellers, George Strahan, John Millan, and Andrew Millar.[65] This is the earliest evidence of Thomson's association with Millar, who had only recently come south from Scotland. The address at which Thomson himself would receive subscriptions was given as the Smyrna Coffee-House, which was near the corner of St James's Street in a highly fashionable quarter; it was the resort of Swift, Pope, and Arbuthnot, and was celebrated humorously in Steele's *Tatler* as the haunt of snuff-taking professors of music, poetry, and politics. Thomson made it his regular address in early 1728, so had certainly left Little Tower Street by then.[66]

The publication of his proposals does not necessarily mean that Thomson had finished writing all four Seasons by January 1728, for it was not unknown at that period for subscriptions to be solicited for incomplete or even unwritten works; but in a letter to Sir John Clerk of 18 January he says, 'I am now almost done with the four Seasons.' Much of the remainder of this letter is given over to tactful suggestions as to how Clerk's long poem, 'The Country Seat', might be improved, and to offers of further help: 'Whatever little Assistance I can contribute toward finishing such a Design You will oblige me by commanding it.' He ends by drawing attention to his subscription proposals and delicately, but far from servilely, alluding to the position of the author: 'Dedications and Subscriptions are the very fundamental Priviledges of us fortuneless Authors— The Tribute of the Muses—levied at Pleasure; but since there is no Coercion in the Matter that Liberty may be the more easily indulged us.'[67]

Clerk was clearly eager to apply the skills of 'the best poets in Britain' to the improvement of his poem; his letter asking cousin Aikman to prod Thomson and Mallet into action crossed the letter from Thomson to Clerk from which I have just quoted. Aikman wrote to him,

Since Receit of yours of 18. Janry it has not been in my power to gett any thing done wt Thomson or Malloch till within these few days, for Thomson is so throng abt his Subcription that he minds nothing else and Mr Malloch has been printing his Excursion which has imployd all his leisure time.

Aikman goes on to say that Mallet would send Sir John a copy of *The Excursion* under the Duke of Montrose's postal frank, and that he (Aikman) has paid three guineas to Thomson on account of the three copies of *The Seasons* for which Sir John has said he will subscribe. As for Sir John's poem, he says, 'The

Restrictions you lay these Gentlemen under in relation to the C——ry Seat makes them both a little backward to meddle', but Mallet, 'one of the best tempered Souls alive', has written a specimen of revised text, which Aikman now sends with Mallet's offer to continue and revise the rest of the poem.[68] It does not appear that Thomson sent so much as a specimen; he was indeed 'throng' or busy about his subscription.

Some friends were helping too, for when the January proposals were reprinted in the *Whitehall Evening-Post* for 19 March 1728 they were prefaced by a long and impressive anonymous puff, which commended the recent improvement of English taste, as evidenced by the success of Thomson's first two publications:

If an Author, altogether unknown to the World, and unsupported by any thing but the native Force of his own Genius, should make his first Attempt in Poetry, on a Subject which can only please by its genuine Worth and Beauty, without gratifying either the ill Nature, irregular Passions, or Levity of Mankind: if he should venture beyond this, and lay aside the favourite Mode of writing in Rhyme; I think the *general Encouragement* of such a Performance would be a very good Proof of my Assertion.

And yet this is exactly true with regard to the Poems of *Winter* and *Summer*, which, tho' introduced into the World under all the Disadvantages I have been supposing, in a little time came to be universally read and approven. The Public, without dwelling on such minuter Faults as they might have found in them, distinguished, with a just Indulgence, that strong and fertile Imagination, which animates the several Representations of Nature they contain.

In similar phrases, in May, the *Present State of the Republick of Letters*, edited by Andrew Reid, took up the praise of Thomson; Reid, an associate of Thomson's friend John Gray in popular science publications, offered additional praise of the *Poem to Newton* and 'the judicious and well-placed reflexions of piety, virtue and humanity which run through his works'. Both periodical articles contained quotations from the forthcoming *Spring*, probably from manuscript or uncorrected proof, since the first edition of that poem has additions, deletions, and other variants from the passages quoted in the journals.

Possibly these puffs for the subscription edition had some connection also with the publication of a fifth edition of *Winter* and a 'second edition' of *Summer*, which were advertised alongside the 'fourth edition' of the *Poem to Newton* in newspapers in March. *Summer* was merely a reissue of the first-edition sheets with a cancel title dated 1728 and giving Millan's new address; the *Poem to Newton* was merely one of the planned reissues of first-edition copies under pre-printed press-variant titles; but *Winter* was a genuinely new edition, with extensive minor authorial revisions to the text of the poem, resulting in a slight increase in length to 478 lines. It was a smaller volume than the second edition, though, because the Preface and complimentary poems were deleted, never to be reprinted in Thomson's lifetime.[69]

Spring was published on 5 June 1728, apparently on Thomson's own account, with Andrew Millar, and for a short while George Strahan, acting as agents to sell the book on commission. It seems that sales were slower than Thomson expected or he in some other way, not for the first or last time, miscalculated his finances, so that Millar stepped in to shoulder the risk. In January 1729, he reissued the evidently large number of remainder copies under a cancel-title and with an added contents page as a 'second edition'.[70] Joseph Warton says that Millar gave Thomson fifty guineas for *Spring*,[71] but it is not clear whether this was for the 1729 issue or was a proportion of the £137. 10s. that we know Millar paid for the copyrights of *Spring* and *Sophonisba* in January 1730. Either way, Andrew Millar was justifying Johnson's later accolade, that he raised the price of literature.

Copies of the first edition of *Spring* in June 1728 contained the *Proposals* for the subscription edition and an advertisement promising that the edition would be ready 'next Winter', even though subscribers were not as numerous as Thomson had hoped:'For *Subscription* is now at its Last Gasp, and the World seems to have got the better of that many-headed Monster.' Though sub-scribers would, as it turned out, have to wait two years rather than six months for their copies of *The Seasons*, *Spring* was a substantial earnest of the work in progress. At 1,082 lines long it is written according to the enlarged conception of the complete work which had become apparent in the writing of *Summer*. Unlike *Summer*, the nature-descriptive passages of *Spring* all paint British scenes: native birds and flowers and weather. Thomson is 'at home' also in the sense that more of this Season than of any other is written out of his own distinctive talent for first-hand observation and unblinking description; here, more consistently than elsewhere, he uses the poetic eye that Johnson praises:

the eye that distinguishes in every thing presented to its view whatever there is on which imagination can delight to be detained ... The reader of *The Seasons* wonders that he never saw before what Thomson shews him, and that he never yet has felt what Thomson impresses.[72]

Like Gilbert White and John Clare, Thomson has a special feeling for birds; this is clear in the well-loved robin passage added to the second edition of *Winter* and is no less apparent in the long central episode of *Spring* describing the mating and nesting of birds and their tricks to protect their broods. He shares the intentness of the swallow as it 'sweeps | The slimy Pool, to build his hanging House | Ingeniously intent'. He enters into the fledgelings' fear of flying:

> O'er the Boughs
> Dancing about, still at the giddy Verge
> Their Resolution fails; their Pinions still,
> In loose Libration stretch'd, to trust the Void
> Trembling refuse: till down before them fly
> The Parent-Guides, and chide, exhort, command,
> Or push them off.

The brutally curt change of language-register in that last phrase nicely partici-
pates in the parent-birds' impatience too. He even goes courting with the birds,
when they,

> In fond Rotation spread the spotted Wing,
> And shiver every Feather with Desire.[73]

Though the rhetorical tone is utterly different, particularly in the affectionate
mock-pedantry of 'Libration' and 'Rotation', there are moments when
Thomson could claim, with Keats, 'if a Sparrow come before my Window I take
part in its existence and pick about the Gravel'.[74] But it is only moments,
because Thomson will always stand back at some point in order to relate bird
behaviour to the order of the universe and the goodness of God.

Thomson has a characteristic attentiveness, for instance in this prelude to a
rain-shower:

> Gradual sinks the Breeze
> Into a perfect Calm; that not a Breath
> Is heard to quiver thro' the closing Woods,
> Or rustling turn the many-twinkling Leaves
> Of Aspin tall. Th' uncurling Floods, diffus'd
> In glassy Breadth, seem thro' delusive Lapse
> Forgetful of their Course. 'Tis Silence all,
> And pleasing Expectation. Herds and Flocks
> Drop the dry Sprig, and mute-imploring eye
> The falling Verdure. Hush'd in short Suspense
> The plumy People streak their Wings with Oil,
> And wait th' approaching Sign to strike at once
> Into the general Choir.

Commenting on such passages, Martin Price observes that Thomson 'foreshadows Wordsworth in giving himself up to a scene, accepting its mysterious
power over him, describing with the exactness of awed attention the least
movement he sees'.[75]

As usual, though, Thomson 'sees' far more than what is visible to the cor-
poreal eye, whether this is the 'twining Mass of Tubes' revealed by the micro-
scopic inspection of a plant, or the transformations of nature in the nightmares

of an unhappy lover, or the imaginative vision of the Deluge that brought to an
end the legendary Golden Age, when

> o'er the highest Hills
> Wide-dash'd the Waves, in Undulation vast:
> Till from the Center to the streaming Clouds
> A shoreless Ocean tumbled round the Globe.

The Deluge provides the occasion for rhetorical and emotional sublimity, but it
is described in accordance with the scientific theories of Thomas Burnet. The
scientific interests apparent in *Summer* reappear in *Spring* also, in, for instance,
an extended discussion of animalcula, in an account of the rainbow, with a
tribute to Newton, and, scattered through the poem, in a deal of botanical lore
from recent books, such as Stephen Hales's *Vegetable Staticks* (1727). Scientific
knowledge serves Thomson's devotional purposes here, as in the earlier-
written Seasons (and as in the scientists he was reading), to display the wisdom
of God in the creation. The 'Breath of Nature' applauded in a sensuous
description of the rich variety of colours, textures, and scents in common
English garden flowers is produced by physical processes explicable (and
explained) in terms of plant physiology; but this 'Breath' is also direct, physical
evidence of a First Cause, that single unifying 'Essential Presence' (literally the
spirit) that orders these processes and generates all being, including that of the
poet.[76]

    Though there are references to tempests, insect-blights, and the self-
induced miseries of pining or jealous lovers, and though the mythical-historical
account of the Golden Age draws attention to the modern Iron Age, *Spring* is to
a far greater extent than *Winter* and *Summer* a representation of joy, kind-
liness, harmony, and beauty in external and human nature. The terrible
God of storms, so manifest in the earlier-written Seasons, does make a brief
appearance:

> The Tempest blows His Wrath, . . .
> The Thunder is His Voice; and the red Flash
> His speedy Sword of Justice:

'But chief', Thomson continues,

> In Thee, Boon *Spring*, and in thy softer Scenes,
> The *Smiling GOD* appears.[77]

In *Spring* we are closest to the Golden Age, when 'Harmonious Nature too
look'd smiling on', and smiling Nature still has power to generate benevolence
in men. The smiling God's 'Creative bounty' is diffused in the form of human
charity; a charitable man enjoys a Godlike pleasure; he 'tastes' the 'The Joy of

GOD to see a happy World!' Thomson is returning to a favourite topic, as he elaborates in verse some expressions in a letter of 1726 to Aaron Hill:

Social love . . . the just and free Exercise of which . . . renders one amiable, and divine . . . Humanity is the very Smile and Consummation of Virtue; 'tis the Image of that fair Perfection of the Supreme Being, which, while he was infinitely happy in himself, mov'd him to create a World of Beings to make them so.[78]

In *Spring* Thomson speculates more searchingly than in earlier poems about the interrelationship between God, nature, and man, and between spirit and matter:

> 'Tis *Harmony*, that World-embracing Power,
> By which all Beings are adjusted, each
> To all around, impelling and impell'd
> In endless Circulation, that inspires
> This universal Smile. Thus the glad Skies,
> The wide-rejoycing Earth, the Woods, the Streams,
> With every *Life* they hold, down to the Flower
> That paints the lowly Vale, or Insect-Wing
> Wav'd o'er the Shepherd's Slumber, touch the Mind
> To Nature tun'd, with a light-flying Hand,
> Invisible; quick-urging, thro' the Nerves,
> The glittering Spirits, in a Flood of Day.

Though he is drawing from Locke's notions of physiology and Shaftesbury's moral philosophy, as he does elsewhere, Thomson's speculations at this point are less ready-made than in much of the *Seasons*. He argues that objects of sense, when charged with the philosopher-poet's projected emotions ('glad Skies', 'wide-rejoycing Earth') have an active power to touch his educated mind and refined sensibility, and stimulate his animal spirits (that is, the thin liquid in the hollow tubes of the nerves which, according to Locke, is the immediate instrument of all motion and sensation), so that he feels a warmth and light ('Flood of Day') which is that 'Creative Bounty', common to God and man, invoked a few lines earlier.[79] The intellectual and moral conception of harmony is felt with bodily senses in a way anticipating Wordsworth.

Political harmony finds a place in *Spring* too, when an affectionate sketch of lambs frisking on the site of an old Border fortress gives rise to reflections on the benefits of the Act of Union, or when vignettes of the ploughman yoking his oxen and scraping his ploughshare are expanded into an historical prospect which takes in the ancient Romans' veneration of agriculture and the import-ance of farming for Britain's export trade. It is implied that the local harmony between the husbandman, his team, his tackle, and his land is part of the larger 'happy Britannia' harmony of a wide mercantile empire which has cultural links with ancient Rome.[80] Thomson here justifies his theme by reminding his readers that it was Virgil's too. Such a claim so near the beginning of the poem that would stand first in the completed *Seasons* perhaps indicates that Thomson now thought his work belonged more to the georgic than to any other of the traditional genres of poetry. The *O fortunatos* rhapsody at the end of *Autumn* would confirm that impression; the completed *Seasons* would still end with *Winter*, where man shelters from the storm and trusts in Providence, and with the devotional 'Hymn', so that both of the seminal nature-poems acknowledged and praised in the Preface to *Winter*, the Book of Job and the *Georgics*, would resound in the final composition. However, from the writing of *Spring* onwards the Virgilian echoes are louder, longer, and more frequent.

Much of *Spring* is concerned with love, with mating in the animal kingdom (echoing Virgil's *Georgics*), with human sexual passion, with parental love in birds and humans, and with Thomson's constant theme of social love. The public voice is less evident than it is in the middle of *Summer* or the end of *Newton*. In the dedications, of which there are, unusually, two (one in prose, like the earlier-written *Seasons*, one in verse, like the later versions), Thomson celebrates the private virtues of the Countess of Hertford, rather than the public activities of the politician-dedicatees of *Winter, Summer,* and *Newton*.

Thomson was in London in the early summer of 1728 to correct *Spring* for the press, probably rewriting it a little in proof, as seems to have been his habit. Savage was finishing his longest poem *The Wanderer* (published January 1729), which offered a broadly similar mixture to Thomson's three *Seasons*, but in couplets. The first of its five cantos contains a compliment to his friend:

> And *Thomson*, in this Praise, thy Merit see,
> The Tongue, that praises Merit, praises thee. (i. 333–4)

Later in the year Thomson was with Mallet in the country. He had been there some time when, on 10 October, Aikman wrote apologetically to Sir John Clerk to explain why he had had 'no conversation' with 'our two Poets' over 'The Country Seat';[81] this is the last we hear of Clerk's poem in the correspondence of Thomson or his friends. If, as seems likely, Thomson was staying with Dodington again, he might well have been writing, or at least been gathering impressions for, his own country-seat poem in *Autumn*, the last of the *Seasons*, which he began to write immediately after *Spring*. There he describes the new beauties of Eastbury as it is growing daily under the hands of builders and gardeners; he relishes the splendours of the great house, the wide prospects of its grounds, the 'inspiring breeze' and ever-open 'book of Nature', but also, perhaps especially, the sunny kitchen-garden wall, which

> Presents the downy peach; the purple plumb,
> . . . the ruddy nectarine; and dark,
> Beneath his ample leaf, the luscious fig;

and which prompts his fancy to no less voluptuous thoughts about

> The Claret smooth, deep as the lip we press,
> In sparkling fancy, while we drain the bowl;
> The mellow-tasted Burgundy; and quick,
> As is the wit it gives, the bright Champaign.[82]

What Christopher Pitt wrote of Edward Young at Eastbury could equally be said of Thomson:

> . . . with your Dodington retir'd you sit,
> Charmed with his flowing burgundy and wit.[83]

Writing of the creature comforts with which Dodington supplied his guests Thomson displays the frank hedonism that impelled Johnson to accuse him of 'gross sensuality'.[84]

Two other poems may be linked with this conjectured visit to Eastbury in the autumn of 1728. The first is 'The Happy Man', in which the well-used Horatian *beatus ille* convention is adapted to compliment Dodington; much of this poem echoes *Autumn*, particularly the praise of Eastbury. The second is 'The Incomparable Soporifick Doctor', a savage satire upon some unidentified dull, gluttonous rural clergyman, perhaps someone known to the house-party at Eastbury; he cannot be the amiable, sprightly Patrick Murdoch (as many editors of Thomson have supposed), if only because Murdoch did not take holy orders until 1738. Both poems are twenty-odd lines long and in heroic couplets.[85] It is likely that Thomson finished *Autumn* in the second half of 1728; he may at that time have been turning over in his mind a long-meditated tragedy; he was certainly writing *Britannia*.

This blank-verse poem, just over three hundred lines long, was published in folio on 21 January; the publisher was Thomas Warner, a bookseller who published nothing else of Thomson's. Unusually for Thomson, there was no dedication and the author's name did not appear on the title page. Though the imprint 'Printed for T. Warner' implies that Warner was the copyright owner, it is likely that he was merely Thomson's or Millan's agent, because it is known that he was one of a small group of 'trade publishers', who were paid to distribute books for which others took the financial risk.[86] A trade publisher could stand between the authorities and someone really responsible for a controversial work or could ensure rapid distribution of a highly topical work. Probably the second was the case with *Britannia*, for it was advertised from

15 February onwards among works of Thomson sold by his regular publishers, Millan and Millar.

Britannia was occasioned by general public clamour for energetic retaliation against Spain's interference with British trade in the Spanish American colonies. Because of very severe limitations placed upon concessions secured by British merchants under the Treaty of Utrecht in 1713, a thriving illicit traffic grew up, which Spanish coastguards sought to check by the seizure of British ships. Consequently relations between Britain and Spain had by 1727 reached the hostile state described above in my discussion of the Dedication of Thomson's *Poem to Newton*. Admiral Hosier's squadron in the West Indies was attacked by a fever which carried off over four thousand men and officers, including Hosier himself, who died in August 1727, whereupon opposition politicians and journalists blamed Walpole for the expedition's failure to engage the Spaniards in battle. Parliament in 1727 and 1728 was loud with the opposition's denunciation of Walpole's over-pacific foreign policy; publication of *Britannia* on 21 January 1729 was timed to coincide exactly with the opening of a new parliamentary session, when it was expected that the opposition attack on the government would be pressed home with even greater vigour. The poem's topicality was intensified by a passage welcoming Frederick, Prince of Wales ('A Freight of future Glory'),[87] on his landing at Harwich on 3 December 1728. This passage includes tactful praise of King George II and Queen Caroline too, but Thomson, like the crowds who cheered Frederick to the echo, must have known that the Prince was coldly regarded by his parents.

Thomson's poem opens 'on the Sea-beat Shore', where there is a statuesque allegorical tableau of a distraught Britannia between departing, discontented Peace and roused-up War, who 'mourn'd his fetter'd Hands'; what follows is Britannia's complaint. She contrasts the shame of recent Spanish depredations and Hosier's fate with the defeat of the Spanish Armada; she enumerates the blessings of peace, but declares the justness and inevitability of war in present circumstances; she urges Britain's need to rule the waves in order to defend its providentially-ordained mercantile empire; she inveighs against luxury, the foe of that liberty which Britain is providentially required to uphold; and she declares she will fly to the first session of Parliament in order to stir up the patriots who will speak for her and 'shed the Spirit of *Britannia* round'.

> This said; her fleeting Form, and airy Train,
> Sunk in the Gale; and nought but ragged Rocks
> Rush'd on the broken Eye; and nought was heard
> But the rough Cadence of the dashing Wave.[88]

With the setting changed to the ruins of Rome and the speaker changed to Liberty herself, Thomson would repeat the same allegorical framework, as he would repeat the same general attitudes and many of the same specific ideas, in his most ambitious later poem, *Liberty*. In neither poem is his talent directed to the happiest effect.

There is a lack-lustre quality about too much of *Britannia*, most evident perhaps in the long invocation to peace, beginning 'Fair *Peace*! how lovely, how delightful Thou!' which at moments unnervingly calls to mind the tones of Mr Chadband. Against this, though, may be set the contextually unexpected bright vision of a flash flood on the Nile, or a series of vivid heroic seascapes, of Hosier's sad returning ships, of the sailing of the Spanish Armada, and the gales, stirred up by Britannia to shatter the Armada's defeated fugitives:

> Then too from every Promontory chill,
> Rank Fen, and Cavern where the wild Wave works,
> I swept confederate Winds, and swell'd a Storm.
> Round the glad Isle, snatch'd by the vengeful Blast,
> The scatter'd Remnants drove; on the blind Shelve,
> And pointed Rock, that marks th' indented Shore,
> Relentless dash'd, where loud the Northern Main
> Howls thro' the fractur'd *Caledonian* Isles.[89]

Hatred of that civil tyranny and religious bigotry which many Britons traditionally associated with Spain communicates some degree of genuine moral energy to *Britannia*. An invigorating patriotism, a love of liberty, and a sense of national destiny make this poem, at its best moments, something more than the expression of temporary war fever.

As one might expect, Thomson's poem was appropriated by political controversialists as soon as it was published. On 28 January the pro-Walpole *Daily Journal* quoted nearly fifty lines of Britannia's invocation to peace as praise of government policy, noting that, although the anonymous author apparently wished to rouse the nation to war, he could not resist the claims of peace. Four days later the opposition paper *Fog's Weekly Journal* printed the first eighty lines of the poem, down to and including the defeat of the Spanish Armada, in order to correct any misapprehension by *Daily Journal* readers. *Britannia* is also referred to in political writings of 1731, but did not make a great stir; it was probably employed more as an opposition political tool in the late 1730s than when it was first published. When the identity of its author was known Walpole's supporters laid charges of inconstancy and base ingratitude against him. For instance, the pro-government *Free-Briton*, 13 August 1730, reviewed Thomson's career from his dedication of the *Poem to Newton*, by way of *Britannia*, and then *Sophonisba* (dedicated to the Queen), to his recent appointment as travelling tutor to Charles Richard Talbot, son of the Solicitor-General:

When Sir *Isaac Newton* died, a young Gentleman, fam'd for the Sublimity of his Genius, drew Bills on a certain *great Man*, by a courtly Dedication prefix'd to his incomparable Poem. *He . . .* was rewarded with a Present of *fifty Pounds*. As he had shew'd his Parts on this Occasion, so he publish'd his Gratitude the following *Winter*, libell'd the Ministry in formidable Poetry; apply'd to them again in the *Spring*, and was ready to *travel* for the Good of the Publick with a Pension of *three hundreds* per Annum.[90]

If 'Sublimity of his Genius' and 'incomparable Poem' are not ironic, this criticism has more of sorrow than of anger; at least it does not have the sweeping animosity usually reserved for clearly identified enemies of the government. The Solicitor-General's patronage, the dedications of *Sophonisba* to the Queen and *Autumn* to the Speaker of the House of Commons, and the subscription list to *The Seasons*, all in 1730, showed that Thomson was not in disgrace with court or government over *Britannia*.

By then Walpole, immune from war fever, had ridden out the storm, and, in November 1729, demonstrated the strength of his government and his own position by concluding with Spain the Treaty of Seville, the terms of which were highly advantageous to Britain. Thomson's flirtation with the opposition, if it was as much as that, might be connected with Dodington's decision about this time to take a more independent line in politics. Very soon Dodington would openly associate himself with the opposition politicians congregating around the Prince of Wales, but would hold on to his Lordship of the Treasury. Perhaps Thomson was trying to perform a similar balancing act: he praises the Prince, but the king and queen also; he calls for war, but praises peace and the 'Man divine', who gives us peace. Such a man, it could be argued, was Walpole.[91]

Whatever were Thomson's motives in writing *Britannia*, his main literary hopes must have been bound up in the subscription edition of *The Seasons*, for which his proposals had appeared and he had collected his first guineas in January 1728. All four *Seasons* had probably been written by the winter of 1728–9; so this may be the period recollected by Duncan Forbes's daughter many years later: 'I remember previous to the publication of his seasons, that many long winter evenings the two were closeted: as I suppose correcting for the press, as I used to see loose pages of the manuscripts lying interlined with my father's hand.'[92] Thomson's friends bestirred themselves also in the slow business of gathering subscriptions. In March, Thomas Rundle wrote to his friend Mrs Barbara Sandys, a well-to-do widow and political hostess, to tell her that he has added her name to Thomson's subscription list. He praises Thomson as a man of genius who employs his muse to make virtue agreeable:

Nature and its explainer, and its author are his themes; what indeed could without prophaneness be joined to the praises of the Great Creator, but his works and NEWTON;

his works are his words; he speaks his sublime wisdom and goodness to us in them, and NEWTON is his interpreter. The poet describes the various scenes of the year with all its contrast of landskip agreeably; and now and then inserts a digression of a short story, which relieves from the uniformity of the prospect, and seems as figures in the works of that sort of painters, to give life and action to what is in itself merely inanimate.

The tone and detail of Rundle's account lead one to believe that he had seen or heard a full report of the whole work; otherwise he would not have implied, with his 'now and then', that *The Seasons* contains more than one short story. It is possible too that Rundle knew of the poet's ambition to be a dramatist, because the letter goes on to refer to plays of old, 'works of a sublime and sacred nature' (presumably Greek tragedy), and to Rundle's hopes that Thomson will reform English letters.[93]

Mrs Rowe also acquiesced in Lady Hertford's suggestion that she should subscribe. In April 1729 Thomson went to Oxford to drum up subscriptions, armed with a letter of introduction from Edward Young to Joseph Spence, Fellow of New College and Professor of Poetry in the University. He could expect a friendly reception from Spence, who had made prompt and favourable mention of *Winter* in the Second Part of his *Essay on Pope's Odyssey* (1727); we have Joseph Warton's testimony that Spence exerted himself to find subscribers. Warton wrote in 1797, 'I have before me a letter of Mr Spence to Pitt earnestly begging him to subscribe to the quarto edition of Thomson's Seasons, and mentioning a design which Thomson had formed of writing a descriptive poem on Blenheim; a subject that would have shone in his hands.'[94] The poet and translator Christopher Pitt duly subscribed, but Spence's letter to him is no longer to be found; Warton's note is the only surviving reference to any plan of Thomson's to write on Blenheim. Thomson might have seen Blenheim Palace during his visit to Oxford; perhaps he was at that time unaware that *Blenheim*, a descriptive poem on the place by his own future patron George Lyttelton, had been published (anonymously) in 1728.

Back in his old haunt, the Smyrna Coffee-House, Thomson sent a copy of the subscription proposals to Sir William Bennet on 10 April, announcing that the book would be ready to be delivered to subscribers at the end of May: 'It is now in the press.'[95] This statement is optimistic or disingenuous, because copies were not delivered for over another year; Sir William, who died in December 1729, did not live to see his. Meanwhile, in April 1729, four of Thomson's more substantial short poems were printed in *Miscellaneous Poems by Several Hands, publish'd by Mr Ralph*, the collection known as *Ralph's Miscellany*. The four are the 'Hymn on Solitude', in a text broadly similar to the one transcribed by Lady Hertford, 'A Paraphrase on the latter Part of the Sixth Chapter of St Matthew', 'The Happy Man', and 'The Incomparable Soporifick Doctor'; all were previously unpublished.

Though Thomson had announced that his subscription quarto was in the press in April, it is unlikely that printing really had begun by then. On 18 July he received £105 from John Millan for assignment of the perpetual copyright of

Summer a Poem, Autumn a Poem, Winter a Poem, Britania a Poem, a Poem Sacred to the Memory of Sir Isaack Newton; a Hymn on ye Succession of the Seasons and an Essay on Discriptive Poetry with all the Corrections, Alterations and Additions &c that will be printed in the Subscription Edition of my forsaid Poems: as also in full for any alterations &c that I may occasionally make hereafter.

The 'Essay' mentioned here may have been an intended revision of the Preface to *Winter*; it was never printed. Millan's advertisements for *Britannia* and the *Poem to Newton* from April 1729 onwards refer to Thomson as the 'Author of Spring, Summer, Autumn and Winter, Etc.[96] The wording of the copyright assignment implies that *Britannia* would form part of the subscription edition, but it seems not to have been included in copies delivered to subscribers; *Spring* is not in the assignment because Andrew Millar had the copyright.

In the autumn of 1729 Thomson was Dodington's guest once again. On 20 September he wrote from Eastbury to Mallet, who was then at Shawford, working at his tragedy on the story of Periander in the intervals of his labours as tutor to the Duke of Montrose's sons:

Dear Mallet, by this Time I suppose You are returned from London to the Downs of Hampshire, and Eurydice. Was you not interrupted, your Forenoons broken, and your Spirits unworthily dissipated by the Business of the Day, how pleasantly would it go on? With what unabated Fire?—Nothing to do, but to seize the rapturous Hour, when Nature prompts, and bids the fine Ferment of the Spirits rise. How delightful! to catch the Passions trembling from the Heart, that deep-felt delicate Harmony, that Enchantment which the least Touch of every ruder Care dissolves.

Thomson's next words reveal that he is chafing under his need for patronage; he even hints that life at Eastbury as Dodington's courtier and bard, for all its comforts, is a sort of Babylonish captivity: 'I too am far from that divine Freedom, that independant Life, which the Muses love. But it shall not be long thus, and soon will I hang up my Harp upon the Willows.' Thomson hoped to achieve some measure of financial independence by means of the forthcoming edition of *The Seasons*, but subscriptions were still slow to come in, possibly because the whole price had been asked for at the time of subscribing, rather than half in advance and half on publication, which was the more common practice. The letter to Mallet wryly continues with a wistful fantasy, where his target is now booksellers and even the reading public, rather than patrons:

I have heard of an Agreement among some of our modern Goths (who by the Bye are even unworthy of that Name) by which they bind Themselves not to encourage any

Subscription what ever under a certain Penalty. Methinks all tolerable Authors in this Age, all who can give Honour and Entertainment to it, should, in Opposition to this and the general Discouragement they labour under, enter into an Association not to write at all; or, if they do write for their own Pleasure and that of their particular Friends, yet never to publish. At the same time Care must be taken that none of your Manuscript-Publishers get what you write into their Hands; but let all be kept as sacred Mysteries from prophane Eyes. Then should we, as the Scripture says, have Joys which the Wicked could not intermeddle with: and if their Vanity, not Taste, prompted any of them to see what was written, they might, for a swinging Sum. There would be no Danger of their carrying much away with them. It is high Time that the Poets, who have been all along Bubbles to the World, given them the greatest Pleasure and received little in Exchange, began to think of some Craft: their Art is the Source of so much Pleasure, so commanding, that it is very capable of it, if thus mysteriously managed. But You destroy my whole Scheme, by saying, that if they have not good Writing, bad will do as well, and better. A Hurlothrumbo or any thing—Evil is their Good. Damn their Corruption, their low Taste, and all their stupid Expence![97]

It was indeed the case that abuses of the subscription system had induced some gentlemen to enter into quasi-legal bonds not to subscribe for any book whatever; such 'bondsmen' were the subject of satire in the late 1720s and 1730s, and would later make Fielding's Mr Wilson one of their victims.[98] Thomson is worried that the 'Tribute of the Muses' (as he called it in his letter to Clerk), the collective patronage represented by a long and high-class subscription list may not be forthcoming; he is impatient of the need to pay court to Lady Hertford and Dodington, generous, cultivated, and charming as those patrons were in their different ways; but he sticks to his view that enlightened patronage is a better guarantor of noble poetry than the commercial judgement of booksellers.

    Authorship had its compensations, though; perhaps Thomson is unconsciously comparing his present life with the life he might have led as a clergyman, when, in a later paragraph of this letter to Mallet, he writes,

I have been in dead Solitude here for some Days bypast. Mr D. went to London to wait upon the King—Now He's return'd. Poor Stubbs kept me alive. He toils here in two Parishes for 40 Pounds a Year—Had I paper I could rail for a Page more at it.

(George Stubbes, minor poet, wit, and longstanding friend and dependant of Dodington's was rector of Tarrant Gunville, the home parish for Eastbury.)
    There is another might-have-been in this same letter:

To turn my Eyes a softer Way, I am really touched with a fair Neighbour of your's—You know Who—Absence sighs it to me. What is my Heart made of? A soft System or Love—Nerves—Too sensible for my Quiet—capable of being very happy or very unhappy—I am afraid the last will prevail. Lay your Hand upon a kindred Heart and despise me not. I know not what it is, but she dwells upon my Thought, in a mingled Sentiment, which is the sweetest, the most intimately pleasing the Soul can receive, and which I would wish never to want towards some dear Object, or another. To have always some secret darling Idea, to which one can still have Recourse amidst the Noise and Nonsense of the World, and which never fails to touch us in the most exquisite Manner, is an Art of Happiness that Fortune cannot deprive us of. This may be called romantic, but whatever the Cause is the Effect is really felt. Pray, when you write, tell me when You saw Her, and with the pure Eye of a Friend; and when you see Her again, whisper that I am her most humble Servant.

Here speaks the man who loves to be in love: his sentimental delicacy in letters and poetry is the obverse and complement of his noted coarseness in convivial male company. Mallet knew who this lady was, but we do not.[99]

Another woman dwelling on Thomson's thought at this time doubtless was the heroine of the tragedy he was writing in the summer of 1729. He was bidding for fame as a playwright no less than as a poet; with what success the next chapter will show.

4

Recognition: *Sophonisba* and *The Seasons*, 1730

IT is likely that Thomson's ambition to write for the stage was aroused soon after his arrival in London. Hill was a man of the theatre, who wanted to see a revival of classical tragedy; at one of Thomson's early meetings with him Hill read aloud to a number of the assembled disciples four acts of the revised version of his *Elfrida* (the play eventually acted in 1731 under the title of *Athelwold*).[1] In 1725 and 1726 Thomson's closest literary associate, David Mallet, was at work on a tragedy 'concerning Xerxes and his brother Masistes' and was encouraging Savage to write a second tragedy.[2] On 15 August 1726 Savage wrote to Mallet, 'As for your story of Massinissa, I still admire it, and am resolved to attempt it, tho' I have not yet begun.'[3] Masinissa's history was also Sophonisba's; so it is possible that Thomson took over the subject from his friends when Savage's resolve to attempt it failed, as so many of his resolves did. The puff for *Spring* in the *Whitehall Evening-Post* of 19 March 1728 referred obliquely to Thomson's plans to write a play:

May I have leave just to hint that the *present* Encouragement of so good a Genius may prove *their future* Entertainment in a nobler way; when the Author shall rise from the *still Life* of Poetry, to represent the Passions of Mankind, those great Springs of Action; and the Distresses flowing from them, which, by exciting our Compassion and Fear, move and delight so exquisitely in the *Scene*.

Whether Thomson had a specific dramatic subject in mind as early as March 1728 is not known, but he was writing his *Sophonisba* by the summer of 1729, when Mallet, having abandoned *Xerxes*, was at work on a tragedy upon another subject from Herodotus, the story of Periander.[4]

Financial rewards for even a moderately successful play were attractive and new plays were in demand at that time; a modern historian of the London stage, Arthur H. Scouten, has noted that in the late 1720s and 1730s the total theatre audience was growing, new houses were opening, and there was 'a remarkable increase in the total number of new plays';[5] but Thomson's motives for turning dramatist were far from mercenary. His defence of the lofty, quasi-religious ends of poetry in the Preface to the second edition of *Winter* in June 1726 is implicitly a defence of the serious drama too, for it includes a hit against the shameful 'sulphureous Attacker of the Stage', William Law, author of *The Absolute Unlawfulness of the Stage-Entertainment Fully Demonstrated* (1726).[6] Thomson believed that the stage, in its proper function as the ancient Greeks had used it, was a powerful moral instructor: not opposed to religion, but complementing it.

For his first attempt upon the stage Thomson took the story of the Carthaginian queen Sophonisba at the time of the Second Punic War. His source was principally Livy, with material also from Diodorus Siculus and Appian,[7] for, in common with other eighteenth-century writers of heroic tragedy, Thomson sought to preserve historical truth as far as this was possible within the bounds of dramatic probability. As the Prologue to Thomson's play reminded its first auditors, this story was the subject of the earliest modern European regular tragedy, the Italian *Sofonisba* (*c*.1514) by Gian Giorgio Trissino. The story had been told by Petrarch, Boccaccio, and Bandello; it was retold in William Painter's *Palace of Pleasure* (1576) and in a narrative poem by Sir David Murray (1611). There were five plays about Sophonisba on the French stage before Pierre Corneille's in 1663; in England there were stage versions by John Marston (1606), Thomas Nabbes (1635), and Nathaniel Lee (1676). The sale catalogue of Thomson's library after his death reveals that he possessed copies of Trissino's and Corneille's plays on Sophonisba in editions dated 1722 and 1723,[8] but the only version Thomson is likely to have seen on the stage is Lee's *Sophonisba*, which was acted at least three times when Thomson was a regular London theatregoer.[9]

Lee's play contains much action and extravagant spectacle, and diffuses action over a large range of characters; Thomson's play, by contrast, is spare, chaste, and correct to a fault; it observes the unities of time, place, and action even more strictly than Corneille's *Sophonisbe*. Thomson added a Preface to the printed edition of his play, where, perhaps intending to forestall criticism such as Dennis had levelled against Addison's *Cato*, that multiple actions had been brought implausibly into one time and place, he justified simplicity of action and unity of design, citing Racine's preface to *Bérénice* in support. Thomson's play has only four main characters: Sophonisba, Scipio, Masinissa, and Syphax, together with a friend or lieutenant attending upon each of the first three, and a messenger.

Sophonisba is the daughter of the warrior Hasdrubal; her ruling passion is love of country. Before the action of the play opens she has married Syphax, King of Masaesylia, who is prepared for her sake to break his allegiance to Rome and fight for Carthage. In marrying Syphax, Sophonisba has extinguished her affection for her other lover Masinissa, who is now a faithful and admiring follower of Scipio, commander of the invading Roman army. When Syphax is defeated and brought back to his own palace in Roman chains Sophonisba, about to endure the same fate, is driven by a passion more political than erotic to abandon her husband and marry Masinissa, who has never ceased to love her. As she explains to the understandably outraged Syphax, she did not prefer one husband to the other, 'But *Carthage* to you both'. It can be no shame to prefer

> Thousands to one, a whole collected people,
> All nature's tenderness, whate'er is sacred,
> The liberty, the welfare of a state,
> To one man's frantic happiness.[10]

Syphax is a man of simple, unregenerate animal passions, and Masinissa's inveterate enemy in love and war. Masinissa is the man of sensibility, the only character whose speeches often echo the nature imagery of the *Seasons*. Like Antony, he is torn between love of an African queen and his duty to Rome. In the relatively animated, because mostly rhymed, soliloquy which ends Act I he reflects upon the wild fury he has just witnessed in his prisoner Syphax:

> O save me from the tumult of the soul!
> From the wild beasts within!—For circling sands,
> When the swift whirlwind whelms them o'er the lands;
> The roaring deeps that to the clouds arise,
> While thwarting thick the mingled lightning flies;
> The monster-brood to which this land gives birth,
> The blazing city, and the gaping earth;
> All deaths, all tortures, in one pang combin'd,
> Are gentle to the tempest of the mind.[11]

It is a theme of *Summer* (1727) that a tropical climate gives rise both to the natural calamities described here and to extreme passions in men. Masinissa, like Syphax, is a Numidian or Berber chieftain, but he has been civilized by contact with Rome and has learned to venerate the ideal of public virtue personified in Scipio. In many respects he resembles Juba, the Numidian prince who admires Cato in Addison's play. Away from Scipio's guardianship, however, Masinissa yields to passion, in this case the tender, rather than the savage, passion of love, and, unlike Sophonisba, who is temperamentally more Roman than African, he loses all sense of public responsibility. On marrying Sophonisba he vows to obtain her release from Roman captivity, but, when Scipio recalls him to his duty in the last act, he can keep his vow only by sending her poison, which she resolutely drinks.

Scipio speaks fewer lines than the other main characters and does not enter until Act V, Scene ii, but his presence is felt throughout the action. He is an old

hero of Thomson's, one of only three Romans among the ten classical worthies
praised in *Winter* (1726):

> Sages of ancient Time, as Gods rever'd,
> As Gods beneficent, who blest Mankind.[12]

Masinissa's early references to him as 'the first of men' and 'a guardian God
below' echo praise of Scipio in *Winter* as the very embodiment of public virtue,
specifically of republican virtue. Scipio's lieutenant reminds the backsliding
Masinissa later in the play that 'A Roman | Would scorn to be a king'.[13] That
locus classicus of ancient Roman virtue and favourite subject of moralized history
painting, the story of 'the Continence of Scipio', is narrated in Act II, Scene ii,
of Thomson's play. It illuminates the character of the still-absent Scipio and
provides a point of reference for later episodes, such as the tableau in the
following scene when Sophonisba kneels as Masinissa's captive and obtains his
protection by overcoming his continence, or the denouement when Scipio does
claim his queenly captive, albeit for Rome not himself.

In *Sophonisba* Thomson is concerned less with the passions of the heart than
with political virtues, the moral qualities in individual persons that create and
sustain a nation. His underlying theme is (to quote the revised text of *Winter*,
awaiting publication in 1730) 'how Empire grew, declin'd, and fell'; he echoes
passages on the growth of civilization and on social love in his newly-written
Autumn.[14] Scipio, explaining the rise of Rome, declares:

> From savage nature,
> 'Tis patience that has built up human life,
> The nurse of arts.

Condemning Masinissa's irrational, self-gratifying, politically dangerous love
for Sophonisba, he contrasts sexual passion with 'sympathy':

> a fountain-love;
> Branch'd infinite from parents to their children,
> From child to child, from kindred on to kindred,
> In various streams, from citizen to citizen,
> From friend to friend, from man to man in general.[15]

This reads like a summary of almost any eighteenth-century treatise on moral
philosophy. Such passages add substance to Johnson's claim that nobody in the
splendid audiences at the rehearsals of *Sophonisba* 'was much affected, and that
the company rose as from a moral lecture'.[16]

The Carthaginian heroine dies by her own hand like a female Cato.
Addison's play had been criticized by John Dennis because, in showing Cato
vanquished by Caesar, it allowed virtue to suffer and vice to triumph: Thomson

escapes such objections by showing the triumph of virtuous republican Rome, while at the same time insisting upon the stoic Roman virtues of Sophonisba herself. The last lines of the play are her epitaph and Thomson's patriotic flourish:

> She had a *Roman* soul; for every one
> Who loves, like her, his country is a *Roman* . . .
> If parent-liberty the breast inflame,
> The gloomy *Libyan* then deserves that name:
> And, warm with freedom, under frozen skies,
> In farthest *Britain Romans* yet may rise.

Thomson is already turning over in his mind the theme of his most ambitious poem, *Liberty*.

The themes of the Prologue too are freedom and cultural imperialism. It opens with allusions to Italian and French plays about Sophonisba, and continues:

> What foreign theatres with pride have shewn,
> *Britain*, by juster title, makes her own.
> When freedom is the cause, 'tis hers to fight;
> And hers, when freedom is the theme, to write.[17]

In the printed editions the Prologue is said to be 'By a Friend'. Johnson was informed by Savage 'that of the Prologue to *Sophonisba* the first part was written by Pope, who could not be persuaded to finish it, and that the concluding lines were added by Mallet'.[18] The editors of Pope's *Minor Poems* in the Twickenham edition attribute the first 26 lines of the Prologue to Pope and the last six to Mallet; they note parallels between lines 1–26 and Pope's Prologue to Addison's *Cato*.[19] Lord Hervey wrote an epilogue, which, in the event, was not used.[20] The Epilogue in the printed text of the play is attributed to 'a Friend'. Both epilogues are in the then fashionable, bantering, ribald style, and, as was the custom, were intended to be spoken by a woman, but the one actually used has the grace to acknowledge Thomson's dislike of the practice of tagging comic epilogues on to tragedies:

> Our squeamish author scruples this proceeding;
> He says it hurts sound morals, and good breeding.[21]

All the objections that Johnson and Joseph Warton, among others, urged against Addison's *Cato* can be brought with greater force against *Sophonisba*. Thomson's play is indeed 'rather a poem in dialogue than a drama . . . Nothing here excites or asswages emotion'; it 'is a fine dialogue on liberty, and the love of one's country', but it 'must be owned to want action and pathos'.[22] Some of the dramatic weakness of Thomson's tragedy was apparent to the Drury Lane management from the outset, to judge by an anecdote of Benjamin Victor. He recalled the author reading his manuscript to the actor Barton Booth, one of the three managers of the Drury Lane theatre:

when he came to the fifth act, it opened thus:

> The breezy Spring
> Sits loosely-floating on the mountain-top,
> And deals her sweets around.

'Very fine, (says Booth)—but what the devil does it do here?—I had rather that pretty flower was stuck in the middle of a love-poem, than in the fifth act of a tragedy!'[23]

Whether or not it was plucked from the acting version, this pretty flower was retained in the printed text.[24] That text also includes, as an appendix, a 'Nuptial Song', in octosyllabic couplets, which, we are informed, was 'intended to have been inserted in the Fourth Act'.[25] The ceremony of marriage between Masinissa and Sophonisba occurs off-stage in Act IV, and the play as it now stands offers no obvious context for a nuptial song, so this song may perhaps be all that Thomson wished to preserve of an entire scene that he had deleted.

Pretty flowers notwithstanding, Booth and his fellow managers, Robert Wilks and Colley Cibber, accepted the play, but for a while there was some doubt as to whether it would come on in the 1729–30 season. At some time near the end of 1729 Mallet wrote to Pope, retailing some gossip from John Upton, the future editor of Spenser and one of several Oxford college fellows who subscribed to the collected *Seasons* (1730):

He has heard, it seems, that Mr D. publickly lays claim to a share in the Writing of that Tragedy, at which he is most divertingly angry. I pity my poor Friend betwixt them. And the kindest Wish I can form for him is, that his Performance may defend it self against the vain Applauses of the One, and the officious Impertinence of the other.

'Mr D.' is annotated 'Dodington' in the hand of Lord Burlington on the manuscript of this letter. As George Sherburn points out, it is Upton who is 'most divertingly angry'.[26] William Aikman was able to report to his patron Sir John Clerk on 13 January 1730 that both Thomson and Mallet had finished their tragedies, but Mallet's was presented to the Drury Lane management too late to be acted that season. Thomson's play, however, was already in rehearsal and 'bears a very great character among the Virtuosi. Mr Dodington is extravagant in its praise as is Mrs Oldfield and several of the players. I wish they may not raise peoples expectations to a height about it that cannot be satisfied.'[27] Johnson says that *Sophonisba* 'raised such expectation that every rehearsal was dignified with a splendid audience'.[28]

On 16 January, perhaps impressed by the expectations of the *virtuosi* at the

Drury Lane rehearsals, Andrew Millar paid £137.10s. for the copyrights of
Sophonisba and *Spring*, together with 'all additions corrections alterations and
amendments whatsoever which shall or may at any time hereafter be made'.
There was a proviso, similar to that in the assignment of the other parts of the
Seasons to Millan six months earlier, that Thomson could print *Spring* 'once and
no more' to go with other poems 'by way of Subscription to make a quarto
Volume', a volume which, the assignment says, is 'now printing'.[29]

With *Sophonisba* in rehearsal, the *Poem to Newton*, *Britannia*, *Winter*, *Summer*,
and *Spring* in print, and a growing subscription list for the long-heralded
complete, revised *Seasons*, Thomson was now making his presence felt on the
London literary scene, but his success aroused resentment in some quarters.
About the same time as the Drury Lane managers accepted *Sophonisba* they
rejected another new tragedy, *Timoleon*, by Benjamin Martyn (1699–1763);
'but by the Author's Interest, it was afterwards sent with a Command which
they durst not disobey'. It seems that rehearsals for *Sophonisba* were interrupted
so that Martyn's play could go forward, because *Timoleon* was only a fortnight in
rehearsal before it opened on 26 January for a successful run of fourteen
nights.[30] As the Prince of Wales attended the fourth night and the printed play,
published on 7 February, was dedicated to the King, it is likely that the
playwright (a government place-holder) had friends at court. A newspaper
article shortly after *Timoleon*'s opening implied that Thomson was taking the
postponement of his own play badly: 'The Tragedy of *Timoleon* has been received with very great Applause by the Town, notwithstanding the Endeavours
of a certain Person (who can give a Preference to none but his own Performances) to depreciate it.'[31] Martyn's own resentment, freely expressed in the
earlier, rasher text of his Preface, is directed against the managers, particularly Cibber,[32] but some satirical couplets by 'Perseus' in newspapers on 14
February conclude:

> Their *Curses* freed *Timoleon* from the Grave,
> But *Miracles* must *Sophonisba* save.

A footnote adds scornfully, 'These People [the managers] have been heard to
say that *Sophonisba* was an excellent Play.'[33]

It is likely that *Sophonisba* was also the target of a satirical letter, dated 19
January 1730, in *The Grub-Street Journal* of 22 January, where it was said that 'a
Parnassian Tragedy of *Corneille* has been made to shine with true Grubaean
honour on the British Stage, by an eminent Dramatick Writer of your Society'.
It would be reasonable to suppose that the eminent dramatic writer was Colley
Cibber, but none of his adaptations of tragedies by Corneille had been acted on
the London stage in the five years before this letter. So one suspects that the
work in question is *Sophonisba*, and that the author of the letter believed that it

was an adaptation of Corneille's *Sophonisbe*. As Thomson's play had only just gone into rehearsal and its authorship may not yet have been widely known, the letter-writer may have imagined that it was Cibber's work, but it is equally possible that he is referring only to Cibber's managerial approval of a play bad enough for Grub Street, and to his playing the shining, honourable part of Scipio in rehearsal.

Whether or not Thomson is directly attacked in this letter, he is certainly one of the targets of an ironic essay by John Martyn (1699–1768, no relation of the author of *Timoleon*), on 'Grubaean' imitations of the 'Parnassian' Milton, which was printed in *The Grub-Street Journal* of 5 February 1730. After ridiculing Ralph and Dennis, Martyn introduces an example of bathos from Thomson's *Winter*, six lines on a storm, ending,

> 'the hollow Chimney howls,
> The Windows rattle, and the Hinges creak.'[34]

Two weeks later, though, on 19 February, *The Grub-Street Journal* printed Martyn's retraction. He declares that Thomson is not a Grub Street writer after all: 'the greatest part' of *Winter* is 'written after the Parnassian manner'. Martyn and the other editor of *The Grub-Street Journal* were Tories, possibly Jacobites, who would have strong enough political motives for attacking as strongly Whig a poet as Thomson. In literary matters, though, they were invariably respectful towards Pope; they generally supported his friends and attacked his enemies, so one suspects that between 5 and 19 February someone told Martyn that Pope and Thomson were friends. Subsequently, *The Grub-Street Journal* reported the success of *Sophonisba* and ridiculed pamphlets attacking the play. When Martyn's essay on Grubaean imitations of Milton was reprinted in *Memoirs of the Society of Grub-Street* (1737) all allusion to Thomson was deleted.

Sophonisba opened at Drury Lane on 28 February and ran for ten performances, the last on 17 March; the author thus enjoyed three benefit nights. It was never revived in the regular London theatre, though on 5 April 1731 it was played publicly by a troupe of child actors, the 'Lilliputians'.[35] The moderate success of its first run is perhaps attributable more to the players than the play.

The name part was taken by Anne Oldfield, whose bedworthiness had so excited Thomson when he first visited a London theatre.[36] In 1730 she was the leading actress of her generation, then aged 46 and in the thirtieth season of her acting career. She had first made her reputation playing ladies of quality in comedies of manners, but was a fine tragic actress too; she triumphed in popular modern tragedies where the leading character was a strongly-drawn suffering woman, such as Ambrose Philips's *The Distrest Mother*, and Rowe's *Jane Shore* and *The Fair Penitent*. Sophonisba was her last new part in tragedy. Thomas Davies, the biographer of Garrick, recalls that, in Act III, Scene iii,

In reply to some degrading expression of Masinissa relating to Carthage, she uttered the following line, 'Not one base word of *Carthage*—on thy soul!' with such grandeur in her action, a look so tremendous, and a voice so powerful, that it is said she even astonished Wilks, her Masinissa; it is certain that the audience were struck, and expressed their feelings by the most uncommon applause.[37]

Another contemporary, the dramatist William Rufus Chetwood, said that the part of Sophonisba was reputedly the cause of Mrs Oldfield's death, 'for, in her Execution, she went beyond Wonder, to Astonishment! From that time her decay came slowly on!'[38] She died in October 1730.[39]

Masinissa was played by the even more experienced Robert Wilks, then in his sixties. He was a joint-manager of Drury Lane and an actor of considerable range and sensitivity; he was noted for his Hamlet, a part he was playing on the stage at the time *Sophonisba* was in rehearsal.[40] When the play was printed Thomson singled out the leading players for praise in his Preface:

Whatever was designed as amiable and engaging in *Masinissa* shines out in Mr *Wilks*'s action. Mrs *Oldfield*, in the character of *Sophonisba*, has excelled what, even in the fondness of an author, I could either wish or imagine. The grace, dignity, and happy variety of her action have been universally applauded, and are truly admirable.[41]

John Mills, fresh from playing the lead in *Timoleon*, took the part of Syphax. Like Anne Oldfield and Wilks, he had begun his acting career in the previous century; he was a competent all-round actor, particularly good in parts 'of the rough, haughty, and *stern* kind'.[42] The cast list in the printed text of *Sophonisba* gives the role of Scipio to Williams, but we learn from Thomas Davies that he did not play this part on the first two nights. According to Davies, when the play was first read to the actors Colley Cibber 'laid his hand upon Scipio, a character, which, though it appears only in the last act, is of great dignity and importance'. Cibber had played several considerable tragic parts at Drury Lane that season, including Syphax in Addison's *Cato* (a different historical Syphax from the one in *Sophonisba*), but audiences greatly preferred to see him play comic parts, in which he excelled. His playing of Scipio met a hostile reaction, as Davies reports:

For two nights successively, Cibber was as much exploded as any bad actor could be: Williams, by desire of Wilks, made himself master of the part; but he, marching slowly, in great military distinction, from the upper part of the stage, and wearing the same dress as Cibber, was mistaken for him, and met with repeated hisses joined to the music of catcals; but, as soon as the audience were undeceived, they converted their groans and hisses to loud and long-continued applause.[43]

Williams spoke the Prologue. The Epilogue was not spoken by the heroine, as was customary, even though Anne Oldfield had a particular talent for the ribald innuendo of such performances: it was delivered instead by Jane Cibber, not a member of the cast.[44] One would like to think that Thomson, who repeatedly made objections to flippant epilogues tagged on to tragedies, put his foot down to the extent of preventing Sophonisba herself crudely breaking the mood in which his tragedy ended, but he was not in a position to dictate to established actors. So a more probable explanation is that the circumstances of *Timoleon*'s staging, already described, made it necessary for its rehearsal and acting to be arranged in tandem with *Sophonisba*, with the main players in one acting lesser parts in the other. Jane Cibber acted in *Timoleon* and Anne Oldfield spoke the Epilogue; in *Sophonisba* these roles were reversed.

A run of ten nights was good, but not exceptional for a new play. Shiels and Murdoch both comment on the audience's favourable response, and Shiels adds an anecdote about Thomson's agitation on the first night:

Mr Thomson who could not but feel all the emotions and sollicitudes of a young author the first night of his play, wanted to place himself in some obscure part of the house, in order to see the representation to the best advantage, without being known as the poet.—He accordingly placed himself in the upper gallery; but such was the power of nature in him, that he could not help repeating the parts along with the players, and would sometimes whisper to himself, 'now such a scene is to open', by which he was soon discovered to be the author, by some gentlemen who could not, on account of the great crowd, be situated in any other part of the house.[45]

On 6 March the *Daily Post* reported that *Sophonisba* 'is allow'd, by the best Judges, in its Poetry, to be hardly inferior to any Piece the Stage has produc'd for many Years: The Habits and Decorations are very magnificent, and Mrs Oldfield's Performance surprizing.' Three days later the *Daily Journal* chimed in, saying that 'The Conduct of the Play is regular and uniform; the Manners perfectly well-mark'd and distinguish'd; the Sentiments strong, natural, and convey'd in the greatest Dignity of Expression. Mrs Oldfield, in particular, has charm'd all the World with the Justness, Force, and Gracefulness of her Action.'

Contemporary readers and auditors, recommending the play to their friends, praised the poetry and moral sentiments, though some had reservations about the heroine's excessive patriotism. Mrs Pendarves wrote, 'Sophonisba is a character that can never be made agreeable; that extravagance of love for her country, had it been softened by a little tenderness, would have been more moving...The language is sublime, and I think excels any play we have had a great while.' Elizabeth Rowe: ''Tis a noble Tragedy, I can't help prefering it to Mr Addison's Cato; the language and Sentiments have all a peculiar Grandeur.' Thomas Rundle:

The story is a bad one, and its being true is the only justification of it; the writing is incomparable . . . There are some roughnesses in the numbers; some poetical extravagancies as nearly related to nonsense, as a note raised to the highest pitch, by a fine singer, is to a scream; some aukward odnesses of expression, which may be observed by one, who is of a taste cold enough to attend to such minute transgressions, when his reason and fancy ought to be fired by good sense, harmony, and nature.[46]

Thomson's profit from *Sophonisba* is difficult to assess precisely. An author's theatre income was by way of his benefit nights, when he received all the proceeds from the sale of tickets, less a fixed house charge of about fifty pounds. The capacity of Drury Lane was about one thousand and the range of seat prices ran from five shillings to one shilling, but aristocratic patrons and royalty in particular would pay far more than the face value of their tickets at an author's benefit. At the very roughest guess, based on scanty records of other benefits, Thomson might have cleared as much as three hundred pounds for all three benefit nights together.[47] Whatever the actual sum, it is virtually certain to have been significantly more than the prices fetched for Thomson's copyrights in works of comparable length.

On 7 March it was announced that *Sophonisba* would be played on 19 March for the benefit of Mrs Oldfield; this was unusual because the players as a general rule were not allowed to choose a new play of the current season for their benefit performances; but in the event her benefit play on 19 March was the old, highly popular repertory piece, Rowe's *The Fair Penitent*. Advertisements for that performance say that 'Tickets for *Sophonisba* will be taken', so it looks as if Thomson's play, which was taken off after 17 March, did not run as long as the management expected.[48]

The author's second benefit performance, on 9 March, was by command of the Prince of Wales and was attended also by the Princess Royal and other, unnamed members of the royal family. Andrew Millar announced that the printed play would be on sale that day, but, as it happened, publication was delayed until 12 March. This delay may have been made necessary by small revisions at press, or the opportunity to make such revisions may have been taken because Thomson had been given the honour of presenting a copy to the Queen and he did not want his play to be on sale earlier.[49] On 13 March the newspapers announced: 'Yesterday Mr Thomson was introduced to her Majesty by the Right Hon. the Earl of Grantham, and presented his Tragedy of *Sophonisba*, which is now acting with great applause at the Theatre Royal in Drury lane, and was graciously received.' It is likely that the Countess of Hertford, who was a Lady of the Queen's Bedchamber, was instrumental in bringing Thomson to the Queen's notice. The printed play carries a royal dedication, couched in the same patriotic terms as *Britannia*, though with less belligerence. Caroline is addressed as a queen 'who commands the hearts of a

People, more powerful at sea than *Carthage*, more flourishing in *commerce* than those *first Merchants*, more secure against conquest, and, under a *Monarchy*, more free than a *Commonwealth* itself'. In private Thomson was less respectful of queen and country, to judge by Spence's report that Thomson 'laughed heartily when we read the passage relating to Caroline, and the other of the glory of our nation'.[50]

Sophonisba brought Thomson greater financial profit and recognition, and in more elevated social circles, than he had hitherto received, but he was not artistically satisfied with his first effort for the stage. He wrote to Dodington later in the year, 'I think of attempting another Tragedy, and on a story more addressed to common passions than that of Sophonisba. People now-a-days must have something like themselves, and a public-spirited monster can never concern them.'[51] The accuracy of this assessment of public taste was strikingly demonstrated by the huge success of George Lillo's domestic tragedy, *The London Merchant, or the History of George Barnwell*, in the following year, but as it transpired, Thomson's next tragedy would not appear for eight years and would be concerned with the somewhat uncommon passions of the House of Atreus.

Though press comment was generally favourable and *The Grub-Street Journal* had come over to Thomson's side, attacks on his work continued from other quarters. During the run of *Sophonisba*, before the play was printed, appeared a thirty-page pamphlet, *A Criticism on the New Sophonisba*, by 'Tim Birch'. The real name of the author is not known, but it looks as if he was a well-wisher of Benjamin Martyn, who feared that Thomson's play might eclipse *Timoleon*; it is conceivable that he was Benjamin Martyn himself. 'Tim Birch' sneers at the Drury Lane managers, who 'have erected themselves Judges of all *Dramatick* Entertainments', and at the claque of 'Scotchmen with tuneful Hands and merry Feet', which, he implies, accounted for the favourable reception of Thomson's play. He asserts that Thomson, 'being present at the Performance of *Timoleon* could not stifle his Envy, which burst into Expressions very unbecoming a Brother Adventurer'. Then, after bestowing a brief encomium on Martyn's play, 'Tim Birch' proceeds to damn *Sophonisba* in general and in detail. His most tediously repeated accusation in this sour and mostly humourless diatribe is plagiarism; he concludes that Thomson has 'been very innocent in borrowing from others, having only taken such Things in his Necessity as they might well spare, and by a peculiar happy Transfiguration made them his own'. The best stroke of wit is a parody of Thomson's 'Oh Sophonisba! Sophonisba Oh!' as 'Oh Jemmy Thompson! Jemmy Thompson Oh!'.[52] But even this witticism is not original if Shiels is to be believed; he says that when the unfortunate line was spoken by Wilks on the first night at Drury Lane 'a smart from the pit cried out, "Oh Jamey Thomson, Jamey Thomson Oh!" '[53] Tim Birch's pamphlet achieved enough notoriety for Joseph Mitchell to be forced to write to the newspapers on 16 March, pompously denying that he was its author.[54]

On 19 January newspapers carried advertisements for *A Defence of the New Tragedy of Sophonisba* alongside *A Criticism on the New Sophonisba*; both pamphlets were published by F. Cogan; it was hinted in *The Grub-Street Journal* a week later that both were written by the same hand. Though Grant takes the second pamphlet to be a genuine defence, 'which appears to have settled the controversy',[55] it is a work of sustained irony and a more damaging attack than the original *Criticism*. The author of the *Defence* claims, for instance, 'Mr *Thomson* is so far from using Words without any Meaning, (as *Tim. Birch* would insinuate) that most of his Sentences will bear two.' He declares that Tim Birch is wrong when he says that Thomson's thoughts are stale, for, rather, they are 'new and bold'. After quoting examples of absurd boldness, he concludes, 'This jumbling Words together till they jingle, puts me in Mind of Boys shaking Halfpence in a Hat, and when they hear 'em chink one against another, toss 'em out for a lucky Throw!' Having the printed text to hand, as the author of the *Criticism* did not, he is able ironically to praise that 'simplicity' to which Thomson drew attention in his Preface.[56] *The Grub-Street Journal* of 26 March claimed that the authors or author of the *Criticism* and *Defence* were qualified to be members of that society of hacks of which the *Journal* was the ironic mouthpiece, whereas Thomson 'will probably be a profest enemy to our society'.

Sophonisba soon found a more powerful and witty antagonist. Henry Fielding's farce *Tom Thumb, a Tragedy* opened on 24 April 1730 and ran very successfully for thirty-three nights, until 22 June. This wide-ranging burlesque includes parodies of the best-known heroic tragedies from the times of Dryden and Lee onwards; Thomson's *Sophonisba* is the most modern object of its ridicule. Not only is Thomson ridiculed, there is some neat parody of Pope's nationalism in Fielding's Prologue:

> *Britons* awake!—Let *Greece* and *Rome* no more
> Their Heroes send to our Heroick Shore.
> Let home-bred Subjects grace the modern Muse . . .
> To-Night our Bard, *Spectators*, would be true
> To *Farce*, to *Tragedy*, *Tom Thumb*, and *You*.[57]

Fielding's play was enlarged during the run and both the original and the revised versions were printed in 1730, but what was to become the most derided line of *Sophonisba* is parodied in neither version. This fact perhaps casts doubt on Shiels's story of the impromptu joke from the audience, or perhaps indicates that the joke (whether originating with 'the smart from the pit' or 'Tim Birch') did not travel around the town fast enough for Fielding to pick it up

while *Tom Thumb* was running. The line 'Oh! *Huncamunca, Huncamunca*, oh'
first appears in Fielding's more considerable revision of his farce, under the
new title *The Tragedy of Tragedies; or the Life and Death of Tom Thumb the Great*,
which ran for twelve nights from 24 May 1731 and has been revived on
innumerable occasions since. The printed text of the play adds a bulky
apparatus containing quotations from the authors parodied in which there are
over a dozen citations from Thomson's play as well as many from Lee's
Sophonisba. It carries also a Preface which parodies Corneille's address to the
reader in his *Sophonisbe*; but in the ironies of Fielding's preface there is,
incidentally, some just criticism:

> The *Sophonisba* of *Mairet*, and of *Lee*, is a tender, passionate, amorous Mistress of
> *Massinissa*; *Corneille* and Mr *Thomson* give her no other Passion but the Love of her
> Country, and make her as cool in her Affection to *Massinissa*, as to *Syphax*. In the two
> latter, she resembles the Character of Queen *Elizabeth*; in the two former she is the
> Picture of *Mary* Queen of *Scotland*.[58]

Shortly before *The Tragedy of Tragedies* was staged at the Little Theatre in the
Haymarket, *Sophonisba* was probably the object of parody at the theatre in
Lincoln's Inn Fields, where, on 30 April 1731 and two subsequent evenings,
was performed *The Contrast; a Tragi-Comical Rehearsal of Two Modern Plays:
Match upon Match, or No Match at All, and the Tragedy of Epaminondas*, by John
Hoadly, son of the Bishop of Salisbury. On 6 May *The Grub-Street Journal*
printed an ironic letter, which purports to be by the play's author writing under
the pen-name 'Salisbury Steeple' to indicate his parentage. This letter admits
that *The Contrast*

> was written with a direct view of *abusing* two or three particular men; more especially that
> strenuous *Antigrubean* the Author of *Sophonisba*; whom I have handled in such a manner
> that on that account I was afraid for some time to own myself the writer, lest some surly
> *North Briton* should have made my b——h suffer for what my fingers had perform'd.

How Thomson was abused we do not know, because, at the desire of Bishop
Hoadly, *The Contrast* was suppressed, and no copy or detailed report of the
play's content survives.[59]

That Thomson was regarded at this time more as the poet of *Sophonisba* than
the *Seasons* appears from verses by the indigent, dissipated Edinburgh poet
Samuel Boyse, 'To Mr Thomson upon his Tragedy of Sophonisba', printed in
1731,[60] and from anonymous verses on 'The Modern Poets' in *The Grub-Street
Journal* of 18 November 1731. These verses praise Swift, Pope, and Young,
and contain a reference to Thomson's play which may or may not be hostile:

> While *Sophonisba* dies by freedom fir'd,
> And mild *Timoleon* rants like W——inspir'd

> While *Oxford* jokes are hiss'd in *Drury-Lane*,
> My muse can't well forbear the sneering strain.

One reason why *Sophonisba* is referred to far more frequently than the *Seasons* at this time is that stage drama is more public than other forms of poetry and so more likely to provoke controversy.

In 1731 Thomson was abroad and not in a position to reply to literary enemies, but he appears to have taken little note of attacks on *Sophonisba* when he was in England.[61] Whether or not, as a young man with his way to make, he depreciated rival authors, as defenders of *Timoleon* would have us believe, the general testimony is that he had an easy-going temperament. Literary warfare never had for him the attractions that it held for Pope or Fielding. There are scornful references to the dunces of Pope's *Dunciad* in Thomson's private letters, in some lines on Joseph Mitchell, beginning 'Why not all faults', and in a curious poem on venereal disease, beginning 'Happy the man',[62] but none of these was published in Thomson's lifetime. What was possibly the first of two public attacks upon men he took to be dunces was a four-line epigram on James Moore-Smythe which was printed in *The Grub-Street Journal* for 28 May 1730. On this printing it was untitled and unattributed, but when reprinted in *A Collection of Pieces publish'd on Occasion of the Dunciad, by Mr Savage* (1732), and again in *Memoirs of the Society of Grub-Street* (1737), volume I, page 108, it was headed 'On J. M. S. *Gent* by Mr Th——n'.[63] The same number of *The Grub-Street Journal* and later ones in June and July 1730 contain other epigrams ridiculing Moore-Smythe which are confidently attributed to Pope in the Twickenham edition.[64] Pope's contempt for Moore-Smythe could have been sufficient reason for Thomson's hostility to the man, but a contributory motive may have been that Moore-Smythe was reputed to be a Jacobite. (Thomson's second public attack on a fellow writer was his retaliation in 1736 against a parody of his work by Isaac Hawkins Browne.) I am not aware that Moore-Smythe attacked Thomson in 1730, but another of Pope's dunces, Bezaleel Morrice, satirized both Pope and Thomson in *Dissectio Mentis Humanae*, and Leonard Welsted, also one of Pope's targets, bore some private resentment of Thomson, who, he thought, had ousted him from Dodington's favour.[65]

Yet another of Pope's dunces, though probably not one of Thomson's, is the subject of a high-spirited letter from Joseph Spence to Thomson, conjecturally dated 12 May 1730, describing a visit to John Dennis:

That great Antient in Criticism! born in the prime grandeur of our poetical world, and yet preserv'd by Heaven to outlive the universal Deluge of it—Never before had my eyes beheld so venerable an aspect. That eye-brow, jetting out unequally like the Natural Arch of a mossy Grotto; with that glare of light dashing from under it to us, and back again into the Caverns of his mind, brought back to my remembrance the famous passage of Puzoli; which I never saw in my life.

It is possible to infer that Spence was storing his belongings at Thomson's lodgings or even staying with Thomson while on a visit to London, because his postscript begs 'the favour of you to give a place to this lumber, and to be so good as to send back by the messenger My best Gown and Cassock, Surcingle, Band, and Beavor, and Shirt'.[66]

Dunces and even old John Dennis were, one imagines, of no more than marginal interest to Thomson in May 1730, when the complete *Seasons* was at last about to be published. Copies of the quarto were delivered to subscribers on 8 June; at the same time copies not subscribed for were offered by Millar and John Brindley, a bookbinder, for general sale at a guinea, in sheets. Samuel Richardson printed the book in the new 'neat style'; that is, he dispensed with the customary initial capital to every substantive and the customary italic for proper names, and instead printed all in roman, with large and small capitals for proper names and 'emphatical words'. It is likely that Thomson insisted on this at Pope's suggestion, for it is unlike the more old-fashioned styles usually employed by Richardson. Someone, almost certainly Thomson himself, tidied up the punctuation to bring the four *Seasons* more in line with one another, but *Winter* is still twice as heavily punctuated as *Summer* and *Autumn*, and nearly three times as heavily as *Spring*. These relative levels of fluency could be seen as reflecting the poems' different subjects.[67] The number of copies of the quarto printed is not known, but it must have been many more than the 457 which had been ordered by the 388 subscribers whose names are listed in the volume.

We do not know how many copies were taken up by the multiple-copy subscribers, or how many subscribers' names were omitted from the printed list, but, whatever the precise number, it is evident that Queen Caroline headed a subscription list crowded with names bespeaking power or wealth or genius or taste. Half the Scottish representative peers in the House of Lords subscribed; so did Walpole and Lady Walpole (two copies). Dodington subscribed for twenty copies, Pope for three, and Duncan Forbes and Burlington for five each. Presumably Burlington was interested as a patron of William Kent, who had drawn the designs (engraved in Paris by Nicolas Henri Tardieu) that illustrate each of the four seasons. The upper half of each design represents an allegorical 'progress' of the personified season as described in the opening lines of each book, while the lower half portrays naturalistically, upon different planes, several episodes and scenes from the book. Such multiple action and mingling of natural and supernatural accords well with Thomson's text. A fifth plate was engraved by Pierre Fourdrinier from Kent's preliminary design for the Newton monument in Westminster Abbey.

The text of the quarto is considerably, but unevenly, revised from earlier editions of the individual Seasons. In *Spring* there are substantive changes affecting about 80 lines of the 1728 text, none of them very significant, and the poem's total length is increased by five lines to 1,087. In *Summer* over 150 new lines are added, including three new episodes; there are substantive changes in another 150 lines; about 70 lines on the autumnal topics of Scotland, wildfire, and meteors are revised and transferred to *Autumn*, and other lines deleted completely, so that the length of the whole poem is increased by only 60 lines over the 1727 text, to 1,205 lines.

The three new episodes all testify to a drift away from the devotional purpose with which Thomson had embarked upon the *Seasons* four years earlier. A description of sheep-shearing, idealized as a scene 'Of happy labour, love, and social glee', makes the poem more of a georgic; an account of a petrified city in North Africa, where the 'nitrous penetrating salts' deposited in a sandstorm have turned every inhabitant to stone, emphasizes the extravagant and exotic elements in the poem; the story of Damon and Musidora, telling how a Stoic is humanized by a naked woman's beauty, has some slight moral import, but its chief appeal lies in the salacious detail. Less considerable additions to *Summer* include an enlargement of the pantheon of British worthies to give it a more distinctly political and Whiggish cast; two preachers are deleted and Hampden, Algernon Sidney, Russell, and (the philosopher) Shaftesbury are added, together with Sir Philip Sidney, Walsingham, Drake, and Ralegh. Thomson himself was distantly related, through his mother, to the Scottish associates of the Whig martyrs, Algernon Sidney and Russell.[68]

Changes to *Winter* are more considerable: over four hundred new lines are added, there are substantive changes in over a hundred lines of the 1728 text, a hundred lines of autumnal description are revised and transferred to *Autumn*, and other lines are deleted. The total effect is to make *Winter*, at 781 lines, over three hundred lines longer than the 1728 version, and markedly different in scope and intention. The new lines include: an episode of a shepherd perishing in the snow, with ensuing moral reflections which lead into a tribute to the work of the Jail Committee that in 1729 investigated reports of cruelty and extortion in prisons; an account of rustic games and city pastimes, with references to plays by Shakespeare, Otway, and Steele; a compliment to his friend Pope as poet and man; a great deal of additional scientific matter in the description of frost; and extended exotic descriptions of northern wastes, the climax of which is an Arctic counterpart to the petrified city newly added to *Summer*, telling of the deaths of Sir Hugh Willoughby and his crew, frozen into statues at their posts. This version of *Winter* recognizes the power of 'the Father of the tempest', and it concludes, as the first version does, with a vision of the Last Day. The overall effect of the 1730 revisions is, however, to dilute the devotional character of the poem.[69]

Autumn is all new, except for the passages transferred and revised from *Summer* and *Winter*, and, at 1,269 lines, is the longest of the four Seasons; it is also the most secular. It belongs to the English georgic tradition in such episodes as the opening scene of harvest plenty, which prompts a dissertation upon the growth of arts and (by way of an animated picture of commercial London as viewed from Thomson's lodgings in Little Tower Street) expansive, optimistic reflections upon Britain's mercantile and naval strength. Praise of Dodington's country estate and references to cider and wine-making are also georgic in character. The ending of the poem is directly modelled upon the classic 'O fortunatos' rhapsody at the end of Virgil's *Georgics* ii, but where Virgil describes principally the joys of the frugal, hardy, pious husbandman (with a short digression on the poet's own happiness in rural retirement), Thomson devotes his account of the 'happy man' almost wholly to the hedonist philosopher-poet. In keeping with *Autumn*'s georgic nature there is a noticeable Latinate element in the diction, for instance in the repetition of what would later become some of Thomson's favourite characteristic words, 'effulgence', 'effulgent', and 'refulgent'.[70]

One of the georgical passages, on reaping, provides the occasion for the interpolated story of Palemon and Lavinia, an edifying illustration of benevolence and gratitude. A more interesting development from georgic material occurs in the hunting scenes, which conclude in the mock-heroic description of a drinking session in the old-fashioned hall of some boorish, rustic, presumably Tory, squire. By the end, the squire's guests have drunk themselves beneath the table, their fuddled perceptions conveyed by a simile drawn from Thomson's own perceptions of nature elsewhere in the poem:

> Before their maudlin eyes,
> Seen dim, and blue, the double tapers dance,
> Like the sun wading thro' the misty sky.
> Then, sliding sweet, they drop. O'erturn'd above
> Lies the wet, broken scene; and stretch'd below,
> Each way, the drunken slaughter.

Lyttelton thought the drinking scene so out of character that he deleted the whole passage of 87 lines from the 1750 edition of the *Seasons*, and rewrote and republished it elsewhere in Thomson's *Works* as 'A Burlesque Poem in the manner of Mr Philips'.[71] Other readers might wish that more of the *Seasons* had been written in this unbuttoned, parodic mood, the mood that contributes so much to the success of *The Castle of Indolence*.

Public and political material, in addition to that tribute to Britain's naval strength already mentioned, includes compliments to the Queen and her daughter, and more extended praise of those leading Scottish Whigs, the Duke of Argyll and Duncan Forbes. There is praise of Scottish enterprise and a plea for the improvement of agriculture, fisheries, and trade, and the development of woollen and linen manufactures in Scotland. A livelier Scottish maritime industry would, Thomson claims,

> united BRITAIN BRITAIN make
> Intire, th'imperial MISTRESS of the deep.

Thomson is consistently the poet of the Union and of 'Rule Britannia'. He also sees Scotland 'in romantic view', in, for instance, his description of autumn bird-migration:

> where the NORTHERN ocean, in vast whirls,
> Boils round the naked, melancholy isles
> Of farthest THULÈ, and th'ATLANTIC surge
> Pours in among the stormy HEBRIDES;
> Who can recount what transmigrations there
> Are annual made? what nations come and go?
> And how the living clouds on clouds arise?
> Infinite wings! till all the plume-dark air,
> And white resounding shore are one wild cry.[72]

Nothing is recounted here; what is captured is a sense of space and movement, an endless confusion and agitation, caught and held at last in the unsettling phrase 'one wild cry'.

The lines on 'Philosophic Melancholy', in the mood of Milton's *Il Penseroso*, which may have been the starting-point of the *Seasons*, are now transferred from *Winter* to *Autumn* and expanded. 'Philosophic Melancholy' is said to inspire feelings of benevolence towards individual men and humankind in general, as in *Winter*; but now, in addition, it inspires political emotions:

> th'indignant scorn
> Of mighty pride; the fearless, great resolve;
> The wonder that the dying patriot draws,
> Inspiring glory thro' remotest time.

More interestingly and appropriately, under its influence,

> Ten thousand thousand fleet ideas, such
> As never mingled with the Vulgar's dream,
> Crowd fast into the mind's creative eye.[73]

Like the three other Seasons, *Autumn* ends with an ascending movement of mind. In *Winter* the mind is drawn upwards to contemplate the Last Judgement and eternity; in *Summer* it rises through the various kinds of philosophy to divine contemplation; in *Spring* it considers the heavenly reward prepared for a virtuous married couple; but the corresponding mental ascent in *Autumn* lifts the poet to a contemplation of 'NATURE! all-sufficient! over all!'.[74] Very little of

Autumn can be read as explicitly religious. What devotional content this poem has is rather to be inferred from the context supplied by the three earlier Seasons and, particularly, the concluding 'Hymn', which is the other entirely new poem in the 1730 *Seasons*.

The 'Hymn' (121 lines long) is modelled in a general way upon Psalm 148, but restates and harmonizes some of the key scientific, philosophical, and religious notions introduced in the other *Seasons*. Its theme is that the four seasons are 'the varied God', for God is immanent in every phenomenon of nature, whether beautiful or terrible:

> HE sustains, and animates the whole;
>
> From seeming evil still educes good,
> And better thence again, and better still,
> In infinite progression.[75]

This is quite unequivocal. Even so, the general tendency of all the additions to and rewriting of the *Seasons* in 1730 is to make the work as a whole less religious and more miscellaneous.

Thomson's first biographer, prompted perhaps by conversation with Johnson (for Shiels was Johnson's amanuensis), writes of the *Seasons*: 'There appears no particular design; the parts are not subservient to one another; nor is there any dependance or connection throughout; but this perhaps is a fault almost inseparable from a subject in itself so diversified, as not to admit of such limitation.' Johnson himself complains that 'The great defect of *The Seasons* is want of method', but he also notes: 'The poet leads us through the appearances of things as they are successively varied by the vicissitudes of the year, and imparts to us so much of his own enthusiasm that our thoughts expand with his imagery and kindle with his sentiments.'[76] For all the digressions, the varied material of the poem is contained within a natural framework, so that all the minutely-observed weather signs and other natural features of the seasons, together with the seasonal activities of insects, birds, animals, and men, are described in due order. The catalogues of worthies are hardly related to the seasonal framework, but the interpolated stories and imaginary voyages to foreign lands are; so the whole work has to a considerable extent the organizational unity that its title implies.

The Seasons also has some kind of unity of focus by its repeated glances at Milton. For instance, Thomson draws upon Milton's account of paradise for his own descriptions of trees, blossoms, fruit, flowers, the 'mazy error' of streams, the nightingale, and many other of the palpable beauties of the present English landscape. There are many echoes of Raphael's narrative of the creation in Book VII of *Paradise Lost* (with the science brought up to Thomson's date), and Milton's geographical excursion in Book XI is extended in *Summer* and *Winter*. Thomson draws equally upon Milton's descriptions of fallen and unfallen nature. However, objects which are the vehicles of heroic metaphor in *Paradise Lost* have a way of reappearing in the *Seasons* simply as themselves; scraps of Milton's epic are naturalized into the georgic mode. Particularly, Milton's similes for Satan reappear in straight descriptions. The ship moored to an iceberg in *Winter* recalls Milton's ship moored to the whale which is a simile for Satan; the morning-walk in *Spring* recalls Satan's walk, 'As one who long in populous city pent'. Thomson briefly echoes Milton in the course of his descriptions of wildfire, or the sun looking through horizontal misty air, or the eclipsed sun, or 'Ships, dim-discover'd, dropping from the Clouds', or a burned forest, or the sea murmuring after a storm, or the fields reviving after rain, all of which in Milton are similes for Satan or for the devils in general.[77] Satanic associations are never explicitly drawn to the attention of the reader of the *Seasons*: Thomson never mentions Hell to ears polite. Nevertheless these occasional brief echoes of the great Miltonic set-piece similes do flit like shadows across the landscape descriptions of Thomson's poem to provide us with unforced reminders that we live in a fallen world. Seasonal changes themselves, while they provide the beautiful variety of this world, also are living evidence of the fact of the Fall. Miltonic echoes always bring a reminder of Milton's high argument.

The first version of *Winter* in 1726, the concluding 'Hymn' in 1730, and some passages of *Summer* and *Spring* in their first versions clearly indicate that the whole work is intended as a theodicy. Its unity lies in the poet's affirmation of a providential order, apprehended by faith, based partly upon a scientific understanding of such natural phenomena as the great chain of being, the planetary system, or the percolating arrangement that refreshes the earth. However, as we have seen, most of *Autumn* and much of the other material added in 1730 (British explorer-heroes, naked girls, stage-plays, and a petrified city) is not explicitly or implicitly referred to that order.

A very different kind of unity, or partial unity, is suggested by the gradual accretion of historical and geographical material. The ideas of patriotism and public virtue animate the catalogues of ancient and modern worthies; the words 'liberty' and 'freedom' in their political sense, and 'patriot' suddenly become prominent in the 1730 additions; 'Britain' and 'Britannia' appear more frequently in 1730 too, when the conditions of foreigners are implicitly or explicitly compared with the wealth, power (especially the naval power), and general blessedness of the British.[78] The newly united kingdom provides a unifying idea for much of the *Seasons*, though Thomson does not choose explicitly to link Britain's destiny with God's designs, as he does, for instance, in the first stanza of 'Rule Britannia'.

'Liberty' and 'Britannia' are female personifications of course, as they were

and would be in the political poems of 1729 and 1735–6, where their names
are used as titles. In the first edition of *Summer* and now more prominently in
Autumn they are accompanied by the male personification 'Industry'. He,
particularly in *Autumn*, foreshadows the overthrower of the Castle of Indolence,
though in 1730 he is not at all antagonistic towards those less industrious
personifications, 'Solitude', 'Philosophic Melancholy', and 'Contemplation',
which preside over *Winter*[79] and which, some would argue, are among the
presiding spirits of the first canto of *The Castle of Indolence*.

   The Seasons is not given over to the systematic promotion of any single truth,
religious or political; the various objects comprehended by the poet's view are,
as objects, miscellaneous; but they acquire a kind of subjective unity through
the poet's perception of them. Johnson wrote of Thomson, 'he looks round on
nature and on life, with the eye that distinguishes, in everything presented to its
view, whatever there is on which imagination can delight to be detained'.[80] In
the *Seasons* there are nearly a hundred references to the poet's eye and its
powers. Often it is the physical eye, 'straining' to see objects in twilight, 'fresh-
expanded' when shade is found from dazzling sunlight, or 'cherish'd' by green,
the restful, central colour of the spectrum. Sometimes it stands for the activity
of visual perception, when it is 'darted' or can 'shoot'. It is both active and
passive when, 'Snatch'd thro' the verdant Maze, the hurried Eye | Distracted
wanders'. Frequently it represents the whole response of the poet to the visual
spectacle: the eye is 'astonish'd', 'charm'd', 'raptur'd', and 'ravish'd'. Just as
frequently, though, the 'eye' represents the mental and spiritual faculties of the
philosopher-poet, the power he has to see beyond appearances: so there is the
'philosophic' eye, which, unlike the vulgar eye, understands the natural causes
of rainbows or comets, and there is the 'purer' eye, which sees God in nature.
This purer eye is also reason's eye, which at last will make clear the providential
scheme; it is complemented by fancy's eye. Together they embody the visual
perceptions, the knowledge, and the faith out of which the poem is made.[81]

   All these eyes are facets of 'the mind's creative eye', which is active when the
poet is in his 'Penseroso' state of 'Philosophic Melancholy', an enhanced self-
awareness and meditative mood. Wordsworth, citing a passage of Thomson as
'a beautiful instance of the modifying and *investive* power of the imagination',
went on to declare that 'much of *The Seasons* is written from himself, and nobly
from himself'. Instead of a narrative or an intellectual system, Thomson offers
only a very loose structure of description and reflection, with interpolated
histories, but this very looseness makes us aware that the associative mental
processes of the poet have to stand in place of narrative or logical continuity.
Such a manner of proceeding accomodated perhaps too easily the new interests
and ideas of a man adjusting himself to a new environment and changing in the
process. Different parts of the 1730 poem spring from different stages of

intellectual growth, different levels of awareness, and perhaps different degrees of emotional involvement with the subject-matter. This may have been what Wordsworth recognized with his qualification 'much of'. By 1730 Thomson's political views are clouding the creative eye just a little; as he tells us in the verse address to the dedicatee of *Autumn* he now wishes 'To mix the Patriot's with the Poet's Flame'.[82]

Similar addresses, similarly emphasizing the patriotism of their politician-dedicatees are added to the 1730 versions of *Summer* and *Winter*, thus bringing more political bias into those poems themselves. The verse dedication of *Spring* (1728) is retained and all the earlier prefatory prose dedications are now dropped. *Autumn* is dedicated to Arthur Onslow (1691–1768), a Walpole supporter of unusual integrity, who was elected Speaker of the House of Commons in January 1728, when Sir Spencer Compton was elevated to the other house as Baron Wilmington. It does not appear that Thomson ever became nearly as intimate with Onslow or Wilmington as with the patrons of the other two *Seasons*, Lady Hertford and Dodington. Onslow is applauded routinely for his 'patriot-virtues', but also for his oratory, described as 'Devolving thro' the maze of eloquence | A rowl of periods'. Lord Hervey noted privately at this time that Onslow 'was a man naturally eloquent, but rather too florid . . . he had kept bad company of the collegiate kind, by which he had contracted a stiffness and pedantry in his manner of conversing'.[83] Setting these two judgements side by side, one may infer that Thomson had a Scottish taste in rhetoric. The florid diction of his poetry was the occasion of a well-known practical joke. Boswell reports that Johnson said:

Thomson had a true poetical genius, the power of viewing every thing in a poetical light. His fault is such a cloud of words sometimes, that the sense can hardly peep through. Shiels, who compiled 'Cibber's Lives of the Poets', was one day sitting with me. I took down Thomson, and read aloud a large portion of him, and then asked,—Is not this fine? Shiels having expressed the highest admiration. Well, Sir, (said I,) I have omitted every other line.[84]

The subscription quarto contained, in addition to the four *Seasons* and the 'Hymn', a revised *Poem to Newton*, without the prose Dedication, with the criticism of Descartes toned down, and with a general polishing of the quickly-written text of 1727. On the same day that copies of the quarto were delivered to subscribers, 8 June, Millan published a second edition of *Britannia*, 'in Quarto, proper to be bound with the Subscription Edition' of *The Seasons*. This edition of *Britannia* carried Thomson's name on the title page; among its revisions from the earlier text is the politically significant deletion of a passage near the end in praise of the entire royal family, while a passage near the beginning in praise of Frederick alone is retained.

Though at first offered for sale separately, *Britannia* was later regularly bound up and sold with remainder copies of the subscription quarto of *The Seasons*, of which there must have been a very large number in view of the fact that advertisements for this composite issue run from November 1730 to late 1760.[85] Although it is convenient to refer to all copies as the 'subscription edition', indications are that this, like Pope's Homer, was a joint enterprise between the trade and an author. In the case of Pope's *Iliad* the bookseller gave the author 660 copies for subscribers and had 1,750 printed in a plainer style and different format to sell on his own account, reducing the number to 1,000 after volume 1. Trade copies of *The Seasons* were from the same impression as subscribers' copies, so we have no means of estimating how many extra copies over and above the 457 for subscribers were printed for sale through the trade, but the long continuance of advertisements implies a large number, as does the fact that surviving copies (considerably more than half of them bound up with *Britannia*) greatly outnumber surviving copies of any other issue of *The Seasons* in Thomson's lifetime. The poem proved to be good business for bookseller and poet; a note appended to the account of a lawsuit in 1769, when Millar was defending his copyright against pirates, said that Thomson 'reaped about a thousand guineas profit while the work was his own property'.[86] If this is accurately reported, Thomson fared almost as well as Pope, who, according to David Foxon's calculations made a profit of about £5,000 from six volumes of the *Iliad* and about the same sum from five volumes of the *Odyssey*; and it is notorious that Pope's contracts with Lintot were sharply advantageous to the poet.[87]

The text of the quarto *Seasons* and *Britannia* published on 8 June was reprinted in octavo several times in the 1730s. By the issue of pamphlets containing individual *Seasons* (with the 'Hymn', *Poem to Newton*, and *Britannia* always printed with *Winter*), and complete sets of pamphlets under a 'Seasons' collective title page, and a continuously-paginated edition, falsely dated '1730', Millar and Millan collaborated to keep in print the poems of which they had bought the copyright down to 1738, when Millan parted company with Thomson. Authorial revision in these reprints is negligible or non-existent. The pamphlet reprints of *Britannia* in 1730 and 1734 add below the title 'Written in the Year 1719', which is altered to 'Written in the Year 1727' or 'first published in 1727' in various reprints in 1738. It has been argued that these misdatings are Thomson's subterfuge, intended to make the poem seem less topical than it was, but it is quite possible that they are simply erroneous editorial additions by his publishers, '1719' being Millan's mistranscription of 'MDCCXXIX' on the first-edition title-page, and '1727' being Millar's near-miss shot at a correction.[88] If 1719 was deliberately chosen, it could possibly have been because it was the year of the only Spanish military invasion of

Britain, when a small army supporting a Jacobite rising was routed by the Hanoverians in north-west Scotland, after the greater part of the armada had been shattered by storms. This event was the occasion of a great tide of anti-Spanish feeling among Scottish Whigs when Thomson was an undergraduate in Edinburgh.[89]

By the middle of 1730 Thomson could have felt that he had done well in the five years since he left Scotland: he had received royal notice as playwright and poet, the subscription had gone well, he enjoyed the friendship and respect of men of wit, and the support of some discriminating patrons. Spence had said of him in late 1729 or early 1730, 'They make him promises, but he has yet nothing substantial.'[90] Something substantial was now coming his way, however, in the shape of his engagement as a paid grand-tour travelling companion to Charles Richard Talbot, the eldest son of Charles Talbot, Solicitor-General and Walpole's trusty lieutenant. Murdoch informs us that this lucrative and honourable position was secured for Thomson by the recommendation of Thomas Rundle.[91] The qualities for which Rundle made this recommendation may be inferred from his commendation of *The Seasons* to Mrs Sandys on 16 July 1730: 'Such writings give dignity to leisure, and exalt entertainment and amusement into devotion'; Thomson has recalled poetry 'to her first high office of adorning piety, and raising an ambition after virtue'; 'the sentiments of liberty, of virtue, of generous manly piety hurry away my approbation'.[92] If such things were said to Thomson's face he would have felt doubly pleased with himself as he prepared to travel on the Continent.

5

The Grand Tour and an Establishment, 1730–1733

THE grand tour was intended to supply taste and a knowledge of the world to young men of wealth and rank who might be expected to play some part in public life. Ideally it would perfect them in languages, also in such accomplishments as fencing, riding, and dancing; it would polish their manners in foreign courts, and inform them in art, music, architecture, antiquities, fortifications, geography, history, and government. This last knowledge would enable them the better to understand and appreciate the British constitution, by which their own freedoms were happily secured. The itinerary of a grand tourist invariably took him through France, with generally an extended stay in Paris; it usually took in Switzerland and those parts of Germany and the Low Countries not too far from the Rhine; but its main destinations were the great cities and classic sites of Italy. The liberal education offered by travel in that country is summarized by Addison in the Preface to his *Remarks on Several Parts of Italy* (1705), the record of his tour in 1701–3:

One finds something more particular in the Face of the Country, and more astonishing in the Works of Nature, than can be met with in any other Part of *Europe*. It is the great School of Music and Painting, and contains in it all the noblest Productions of Statuary and Architecture, both Ancient and Modern. It abounds with Cabinets of Curiosities, and vast Collections of all kinds of Antiquities. No other Country in the World has such a Variety of Governments, that are so different in their Constitutions, and so refined in their Politics. There is scarce any Part of the Nation that is not famous in History, nor so much as a Mountain or River, that has not been the scene of some extraordinary Action.

Johnson declared some seventy years later, 'A man who has not been in Italy, is always conscious of an inferiority, from his not having seen what it is expected a man should see. The grand object of travelling is to see the shores of the Mediterranean.'[1]

With this grand object in view Thomson was learning Italian in the summer of 1730 under the tutorship, McKillop conjectures, of Paolo Antonio Rolli (1687–1767), at that time the leading member of the Italian literary and scholarly circle in London. Rolli wrote opera libretti, on account of which he is named in Pope's attack upon Italian opera in *The Dunciad* (1728), but he was an eminent scholar and poet. He was at work in 1730 on an important Italian translation of *Paradise Lost*, in the intervals of teaching Italian to the Prince of Wales, the Prince's sisters, and various members of the nobility, including the Countess of Hertford.[2]

Other letters in the autumn of 1730 refer to Thomson's studies in French and to a short excursion to Bath, where he encountered one of the town's most famous residents, the corpulent, indeed mountainous, Scottish physician George Cheyne, whose notions on vegetarianism had found their way into Thomson's *Spring*, but not into his diet.[3] His companion in Bath and probably on his journey there was John Upton, seven years younger than Thomson, with whom he had struck up an easy-going friendship, to judge by the tone of a letter, dated 27 October, to a common acquaintance of theirs, a certain Valentine Munbee:

Your civilities to me dwell upon my mind in a very agreeable manner, and I heartily wish that I could have added to their number by passing some part of the season with you according to your kind Invitation. Mr Upton and I much desired, and often designed it; but what prevented him I know not, and what hindered me I cannot exactly tell. It was, it seems, predestinated that I should not be so happy. For him, who denies predestination, he must own it to be the fault of his free-will, or, if he pleases, of his platonic passion and attachment to some Ladies here in town. Now he innocently luxuriates amidst the Fair and Quadrille at Bath, which was lately to me for a few days the Limbo of vanity.[4]

As Upton, a Fellow of Exeter College, Oxford, was in Anglican orders, he would certainly have professed the Arminian theology that Thomson banteringly attributes to him. One would like to know how strongly Thomson adhered to the Calvinistic belief in predestination, which he must have been taught in his youth and which he now jokingly refers to. Thomson promised to write to Munbee, but if letters were exchanged none has been traced.

Perhaps Thomson agreed to exchange letters with Pope also; so much may be inferred from Pope's remark to Mallet in a letter of 29 December 1730: 'I have not heard from Mr Thomson.' Johnson testifies to some communication between Pope and Thomson at this time; he writes that Pope 'had much regard for Thomson, and once expressed it in a poetical Epistle sent to Italy, of which, however, he abated the value by transplanting some of the lines into his *Epistle to Arbuthnot*'. Joseph Warton repeats the anecdote and remarks that, though Thomson was displeased by having the lines transferred from himself to another, he and Pope 'lived always on terms of civility and friendship'. A letter from Pope to Aaron Hill on 3 September 1731 appears, at first sight, to confirm Johnson's statement, because it contains 'a few Lines I sent t'other Day . . . to a particular Friend', these lines, addressed to a 'successful Youth', reappear duly revised as the last paragraph of the *Epistle to Arbuthnot*. Their subject is of course Pope's care for his mother in her last illness and his hope that some friend's 'kind Hand, like B***'s or thine', will care for him as he dies. Most of Pope's editors after Warton have conjectured that the successful youth was Murray or Lyttelton, not the 30-year old Thomson, but Sherburn leaves open the possibility that he was indeed Thomson.[5]

In 1730, though, quite another poetical communication between Pope and Thomson was alleged when Thomas Rundle complimented Mrs Sandys by writing, 'The temper of your mind is most exactly described in a line of Pope's, corrected and improved by Thomson:

> ____ *A friend to learned ease,*
> *Content with science in the vale of peace.*'[6]

The couplet is in Pope's 'Epitaph. On Mr Elijah Fenton'; its complete first line is 'Foe to loud Praise, and Friend to learned Ease'. Pope wrote the epitaph after 29 August 1730; it was printed anonymously in various newspapers between 22 and 29 October, when the word 'arms' appeared, instead of 'vale'; 'arms' is the reading of Pope's autograph, where the correction to 'vale' is said to be in the hand of Lord Oxford.[7] I have found no other claim that Thomson corrected Pope's work.

Thomson's circumstances, financial and social, as he set out with Talbot for Paris in November 1730 were very different from what they had been when he embarked for London in 1725. As a 'companion' he enjoyed a higher status than a tutor; also, his allowance of £200 a year was more than a travelling tutor would ordinarily have received.[8] He could call upon prominent men for introductions, as he did in a letter to Dodington two weeks before his departure: 'I shall be very proud of being mentioned by you to any you may think it proper to mention me to at Paris.' Evidently he has already received advice from Dodington, for he now explains his 'grand object' to his patron:

Travelling has been long my fondest wish for the very purpose you recommend: the storing one's Imagination with Ideas of all-beautiful, all-great, and all-perfect Nature. These are the true materia poetica, the light and colours with which Fancy kindles up her whole creation, paints a sentiment, and even embodies an abstracted thought. I long to see the feilds whence Virgil gathered his immortal honey, and to tread the same ground where men have thought and acted so greatly! If it does not give, it must at least awaken some what of the same Spirit. But not to travel intirely like a Poet, I resolve not to neglect the more prosaic advantages of it; for it is no less my ambition to be capable of serving my country in an active than in a contemplative way.

In thus proclaiming his ambition to serve his country actively, Thomson is, no doubt, reinforcing his delicate hint in an earlier paragraph of this letter, to the

effect that man cannot live by poetry alone, and that he would welcome some
sort of government employment, which Dodington, as a Lord of the Treasury,
should be able to secure for him:

One would not however climb Parnassus, any more than your mortal hills, to fix forever
on the barren top. No, it is some little dear retirement in the plain below that gives the
right relish to the prospect; which without that is nothing but inchantment, and, tho'
pleasing for sometime, yet at last leaves us in a desart. The great fat Doctor at Bath told
me, that Poets should be kept poor, the more to actuate their Genius. This is like the
cruel custom of putting a Bird's eyes out that it may sing the sweeter: but surely they sing
sweetest amidst the luxuriant woods, while the full spring blows around them.

The great fat Doctor is George Cheyne.

Most of the remainder of this letter to Dodington is taken up with literary
projects:

At my times of leisure abroad, I think of attempting another Tragedy, and on a story
more addressed to common passions than that of Sophonisba. People now-a-days must
have something like themselves, and a public-spirited monster can never concern them.

If anything could make me capable of an Epic performance, it would be your
favourable opinion in thinking me so. But, as you justly observe, that must be the work of
years, and one in an Epic situation to execute it. My heart both trembles with diffidence
and burns with ardor at the thought. The story of Timoleon, as to the subject-matter of
it, is certainly a fine one: but an Author (I think) owes the Scene of an Epic Action to his
own country; and besides, Timoleon admits of no machinery except it be that of the
heathen Gods, which will not do at this time of day.[9]

Timoleon, one of Plutarch's worthies praised in the first edition of *Winter*, was
the ancient Corinthian who acquiesced in the deposition and killing of his
tyrannical brother, so that liberty could be restored to the people. He was
equated with William III and his story was paralleled with the Glorious
Revolution in Benjamin Martyn's play, acted at Drury Lane just before
Sophonisba was brought on. The reasons given by Thomson for declining
Dodington's suggestion have nothing to do with Martyn, though, and everything to do with the state of mind in which *Liberty* was conceived; the action of
that poem reaches its climax in contemporary Britain and the machinery
consists of allegorized abstractions which were the subject of contemporary
moral, aesthetic, and political discussion.

Our impression of Thomson on the grand tour has necessarily but regrettably to be received mainly by way of the distorting mirror of his poem *Liberty*,
where broadness of effect, to say nothing of political intentions, must have
generalized and falsified the discrete sensations of over two years' travel.
Murdoch, an experienced travelling tutor himself, says nothing of Thomson
and Talbot's itinerary beyond that 'they visited most of the courts and capital

cities of *Europe*'. Shiels mentions only France and Italy as the countries visited, 'where no doubt he inriched his mind with the noble monuments of anti- quity, and the conversation of ingenious foreigners'.[10] Tantalizingly few of Thomson's own direct records of his grand tour survive. Topographical references in *Liberty* are too generalized for us to be able to infer more than a little of its author's itinerary. There are only three surviving letters of his dated from the Continent; they are spaced at intervals of nearly a year: Paris, December 1730; Rome, November 1731; and Paris, October 1732. In none of them does he refer to other cities he has visited, though in the letter from Rome he writes: 'We have been over the most part of France and Italy.' Joseph Spence's copious records of his own grand tour at this time record a meeting with Thomson in Lyons in July 1731 and further meetings at unspecified dates in Venice and Florence. Lady Hertford reported that Thomson had seen the Fontaine de Vaucluse, near Avignon.[11]

Of Thomson's first letter from abroad, addressed to Dodington from Paris on 27 December 1730, only a fragment survives. It opens:

M. de Voltaire's Brutus has been acted here seven or eight times with applause, and still continues to be acted. It is matter of amusement to me to imagine what ideas an old Roman Republican, declaiming on *Liberty*, must give the generality of a French audience. Voltaire, in his Preface, designs to have a stroke at criticism; and Lord have mercy on the poor similes at the end of the acts in our English Plays; for these seem to be the very worthy objects of his French indignation. It is designed to be dedicated to Lord Bolingbroke.

Voltaire's intentions, referred to here, were not carried out in the 'Discours sur la Tragedie, à Mylord Bolingbrooke', which prefaced the printed edition of *Brutus*, but in the Preface to the second edition of *Zaïre* (1733), so it is more than possible that Thomson had heard of them from Voltaire himself. Thomson is not prompted by *Brutus* to mention his own plans for an epic or for a tragedy more addressed to common passions than his *Sophonisba*, because another poetical design is evidently forming in his mind. He writes,

Your observation I find every day juster and juster, that one may profit more abroad by seeing than by hearing; and yet, there are scarce any travellers to be met with, who have given a *landscape* of the countries through which they have travelled; that have seen (as you express it) with the *Muse's* eye; though that is the first thing that strikes me, and what all readers and travellers in the first place demand. It seems to me, that such a *poetical* landscape of countries, mixed with moral observations on their governments and people, would not be an ill-judged undertaking. But then, the description of the different face of Nature, in different countries, must be particularly marked and characteristic, *the Portrait-painting of Nature*.

This is a design for something rather closer to Goldsmith's *The Traveller* than to any poem Thomson wrote, but we can just recognize here the germ of his *Liberty*.

That reference to liberty in connection with Voltaire's *Brutus* sounds the main theme of all Thomson's later reports, in prose and poetry, of his grand tour. This letter to Dodington, for instance:

> You must, however, give me leave to observe, that amidst all that external and shewy magnificence which the French affect, one misses that solid magnificence of trade and sincere plenty which not only appears to be, but is, substantially, in a kingdom where industry and liberty mutually support and inspirit each other. That kingdom, I suppose, I need not mention, as it is, and ever will be, sufficiently plain from the character. I shall return no worse Englishman than I came away.[12]

John Carswell notes the parallel with Voltaire's words on industry and liberty in the *Lettres Philosophiques*, 'Le commerce qui a enrichi les Citoyens en Angleterre a contribué à les rendre libres, et cette Liberté a étendu le Commerce à son tour', and observes of Thomson's repetition of the idea in this letter, 'Since it is the most elementary flattery to repeat a man's own words to him as profundities, one may suspect that this was one of Dodington's own favourite maxims.'[13] He may have uttered this profundity when Thomson and Voltaire were guests together at Eastbury; even so, his two hearers made it very much their own.

Young Talbot was evidently just as good an Englishman as his Scots companion, if not more so. Thomas Rundle wrote in a letter of 30 January 1731 that Charles Talbot 'is at Paris, and behaves as one would wish that he should behave. His rough *English* love for liberty, disdains the embroidered slavery, that glitters in that trifling Court.'[14] Both Talbot and Thomson were reacting as most English travellers did. For all that, Thomson was impressed by French public works and cultural achievements, nursed, as he points out in the last Part of *Liberty*, by enlightened royal patronage.[15]

It is very probable that Talbot and Thomson spent the rest of the winter in Paris. The next we hear of them is when they arrive in Lyons early in July 1731, and take lodgings in the street where Thomson's friend Joseph Spence and his pupil Lord Middlesex were already lodged; this street was alongside the River Saône, a quarter of a mile above its confluence with the Rhône. Spence observes that the latter 'runs as violently as the other does slowly';[16] Thomson figuratively describes the same phenomenon, if he is the author of some lines attributed to him in Richard Colt Hoares's *Recollections Abroad*:

> She meek and modest, with a virgin grace
> Winds round and round, as shunning his embrace.

He rushes rapid with a bridegroom's air,
And pours his torrent in the yielding fair.[17]

These personifications were commonplace; the great equestrian statue of Louis XIV in the Place Royale of Lyons was at this time flanked by figures of a river goddess, representing the Saône, and a river god, representing the Rhône.

Spence writes on 13 July that he and Thomson and their pupils 'are got greatly acquainted here', and then gives a full and graphic account of a nun's profession of vows, which he and Talbot witnessed together. Thomson's only record of a Continental meeting with Spence is in a Gallic jingle, written presumably when the two friends met again later in England:

Mon Frère, vous souvenez-vous
du feu Roi notre Père?
Ma foi, si je m'en souviens
je m'en souviens guère.[18]

One assumes that these lines are a private joke, perhaps alluding to a line in Corneille's *La Mort de Pompée* (Act I, Scene ii): 'Suivant le testament du feu Roi votre père.' Corneille's dead ('fated') king is the father of Ptolemy and Cleopatra, but neither Spence nor Thomson strikes one as a latter-day serpent of old Nile. It is likely that Thomson also met, somewhere in France or Italy, an older friend Patrick Murdoch, who was travelling between 1729 and 1732 as tutor to John, son of Duncan Forbes. Writing to Duncan Forbes's agent in 1736, Thomson asks to be remembered 'heartily heartily' to John Forbes, and adds 'Tho' my Affection to him is not fann'd by Letters, yet it is as high as when I was his Brother in the Virtu, and played at Chess with him in a Post-Chaise.'[19]

Apart from Paris and Lyons, the only place in France that we know was visited by Thomson is the Fontaine de Vaucluse. Years after he returned to England, Lady Hertford wrote to a friend 'Mr Thomson told me he had seen this fountain; and he promised to give me the description of it in verse: but the promises of poets are not always to be depended upon.'[20] If this visit was made on the outward journey to Italy a conjectural itinerary would have Talbot and Thomson travelling down river, perhaps by water-coach, from Châlons to Lyons and on to Avignon, then by chaise to Marseilles; they would have entered northern Italy along the very difficult coast road, or track, or they would have taken small sailing vessels (tartanes or feluccas) from port to port, to Genoa or Leghorn, or to both. Their avoidance of Switzerland on the outward journey is confirmed in the first and only surviving letter by Thomson from Italy. Writing to Dodington from Rome on 28 November 1731, he rather too disarmingly declares,

I will not make any apology for neglecting to do myself the honour of writing to you since we left Paris, when I may rather plead a merit in not troubling you with long scrolls of that travelling stuff of which the world is full even to loathing. We have been over the most part of France, and Italy: what is remarkable and curious in that tour you know much better than I do, tho' actually here on the field of staring.[21]

Spence was in Venice from 15 November to March and in Florence from 11 July 1732 until after Thomson's return to France; he records meetings with Thomson in both cities; so, if Thomson and Talbot did not go back far on their tracks, they must have been in Venice immediately before going on to Rome. In Rome, in November, they met a party of Scots, including Thomson's old patrons, Lord Binning and Lady Grizel Baillie, who were travelling on to Naples.[22] Spence notes that Binning went there 'for a decayed constitution: the goodness of the air kept him alive for some time, but it could not cure him';[23] he died of consumption in Naples on 13 January 1733. Naples was the furthest point from Britain reached by most healthy grand tourists too. It is virtually certain that Talbot and Thomson made an excursion to Naples, probably early in 1732.

Thomson's letter to Dodington from Rome is mostly a complaint of travel-weariness; it conventionally deplores the futile expence of travel, and reiterates the political points made nearly a year earlier in Paris:

That Enthusiasm I had upon me with regard to travelling goes off, I find, very fast. One may imagine fine things in reading of antient authors, but to travel is to dissipate that vision. A great many beautiful antique Statues, where several of the fair Ideas of Greece are fixed for ever in marble, and the paintings of the first masters are indeed most inchanting objects. How little however of these suffices? how unessential are they to life? And surely not of that Importance as to set the whole world, man woman and child a-gadding. I should be sorry to be Goth enough not to think them highly ornamental in life, when one can have them at home without paying for them an extravagant price; but for every one who can support it to make a trade of running abroad only to stare at them, I cannot help thinking something worse than a public folly. Instead of travelling so furiously, it were a wiser and more public-spirited thing, with part of those vast sums of money spent that way, to send people of genius for architecture, painting, and sculpture, to study these arts here and to import them into England. Did they but once take root there, how they might flourish in such a generous and wealthy country. The great architect, painter, and statuary Nature is the same she ever was, and no doubt as profuse of beauty proportion lovely forms and real genius as formerly to the sunny realms of Greece, did we but study the one and exert the other. In England tho', if we cannot reach the gracefully superfluous yet I hope we will never lose the substantial necessary and vital arts of life, such as depend on liberty, labour, and all-commanding trade. For my part, I who have no taste in the least for smelling to an old musty stone look upon these other curiosities with an eye to poetry, in regard that the sister-arts reflect lights and Images on one another. Now that I mention poetry, should you enquire after my Muse, all that I can answer is that I belive she did not cross the channel with me. I know not whether your gardiner at Eastbury has heard any thing of her among the woods there, she has not thought fit to visit me while in this once poetic land—nor do I feel the least presages that she will—But not to lengthen out a letter that has no pretence to Intertain you, give me leave only to add that I can never lose the pleasing sense I have of your goodness to me, and it is a hope I must flatter myself with—your continuance of it on my return to England—to England, for whom my veneration and love, I will be vain enough to say, increase every day even to devotion and fondness.[24]

Such feelings cast an ironic light upon the greater part of Johnson's summary of the effect that the grand tour might be supposed to have had on Thomson:

He was yet young enough to receive new impressions, to have his opinions rectified, and his views enlarged; nor can he be supposed to have wanted that curiosity which is inseparable from an active and comprehensive mind. He may therefore now be supposed to have revelled in all the joys of intellectual luxury; he was every day feasted with instructive novelties; he lived splendidly without expence, and might expect when he returned home a certain establishment.[25]

The hope of what Johnson calls 'establishment' appears in Thomson's last sentence, but the traveller's general mood is far from Johnson's conjecture. His account of his situation puts one in mind of Mr Weller's charity-boy, who, when he reached the end of the alphabet, wondered whether it was worth going through so much to learn so little.

Such matters are, as Mr Weller sagely observed, 'a matter o' taste'. Despite his weariness and homesickness, Thomson's taste was being educated and his imagination stored with *materia poetica*. It was probably on the grand tour that he began his large collection of prints by French and Italian engravers, and bought some of the French and Italian works on art and architecture which are recorded as being in his library at the time of his death.[26] The antique statues of Florence and Rome appear in *Liberty* and ceiling frescoes of Aurora influence a remarkable description of sunrise added to the revised edition of *The Seasons* in 1744. When Mrs Piozzi was in Rome in 1785 she saw three ceiling paintings of this subject; she wrote of the versions by Guido Reni and Guericino: 'Surely Thomson had been living under these two roofs when he wrote such descriptions as seem to have been made on purpose for them.'[27]

The most striking images, though, that Thomson was accumulating in his travels were of the poverty and misery brought about by bad government, civil and religious, and of a potentially beautiful landscape made barren. His sketch of the Roman Campagna reads like first-hand observation:

> Far as the sickening Eye can sweep around,
> 'Tis all one Desart, desolate, and grey,
> Graz'd by the sullen Bufalo alone;
> And where the rank uncultivated Growth
> Of rotting Ages taints the passing Gale.
> Beneath the baleful Blast the City pines,

> Or sinks infeebl'd, or infected burns.
> Beneath it mourns the solitary Road,
> Roll'd in rude Mazes o'er th' abandon'd Waste;
> While Antient Ways, ingulph'd, are seen no more.

Though Spence is an enthusiastic traveller, ready to enjoy most things unless they have too noxious a taint of Popery, he confirms this observation of Thomson's: 'The country about Rome is almost a desert: scarce half of the ground is ever cultivated, and there is sometimes not a house to be seen for five or six miles together. This is one great occasion of the 'mala aria' which lies over Rome in July and August, and in some parts for forty miles round it.'[28] Thomson notes in *Liberty*, as many travellers, did, that modern Rome is far more sparsely peopled than the ancient city:

> Within the City Bounds, the Desart see.
> See the rank Vine o'er subterranean Roofs,
> Indecent, spread; beneath whose fretted Gold
> It once, exulting, flow'd.

He finds modern Romans beneath contempt:

> A thin despairing Number, all-subdu'd,
> The Slaves of Slaves, by Superstition fool'd,
> By Vice unman'd and a licentious Rule,
> In Guile ingenious, and in Murder brave.

Even unhappy memories of verminous Italian inns find their way into *Liberty*:

> No clean Convenience reigns; even Sleep itself,
> Least delicate of Powers, reluctant, There,
> Lays on the Bed impure his heavy head.[29]

Thomson must have visited Florence, and visited it probably on the way back to England, because Spence, who arrived in that city on 11 July 1732, has an undated reference to meeting him there, and we know that Talbot and Thomson were back in Paris by October. When in Florence Thomson's fascination for the statuesque would, one imagines, have drawn him to the Grand Duke's gallery, now the Uffizi, but any such visit seems not to be reflected in his poetry. Of the eight famous pieces of ancient statuary described in *Liberty*, seven were in Rome at the time of his grand tour; the only one in Florence, the Venus de' Medici, had already made its appearance in his poetry, in the 1730 edition of *Summer*. In Florence too he could hardly be unaware of the presence of Don Carlos, the Bourbon heir to the Spanish throne, whose succession to the Grand Dukedom of Tuscany was guaranteed by six thousand Spanish troops, ceremonially escorted into Leghorn harbour on 15 October

1731 by a British battle fleet. This combined operation was part of the price Britain was paying for a cessation of Spanish hostilities against those sore spots Gibraltar and Minorca, and for its commercial advantages under the Treaty of Seville; it concluded in Spain's favour a long chess game of dynastic manoeuvres in which Continental despots used small republics as pawns. Such a conspicuous act of great-power *realpolitik*, a triumph, if triumph it may be called, of Walpole's pacific foreign policy, seems to have prompted no direct comment from the author of *Britannia*, apart from a footnote in *Liberty*, referring to the peaceful state of the historic republics of Florence, Pisa, and Siena, which were subject to the Grand Duke.[30]

The details of Talbot and Thomson's homeward route from Italy are unknown. Addison and many other grand tourists, but not Spence, returned from Italy by way of Germany and the Low Countries, but Thomson's presence in Paris in October 1732 suggests that he and Talbot did not take that route. There is no hard evidence even that they entered Switzerland, though it is tempting to infer that Thomson had seen the Alps when we read one of the more vivid word paintings in *Liberty*:

> The hollow-winding Stream: the Vale, fair-spread
> Amid an Amphitheatre of Hills;
> Whence, vapour-wing'd, the sudden Tempest springs:
> From Steep to Steep ascending, the gay Train
> Of Fogs, thick-roll'd into romantic Shapes:
> The flitting Cloud, against the Summit dash'd;
> And, by the Sun illumin'd, pouring bright
> A gemmy Shower: hung o'er amazing Rocks,
> The Mountain-Ash, and solemn-sounding Pine:
> The snow-fed Torrent, in white Mazes tost,
> Down to the clear Ætherial Lake below:
> And, high o'er-topping all the broken Scene,
> The Mountain fading into Sky; where shines
> On Winter Winter shivering, and whose Top
> Licks from their cloudy Magazine the Snows.[31]

Nevertheless, this is no more specific or graphic than some descriptions in the *Seasons* of tropical or northern places that Thomson certainly never visited.

Thomson's last surviving letter from the grand tour is his longest; it is addressed to the Countess of Hertford and is dated from Paris, 10 October 1732. It begins with the same kind of disarming apology that was offered to Dodington eleven months earlier:

It was but yesterday that I received a letter you did me the honour to write April last, the Banker here not having known how to send it me.—I mention this only to prevent my being judged altogether inexcusable, and not by way of apology for having so long neglected to pay my respects where they are so justly due. To speak naturally, as one who longed mightily to hear of your Ladyship's health I resolved a thousand times to write, and continually reproached my self for neglecting it; but then a vain Imagination of writing in the character of a traveller still prevented me: and like one who finds himself quite unable to answer his Ingagements, I desperately turned bankrupt. The letter however you have honoured me with has awakened me to such a lively remembrance of your goodness, as makes me flatter myself that, upon this ingenuous confession, you will absolve me from any rash promises I made while the fairy prospect lay before me.

The boy from the manse has evidently become a confident courtier; there is always something disingenuous about confessing to making an ingenuous confession. A courtly compliment is slipped into the demonstration of his progress in *virtu*; he praises several pieces of 'divine' Grecian sculpture, then adds:

Was I writing to another than your Ladyship, I might forget myself, and say that they represent a finer nature than is to be found now-a-days. The famous Italian painters having taken their Ideas from them, no wonder that their works should be so vastly superior to the paintings of all other nations, as they beyond comparison are.

For all his pleasure in art, now that his journey is mostly behind him, he finds it altogether less of a fairy prospect. His observations upon France, for instance, display the same truculence as his letter to Dodington nearly two years earlier. Now he is irritated by French leadership in the world of fashion:

It is hard that such a great nation as England cannot be decently proud enough, to have a standard of dress exercises & polite behaviour among themselves, without their always awkwardly imitating a people they neither ever can nor ought to be like. I wish we would also imitate them in one thing, and that is being as indifferent about them as they are about us.[32]

In Thomson's case, travel had the not uncommon effect of confirming the traveller's insularity.

Most of this letter consists of a carefully composed review of Thomson's impressions of Italy:

There are certainly several very fine natural Scenes to be seen abroad, but they are saddened by the misery of their Inhabitants; and Scenes of human misery ought never to please but in a tragedy. The bad Government in Italy, and perticularly that of the Preists, has not only extirpated almost human Arts and Industry, but even disfigured Nature herself. Tho' they might command all that can tend either to the convenience pleasure or magnificence of life, yet are they in some sort destitute of all. The gracious sun indeed still dispenses to them his powerfull smiles, but him they are afraid of. It ought to be considered rather as the land of the dead than of the living. Suppose one who is perfectly master of the antient Poets and Historians suddenly transported there, without knowing what country it was; he would scarce, I fancy, find it out by their descriptions. After, 'tis true, having wandered thro' a vast desolate plain, where by degrees began to appear the tombs of Heroes broken arches and aqueducts, till at last thro' many majestic ruins he came to the palatine Mount, the seat of the Imperial palace: here, would he say, astonished at the awful prospect, here must have stood Rome, the mistress of the world. Behold an Empire dead! and these venerable ruins all around, these triumphal Arches, pillars, remains of temples, Baths, aqueducts and amphitheaters, are her wide-spread monument—a monument, tho' made up of ruins, infinitely infinitely more noble than all the other monuments of the world put together.[33]

This passage contains parallels with themes, ideas, and images of *Liberty* close enough to indicate that the first Part of the poem was forming in the poet's mind, and possibly that something had already been committed to verse. Another passage, on the languishing music of Italy and on indolence, contains perhaps the germ of *The Castle of Indolence*, a poem that we know Thomson began to write when he was at work on *Liberty*:

As for their Music, it is a sort of charming malady that quite disolves them in softness, and greatly heightens in them that universal Indolence men naturally (I had almost said reasonably) fall into when they can receive little or no advantage from their Industry.[34]

However, the only verse that Thomson is known to have written during the grand tour itself is the poem on the death of William Aikman, a copy of which he sent to Lady Hertford from Paris in October 1732. Aikman, 'that worthy modest Man' as Pope called him in a letter to Mallet, had died in London 'after a tedious, lingering consumption' on 7 June 1731. Thomson's forty-line elegy in heroic couplets pays dignified and measured tribute to Aikman's moral qualities,

> Worth above show, and goodness unsevere . . .
> So did his mind reflect with secret ray,
> In various virtues, heaven's internal day;

and points to the religious comfort that such a life can offer to a Christian:

> A friend when dead is but remov'd from sight,
> Hid in the lustre of eternal light;
> Oft with the mind he wonted converse keeps,
> In the lone walk, or while the body sleeps,
> Lets in a wandring ray, and all elate
> Wings, and attracts her to another state.

Sending this poem to Lady Hertford, Thomson described it as 'rather a plain testimony of Friendship, than an attempt of poetry'; so it was probably not intended for publication. It can be inferred that a copy was sent to Aikman's daughter. How, when, and where the news of Aikman's death reached Thomson is not known, but it is reasonable to suppose that he was in correspondence with members of the London–Scottish literary circle.[35]

Possibly one of that circle arranged the publication of what would become one of Thomson's best-known lyrics 'For ever Fortune' in *The Hive, a Collection of the most celebrated Songs*, in 1732. In later reprints this love-song is said to be sung to the tune of 'Logan Water'; its eventual inclusion in Joseph Ritson's *Scotish Songs* (1794) might be regarded as its admission to the canon of traditional Scots songs.[36]

A more significant advance of Thomson's poetic career during his absence abroad is referred to in the letter from Paris to the Countess of Hertford:

Give me leave to return you my most humble acknowledgements for the honour you did me in presenting my Book to the Prince of Wales. I wish it had been something more worthy of You to present, and of him to read. The approbation he was pleased to give a first Imperfect Essay does not so much flatter my Vanity, as my hope, of seeing the fine arts flourish under a Prince of his so noble equal humane and generous dispositions; who knows how to unite the soveraignty of the prince with the liberty of the people, and to found his happiness and Glory on the publick Good. Oh happy as a God he, who has it both in his hand and in his heart to make a people happy!

McKillop conjectures, reasonably enough, that the 'Book' is a copy of the quarto edition of *The Seasons* with *Britannia* bound in, so the 'first Imperfect Essay' might be *Britannia*, where the Prince is praised as a future benefactor of his country.[37]

It is not known exactly when Thomson returned home, but he was certainly back in England before 26 March 1733, when Mrs Rowe, replying to a letter from the Countess of Hertford wrote, 'I am pleased to hear of any improv'ment that so fine a Genius as Mr Thomsons has gained by His Travels.'[38] It would seem that one of the poet's first engagements after his return was to wait upon the amiable patroness who was now furthering his interests with the Prince of Wales as she had done earlier with the Queen. Dodington was probably giving some assistance in this quarter too, for during Thomson's absence abroad he supplanted Lord Hervey as principal political adviser to the Prince.

Dodington's closeness to the Prince did not mean that he had actually joined the growing band of Whigs opposed to Walpole, but this was a period when any close association with the heir to the throne would eventually draw almost any politician into opposition to the king's ministers. As John Carswell wittily observes, 'Politics, like tennis, had been a game played in two opposing Courts for more years than any man living could remember.' Antagonism between these courts, 'each headed by a royal personage, allowing politicians to "sell spot and buy futures", helped indeed towards the development of our peculiar notion of a constitutional opposition'.[39] The buyers of 'futures' gravitated towards the heir 'and for them to accentuate every difference was the surest means of guaranteeing that the son on his accession would displace his father's ministers in their favour'.[40] Such polarization could be over substantial matters, such as religion and foreign policy, when the poles were, say, James II and William of Orange. Frederick, however, whose political differences from his father were altogether less substantial, was detested by both his parents with an intensity that went far beyond the jealousy that a monarch naturally feels for his heir. So much was clear from the Prince's first landing, for the King decreed that his arrival in England should be insultingly unceremonious, a fact of which Thomson may well have been aware when he celebrated this event in *Britannia*. To quote John Carswell:

The King was testy, strict in his habits and limited in his intellect. He once so far forgot himself as to say, in the course of an argument with his ministers, that he would show them they had not got a Stuart to deal with. But the Prince, though equally impulsive and autocratic, was more generous, more warm-hearted, and perhaps more intelligent. Unlike his father, who had no use for 'bainting and boetry' he made claims to sensibility, being an enthusiastic playgoer and a fair 'cellist, singing French songs at an open window to his own accompaniment for hours together, oblivious of the crowd of ragamuffins that had gathered in the street. England interested and attracted him; he thought he understood its politics, and he looked forward with excessive enthusiasm to the time when he would reign.[41]

In the years Thomson was abroad Dodington was building a large and splendid town house in Pall Mall, next to Carlton House, newly acquired by Frederick; he was now spoken of as the Prince's 'prime minister'; the state of their relationship is outlined in a private letter from Dodington to Frederick in September 1733:

You know it has always been my lot to be represented as an arrogant, self-sufficient, empty coxcomb, and in the same quarter of an hour . . . a deep, designing, dangerous spirit.

As to myself, I am a private man whom your Royal Highness was pleased to call to your acquaintance. Your partiality for me grew very fast, till at last, without any merit even in my own vain opinion, you were pleased to honour me with so unreserved a confidence that I believe there was nothing that was most near and dear to us that we could not, nay that we did not communicate to each other. In the beginning I found you in no favourable disposition towards the Minister [i.e. Walpole]; I used all my endeavours at that time, nay always have endeavoured, to soften it.[42]

Dodington, unlike the rasher (or more highly principled) advisers who later guided the Prince's political activities, steered a moderate and conciliatory course. For instance, it was he who effected a formal reconciliation between Prince and King in January 1734.

Conciliation, though, was far from most politicians' thoughts when Thomson returned from the grand tour for Britain was then in the thick of the biggest political storm since the trial of Dr Sacheverell in 1710. James Ralph claimed that 'Never, in the Memory of Man, was the Nation so alarm'd at the Design of a Minister, as in the Case of the projected *Excise* on Wine and Tobacco in 1733.'[43] When Parliament opened in January a sizeable but motley combination of Tory and dissident Whig members, assisted by a well-orchestrated public clamour, were determined to topple the Prime Minister. Though they did not succeed in their principal aim, they compelled Walpole to withdraw his unpopular bill in April. One of the men who spoke most eloquently for the Excise Bill in the Commons was Thomson's patron Charles Talbot, the Solicitor-General; his contribution was less controversial than most because he was a man whose integrity and competence were respected on both sides of the House.

The bill did not reach the Lords, but among its known opponents in that House were Thomson's hero the Duke of Argyll, Mallet's patron the Duke of Montrose, Lady Grizel Baillie's brother the Earl of Marchmont, and the Earl of Stair, all leading Scottish Whigs. Lord Hervey, the Queen's confidant and Walpole's man (of sorts), reported that Lord Stair spoke for this faction to the Queen, arguing against the bill and telling her that Walpole 'is hated by all the Scotch to a man, because he is known to have combated every mark of favour the King has been so good to confer on any of that nation'. The Prince and Dodington were silent in public on the excise question, but, writes Hervey, 'by the distinction the Prince showed on all occasions to Lord Cobham, Lord Stair, Lord Chesterfield, and all that were the most violent against this scheme, it was not difficult to guess what His Royal Highness's opinion of it was, or which way his wishes pointed'.[44] There was no breach between Dodington and Walpole on this occasion; but Lords Chesterfield, Cobham, Marchmont, Montrose, and Stair were all promptly dismissed from some or all of their offices under the Crown.

While Thomson's politician patrons were divided in 1733 over support for Walpole, his most admired literary friend, Alexander Pope, was committing himself to political opposition. His first Horatian imitation *The First Satire of the Second Book of Horace, Imitated*, published in February, just about the time of Thomson's homecoming, was far more openly hostile to the government than anything he had published earlier. Mallet publicly proclaimed his discipleship of Pope in April, with *Of Verbal Criticism*. Where Thomson placed himself politically would not be publicly declared for a year or two, but on his return from the grand tour he resumed a place near the centre of literary society. The reference to him in James Bramston's *The Man of Taste*, published in March 1733, indicates that he was recognized as an associate of Pope and the leading modern writer of blank verse. The speaker in Bramston's poem is a man of bad taste, who praises Curll and believes that Cibber better deserves the laureateship than Pope; he boasts that 'Milton's an universal blank to me'; so his unfavourable comparison of Thomson with himself must be read as irony:

> *Thompson*, write blank; but know that for that reason,
> These lines shall live, when thine are out of season.

Using the same strategy, James Miller had praised Thomson in *Harlequin-Horace; or the Art of Modern Poetry* (1731), where his sense is condemned as unsuited to the bad taste of the age:

> But think not that an Audience will excuse
> The *Fool* that *purposely dull Sense* pursues,
> That *Young* or *Thomson* like, will never write,
> Unless at once to profit, and delight.

Thomson was a literary presence, but we have little information about his doings in 1733. He saw Lady Hertford near the beginning of the year and he was in the country in November and part of December, during which period he called on Pope in Twickenham.[45] He might have spent some time with the Talbots at Ashdown Park in Sussex. A letter from Thomas Rundle, impossibly dated '1731' in the printed edition, may belong to this year; it gives some notion of the atmosphere of Talbot house-parties:

Philosophy, exercise, and cards, hospitality profuse in generosity without luxury, freedom uncontrouled by any thing but voluntary decency and ever-wakeful reason, mirth that seems to neglect thoughtfulness, but shews by its becoming ease and gracefulness ... that it hath used it much in private ... vary our hours and heighten each others pleasures by the perpetual change. All the nine MUSES came hither with Mr THOMSON, wit and sprightliness with BILLY, and wisdom (tho' she left her solemn state behind her) with the Sollicitor.[46]

Billy is William Talbot, the Solicitor-General's second son, born in 1710. Charles Richard Talbot is not mentioned, perhaps because he was away in Glamorgan, where, it was reported in September 1733, he intended to stand for Parliament at the election due in 1734.[47]

This was not to be, because he died suddenly on 27 September, at the age of 24, a calamity that is likely to have been the most important event of 1733 in Thomson's personal life. His reaction was remembered fifteen years later, when Patrick Murdoch wished to console a friend upon Thomson's death:

Think likewise on his own behaviour on the like occasions. He lost Charles Talbot, as we have him; and tho' he retained to his latest hour a most devout veneration of that excellent person, yet he did not consume himself in unavailing grief. He remembered, and commemorated him, in that pious and affectionate manner, that we shall ever remember them both. At the same time he acquiesced in the sovereign will of Providence; and bore his loss (the greatest, in all respects, that could possibly befall to him) with a manly fortitude.

Thomson wrote memorial lines in blank verse to his dead young friend, which, like the elegy on Aikman, take Christian hope as their theme; the verses end:

> ETERNAL GOODNESS reigns: be this our Story;
> A Subject for the past of grateful Song,
> And for the future of undrooping Hope.

As with the Aikman elegy, these lines were not published, though a different tribute to Charles Richard Talbot forms the opening lines of *Liberty*.[48]

Although such a visit is not documented for 1733, we can be reasonably certain that Thomson called on Dodington after his return home, and presumably before Dodington went to Ireland in the autumn. That Thomson was known as Dodington's man is implicit in a letter to him from Aaron Hill on 10 November, a letter which, with sad irony, reverses the roles the two poets had played at the outset of their correspondence seven years earlier. After a flattering opening Hill asks Thomson's opinion of his new tragedy *Zara*, an adaptation of Voltaire's *Zaire*, and continues,

If, after having read it yourself, you find it fit to be read by, or to such of your friends, as can promote its success, by their influence, I flatter myself you will do it that favour. And, if I might be particular, in tasking your indulgence, Mr *Dodington* should be the first of the number. I have not enough the honour of his acquaintance to sollicite his concern for support of this Tragedy.

A few days earlier Hill had sent copies of *Zara* to Pope, with a request that two of them might be put in the hands of Lords Burlington and Bolingbroke. In his very brief acknowledgement of these papers, on 13 November, Pope reveals that Thomson is visiting him at Twickenham: 'I am just taken up by Mr *Thomson*, in the Perusal of a new Poem he has brought me.'[49] The poem has not been identified, but it could very well have been some of the first Part of *Liberty*.

Hill had to wait another five weeks for Thomson's reply on 18 December; it offered effusive praise and a promise to show *Zara* to Dodington when he returned from Ireland in a few days' time; it also gave Thomson's plans for the immediate future: 'Soon I propose to fix in Town for the Winter, during which time I hope to pass several happy Evenings in your Company: Mr Pope earnestly wishes the same.' These concluding words suggest that Thomson had seen Pope more recently than 13 November, and may mean that his spell in the country had included more than one visit to Twickenham. There is a small irony of which all three playwrights were probably unaware when Thomson in this letter implicitly condemns the coldness of Voltaire's tragedy: 'I deeply feel the Difference betwixt Mr Voltaire and Mr Hill. The more generous Warmth of your Heart more animates the Scene, raises the dear Tumult in the Breast, and moves me much more.' Coldness, though, was the very charge that Voltaire would later bring against Thomson's (otherwise admirable) tragedies: 'they want perhaps some fire; and it may be that his heroes are neither moving nor busy enough'.[50] Whatever help Pope, Thomson, and their highly-placed friends might have been able to offer, it was not immediately effective, because *Zara* did not reach the public stage until 1736.

Thomson excuses the brevity of his letter to Hill about *Zara* by explaining that 'The two or three Days since my Return to Town have been rather hurry'd than employ'd in solliciting for the Benefit of old Dennis.' John Dennis, now in his seventies, was blind and sunk in poverty. As early as 1731 Pope had tried to raise a subscription to relieve the wants of his former enemy, and in 1733 he was sending sums of money to him indirectly, by way of Mallet. Dennis's well-wishers, including Pope, Thomson, and Mallet, then arranged a benefit performance of Vanbrugh and Cibber's *The Provoked Husband* at the Haymarket theatre on 18 December. Pope wrote a Prologue for the occasion, though it is not certain that it was actually spoken on the night.[51]

The success of the performance was reported in the *Daily Advertiser* and other newspapers on 19 December: 'There was an exceeding crowded Audience of Persons of Distinction last Tuesday Night at Mr Dennis's Benefit, and his Royal Highness the Prince of Wales was pleased to send twenty Guineas as a present to that Gentleman.' That Thomson played a leading part in organizing this benefit is evident from some couplets printed in the *Daily Journal* on 22 December and reprinted in other newspapers and journals. The verses are headed 'To Mr *Thomson*, Author of the Poems on the 4 Seasons, on Occasion of the Part which that Gentleman took, in the Concern for Mr *Dennis*'s late Benefit', and are signed 'J. D.' They assert that the first three seasons of the year are reflected in Thomson's flowery fancy, strength of expression, and rich fruits of instruction, whereas winter is reflected in Dennis's own decayed state; they conclude:

> Yet, shall my propless *Ivy*,—pale, and bent,
> Bless the short sunshine, which thy pity lent.

When the lines were reprinted in *The Grub-Street Journal* a caustic comment was added, as if from the pen of Dennis's brother hack:

> I'm glad to find my *brother*'s grateful lay,
> Like *medlar fruit, delicious in decay*.

Dennis himself felt a similar contempt for the verses that had been written in his name, for, according to an anonymous *Life of Mr John Dennis* (1734), he exclaimed when they were read aloud to him, 'by God, they could be no one but that Fool Savage's'. This *Life* tells us that the benefit performance raised a hundred pounds for Dennis and confirms Thomson's leading part in the affair, though it refers to him, perhaps disingenuously, as 'Some Gentleman, who it seems writes Verses in Imitation of Milton'.[52] Dennis did not long enjoy the proceeds of his benefit; he died on 6 January 1734 and, thanks to his late financial windfall, was handsomely interred.

Though Pope was prepared to give money to relieve Dennis's poverty, he refused to the last to give any respect to the old man's writings; so much is clear even in the benefit Prologue. Thomson, on the other hand, seems to have corresponded with Dennis on friendly terms; along with Savage, Mallet, Hill, and Edward Young, he subscribed to Dennis's *Miscellaneous Tracts* (1727). More significantly, he revealed in his Preface to *Winter* the influence of Dennis's critical writings on Milton and the sublime.

A particularly important event for Thomson's own fortunes was the appointment of Charles Talbot, the Solicitor-General, to the office of Lord Chancellor on 29 November 1733, and his elevation to the peerage a week later.

Lord Hervey's account of this event and the near-simultaneous elevation of Sir Philip Yorke (later Lord Hardwicke) offers some insight into the respected character of Thomson's patron and into Walpole's manipulation of state patronage for the public good:

Sir Philip Yorke, being first in rank, had certainly a right to the Chancellor's seals; but Talbot, who was an excellent Chancery lawyer and knew nothing of the common law, if he was not Chancellor, would be nothing. Yorke therefore, though fit for both these employments, got the worst, being prevailed upon to accept that of Lord Chief Justice, on the salary being raised from £3,000 to £4,000 a year for life, and £1,000 more paid him out of the Chancellor's salary by Lord Talbot. This was a scheme of Sir Robert Walpole's, who, as Homer says of Ulysses, was always fertile in expedients, and thought these two great and able men of too much consequence to lose or disoblige either. Sir Robert communicated this scheme secretly to the Queen, she insinuated it to the King, and the King proposed it to Sir Robert as an act of his own ingenuity and generosity.

Lord Talbot had as clear, separating, distinguishing, subtle, and fine parts as ever man had. Lord Hardwicke's were perhaps less delicate, but no man's were more forcible. No one could make more of a good cause than Lord Hardwicke, and no one so much of a bad one as Lord Talbot. The one had infinite knowledge, the other infinite ingenuity: they were both excellent, but very different; both amiable in their private characters, as well as eminent in their public capacities; both good pleaders, as well as upright judges; and both esteemed by all parties, as much for their temper and integrity as for their knowledge and abilities.[53]

Lord Campbell, reviewing the lives of all the Lord Chancellors down to his own day, said of Talbot: 'from the reign of Ethelred to that of George IV, I find this Chancellor alone without an accuser; without an enemy; without a detractor;

without anyone, from malice or mistake, to cavil at any part of his character, conduct, or demeanour.'[54]

The immediate benefit to Thomson of his patron's elevation was an appointment as Secretary of the Briefs in the Court of Chancery. This institution may at that time have been less scandalous than when Dickens was collecting material for *Bleak House*, but was even less reformed and its doings shrouded in even deeper mystery. Among its more than a hundred paid offices in the gift of the Lord Chancellor at the date of Thomson's appointment were some that would not disgrace the pages of Rabelais:

> The Comptrollers of the Hanaper,
> The Clerks of the Petty Bag,
> The Chaff-wax,
> The Clerk of the Dispensations and Faculties,
> The Patentee of the Six-peny Writ Office,
> The Gentlemen of the Chamber, and
> The Secretary of the Briefs.[55]

The 'briefs' with which this Secretary, or to be more exact his deputy, was concerned were 'letters patent under the Privy Seal, issued by the Court of Chancery, in the name of the Crown, directed to the Archbishops, Bishops, Clergy, Magistrates, Churchwardens and Overseers of the poor ... requesting them to assist in promoting the pious objects with which they were issued'.[56] Their issue was an ancient practice, which became common in the Elizabethan period, was now regularized by an Act of 1705, and would be abolished in 1828, along with many timeworn sinecures.[57] Briefs were read by clergy to their congregations; they were appeals for alms, usually for the repair of church fabrics, but sometimes for making good damage caused by fire, storm, flood, shipwreck, and other acts of God, or for the relief of suffering Protestants in other countries. Then, as now, a proportion of charitable contributions were swallowed in administrative costs. A House of Commons committee discovered in 1732:

Among the various Claims of those, who now call themselves Officers of the Court of Chancery, none appeared more extraordinary to the Committee, than the fee of the Secretary and Clerk of the Briefs; who, upon Grants, to enable Persons to beg and collect Alms, claim, and frequently receive, a Fee of Forty, Fifty, or Sixty, Pounds; and the Register takes, besides, Twelve or Thirteen Pounds, for stamping and telling the Briefs; which Fees with other great Charges upon the Collection, devour Three Parts in Four of what is given for the Relief of Persons, reduced to extreme Poverty by Fire, or other Accidents.[58]

The fees extracted by Chancery for briefs are the subject of satire by Charles Churchill in *The Duellist* (1764), lines 277–80, and by William Cowper in

Charity (1782), lines 469–84. Thomson's income from the secretaryship was estimated at £300 a year, but only for a short period because he held the post for about three years in all; at some unspecified date during his tenure the income was reduced to £100 a year, and, as it happened, he did not 'receive a shilling from it during its reduced state'.[59] Such income as he received would, one supposes, be after he had paid a deputy to carry out the duties of the post. Murdoch notes that the secretaryship was 'a place of little attendance, suiting his retired indolent way of life, and equal to all his wants'.[60] Thomson thus obtained the 'establishment' which, Johnson observed, he might have expected on his return from the grand tour.

6

The Poet of Liberty, 1734–1736

THE renewed hospitality of Dodington, Talbot, and Lady Hertford was gratifying, the income from the Secretaryship of Briefs was, doubtless, even more comforting, but Thomson enjoyed hopes of patronage from a higher quarter even than the Lord Chancellor. The Prince of Wales had taken notice of *Sophonisba* by ordering a command performance and had praised a presentation copy of one of Thomson's books. The terms in which Thomson thanked the Countess of Hertford for presenting the book to the Prince and in which he spoke of the arts flourishing 'under a Prince of his so noble equal humane and generous dispositions; who knows how to unite the sovraignty of the prince with the liberty of the people'[1] suggest that he had Frederick in mind as a possible dedicatee for his work-in-hand, *Liberty*; indeed, the carefully turned phrases of the letter anticipate some expressions in the Dedication of that poem and the panegyric upon the Prince at the end of Part One of it.

On New Year's Day 1734 the Prince of Wales was persuaded by Dodington to attend the King's levee, where he had not been seen for some months. The King spoke to him, so a public rupture was avoided; but the mutual antagonism between the royal parents and their son persisted, with little attempt at concealment. In the summer of that year, when the first general election was held since the Prince's arrival in England, he was inevitably a rallying-point for the opposition again. Among the prominent English Whigs who went openly into opposition over the Excise Bill in 1733 were the Earl of Chesterfield and Viscount Cobham. In the year following, Cobham's 25-year-old nephew George Lyttelton was introduced to Frederick by Dodington, was appointed equerry to the prince, and rapidly became, with Chesterfield, his new political adviser. As their influence over the Prince increased, Dodington's was diminished; he lost the Prince's confidence without regaining Walpole's. In October 1734 his witty and malicious enemy Lord Hervey gleefully noted that he had 'managed things so ill, that he is in disgrace with both sides. Two stools never made a wider gap for a poor broken rump than on this occasion. He has in truth followed his nose, for he has fallen quite flat.'[2]

Though Thomson would slowly gravitate towards Dodington's rival George Lyttelton, and to a more outspoken association with the opposition group surrounding the Prince of Wales, he always remained on good terms with Dodington. He was also still very much Talbot's man, and Talbot was one of that smallish body of public figures respected for their abilities and moral integrity who had not been driven into opposition to Walpole. Nevertheless, relations between the two great men were somewhat strained in 1734, over the matter of a bishopric for Talbot's (and Thomson's) friend Dr Thomas Rundle. When the Bishop of Gloucester died in December 1733 the Queen and the Lord Chancellor both wished Rundle to be consecrated to the see, but Edmund Gibson, Bishop of London and Walpole's chief adviser on ecclesiastical preferments, would not agree. His stated objection was to Rundle's Arian and liberal theology, particularly some heretically humane opinions on the sacrifice of Isaac, or, as Hervey declared, that 'about fourteen or fifteen years ago he had in private company spoken disrespectfully of Abraham'; but, Hervey adds:

Nobody doubted but that the Bishop of London's sole reason for opposing Rundle was because my Lord Chancellor had made application to the Court in his favour, not through the Bishop of London, but merely upon his own weight and interest; and as the Bishop of London had always disliked what he called lay recommendations, he was determined to make a stand upon this occasion, thinking, if he could show that even so great a man as my Lord Chancellor could not get any one preferred in the Church without applying to him, for the future no other person would attempt it.

Walpole was so dependent upon the support of Gibson's well-drilled bishops in the House of Lords that he could not afford to let Rundle succeed to Gloucester, but he did not wish to disoblige the Queen and the Lord Chancellor, so he procrastinated. The bishopric remained vacant throughout 1734, the subject of a tense and well-publicized political struggle, during which Gibson roused most of the clergy against the heretical Rundle, while himself becoming very unpopular in the country at large, where he was seen as a latter-day Laud, seeking to exalt Church over State. Hervey reports:

Many pamphlets were written, and with great virulence, on both sides; but the two principals were very differently treated in these productions, for, whilst my Lord Chancellor's name was never mentioned but with decency, the Bishop of London was pelted with all the opprobrious language that envy and malice ever threw at eminence and power.[3]

Thomson's public comment was deferred until his *Poem to the Memory of Lord Talbot*, where Gibson's intrigues and Walpole's weakness are characterized as 'slanderous Zeal, and Politics infirm, | Jealous of Worth'.[4]

The year-long battle in the public press was the reflection of a struggle in the ante-rooms of Westminster and St James, where, it would appear from Hervey's detailed verbatim reports, the Prime Minister deployed forensic skills equal to those of the Lord Chancellor himself. Talbot nevertheless insisted 'that he could not so far abet the injustice done to the character of Rundle on this occasion as to give his consent to Rundle's being put by, and by naming another man seem tacitly at least to admit that he had before named an improper man'.[5] He believed that his own credit and judgement were so far impugned by Gibson's objection to his nominee's orthodoxy that by December 1734 he was secretly considering the possibility of resigning the Great Seal if Rundle was passed over. This threat was conveyed by his eldest son William to the court-haunting Prebendary of Westminster, Dr Alured Clarke, who passed it on to Mrs Clayton, one of the Ladies of the Queen's Bedchamber, in a letter of 15 December 1734. Something of the quality of life in Walpole's England is revealed by Clarke's great alarm that William Talbot's letter, containing 'strong expressions' about the Rundle affair, had been sent to him through 'the common post', where it could be read by 'the searchers', that is, Walpole's spies in the Post Office, Clarke's own letter was sent 'by a private hand' in order to avoid such a possibility.[6]

A compromise was eventually patched up. Gloucester was given to the pious, learned, and charitable Martin Benson, who was a friend of Talbot; then, a few months later, in July 1735, Rundle was rewarded with the much richer but more remote bishopric of Derry. Perhaps it was thought that the Irish would have a less tender concern for the reputation of Abraham than would the good folk of Gloucester. Talbot remained Lord Chancellor, but his son William, who was a Member of Parliament, declared against Walpole and in 1735 voted against the government. His reasons are implicit in a letter written to a fellow landowner concerning the use of their influence in Gloucestershire during the parliamentary elections of 1734. The other landowner (Sir John Dutton) had accused Talbot of supporting a Tory candidate while professing Whig principles. Talbot replied that there was no difference between 'a ministerial Whig and a State Tory, when in power'. He then listed in detail the principles of a 'real Whig': the balanced constitution, the need for free elections and a free press, detestation of a standing mercenary army and of 'a Minister who endeavours to govern by corruption', and all the other familiar opposition ideas that Thomson was to weave into *Liberty*. Talbot then lists ironically all the 'Tory sentiments' which are hostile to liberty, concluding with the 'Tory' opinion

that whatever reflects upon the character of a man in power is a libel; that even the public spirited sentiments of a patriot, delivered on the *Stage* in the character of a BRUTUS, or a CATO, may be injurious to the peace of the nation; and villainy made odious by the representation of a SEJANUS or a BUCKINGHAM, may by popular malignity be interpreted to reproach those at the helm of affairs with the like dispositions; that therefore the *Stage* ought to be under the immediate directions of a Court Officer.

Talbot argues that, as the candidate supported by Dutton 'hath invariably voted with the Minister' and as his own candidate's 'promise to act as a Tory' means that he will 'oppose the measures of Sir Robert Walpole, should things continue to proceed as they have gone of late', the two candidates could justly exchange their party labels.[7] Young Billy, a political manager at the age of 24, displays, in his paradoxical reversal of Whig and Tory, something of the wit and sprightliness that Rundle (and, doubtless, Thomson) enjoyed in him, but his analysis also makes good sense.

Admiration for Rundle and the Talbots would have been sufficient cause for Thomson to dislike Walpole and his style of government, but there were also more substantial and less self-interested motives. The judicious modern biographer of Walpole, Sir John Plumb, writes:

All that he does and says in the early thirties argues a growing inflexibility of temperament, a greediness to grasp and exercise power ... He was hated more for being himself than for his conduct of affairs. Not only was his power resented; and his royal favour loathed; his whole manner of life bred detestation wherever he went ... The good that he did—the stability, the peace, the prosperity, were taken for granted—the evil magnified to phantom proportions.

Public life and the institutions of government were thereby brought into disrepute: by 1734 Parliament had lost much of the respect it had enjoyed in the early years of the century; an ever franker acceptance of the greedier side of human nature strengthened self-seeking, weakened altruism and vulgarized politics, until critical issues of state became a matter of personal vendetta.[8]

For many observers 1734 was a watershed, because the scale and openness of government bribery in the election of that year was unprecedented; the tone of politics was perceptibly lowered. Thomson was not blind to this development. It was force of circumstances as much as maturing ambitions which made him a voice of public protest, with the result that, after the early 1730s, he wrote more new poetry upon the moral qualities of men in public life than upon his 'own' subject, the natural scene.

The literary opposition to Walpole at this time was led by Pope; to some degree it was orchestrated by Bolingbroke, until his retirement to France in May 1735. In the earliest full-scale 'Life' of Bolingbroke it is claimed that Thomson enjoyed Bolingbroke's patronage;[9] but, though it is true that Bolingbroke, as the friend of Thomson's friends Pope and Mallet, was in a position to meet Thomson, I have been able to find no evidence that he became his patron. One imagines, indeed, that Thomson would have been disinclined to put himself in the debt of one who had been so conspicuous a Jacobite, and who was thought in many quarters still to be one. Thomson's association with the opposition was sufficiently well known by September 1734 to be acknowledged in a verse squib on the subject of patronage. The *Grub-Street Journal* of 19 September printed some verses comparing Walpole's patronage of miserable scribblers with his predecessors' patronage of great poets; then, in the same journal a week later, an answering rhyme lists half a dozen writers who were once patronized by Walpole and now oppose him; they are a mixed bag of 'Pope, Young, Welsted, Thomson, Fielding, and Frowde'.

Thomson's name was now famous enough for a literary adventurer to attempt to capitalize upon it. In November 1734 the *London Magazine* printed a flattering verse epistle 'To Mr James Dalacourt in Ireland, upon his Prospect of Poetry', signed 'J. Thompson'. When this same poem was sent to *The Gentleman's Magazine* a year or two later, perhaps by Dalacourt himself, the editor Edward Cave consulted Thomson, who denied authorship. Thomson's disclaimer, printed in *The Gentleman's Magazine* for August 1736, did not trouble Dalacourt (or De la Cour, as he later styled himself), for he continued to reprint the poem alongside his own 'Prospect of Poetry' in the various collected editions of his verse; as a result, the epistle was reprinted in some editions of Thomson from the late eighteenth to the mid-nineteenth century. Thomson himself was working at *Liberty* during 1734; on 17 September Alured Clarke reported his progress to Mrs Clayton:

I believe it will not be long before Mr Thomson's Poem on 'Liberty' is published. I have seen the first book, and there are such worthy sentiments in it, and his plans are so well calculated for the promoting of good public principles, that though his poetry does lie open to some objections, I cannot but wish him a multitude of readers.

Clarke then summarizes the book he has seen and quotes from a passage near the end (lines 341–58), where the poet dedicates his verse to the service of Liberty.[10]

Thomson's copyright assignment to Andrew Millar of 'a poem called Liberty in five parts', for the sum of £250, is dated 16 December 1734, and Millar's advertisements of the forthcoming publication of *Liberty, a Poem* appeared in newspapers from 12 December, but in the event the work was printed and issued serially. On 13 January 1735 appeared *Antient and Modern Italy Compared. Being the First Part of Liberty, a Poem*; on 7 February appeared *Greece. Being the Second Part*, etc.; on 24 March appeared *Rome, Being the Third Part*, etc. Three thousand ordinary-paper copies of the First Part were printed, but only two thousand of the Second and Third Parts; in addition, 250 copies of each part were printed on fine paper; the format is quarto. Millar's price for the copyright and his initial print order indicate that he thought the poem was a valuable property.[11]

The first three Parts were probably complete before Part One was printed; each is between four hundred and six hundred lines long and they form a unity. The work opens in the ruins of ancient Rome, where the Goddess of Liberty appears to the poet and provides him with a vision of that land in all the magnificence and glory of the Roman republic, which she contrasts with the decayed state of modern Italy that has resulted from the loss of liberty. The poet then dedicates his own verse to the service of liberty and asks the goddess to recount the progress of her reign; 'She assents and commands what she says to be sung in *Britain*; whose Happiness, arising from Freedom, and a limited Monarchy, she marks.' The First Part ends with an invocation in which Thomson declares that the source of poetic inspiration is now in the North, not the Mediterranean; he aspires to something 'nobler than Poetic Fame'; he wants to be a teacher more than a poet:

> Oh THOU! to whom the *Muses* owe their flame;
> Who bid'st, beneath the Pole, *Parnassus* rise,
> And *Hippocrenè* flow; with thy bold Ease,
> The striking Force the Lightning of thy Thought,
> And thy strong Phrase, that rolls profound, and clear;
> Oh gracious GODDESS! re-inspire my Song;
> While I, to nobler than Poetic Fame
> Aspiring, thy Commands to BRITONS bear.

The Second and Third Parts trace the rise, flourishing, and decline of liberty in Greece and then in Rome; at the end of Part Three, *Rome*, the Goddess tells how she invigorates the northern nations and 'sends them in Vengeance on the *Roman* Empire, now totally enslaved; and then, with *Arts* and *Sciences* in her Train, quits Earth during the dark Ages'.[12]

The First Part is prefaced by a prose Dedication to the Prince of Wales, in whom, declares Thomson, 'an overflowing Benevolence, Generosity, and Candour of heart' is 'joined to an enlightened Zeal for Liberty, an intimate Persuasion that on it depends the Happiness and Glory both of Kings and People'. By expressing his satisfaction that such princely and patriotic qualities are now 'shining out in Public Virtues, as they have hitherto smiled in all the Social Lights and Private Accomplishments of Life', Thomson is, in effect welcoming the Prince's increasing political activity, and therefore aligning himself publicly with the opposition. In a complimentary passage towards the end of the First Part he praises the prince and his parents as if there were no hostility between them, but pointedly gives more prominence to the Prince's zeal for liberty than the King's. The Goddess of Liberty declares that the House of Hanover is 'Fix'd on my Rock'; the King and Queen 'To steady Justice yielding Goodness join':

> While there, to finish what his Sires began,
> A PRINCE behold! for ME who burns sincere,
> Even with a Subject's Zeal. He my great Work
> Will Parent-like sustain; and added give
> The Touch, the *Graces* and the *Muses* owe.
> For BRITAIN's Glory swells his panting Breast;

And *Antient Arts* He emulous revolves:
His Pride to let the smiling Heart abroad,
Thro' Clouds of Pomp, that but conceal the Man;
To please his Pleasure; Bounty his Delight;
And all the Soul of TITUS dwells in Him.[13]

Thomson could not have been unaware that Titus was on good terms with his father Vespasian, who allowed him to share the government of the Roman empire; together they restored honest and efficient administration after a period of corruption under Nero and his immediate successors. In his characterization of Frederick as an upholder of the constitutional liberties of his people and an enlightened patron of the arts Thomson adumbrates the notion of a patriot prince and anticipates Bolingbroke's *Idea of a Patriot King*.

The wording of the Dedication makes it clear that Thomson had the Prince's permission to write and publish it; but it seems that the two men had not met at this stage; at least, Murdoch implies that they did not meet until after the death of the Lord Chancellor in 1737. Publication of *Liberty* did not begin until after the Prince of Wales had broken with Dodington in late 1734, by which time Lady Hertford would be less inclined to communicate with a Prince now so opposed to the Queen, her mistress. So Thomson's introduction to Frederick's court was probably effected by someone else. This someone may have been William Talbot, as is claimed by an anonymous writer in the *Critical Review* in 1765.[14]

Thomson sent a copy of Part One of *Liberty* to Aaron Hill, who replied on 17 January with characteristically effusive praise, tempered only by certain reservations about the 'transposition and obscurity', resulting from Thomson's endeavours 'after beauties, which, I am sure, are unnecessary to your *poem*, and (I fear) unnatural to our *idiom*'. Hill helpfully marks the places where a difficulty 'might be removed, by change of a word, here and there; and the glowing *felicity* of the *thoughts*, by that means, unveiled from a kind of *cloudiness*, the effect of your new turn, in expression'. His letter ends, however, with high praise ('while you are writing of *old Rome*'s liberty, you seem to have sucked in, with the *Roman* air, the *soul of an old Roman*') and an exhortation:

Go on, in your glorious endeavours, to *light up* the north, with this *fire*. We have always been lovers of liberty, in her coarseness, and rugged simplicity; teach us to *taste* her, in her *politeness*; teach us to be *free*, without *insolence*; and *elegant*, without *luxury*; to be *learned*, at once, and warlike; to be *traders*, but not *tradesmen*; and, in fine, to *deserve*, by our happiness, the *envy* of the rest of the world, but to *escape* it, by our *humanity*. If this is in *verse*, you can do it.[15]

A tall order.

On 7 February Thomson wrote a brief note of thanks and sent the Second Part of *Liberty*. Hill duly praised the harmony and sentiment of this work in his periodical *The Prompter* (number 28) on 14 February, and, on 17 February, wrote a letter to Thomson in which he compares him with Homer and declares that his poem is a landmark of public virtue and genius in a generally corrupt and declining age:

I look upon this mighty work, as the last *stretched* blaze of our expiring genius. It is the dying effort of despairing and indignant virtue, and will stand, like *one* of those immortal *pyramids*, which carry their magnificence thro' times, that wonder, to see nothing round them, but uncomfortable *desart*.[16]

Hill displays considerably more enthusiastic friendship than sound judgement, in view of the fact that during the thirteen months before these words were written Pope had published six substantial poems: the *un*stretched effort of indignant virtue and far-from-expired genius.[17] One imagines that Thomson ingested Hill's flattery *cum grano salis*.

Publication of *Rome*, the Third Part of *Liberty*, on 24 March 1735, was accompanied by an announcement from Millar that the Fourth Part, *Britain*, would speedily be published; its publication, however, was delayed for ten months. We do not know the reasons for this long interruption of the sequence of monthly publication, but the greatly enlarged scale and polemical tone of the last two Parts when at last they appeared, suggest that Thomson extensively rewrote the later parts of his poem.

The summer of 1735 saw him staying, as usual at this season, in the country houses of his patrons. In June he was at St Leonard's Hill, near Windsor, with Lord and Lady Hertford. There he wrote his stanzaic ode 'To Retirement', a conventional minor 'local' poem, in which the poet first invokes his subject and his patron:

> Come calm Retirement! Sylvan Power!
>   That on St Leonard's lov'st to walk,
> To lead along the thoughtfull Hour
>   And with the gentle Hartford talk;

he reviews the visual delights and beneficial moral influences of the natural scene as he plunges into the woods around the hill; eventually he reaches the 'airy Steep' from which London is visible, at which point his poem ends:

> And lo! where on Augusta's Shore,
>   The Human Tempest roars amain;
> What Wretches there their fate deplore!
>   Oh cover me ye Woods again![18]

'To Retirement' is dated 13 June in Lady Hertford's commonplace book; another poem by Thomson, though undated, is close enough to this one in the commonplace book to suggest that it too might have been written during the same visit to St Leonard's Hill. This is 'On a Lady's undertaking to tell a

Gentleman what he thought on by feeling his Pulse', the memento perhaps of some drawing-room game. It is a charming trifle in which the poet gallantly admits to the sweet disorders that arise in his blood at 'Clarinda's' touch and, despite himself, proclaim a love which cannot be spoken. We cannot tell whether the Countess herself is 'Clarinda', any more than we can be certain she is 'Seraphina', an ideal mistress, worshipped from afar and chastely associated with the moon, in two, or perhaps three, undated poems by Thomson. Such poems belong, with pulse-feeling and walks by moonlight, among the senti- mental games of well-bred, platonic, courtly love. Some sentimental literary play in the Countess's circle was probably the occasion of two love-songs, one attributable to Thomson, the other attributed by Lady Hertford to 'Mrs M——', who was perhaps Mrs Arabella Marrow, friend and correspondent of Lady Hertford and Elizabeth Rowe. Both poems begin 'Sweet Tyrant Love'; they continue in identical terms, almost word for word, except that Thomson's is the address of a bashful man to a woman and Mrs M——'s the address of a bashful woman to a man; it is not known which is the earlier, but Mrs M——'s was probably transcribed by the Countess in 1732.[19] Few of Thomson's not inconsiderable number of love-poems can be dated; most of those that can be have links with his courtship of Elizabeth Young between 1742 and 1745 or with his attendance upon the Countess of Hertford from 1727 onwards. Only four of his love-songs were published in his lifetime; it is not certain that any was printed with his consent.

Lady Hertford's dating of 'To Retirement' indicates that it was a leaving gift, because her husband wrote on 14 June from London, 'I got hither very well, but left Mr Thomson at Hammersmith where he took a boat as he said in order to go to Mr Doddington, but I fancy he will go a little farther.' Evidently Thomson was to visit Dodington's house at Chiswick; the farther destination proved to be Dodington's country seat, Eastbury. One of the house-party at St Leonard's Hill was Baron Brooke, the 16-year-old nephew of Lady Hertford and heir to the earldom of Warwick, who was preparing to depart on the grand tour with his tutor Robert Symmer, an old friend of Thomson's from his Edinburgh years. Thomson wrote from Eastbury on 30 June to wish him well and to reflect upon the kind of character he hoped the young lord would develop in his travels abroad:

our Characters ought to resemble in a great Measure our staple Commodity, substantiall Broad-Cloath; tho' Silk, upon some gay Occasions, must be own'd to be very becoming and gracefull. To accommodate the Matter then, let the Coat consist of Cloath, and the Wastcoat, of Silk; and even that silk Wastecoat ought to be left off as we grow in Age.[20]

This metaphorical silk waistcoat is not quite the 'embroidered slavery' that Charles Richard Talbot disdained in Paris, but one still has the impression that

Thomson hopes that Lord Brooke, like young Talbot, will return from the Continent no worse an Englishman than when he went away. As Symmer set out with his charge Thomson may have congratulated himself on having attained, even at Eastbury, rather more independence than some of his oldest and closest friends, for at this date Murdoch was travelling tutor to the nephew of Admiral Vernon, and Mallet was performing the same office for the wealthy politician and literary dabbler Robert Nugent; in addition, it was widely thought, Mallet was writing the once-celebrated poems published over Nugent's name.

The needs of his younger brother John, who was suffering from consumption, brought Thomson back from Eastbury to London, presumably to see his banker as well as his brother. On 7 August he wrote to his old friend Dr William Cranstoun:

The Bearer hereof, my Brother, was seized last Spring with a severe Cold, which seems to have fallen upon his Lungs, and has reduced him to such a low Condition that his Physician here advises him to try what his native Air can do, as the only remaining Means of Recovery. In his present melancholy Circumstances, it gives me no small Satisfaction to think that he will have the Benefit of your Directions: and for me to spend more Words in recommending Him to your Care, were, I flatter myself, a superfluous Formality. Your old acquaintance Anderson attends him; and, besides what is necessary to defray the Expences of their Journey, I have only given my Brother five Guineas, chusing rather to remit him the Money he will afterwards want, which shall be done upon the first Notice.

John Thomson was to stay with his aunt at Chesters, a hamlet close to his birthplace in Southdean, because it was a widely held medical theory that a man's health could best be restored in the air of the place where he was born. Of his own circumstances Thomson writes: 'They blossomed pretty well of late, the Chancellor having given me the Office of Secretary of the Briefs under him: but the Blight of an idle Inquiry into the Fees and Offices of the Courts of Justice which arose of late, seems to threaten it's Destruction.'[21]

Thomson refers to the second of two successive enquiries. The first was by a committee of the House of Commons, sitting from 1729 to 1733, which found 'that many new offices had sprung up since a committee had enquired into the subject in 1598; but it was found very difficult to say what officials were attached to the courts or what were their fees'. On this committee's recommendation a royal commission of inquiry was appointed, whose report, issued in 1740, noted *inter alia*: 'There was hardly an office in Chancery which was not a patent office, and whereof the duties were not systematically discharged by deputy . . . Deputies were appointed to do the work, and to earn for themselves and their patrons the fees taken from the public.'[22] Though the administrative reforms proposed by the commission were not effected until the following century, it would appear from a near-contemporary anecdote that changes were made in Thomson's circumstances (and, incidentally, that the poet understood his deputy's duties). The anonymous writer in the *Critical Review* (1765) states:

About the year 1732, a commission, consisting of the great officers of state, heads of the law, and others, was established, for enquiring into and stating the income and perquisites of public offices, particularly those under the lord chancellor. Mr Thomson's place of secretary of the briefs fell under the cognizance of this commission; and he was summoned to attend it, which he accordingly did, and made a speech, explaining the nature, duty, and income of his place in terms that, tho' very concise, were so perspicuous and elegant, that lord chancellor Talbot, who was present, publicly said he preferred that single speech to the best of his poetical compositions. The income of the place was by the commissioners, from above 300 reduced to 100 l a year; but Mr Thompson waited on his patron and offered to resign it; nor did he ever receive a shilling from it during its reduced state.[23]

One trusts that Talbot's compliment, if correctly reported, was not left-handed.

Thomson completes his August letter to Cranstoun with notes upon some books he is sending by his brother John and Anderson:

You will see by the three first Parts of a Poem called Liberty, which I send you, that I still attempt the barren but delightful Mountain of Parnassus. I have pour'd into it several of those Ideas which I gathered in my Travels, and particularly from Classic Ground. It is to consist of two Parts more, which I design to publish next Winter. Not quite to tantalize You, I send you likewise some of the best Things that have been printed here of late, among which Mr Pope's Second Volume of Miscellanies is eminent, and in it his Essay on Man. The first Volume of his Miscellany Poems was printed long ago, and is every where: His Letters were pyratically printed by the Infamous Curl. Tho Mr Pope be much concerned at their being printed, yet are they full of Wit, Humour, Good Sense, and what is best of all, a Good Heart. One Mr Littleton a young Gentleman, & Member of Parliment wrote the Persian Letters. They are reckoned prettily done. The Book on the Sacrament is writ by Hoadley Bishop of Winchester. All Bigots roar against it: consequently it will work your Miss-Johns. I wish I could send you more Entertainment of this Kind; but a new Gothic Night seems to be approaching, the Great Year the Millenium of Dulness.[24]

Thomson was as fully deceived as everybody else by Pope's ruse to make Curll print his letters; the other Pope references are to the verse collections of 1735 and 1717, and, not for the first time in Thomson's letters to Scotland about the London literary scene, *The Dunciad* of 1728–9. As a true Whig, as an out-and-out Erastian in the Rundle affair, and as a man with liberal theological views, Thomson would approve of Hoadly the more the clerical bigots roared against him. This is one of several letters to Cranstoun that contain disparaging references to narrow-minded Scots Calvinist ministers ('Mis-Johns') of their acquaintance. His third author is more significant for his own future: this is the earliest reference to Lyttelton in Thomson's surviving correspondence.

The book Thomson sends, *Letters from a Persian in England to his Friend at Ispahan* (1735), written in frank imitation of Montesquieu, is a satire against Walpole's government. Lyttelton was in the service of the Prince of Wales, who was very much in the public eye in the summer of 1735, not least because the King was away on one of his unpopular visits to Hanover between May and October. On 6 September it was reported in several journals that the Prince had commissioned a statue of King Alfred with an inscription in which Alfred was said to be 'the Founder of the Liberties and Commonwealth of England', and also a statue of the Black Prince with an inscription promising that Frederick would make 'that amiable Prince the pattern of his own Conduct'. On 4 October the Prince honoured Pope's house at Twickenham with a visit; this conspicuous approbation of England's greatest poet and the opposition's leading wit received wide publicity. Pope thereupon added some praise of Frederick to his (or Swift's) *Bounce to Fop*, a mock 'heroick epistle' as from his bitch Bounce to a lap-dog at court; he also gave Frederick one of Bounce's pups, with a couplet engraved on its collar which neatly declared Pope's attitude to sycophants who waited upon the Prince and implied that, though Pope was prepared to align himself with the opposition court, he was not the Prince's creature:

> I am his Highness' Dog at *Kew*;
> Pray tell me Sir, whose Dog are you?[25]

Meanwhile, Thomson's *Liberty* was quoted and praised in the opposition press: *The Craftsman* of 16 August reprinted the address to liberty near the end of Part One (including the lines quoted by Alured Clarke in his letter of September 1734), and a long passage from Part Three on public virtue in republican Rome:

> The great the reigning Passion of the *Free*.
> That Godlike Passion! which, the Bounds of *Self*
> Divinely bursting, the whole Public takes
> Into the Heart.[26]

These are texts for an attack upon the selfish great who indulge in 'publick Plunder' and the mercenary, servile, 'abandoned Crew of Scribblers' who traduce the upholders of 'the Cause of Liberty and Virtue'.

The function of literature in a corrupt age is also the theme of Aaron Hill's periodical *The Prompter*. For years before this periodical began to appear in 1734, Hill campaigned for a moral and artistic reform of the stage; he wanted the power of the tasteless, profit-seeking theatre managers to be broken, without putting theatres under puritanical or political restrictions. His ideal, like Thomson's, was the theatre of the ancient Athenians: 'From the *moving* Enthusiasm of their Stage', directed 'by the *Poets*, who were the only *State*

Pensioners of those Days, youth grew to love liberty, and hate tyranny, and acquired a propensity to arms and eloquence'. These words are from *Advice to the Poets* (1731), where Hill also calls for a royal fund or public subscription to reward the authors of a stated number of improving 'Prize-Tragedies' each year. A major theme of *The Prompter* in 1735 is the need for public regulation of the theatre by 'Commissioners of Taste'; it is to be wished 'that the *Direction* of our Theatres might be consign'd to the most *qualify'd* hands, under *Regulation* rather than *Restraint*'.[27]

Responding to the gift of a packet of these *Prompter* essays and echoing their opinions, Thomson wrote to Hill on 23 August:

As the Stage is a powerful School of humane polite Morality, so nothing can contribute more to barbarize the Age than the present Condition of ours. There, human Nature is represented in as aukward, false, and monstrous a Manner, as the human Form was in antient Gothic Sculpture and Painting. If that were all, it might be laugh'd at, and contemn'd: But since it tends, at the same time, to confound the Head, and corrupt the Heart; since Crouds grow stupid, or barbarous, as they gaze; who can consider it in that View, without feeling an honest Indignation? And what crowns the Misfortune is, that there is no Hope of its ever being otherwise: The Root of the Evil lies too deep to be pluck'd up. Was there ever an equal Absurdity heard of, among a civiliz'd People? That such an important public Diversion, the School which forms the Manners of the Age, should be made the Property of private Persons; who, did they happen in the first Instance, by an infinite Chance, to be Judges of the Matter, yet may transfer that Property to the most profligate, tasteless, and ignorant of Mankind! But this, alas! is only one of the Pillars of that vast Temple of *Corruption*, under which this Generation, more than any other that ever boasted Freedom, worships the dirty, low-minded, insatiable Idol of Self-interest.

Hill's reply on 5 September enlarges on his plans for reform. He wishes to see the establishment of 'a *tragic academy* for extending, and regulating *theatrical* diversions, and for instructing and educating *actors*'; such an academy 'might establish the *reputation* of the stage, by appropriating its *influence*, to the service of *wisdom*, and *virtue*'; it would be set up by subscription and Hill hoped to see the Prince of Wales's name at the head of the list of subscribers.[28]

Thomson was Dodington's guest from mid-June to mid-October, except for part of August, when he returned to London to make travelling arrangements for his brother (when, too, he picked up the *Prompters* sent by Hill); before mid-June he was Lady Hertford's guest at St Leonard's Hill; it is likely that he was also the guest this year of the Talbots, father or son or both; all in all, he was as much of a 'rambler' as Pope at this time. He was at Eastbury when brother John died in his native air, so it was over a month before he heard the news of this not-unexpected event from Cranstoun. He replied philosophically on 20 October, 'What you mention is the true Point of View, wherein to place the Death of Relations and Friends. They then are past our Regret: the Living are to be lamented, and not the Dead.' This reflection leads him to affirm that the future life is the infinite ascent of mind from stage to stage, and immortality is an endless extension of knowledge, a notion he had already versified in *Winter* (1730): 'This, I think, we may be sure of: that a future State must be better than this; and so on thro the never-ceasing Succession of future States; every one rising upon the last, an everlasting new Display of infinite Goodness! But', he adds, mindful of what was orthodox doctrine in Jedburgh Presbytery, 'hereby hangs a System, not calculated perhaps for the Meridian where you live tho' for that of your own Mind.' He transcribes the unpublished lines in memory of Charles Richard Talbot, with their cheering message that earthly friends will meet again in Heaven: 'Attend we, chearful, the rejoining Hour.'[29] He gives instructions as to the disposing of his brother's effects, over which it seems his country cousins were quarrelling, and arranges to pay his debts, for, though he is many miles from his relations, James is head of the family.

The last month or two of 1735 was occupied in preparing the unpublished books of *Liberty* for the press. *Britain*, the fourth Part, was published in January and *The Prospect*, the fifth, in February 1736. The print order for ordinary-paper copies of each Part was 1,000 (that is, half that for Parts Two and Three, and a third that for Part One), thus painful evidence of poor sales of the earlier Parts; 250 fine-paper copies were ordered, as before. The printer's account for 13 January includes a charge for 'alterations', which were presumably revisions of *Britain* in proof, such as those which Thomson is known to have carried out on the *Seasons*.[30]

In *Liberty* as in the *Seasons*, Thomson works to a larger scale in the later books; one has the impression that he makes long poems more by accretion than all-controlling design. So *Britain* is over twice as long and *The Prospect* about half as long again as any of the first three Parts; the last two Parts together are slightly longer than *Spring* and *Winter* (1730) combined. The enlargement of scale may have been a late decision, explaining the ten-month interval between publication of Parts Three and Four; if so, it may be associated with the undoubted sharpening of the poem's political intentions between *Rome* and *Britain*.

Part Four is a narrative of post-classical European history, followed by a more detailed history of Britain down to the Glorious Revolution, when 'dawn'd *the Period* destin'd to *confine* | The Surge of wild *Prerogative*'. Throughout, Thomson gives free rein to his anti-Papist, anti-Jacobite sentiments; thus his opening allegorical tableau represents medieval Europe as prey to savage furies, the wildest of which is Ecclesiastical Tyranny, whose associates are Scholastic Discord, Cleric Pride, Holy Slander, Persecuting Zeal, and Idiot Superstition; later in the poem James II is 'The *Bigot King* ... his Zeal |

Outflaming *Rome* herself'. The earlier struggle for liberty is described not without implicit reference to the politics of Thomson's own day. Thus the barons who confront King John at Runnymede are 'a Band | Of *Patriots*, ardent as the Summer's Noon'. From their time

> the wholesome Winds
> Of *Opposition* hence began to blow,
> And often since have lent the Country Life.
> Before their Breath *Corruption*'s Insect-Blights,
> The darkening Clouds of *evil Counsel* fly;
> Or should they sounding swell, a putrid Court,
> A pestilential Ministry, they purge.

This, of course, is the Goddess of Liberty speaking; later she rhapsodizes the benefits of limited monarchy in terms of the canonical 'O fortunatos' passage in Virgil's *Georgics*:

> Thrice happy! did they know
> Their Happiness, BRITANNIA'S BOUNDED KINGS.

The goddess looks upon her work in Britain and finds it good; but there is a danger, as she admits in the very last lines of *Britain*:

> Nor outward Tempest, nor corrosive Time,
> Nought but the felon undermining Hand
> Of dark CORRUPTION, can its Frame dissolve,
> And lay the Toil of Ages in the Dust.[31]

That danger is enlarged upon in the last part, *The Prospect*; but, for all its familiar opposition rhetoric, this part is largely devoted to the prophetic vision of a flowering culture of arts, sciences, and public works which will flourish if political corruption can be eliminated. Paradoxically, specific cultural models and especially models for enlightened public works are to be found in despotic France, but the goddess argues that the fruits of culture would grow better in Britain, 'by the potent Juice | Of *Freedom* swell'd'. The poet's own eyes are now opened to the vision of future national grandeur and happiness, but his poem ends ambiguously;

> As thick to View THESE VARIED WONDERS rose,
> Shook all my Soul with Transport, unassur'd,
> The VISION broke; And, on my waking Eye,
> Rush'd the still RUINS of dejected ROME.[32]

Liberty is aptly characterized by A. D. McKillop as 'dissident Whig panegyric'.[33] Dissidence became more apparent while Thomson was composing it, but the high, patriotic, panegyrical idea of the poem was a natural development from the concern for public spirit and social love and the interest in history and politics observable in *Sophonisba* and additions to the *Seasons* in 1730. His grand tour provided an immediate stimulus and some material, but his theme had already been anticipated in the poetical fruit of Addison's grand tour, *A Letter from Italy* (1703). This treats of classic ground, stupendous ruins, sculpture, and painting, before asking what avail the charms of nature and the smiles of art,

> While proud Oppression in her vallies reigns,
> And Tyranny usurps her happy plains? (111–12)

Addison concludes with an address to the Goddess Liberty:

> 'Tis Liberty that crowns *Britannia*'s Isle,
> And makes her barren rocks and her bleak mountains smile. (139–40)

There is evidence of a direct link between Addison's poem and *Liberty* among Thomson's manuscripts, in his transcription of a passage from *A Letter from Italy*, which describes the beauty of the Italian landscape, followed by his own point-by-point reply, describing the hideousness of that landscape. Thomson's transcription (perhaps from memory, because he transposes couplets and slightly misquotes) begins:

> Bear me some God to Baia's gentle seats,
> And cover me in Umbria's green retreats;
> Where even rough rocks with tender myrtle bloom,
> And trodden weeds send out a rich perfume.

He replies thus:

> Snatch me some God from Baia's desart seats,
> And bear me swift o'er Umbria's wild retreats;
> Where rifted rocks with steaming sulphur glow,
> And the whole earth is vaulted fire below.

Both impressions appear in the First Part of *Liberty*: Thomson's parodic reply is closely echoed in his description of modern Italy; Addison's lines are more faintly and perversely echoed in a vision of the long-lost landscapes of the Roman republic:

> In *Umbria*'s closing Vales, or on the brow
> Of her brown Hills that breathe the scented gale:
> On *Baia*'s viny Coast; where peaceful Seas,
> Fan'd by kind Zephirs, ever kiss the Shore.[34]

The political observations of Addison and Thomson, as they contrasted contemporary Italy with contemporary Britain on the one hand and ancient

Rome on the other, were commonplaces of the day, repeated in most of the histories and travel books which Thomson used in the writing of *Liberty*. Independently of Thomson, the patriotic young George Lyttelton, addressing his verse *Epistle to Mr Pope* from Rome in 1730, writes of Mediterranean lands:

> Fall'n is their glory, and their virtue lost:
> From Tyrants, and from Priests, the Muses fly,
> Daughters of Reason and of Liberty. (10–12)

'The grandeur that was Rome' was an old literary theme, given freshness for Thomson by his own visit to the city and possibly by his friendship with John Dyer, whose *Ruins of Rome*, though not published till 1740, was partly written by 1729;[35] but 'the glory that was Greece' was perhaps a little less hackneyed in the 1730s, so that the idealization in Part Two of *Liberty* not merely of Greek political wisdom but of Greek culture as a whole was an early manifestation of the Grecian taste which flowered in mid-eighteenth-century Britain.

The most striking tribute to Greek culture appears, however, in Part Four, with a set-piece description of the most admired antique statues, each one the expressive form of ideal nature. These are the Farnese Hercules, the Vatican Meleager, the Fighting Gladiator (the Borghese Warrior), the Dying Gladiator (the Dying Gaul), the Apollo Belvedere, the Farnese Flora, the Venus de' Medici, and the Laocoön: all of them thought to be ancient Greek works and invariably listed by connoisseurs among the top twenty known works of sculpture. Thomson himself owned drawings by Castelli of seven of the eight he described. The sculptural parallels for Celadon and Musidora in *Summer* (1727 and 1730) show that Thomson was fascinated by the aesthetic and sentimental possibilities of expressing emotional agitation through frozen physical motion. In *Liberty* he explores such effects along a regular gallery of varied figures and actions, for instance, in the Dying Gladiator:

> Supported on his shorten'd Arm he leans,
> Prone, agonizing; with incumbent Fate,
> Heavy declines his Head; yet dark beneath
> The suffering Feature sullen Vengeance lowrs,
> Shame, Indignation, unaccomplish'd Rage,
> And still the cheated Eye expects his Fall.

In this poem, though, where the poet's concerns are more public than in the *Seasons*, references to Greek art in general, and perfect statues in particular, also remind the reader that beautiful or sublime forms possess a moral beauty or sublimity, and that an imitation of ancient models might lead to a revival of ancient virtue.[36]

The progress of liberty traced in the poem is the reawakening of ancient virtue, of public spirit, of godlike, heaven-directed social love, which, in Thomson's opinion, has always inspired patriots and true heroes:

> The great the reigning Passion of the *Free*.
> That Godlike Passion! which, the Bounds of *Self*
> Divinely bursting, the whole Public takes
> Into the Heart.[37]

The actions of these heroes, many of whom are also celebrated in the *Seasons*, are associated with a familiar cycle in the histories of nations: 'need engenders virtue and courage, courage results in aggression, leading to success and prosperity; prosperity leads to the self-indulgence of luxury, eventual ener-vation, and final defeat.'[38] The notion that luxury enfeebles and destroys was a commonplace of Greek and Roman histories from Herodotus to Tacitus and a constant theme of political writers and historians in Thomson's day. Thomson duly traces the catastrophic effects of luxury upon Greece and Rome, and delivers a warning to the British, for whom, it may be presumed, there is still hope.

Hope for Britain lies in its potential heroes and patriots, and in its 'mixed' government, a balance of monarchy, aristocracy, and democracy, which, if maintained uncorrupted, will ensure the perpetuity of liberty and prosperity. Thomson points to classical models of mixed government in the Spartan constitution drawn up by Lycurgus and in republican Rome, where the monarchical element was represented by the consuls, but he associates the history of the British constitution with a persuasive myth of Gothic liberty. According to the goddess's account, when liberty died in Rome its seed was preserved in the North, in

> A sullen Land of Lakes, and Fens immense,
> Of Rocks, resounding Torrents, gloomy Heaths,
> And cruel Desarts black with sounding Pine;

where

> a Race of Men prolific swarms,
> To various Pain, to little Pleasure us'd;
> On whom, keen-parching, beat *Riphæan* Winds;
> Hard like their Soil, and like their Climate fierce;
> The Nursery of Nations!

These were the ancestors of 'the blue-ey'd Saxon', who is given credit for the introduction of a limited monarchy into Britain:

> Untam'd
> To the refining Subtilties of Slaves,

> They brought an happy Government along;
> Form'd by that *Freedom*, which, with secret Voice,
> Impartial *Nature* teaches all her Sons,
> And which of old thro' the whole *Scythian Mass*
> I strong inspir'd. *Monarchical* their State,
> But prudently *confin'd*, and *mingled* wise
> Of each harmonious Power.[39]

Thomson's roll-call of English heroes in *Britain*—Alfred, Edward III, Henry V, Elizabeth, Algernon Sidney, and William III—is a Whig pantheon, and one particularly dear to self-styled 'real Whigs' and the parliamentary opposition to Walpole in the 1730s. There is nothing new in his notion that the spirit of English liberty was embodied first in the Saxon constitution, was checked by the Norman yoke, flourished under some patriot-monarchs, notably Elizabeth, was checked again by the first four Stuarts, was re-established at the Glorious Revolution, but is now endangered by a Prime Minister who corrupts a free Parliament. This is what Bolingbroke claims at this time in *The Craftsman* and Lyttelton in his *Persian Letters*.

Liberty, however unsuccessful in the execution, was the kind of poem that Lyttelton had asked for when in 1730 he viewed the ruins of Rome on his grand tour and appealed to Pope to turn from satire and raise

> A lasting column to thy Country's Praise,
> To sing the Land, which yet alone can boast
> That Liberty corrupted Rome has lost.

Joseph Warton's note to this passage says that Lyttelton informed him that, 'in many conversations' he urged Pope to employ 'his great genius in the higher species of poetry'.[40] Pope followed his advice no further than to plan his never-completed, blank-verse, heroic *Brutus*, so Lyttelton was obliged, in effect, to carry out the task himself, when he completely rewrote *Liberty* just after Thomson's death.[41] Lyttelton's *Liberty* (published as Thomson's) keeps only the better lines of the original and adds hundreds of Lyttelton's own composition which are no worse than bad Thomson. It is superior to the poem published in 1735–6, not merely because it is very much shorter; its narrative has less repetition and its syntax is tighter, so it makes a more readable politico-historical tract. Beyond that, no effort of Lyttelton's could bring *Liberty* to imaginative life. Except for a few 'prospects' and occasional descriptions of the works of nature and of art,[42] Thomson never manages to embody his high ideas in living forms; for most of the time he is writing far out of his natural grain. The shift from the *Seasons* to *Liberty* might be seen as a sad, almost parodic counterpart to Pope's triumphant change in purpose, noted in his *Epistle to*

Arbuthnot, published coincidentally in the same month as the First Part of *Liberty*. Could it be that Thomson believed that 'pure Description held the place of Sense' in his own early verse, so it was time he 'stoop'd to Truth, and moraliz'd his song'? If so, he stooped in the commoner meaning of that word, not Pope's. Mere historic truth, tortured into verse by unnatural syntax and adorned with vapid, pompous diction, is, however strong the versifier's political convictions, no basis for poetry.

Thomson thought highly of *Liberty*. Murdoch writes: 'He employed two years of his life in composing that noble work: upon which, conscious of the importance and dignity of the subject, he valued himself more than upon all his other writings.' Johnson echoes Murdoch's words and adds:

but an author and his reader are not always of a mind. *Liberty* called in vain upon her votaries to read her praises and reward her encomiast: her praises were condemned to harbour spiders, and to gather dust; none of Thomson's performances were so little regarded.

The judgement of the publick was not erroneous; the recurrence of the same images must tire in time; an enumeration of examples to prove a position which nobody denied, as it was from the beginning superfluous, must quickly grow disgusting.[43]

Most readers over the past two and a half centuries have been broadly of Johnson's mind, for all the occasional felicities they have chanced upon in this heavy, hectoring poem.

It was probably Thomson's tenderness for his poem as well as for the memory of his grand tour companion that led him to resent a parody by Isaac Hawkins Browne of the lines on Talbot at the beginning of *Liberty*. This parody was first printed, along with parodies of Pope and Young, in a series 'Of the Praise of Tobacco' in some journals of December 1735.[44] Spence reports that when Pope was shown the parodies he remarked: 'Browne is an excellent copyist in his imitations on tobacco, and those who take it ill of him are very much in the wrong', to which Spence adds a note from Thomson's friend John Armstrong: 'Mr Thomson did so, and soon after they were printed published a warm copy of verses against Mr Browne in some of the magazines or newspapers.'[45] The 'warm verses' are 'The Smoaker Smoak'd', printed anonymously in *The Gentleman's Magazine*, December 1736. They begin:

> Still from thy *pipe*, as from dull *Tophet*, say,
> Ascends the smoak, for ever and for aye?
> No end of nasty impoetic breath?
> Foh! dost thou mean to stink the town to death?[46]

Thomson never acknowledged this ponderous and far from witty piece of invective.

A more characteristic short poem of his at this period is the sentimental love song printed over his name in *The Gentleman's Magazine* for February 1736; it is addressed to 'Amanda', and begins:

> Come gentle god of soft desire,
>   Come and possess my happy breast.

Following it on the same page of the *Magazine* is a similarly sentimental reply by a 'Mr Blythe',[47] in which Thomson is addressed as 'Thyrsis'. It is not known whether the 'Amanda' ('she who is to be loved') of these two poems and of Thomson's song 'For ever Fortune', printed in 1732, was a real person; this same conventional literary name would be attached to Elizabeth Young, the object of Thomson's affections in the 1740s, but it is virtually certain that he had not met Miss Young as early as 1736. Another, undated, 'Amanda' poem, not published until after Thomson's death, displays the mild Arcadian charm that earned him the name of Thyrsis:

> Unless with my *Amanda* blest,
>   In vain I twine the woodbine bower;
> Unless to deck her sweeter breast,
>   In vain I rear the breathing flower:
>
> Awaken'd by the genial year,
>   In vain the birds around me sing;
> In vain the fresh'ning fields appear:
>   *Without my love there is no spring.*[48]

Like other love lyrics by Thomson, this was printed with a musical setting. In addition to Mr Blythe's piece, three other poems commending Thomson's verse appeared in *The Gentleman's Magazine* in 1736:[49] two of them, 'To Mr Thomson on his excellent Poems' and 'On hearing Lady *** commend his Seasons', praise the gentle, warbling nature poet, but the third gives him a sterner character. This poem is 'On Mr Thomson's Picture drawn by Mr Slaughter, with the Figure of Liberty in his hand, as describ'd by him in his Poem on that Subject'; its attribution to 'G.W.' may well mean that it is the work of Gilbert West, who was Lyttelton's cousin; certainly, it utters the opposition sentiments one might expect to hear from one of Cobham's nephews:

> Yes, SLAUGHTER, in these lines a soul I trace
> That scorns a falsehood ev'n to gain a place.[50]

Meanwhile, Thomson and Aaron Hill had been in correspondence over the last two Parts of *Liberty*. On 11 May 1736 Thomson wrote to thank Hill for his

5. James Thomson with the Figure of Liberty, by Stephen Slaughter, *c*.1736.

6. James Thomson(?), by Stephen Slaughter.

comments, beginning his own letter with his usual courtly apologies for tardiness:

It is far from being the want of a due Sense of the Honour, your two last Letters did me, that has prevented my thanking you for them before now: The Truth is, they plung'd me so deep into your Debt, that I was dispirited, thro' mere Despair, of clearing it. But now I am rather willing to declare myself an irrecoverable Bankrupt, than any longer neglect to acknowledge the refin'd Pleasure, which your generous Approbation of my late Performance gives me.

By this time, sales of *Liberty* were revealing all too clearly that Hill's good opinion was not widely shared and that Millar would lose money by it. Thomson's letter continues:

Allow me here, by the bye, to remark, that tho' Poets have been long us'd to this truly-spiritual and almost only Emolument arising from their Works; yet I doubt much, if Booksellers have any manner of Relish for it: I think, therefore (notwithstanding that the Ghosts of many Authors walk unreveng'd), of annulling the Bargain I made with mine, who would else be a considerable Loser, by the Paper, Printing, and Publication, of Liberty.

He did not put this quixotic proposal into effect; his own ghost could perhaps be consoled by the fact that whatever his bookseller may have lost on *Liberty* he made up many times over in profits from nearly forty years' exclusive rights to print *The Seasons*. The letter to Hill continues on the question of copyright, with Thomson linking his own grumbles to Hill's pessimistic observations on the contemporary stage:

With regard to Arts and Learning, one may venture to say, that they might yet stand their Ground, were they but merely protected. In lieu of all Patrons that have been, are, or will be, in England, I wish we had one good Act of Parliament for securing to Authors the Property of their own Works; and that the Stage were put upon the Footing of common Sense and Humanity. And can it be, that those who impress Paper with what constitutes the best and everlasting Riches of all civiliz'd Nations, and of all Ages, should have less Property in the Paper, so enrich'd, than those who deal in the Rags, which make that Paper? Can it be, that the great, the delightful School of Manners, should be abandon'd to common Sale, and become the Property of any one, who can purchase it, to be, perhaps, the School of Folly, and Corruption? — A Simony this, in *Virtue*; which, if not so wicked, yet is as pernicious as that in *Religion*. What would Athenians have said to this! what Laughter, what Contempt, what Indignation, would it have rais'd among them!

Thomson's complaint seems odd at first sight, in view of the fact that the Copyright Act of 1709 stipulated that, fourteen years after assignment, a bookseller's copyright would revert to the author, if still living, for a further term of fourteen years; but the booksellers' claim that their copyrights were perpetual under common law, notwithstanding the Act, was upheld in the courts in two cases in 1735 and 1736, one of them adjudged by Thomson's patron the Lord Chancellor.[51] Thomson's assignments to Millan and Millar, like this letter, assume that booksellers can purchase perpetual copyright. It would not be until 1774, after test cases over that valuable property *The Seasons*, that the House of Lords adjudged that the Copyright Act did indeed supersede common law.

In a prompt reply on 20 May Hill applauds the generosity of purpose in Thomson's proposal to free Millar from his contract, but expresses his fear that, because so morally beautiful an action would never be forgotten, the shameful fact that *Liberty* found so few readers would not be forgotten either; this would entail 'a kind of national infamy, which must disgrace us to posterity'. Hill praises the later Parts with his accustomed fulsomeness, but again remarks upon obscurities of expression in the poem. He then continues his earlier discussion of the hoped-for new tragic theatre 'for extending and regulating the conduct of the stage, and appropriating its influence to the service of wisdom and virtue'.[52] Hill himself was trying to supply those needs on the far-from-ideal professional London stage, with two adaptations by him from Voltaire playing there in 1736: *Zara* in January and *Alzire* in June.

A letter by Thomson late in 1736 reveals that he is writing another tragedy too. He would have sufficient aesthetic, moral, political, and financial motives for returning to the stage, but he may also have been prompted by Hill's reforming plans in 1735–6, and perhaps, too, by the great stir caused by a visit to England, from May 1735 to August 1736, by Scipione Maffei, the great reviver of classical tragedy and advocate of a national theatre in Italy. Thomson owned a copy of Maffei's *Teatro Italiano* (three volumes, Verona, 1723–5), a collection of early Italian tragedies, including Trissino's *Sofonisba*, prefaced by an important introduction in which Maffei stresses the moral purpose of the drama (noting the connection between the ancient Greek theatre and religion) and calls for proper instruction in the art of acting and verse-speaking. He argues for everything that Hill and Thomson wanted of drama. Maffei was received by the Prince of Wales, visited Pope at Twickenham, and was fêted generally; it is not known whether Thomson met him in England (or earlier in Verona, or in Paris, where both men were in the winter of 1732–3), but he could hardly have been unaware of his visit and he certainly knew his work. Perhaps it is no mere coincidence that in the three or four years after his visit the English stage sprouted a crop of morally high-toned verse tragedies patriotically celebrating the Prince of Wales.

It may have been Thomson's dissatisfaction with the commercialism of bookselling that impelled him to become, on 14 May 1736, one of the founder-managers, and very much the most celebrated literary member of the Society for the Encouragement of Learning; this was a pioneer venture in collective private publishing, by which members' subscriptions provided capital to print books, the sale of which was intended to generate more capital for more publications. The hopes that accompanied its foundation are proclaimed in the Prospectus, which declares the intention 'to institute a republick of letters, for the promoting of arts and sciences, by the necessary means of profit, as well as by the nobler motives of praise and emulation', and are represented in the society's emblem (designed by William Kent and Thomsonian in spirit), which shows Britannia raising drooping Knowledge. The society issued a handful of learned works before its dissolution in 1749, but its death was inevitable because it competed with the publishing business of those very booksellers whose co-operation it needed in order to distribute its own books through the trade.[53] James Ralph summed up the venture in his *The Case of Authors* (1758):

There was, not many Years ago, a Society for the Encouragement of Learning, who rais'd a Fund, hir'd a House, employ'd a Secretary, and undertook to furnish Paper and Print to Authors, on Condition of being re-imburs'd out of the Sale of the Work.

I do not expect to see such another — Their Plan was too narrow, — They also forgot, that the Booksellers were Masters of all the Avenues to every Market, and, by the Practice of one Nights Postage, could make any Work resemble *Jonahs Gourd* after the Worm had *smote* it: It miscarried, consequently.[54]

Thomson did not allow his interest in the society to influence his pocket unduly, as it is recorded that he paid no subscription for five years. Perhaps charity began at home: on 6 November 1736 he wrote to his friend George Ross, then in Edinburgh, concerning his unmarried sisters Jean and Elizabeth, who were still living in William Gusthart's household in that city:

My Sisters have been advised by their Friends to set up at Edinburgh a little Millener's Shop, and if you can conveniently advance to them twelve Pounds, on my Account, it will be a particular Favour. That will set them a-going, and I design from Time to Time to send them Goods from hence. My whole Account I will pay you when you come up here, not in Poetical paper-Credit, but in the solid Money of this dirty World.[55]

Like the Society for the Encouragement of Learning, the millinery business would fail.

Towards the end of this letter Thomson tells Ross that he was 'whipping and spurring to finish a Tragedy for You this Winter; but am still at some Distance from the Goal'. A letter from Bishop Rundle to Mrs Sandys, probably written a month or two later, tells us more about this tragedy and incidentally illustrates the sometimes officious concern in the poet's work taken by his social superiors:

My friend THOMPSON, the *Poet*, is bringing another untoward Heroine on the stage; and has deferred writing on the subject you chose for him, though he had the whole scheme drawn out into acts and scenes, proper turns of passion and sentiments pointed out to him, and the distress made, as touching and important, as new, and interesting, and regular as any, that was ever introduced on the stage at *Athens*, for the instruction of that polite nation. But, perhaps, the delicacy of the subject, and the judgment required in saying bold truths, whose boldness should not make them degenerate into offensiveness, deterred him.—His present story is the death of AGAMEMNON. An adultress, who murthers her husband, is but an odd example to be presented before, and admonish the beauties of *Great Britain*. However, if he will be advised, it shall not be a shocking though it cannot be a noble story. He will enrich it with a profusion of worthy sentiments, and high poetry, but it will be written in a rough, harsh stile, and in numbers great, but careless. He wants that neatness and simplicity of diction, which is so natural in dialogue. He cannot throw the light of an elegant ease on his thoughts, which will make the sublimest turns of art appear the genuine unpremeditated dictates of the heart of the speaker. But with all his faults, he will have a thousand masterly strokes of a great genius seen in all he writes. And he will be applauded by those, who most censure him.

Elsewhere in this letter Rundle refers to the long delay of the king's homecoming, but he prudently does not draw attention to the parallels with Thomson's play. The King had set out for Hanover on 22 May 1736 and did not return to England until the following January; the country was ruled in his absence by Queen Caroline, as Regent, and by Walpole. These two are unmistakeably portrayed in Thomson's characterization of Clytemnestra and her wicked counsellor Egisthus. We do not know what subject Mrs Sandys chose for Thomson, but if it was the death of Socrates the choice was Rundle's too, for we know from a later letter written by Lyttelton to Mallet that Rundle sent Thomson the plan for a tragedy on this subject. One wonders, indeed, if Rundle is referring immodestly to his own scheme in the words quoted above.[56]

Before he started *Agamemnon* or finished *Liberty* Thomson was at work (if that is not an overstatement) upon a much finer and much longer-considered poem than either; for, by the poet's own account, *The Castle of Indolence* was begun or, at least, conceived in 1733 or 1734. Thomson wrote to his old college friend William Paterson in April 1748, when the poem was at press:

after fourteen or fifteen Years, the Castle of Indolence comes abroad in a Fortnight... You have an Apartment in it, as a Night-Pensioner; which, you may remember, I fitted up for you during our delightful Party at North-Haw. Will ever these Days return again? Dont you remember your eating the raw Fish that were never catched?[57]

Northaw is in Hertfordshire, just north of Potter's Bar; Thomson and his merry friends may have gone there for the sake of its once well-known mineral springs. However much he invokes solitude in his best poetry, Thomson was a man who kept his friendships in good repair. There are glimpses of the haunts and habits of these friends in, for instance, an undated note to John Forbes, 'at the Rainbow Coffee-House in Lancaster Court':

I sent about Seven of the Clock to the Rainbow, but they told you was gone to the Play, and would return after it. If you please to come hither I shall be very glad of your Company. I am at the Bedford Arms in the Piazza of Covent-Garden;

and in another note, dated 25 April 1736, addressed 'A Monsieur Smith, Banquier, pour faire tenir a Monsieur Forbes de Colodden, a son arrivee a Boulogne sur mer':

Dear Jock,

   I am willing to inform you before you leave France that Salmon are very salt, and that we often drink your Health with more than Devotion—with Love. Had I Time, I have many things to say to You, but must defer them till another opportunity. Here are some, and Peter among the Rest, who are heartily heartily Your's.[58]

Such evenings and their mornings after were recalled when Jock Forbes was introduced into *The Castle of Indolence*:

> One Day there chaunc'd into these Halls to rove
> A joyous Youth, who took you at first Sight;
> Him the wild Wave of Pleasure hither drove,
> Before the sprightly Tempest tossing light:
> Certes, he was a most engaging Wight,
> Of social Glee, and Wit humane though keen,
> Turning the Night to Day and Day to Night; . . .
>
> But not even Pleasure to Excess is good,
> What most elates then sinks the Soul as low;
> When Spring-Tide Joy pours in with copious Flood,
> The higher still the' exulting Billows flow,
> The farther back again they flagging go,
> And leave us groveling on the dreary Shore:
> Taught by this Son of Joy, we found it so; . . . [59]

This sociable, good-natured, high-spirited son of Duncan Forbes was a favourite among Thomson's group of Scottish friends; he was the pupil of Patrick Murdoch on the grand tour, when he met Thomson and they played chess in a post-chaise; after he was commissioned in 'the Blues' (the Royal Horse Guards) and had seen action at Dettingen and Fontenoy, he was described by another member of Thomson's circle as 'possest of as much honesty as his father, and as much courage as any man in the army: in short he has his father's good qualities without his talent'.[60]

   The writer of this testimonial was Andrew Mitchell, who was about the same age as Jock, but displayed quite early some of the great talents of a Duncan Forbes. At Edinburgh University he was a pupil of that notable Newtonian Colin McLaurin; he was called to the English Bar and became a Fellow of the

Royal Society. After the resignation of Walpole in February 1742 the Marquis of Tweeddale became principal Secretary of State for Scotland and appointed Mitchell, aged 34, as his under-secretary; subsequently, during the Seven Years War, Mitchell held the important diplomatic post of British envoy to the court of Frederick the Great, for which service he was knighted. He was one of Thomson's executors and, it would seem from a letter of 1754 from Murdoch to John Forbes, he was also a benefactor of the poet:

Has he not been as a father to us both? the same to MacLaurin's family, to Thomson, and of late to Warrender; and to many others that we never heard of? and all with a narrow fortune, and moving in an inferior sphere. In a word, I can find no one to compare with him, but Sir Charles, in Richardson's last book.

This Scottish Grandison's regard for Thomson is confirmed in a letter of 14 September 1742 from Paterson to Mitchell: 'Remember to see the Bard and think for him as you have done for many others. I know you love him.'[61]

John Forbes and Mitchell were eight or nine years younger than Thomson, as were the mathematician George Lewis Scott and the physician John Armstrong, two more Scotsmen who joined their circle about 1735.[62] Scott was one of the managers of the Society for the Encouragement of Learning, but rather less indolent in its affairs than Thomson; after Thomson's death he became tutor to the Prince of Wales's son, the future George III, in whom, it was said, he attempted to inculcate Bolingbroke's idea of a patriot king. Armstrong proceeded to his MD in Edinburgh, was practising medicine in London by 1735, and by the following year had published medical papers, a satirical 'Essay for abridging the Study of Physick', and (anonymously) a scandalous poem, *The Oeconomy of Love*; his celebrated *Art of Preserving Health* would appear in 1744. He is the original of the melancholy man described in *The Castle of Indolence*, canto I, stanza lx, and he contributed the last four, melancholy-diagnostic, stanzas to this canto. An undated note of his to John Forbes is revealing: 'As the D——l, my particular Enemy, would have it, I can't go with you. God send us good Luck in the Lottery. If mine comes up a ten thou.d, I intend to turn Gentleman; for if I drudge more, poyson me. My service to Thomson.'[63]

The majority of Thomson's close friends were expatriate Scotsmen of about his own age, some of them fellow students at Edinburgh, such as Robert Symmer, William Paterson, the ever-constant Mallet and Murdoch, and Hugh Warrender, who, like Murdoch, made his clerical career in the Church of England. Symmer was a tutor and later was employed by Mitchell as his London agent when he was abroad on diplomatic missions: Paterson found employment in the early 1740s with Mitchell's superior the Marquis of Tweeddale, perhaps on Mitchell's recommendation.[64] Warrender was in

Andrew Millar's bookshop in December 1734 to act as a witness of Thomson's copyright assignment; Millar himself was becoming Thomson's personal friend as well as business associate. John Gray, FRS, who helped Thomson with scientific references in the *Poem to the memory of Newton* was of this Scottish circle also. Other Edinburgh near-contemporaries with whom Thomson had at least a fleeting acquaintance in the late 1730s included David Hume (no less) and the physician Alexander Cunningham, later Sir Alexander Dick.[65] In 1764 Dick wrote to Hume, 'This comes to your hand by . . . Mr Sargent, who I dare say you will remember a great while ago in the days of Mr Thomson and Mr Mitchel the ambassador with whomme we used to associate in those days.'[66] The John Sargent mentioned here was a linen draper near Mercer's Chapel in London.

Though the surviving letters do not refer to him, George Turnbull (1698– 1748), a former fellow student of Thomson's, probably re-entered the circle of friends about this time. After teaching philosophy at Marischal College, Aberdeen, Turnbull came south in the 1730s, was a travelling tutor, and associated with London literary figures; like Murdoch and Warrender, he took Anglican orders; by 1742 he was a chaplain to the Prince of Wales. He praised Thomson's work and implied a friendship with him in two books published by Millar in 1740; in 1742 he dedicated another treatise to Thomas Rundle, Bishop of Derry, in whose esteem, he says, 'he had long had a share'. Turnbull's *Treatise on Ancient Painting* perhaps influenced a passage in Thomson's *Castle of Indolence*, but it is now remembered largely because it is one of the large folios being carried as waste-paper to a trunk-maker in Hogarth's *Beer Street*.[67]

Paterson, Mitchell, and Mallet were all associated with the Society for the Encouragement of Learning; William Talbot was one of its founder-managers, though no more active a one than Thomson. Much of the business of the society devolved upon another manager, the antiquarian Thomas Birch, FRS, who became a convivial friend of Thomson's in the late 1730s. Birch was described by Horace Walpole as 'a worthy good-natured soul, full of industry and activity, and running about like a young setting dog in quest of anything, new or old, and with no parts, taste or judgement', but Johnson praised the liveliness of Birch's conversation, particularly his unfailing stream of anecdotes, a gift which would have appealed to Thomson too.[68]

Birch was acquainted with Savage from 1734,[69] though his communications with that elusive Bohemian were as intermittent as Thomson's and Hill's were. On 11 May 1736 Thomson wrote to Hill: 'Poor Mr Savage would be happy to pass an Evening with you; his Heart burns towards you with the eternal Fire of gratitude: But how to find him, requires more intelligence than is allotted to Mortals.'[70] The year before, Savage had been charged with uttering an obscene libel upon the Bishop of London in a satire arising from the Rundle affair and prompted, Johnson claims, by Savage's friendship with Rundle's friend Thomson.[71] Though Savage was acquitted, the episode damaged still further his always doubtful prospects of long-term patronage. Hill mildly observed, in a letter to Thomson on 20 May 1736: 'Some of his friends make complaints of certain little effects of a spleen in his temper, which he is no more able to help and should, therefore, no more be accountable for, than the misfortunes to which . . . his constitution may have owed it originally'; a pension from the king should place him above those mortifications in life which 'must have soured his disposition, and given the unreflecting part of his acquaintance occasion to complain, now and then, of his behaviour'. A month later Hill wrote to Savage himself,[72] trying without success, to persuade him to be reconciled to his putative cousin Lord Tyrconnel, whose hospitality he had greatly abused and from whom he had received a pension of £200 a year until they quarrelled in 1735; but by that date Savage's style of addressing his one-time patron was 'Right Honourable Brute and Booby'.[73] Perhaps encouraged by Thomson's success in that quarter, Savage was now setting his sights on the Prince of Wales; in 1736 he published a poem on the Prince's birthday, which was rewritten and enlarged, a little after the fashion of Part Five of Thomson's *Liberty*, and published in 1737 as *Of Public Spirit in Regard to Public Works*. Savage's Goddess of Public Spirit proclaims:

> Know *Liberty* and I are still the same,
> Congenial! — ever mingling Flame with Flame!

and her poet moves to his peroration:

> Thus (Ah! how far unequal'd by *my* Lays,
> Unskill'd the Heart to melt, or Mind to raise),
> Sublime, benevolent, deep, sweetly-clear,
> Worthy a THOMSON's Muse, a FREDERICK's Ear,
> Thus spoke the *Goddess*.

Whereas the influence of the *Seasons* was deep and long-lasting upon several generations of poets, including the greatest, the best poem modelled upon *Liberty* is this respectable but mediocre piece by Savage.

7

His Highness' Man at Kew: *Talbot* and *Agamemnon, 1737–1738*

SAVAGE was Thomson's house-guest when *Of Public Spirit in Regard to Public Works* was going through the press, for Thomson by that date had been in possession for over a year of a house of his own in Kew Foot Lane, Richmond. In the copyright assignment of *Liberty*, dated 16 December 1734, Thomson is said to be 'of the parish of St. Clements Danes', his surviving letters of 1735 are dated from London and he asks that incoming letters should be directed to him 'at the Lancaster Coffee-House, in Lancaster-Court, in the Strand'. However by 25 April 1736 he had begun to date letters from Richmond and his letter to Hill on 11 May ends: 'Please to direct to me in Kew-Lane, Richmond, Surrey'. His move came as news to Hill, who, in his reply on 20 May, evidently did not know whether the address was temporary or permanent.[1]

The expanding village of Richmond, nine miles from Hyde Park Corner, provided to some degree the rural peace and beauty praised in the *Seasons*, while still being close enough to the London theatres and bookshops where Thomson had business. Its magnetism for fugitives from the smoke and noise of the metropolis is disarmingly epitomized by Thomson's friend John Armstrong, when, in *The Art of Preserving Health* (1744), he praises

> *Richmond's* green Retreats
> (*Richmond* that sees an hundred villas rise
> Rural or gay).   (I. 112–14)

The matchless beauty of the view along the Thames from Richmond Hill was hymned by innumerable writers from Defoe in his *Tour* to Scott in *The Heart of Midlothian*; Thomson added his enthusiastic tribute in the 1744 revisions to *Summer*:

> Inchanting Vale! beyond whate'er the Muse
> Has of *Achaia* or *Hesperia* sung!
> O Vale of Bliss! O softly-swelling Hills!
> On which the *Power* of *Cultivation* lies,
> And joys to see the Wonders of his Toil.[2]

Richmond may have been rural in the 1730s but it was not rustic, for it boasted in addition to its sprouting, gleaming villas, a theatre, assembly rooms, and medicinal waters. Richmond Green was the scene of bull-baiting, prize-fights, cricket, and other manly diversions; Richmond Wells was a place of fashionable, albeit raffish resort. An advertisement of 1730 reads:

This is to give notice to all Gentlemen and Ladies that Richmond Wells are now opened and continue so daily; where attendance is given for Gentlemen and Ladies that have a mind either to raffle for Gold Chains, Equipages or any other Curious Toys, and fine old China, and likewise play quadrille, ombre, wisk, etc. And on Saturdays and Mondays during the summer season there will be dancing as usual.

Six years earlier a visitor had observed,

Here are men of all professions and all religions—Jews and Gentiles, Papists and Dissenters—so that be one's inclination what it may, you will find one's own stamp to converse with. If you love books, every gentlmen hath a library ready at your service; if you will make love, a stranger is everywhere welcome. At play, they will indeed be a great deal too cunning for you; even the ladies think it no crime to pawm handsomely; and for drinking, you may be matched from night to morning. Field exercise, also, as much as anywhere. In short, for a man of no business, whose time hangs on his hand, recommend me to Richmond.

Douglas Grant quotes this passage and adds: 'Who could have resisted such a catholic appeal?'[3]

Part of Richmond's appeal, though, was the presence of rather more exclusive society. Richmond Lodge was Queen Caroline's favourite residence, as it had been since she spent her summers there as Princess of Wales. She improved the gardens and in 1735 installed the 'Thresher Poet' Stephen Duck as her librarian in the strange thatched building there, known as 'Merlin's Cave'. Her daughter Amelia, the Princess Royal, and, less to her liking, her son Frederick, prince of Wales, had houses very close by at Kew. Her husband's Prime Minister and her confidant Walpole hunted once or twice a week in Richmond New Park, of which he was effectively the Ranger (though the post was nominally held by his son); he conducted state business at weekends from the lodge he had built there and he continually defended his game rights against former commoners of the neighbouring parishes with all the apparatus of state power at his command. By contrast, the ever-popular Prince of Wales could be found playing cricket with his father's subjects on Kew Green in 1737.[4] The Duke of Argyll lived on the edge of the park in a fine new house, Sudbrooke Lodge.

The move to Richmond may have improved Thomson's access to his new patron the Prince of Wales; it certainly enabled him to see more of his old friend Pope, whose Twickenham villa was only a short distance upstream on the other side of the Thames. In the letter to Hill on 11 May 1736 Thomson writes: 'Mr Pope was the other Day inquiring kindly after you: I should be glad we could, at the same time, engage him', that is, for dinner at Thomson's house. A Richmond neighbour recalled that Thomson was frequently called upon by Pope, dressed in a light-coloured great coat which he commonly kept on in the house; another recollected that Pope 'courted Thomson, and Thomson was always admitted to Pope, whether he had company or was alone'.[5] These two men were the greatest of the poets newly recruited by the parliamentary opposition. When, during his first months at Richmond, Thomson was writing *Agamemnon* in a small cottage roughly midway between the residence of Clytemnestra at Richmond Lodge and the hunting grounds of Egisthus in New Park, while Agamemnon was away in Hanover, his situation paralleled Pope's when he sat in his grotto composing satires against court and city while the traffic between London and Hampton Court rumbled over his head.

Agamemnon was not finished in time for the 1736–7 season, but if it had been the theatre management might have thought it impolitic to stage the play so close to the date of the King's return from Hanover, which occurred on 15 January 1737 after he had been delayed by storms which many of his subjects wished had drowned him. In February the political scene was dominated by the parliamentary debate on the Prince of Wales's annuity. The Prince had married in the previous April, on which occasion the motion for an address of congratulation to the King was put by the opposition, with the 'Boy Patriots' George Lyttelton and William Pitt paying tribute to the Prince as the embodiment of public spirit and patriotism. Pitt spoke pointedly of Frederick's 'generous love of liberty' and his 'just reverence of the British constitution'. The Prince expected to receive on his marriage a civil-list annuity of £100,000, the sum that his father had enjoyed when he was Prince of Wales ten years earlier, but the King was resolved that he should have no increase of his existing £50,000. Walpole agreed with the King, for the 'Civil List of £800,000 was, among other things, a political patronage fund of the first importance. The transfer of £50,000 out of it to the Prince would be a transfer from the political funds of the Government to those of the opposition.' The Prince thereupon appealed to Parliament against his father. The address on the annuity was introduced in the Commons on 22 February by William Pulteney, who quoted precedents in the honourable provision made for the Black Prince and the princes who became Edward I and Henry V. He more pointedly claimed that there was a creditably Gothic precedent for a parliamentary application on behalf of the heir apparent against the king's advisers in the case of Richard, son of the Black Prince, who was given the honours and revenue of a Prince of Wales despite opposition from the then king (Edward III)—who was, Pulteney said, 'in a sort of dotage' to his mistress.[6] The government defeated the address by narrow majorities in both houses and the breach between Frederick and his parents widened.

Thomson, as a Scot, may have been more perturbed by events in Parliament during April, when the government brought in a Bill of Pains and Penalties intended to impose harsh punishment on the provost, magistrates, and citizens of Edinburgh, on account of the Porteous riot (the incident on which the plot of Scott's *The Heart of Midlothian* turns). This vindictive and unjust bill threw into contempt the status and honour of Scots magistrates and Scots law; it was very properly resented by loyal Scots, however well disposed they might have been towards the Union. Thanks to a vigorous opposition, led by the Duke of Argyll in the Lords and Duncan Forbes in the Commons, the penalties stipulated in the bill were greatly lightened, but the whole affair could only have increased Thomson's dislike of Walpole's authoritarian government.

The opposition's literary assault on the government continued with renewed vigour, stage-managed, according to the government press, by the Prince of Wales's equerry George Lyttelton. He is satirized in the *Daily Gazeteer* of 14 April 1737 as 'Littledone', a foolish malcontent who has urged the hack playwrights of his acquaintance 'to put into their Plays all the strong things they can think of against Courts and Ministers, and Places and Pensions'. Whether prompted by Lyttelton or not, Fielding's company at the Little Theatre in the Haymarket produced a series of anti-Walpole plays, including Fielding's own *Historical Register for the Year 1736* in March and *Eurydice Hiss'd* in April. Another long-running, contentious opposition piece, William Havard's *King Charles the First*, was being acted at the same time at the Covent Garden theatre.

Off-stage, the journal *Common Sense*, founded by Lyttelton and Chesterfield published, among other satiric libels, the outrageous 'Vision of the Golden Rump' (19 and 26 March), a particularly obscene attack upon the King, Queen, and Prime Minister; a complementary stage play *The Golden Rump* was written, but the manager of Lincoln's Inn Fields theatre, instead of having it acted, took the copy to Walpole. This apparently indefensibly scurrilous play gave Walpole the opportunity to introduce the Licensing Bill which became law on 24 June. It put the theatre 'under the immediate directions of a Court Officer' and thus fulfilled William Talbot's ironic prophecy about 'Tory' policy in the 1734 election (see p. 130 above). By this time the Prince had publicly involved himself in the theatrical campaign against his parents and their minister. On 18 May he attended a performance of Fielding's *Eurydice Hiss'd*, and , 'when any strong passages fell', he clapped, 'especially when in favour of liberty'. On 25 May, while the Licensing Bill was going through Parliament, the Little Theatre management advertised that 'a new Farce of two Acts, call'd *The King and Titi; or The Medlars*'[7] would be staged the following week. Though the play was never acted or printed, we can be certain that it was based upon the scandalous

Histoire du Prince Titi (1735, English translation 1736), which the Prince caused to be written in order grossly to caricature his parents.

The shrewdest opposition literary work of this year was Pope's *Epistle to Augustus*, published in May 1737, but the Prince's circle lavished their greatest praise upon Richard Glover's epic poem *Leonidas*, which appeared at the end of March. The poem was dedicated to Viscount Cobham and its hero, the defender of liberty, was very clearly identifiable with the Prince of Wales. Fielding praised it extravagantly in *The Champion* and Lyttelton wrote in *Common Sense* on 9 April: 'never yet was an epick poem wrote with so noble and so useful a design; the whole plan and purpose of it being to show the superiority of freedom over slavery; and how much virtue, public spirit, and the love of liberty, are preferable, both in their nature and effects, to riches luxury, and the insolence of power.' Disingenuously, he adds that such a story, set in ancient Greece, 'will not bear the least suspicion of a parallel to any circumstance or character of these times', so it can be praised by men of all parties 'since none can say that he meant it against them, unless by declaring that they are against liberty'.[8] Lyttelton, perhaps disingenuously again, asserts that Glover is the equal of Milton and Pope; he regrets that Pope has not written an original epic poem, and hopes that Pope might, at least, praise Glover's effort. It is difficult to believe that this was Lyttelton's considered judgement; his intention, one assumes, was to provoke Pope into writing the serious, patriotic epic that so many of his admirers wanted from him. *Leonidas* was from the same stable as *Liberty*, but it was so cried up by the opposition that it left Thomson's poem standing at the post. Thomson's friends, and perhaps Thomson himself, were envious of Glover's sudden rise to fame. Savage sarcastically echoes Fielding's and Lyttelton's praises when he exclaims, 'Leonidas! who has left David, Homer, Virgil, Spenser, and Milton, as far beneath him as the eagle in her flight does the wren . . . thou ravishing, soul-entrancing, all-immortalized, and all-immortalizing, Leonidas Glover!' It is said that when Thomson was told that Glover was writing an epic poem, he exclaimed 'He write an epic poem, a Londoner, who has never seen a mountain!'[9]

For Thomson's fortunes, though, an event more significant than the total eclipse of *Liberty* was the death of the Lord Chancellor on 14 February 1737, bringing with it the loss of the poet's sinecure. It was said that Talbot's successor, Philip Yorke, Earl of Hardwick, kept the Secretaryship of Briefs vacant for some time in the expectation that Thomson would apply to him for it, but the poet, according to Murdoch, 'was so dispirited, and so listless to every concern of that kind, that he never took one step in the affair: a neglect which his best friends greatly blamed in him'. Shiels attributes this neglect to 'unaccountable indolence'. An anonymous contributor to the *Critical Review* in 1765 declares however that we have Thomson's 'own authority for saying, that it was not optional to him, whether he should remain in the place or not, after his patron's death'.[10] Hardwick was much closer to Walpole than Lord Chancellor Talbot ever had been; Thomson had now moved with Talbot's oldest son William into the opposition camp, so unless Hardwick wanted to buy off a political-literary opponent there would be no motive for the secretaryship to be offered to Thomson or accepted by him.

Whether or not Thomson was unaccountably indolent in applying for the secretaryship, he lost no time in writing an elegy on his dead patron. *A Poem to the Memory of the Right Honourable the Lord Talbot*, in nearly four hundred lines of blank verse, was completed before the end of May and published by Millar on 17 June 1737.[11] Thomson's poem commemorates a man who was widely respected as an unusually honest lawyer, but more than this it celebrates the ideal of public virtue, which is exemplified in this man as it was in the heroes praised in the *Seasons* and *Liberty*. Talbot is praised as a man of extraordinarily comprehensive view; he was to society what Newton was to the physical world:

> steady calm,
> Diffusive, deep and clear, his Reason saw,
> With instantaneous View, the Truth of Things;
> Chief what to Human Life and Human Bliss
> Pertains, that kindest Science, fit for Man:

He is the impartial patriot, who, disdainful of 'sneaking Int'rest', 'sits superior to the Little Fray', and concerns himself with 'the Good of All'; so, as Thomson claims at the end of the poem:

> The Good the Bad,
> The Sons of Justice and the Sons of Strife,
> All that or Freedom or that Int'rest prize,
> A deep-divided Nation's Parties all,
> Conspire to swell thy spotless Praise to Heaven.[12]

One object of the poem is 'to vindicate Talbot in his willingness to work alongside an administration which Thomson regarded as venal, thus perhaps to correct and regulate, by an impartial occupation of the highest legal office, the consequences of Walpole's government',[13] and the poet leaves his readers in no doubt as to his own attitude towards that government. Allusion to Talbot's friendships allows the introduction of a compliment to Thomas Rundle in the Irish bishopric,

> Driven from your Friends, the Sun-shine of the Soul,
> By Slanderous Zeal, and Politics infirm,
> Jealous of Worth.

7. Charles Talbot, 1st Baron Talbot of Hensol, by Jonathan Richardson.

8. James Quin, by William Hogarth.

Repeatedly we are reminded that Talbot's virtues shine all the more in contrast to the general darkness of a corrupt and discreditable age.

Near the opening of the poem Talbot's life of active virtue is contrasted with the retired state which ordinarily would be thought virtuous. Talbot could not

> brook in studious Shade to lie,
> In soft Retirement, indolently pleas'd
> With selfish Peace. The SYREN of the Wise,
> (Who steals th' *Aonian* Song, and, in the shape
> Of Virtue, wooes them from a worthless World)
> Tho', deep he felt her Charms, could never melt
> His strenuous Spirit.[14]

One wonders if Thomson is brooding in his parenthesis more upon himself than Talbot, as he touches on the theme of his work- (negligently)-in-hand, *The Castle of Indolence*. There is an anticipation of the 'Syren Melody' with which the Wizard Indolence charms his victims; the 'Aonian Song' is stolen because, under the cloak of virtue, it is put to the evil purpose of counselling retirement from the world, rather than action.

Thomson's poem is dedicated to the former Lord Chancellor's eldest surviving son, William, now Baron Talbot, who is duly enjoined to keep by virtue the title and reputation that his father gained by virtue. His ill success in this was apparent when he separated from his wife in 1742 and was named as an adulterer in divorce proceedings against the Duchess of Beaufort. Horace Walpole, no friend of Talbot, reported that the Duke of Bedford said, 'He pities Lord Talbot to have met with two such tempers as their two wives.' The Duke could afford to be magnanimous, as he was suing Talbot for £80,000 damages. Talbot (if it was he) had performed an important service to Thomson in drawing him to the Prince of Wales's attention; presumably, he rewarded the poet for the dedication of the verses to the memory of his father, but there is no further reference to him after 1737 in the, admittedly scanty, record of Thomson's affairs. He survived Thomson by many years, living on to fight an uninjurious duel with John Wilkes, to serve Frederick's son George III as Lord Steward of the Household, and to attract the satire of Charles Churchill.[15]

The *Poem to Talbot* did nothing for Thomson's reputation. The Duchess of Portland wrote to Mrs Ann Granville on 21 June 1737: 'There is a poem come out upon the late Lord Chancellor (in blank verse), by Thomson, which they say is execrable, or else I would have sent it you.'[16] The rest is silence. The poem probably did very little for its author's pocket either, beyond whatever gift was made by the dedicatee; indeed, as he had kept the copyright (and the risk) he may even have lost money. Thomson's literary profits could not have been high in 1737; sales of the relatively well-received *Seasons* and *Sophonisba* (both in their 1730 texts) had tailed off and the later poems were selling badly. Murdoch says that after the loss of the secretaryship Thomson 'found himself, from an easy competency, reduced to a state of precarious dependance, in which he passed the remainder of his life; excepting only the last two years of it'. Nevertheless, Murdoch informs us, he

never abated one article in his way of living; which, though simple, was genial and elegant. The profits arising from his works were not inconsiderable; his tragedy of *Agamemnon*, acted in 1738, yielded a good sum; Mr *Millar* was always at hand, to answer, or even to prevent his demands; and he had a friend or two besides, whose hearts, he knew, were not contracted by the ample fortunes they had acquired; who would, of themselves, interpose, if they saw any occasion for it.[17]

Despite Murdoch's assurances that Thomson's demands were always answered or even prevented, there is a story about Thomson being arrested for debt; it is not in the earliest biographies of the poet, but is found in two apparently independent versions at roughly the same date as Shiels and Murdoch. The best-known version first appeared in the anonymous *Life of James Quin, Comedian* (1766), where it is said that when Thomson was reduced to that 'state of precarious dependence' after the death of Lord Chancellor Talbot, 'his creditors, finding that he had no longer any certain support, became inexorable, and imagined by confinement to force that from his friends which his modesty would not permit him to ask'. This seems to have had the desired effect on Thomson's actor friend James Quin:

Hearing that Thomson was confined in a spunging-house, for a debt of about seventy pounds, he repaired to the place, and having enquired for, was introduced to the bard. Thomson was a good deal disconcerted at seeing Quin in such a place, as he had always taken great pains to conceal his wants, and the more so, as Quin told him he was come to sup with him, being conscious that all the money he was possessed of would scarce procure a good one, and that there was no credit to be expected in those houses. His anxiety upon this head was however removed upon Quin's informing him, That as he supposed it would have been inconvenient to have had the supper dressed at the place they were in, he had ordered it from an adjacent tavern; and as a prelude, half a dozen of claret was introduced. Supper being over, and the bottle circulating pretty briskly, Quin said, 'It is time now we should balance accounts': this astonished Thomson, who imagined he had some demand upon him—but Quin perceiving it, continued, 'Mr Thomson, the pleasure I have had in perusing your works, I cannot estimate at less than a hundred pounds, and I insist upon now acquitting the debt: on saying this, he put down a note of that value, and took his leave, without waiting for a reply.[18]

The other version of this story was printed during Quin's lifetime in a collection of anecdotes, *The Tell-Tale* (1756), and is repeated in periodicals in the 1760s and in the anonymous Life of Thomson prefixed to some editions of his *Works* from 1766. According to it, the sponging house was located in Holborn, Quin and Thomson had never met before this incident, and Quin's explanation when he handed over the banknote was that after reading *The Seasons* he had determined to bequeath its author a hundred pounds in his will, but 'this day hearing that you was in this house, I thought I might as well have the pleasure of paying the money myself, as to order my executors to pay it, when perhaps you might have less need of it'.[19]

In 1770 another story about Quin's generosity surfaced, according to which Thomson invited Quin (now described as his intimate friend) to dine with him at Kew Foot Lane and after dinner asked his guest 'with much hesitation' for the favour of a loan of fifty pounds. Quin refused roughly and nothing more was said on the matter that night. Next morning, however, Thomson received a letter from Quin, saying that 'he hates the word *lend*' but enclosing the gift of a banknote for two hundred pounds and promising a hogshead of claret, 'which I will come and help you to demolish, as often as health, leisure, and inclination, will permit'.[20]

Whatever the circumstances of their first meeting, the two men became close friends. Before the rise of Garrick, Quin was the most famous actor of his day. He was a witty and epicurean Irishman with the reputation of a proud, fiery temper, borne out by his fighting at least three duels with fellow actors, but the testimony of Thomson's Richmond neighbour William Robertson is that Quin 'was naturally a most humane and friendly man, and he only put on the brute when he thought it was expected from him, by those who gave him credit for the character'. A good example of such a 'put-on' occurs in a professional reminiscence by William Taylor, who regularly came to Kew Foot Lane to shave Thomson and his guests:

I have often taken Quin by the nose too, which required some courage, let me tell you. One day he asked particularly if the razor was in good order; protested he had as many barbers' ears in his parlour at home as any boy had of birds' eggs on a string, and swore if I did not shave him smoothly, he would add mine to the number! 'Ah', said Thomson, '*Wull* shaves very well, I assure ye.'[21]

Taylor said that he had heard Pope and Quin and Paterson 'talk so together at Thomson's, that I could have listened to them for ever'; also that Mrs Hobart, Thomson's housekeeper, 'often wished Quin dead, he made her master drink so. I have seen him and Quin coming from the Castle [Inn] together at four o'clock in the morning, and not over sober, you may be sure.' Drunk or sober, Quin's political opinions, which were those of an old-fashioned Common-wealthman, would have been congenial to Thomson. They are fairly rep-resented by his remarks on Charles I, as recorded by Thomas Davies:

on a thirtieth of January, he said, that every king in Europe would rise with a crick in his neck. This has been attributed to Voltaire, but unjustly. Contending one day with a gentleman about the rectitude of taking away the life of Charles, Quin was asked by what law the judges deprived him of his life? By all the laws, he replied, which he had left them.[22]

Quin was thus added to a circle of friends who continued at Richmond the convivial life that Thomson had led in London. Richard Savage, staying with him at Richmond in May 1737 and writing to a common friend, the prosperous Jewish merchant and literary amateur Solomon Mendez, reports that Pope had just sent Thomson a letter 'full of affectionate expressions both to him and me'. Savage also tells Mendez that, at the time of writing, Thomson is still abed, and 'is quite ashamed in regard to you.—He calls himself names about it; and accuses and curses his evil genius for laying a spell upon him in regard to writing letters.' Though Savage promised that Thomson would write 'in a post or two', it was not until 21 July that a typically apologetic letter was sent. Thomson begins it in the disarming style that he had now refined by all too frequent practice:

Without designing it, I have made a great trial of your goodness; and yet none, I am persuaded, which it cannot sufficiently bear. The full persuasion of that has had a very perverse influence with me; it has encouraged my negligence: for had I imagined you a peevish man, capable of being disobliged at your friends for venial faults, then had I been exceeding punctual in answering a truly kind letter which I received from you some months ago. This, I must own, is doing what your forefathers were charged with of old—turning the grace of God into wantonness.—But since it is a kindred sin, you must forgive me. If all my friends were inexorable to me in like instances, I should become a solitary being; but as there is no malice prepense in the case, only the sweet blood of indolence, I demand forgiveness.

Thomson promises to visit Mendez' house at Clapton, on the far side of London, for two or three days soon, and ends with a mixture of coarseness, self-mockery, and piety which indicates that he has taken 'forgiveness' for granted.

Berkley, I hope, has led your brother-in-law so deep into the world of spirits, that when he sees me, big as I am, he will see no *body*. But, I am afraid, he will never consent to one half of our species losing their bodies. All the senses, I am apprehensive, will be stiff against such a philosophy. Why, then, let us rub on in the old way, till we wear out these present bodies, and are cloathed with finer.[23]

A spirit of good-natured ribaldry characterizes most of the exchanges between Thomson and the men of that family. There is, for instance an undated mock epitaph 'On Mr Jacob Mendes':

Here Jacob lies, grave, just, and sage,
The chastest person of the age:
Who, had he been in Joseph's place,
Had dy'd, not run away—Alas![24]

The main subject of Thomson's letter of 21 July to Solomon Mendez is Savage, who has now left Kew Foot Lane, 'though where the Muses, or some sweeter girls, have hid him, I know not'. Thomson refers to Savage's 'fine poem on Public Works' and, in a complex mock-puff, expresses some of his own real discontent about the 'state of the nation'. He argues that such a poem as Savage's would be easier to justify in a perfect world where poets are rewarded; Savage should write panegyrics only when his present annual pension of fifty pounds from the queen is turned into a thousand:

He will be driven in his coach and six, when he sees noble public roads without, even with turnpikes. When he sees a senate uncorrupted, he will see a magnificent senate-house; and when a court becomes the patron of arts, another Whitehall. He will see a play-house such as he recommends, when a chamberlain shall be the proper judge of plays, and when slavery more exalts the genius than liberty. When he has begot bastards enow to fill an hospital for foundlings, he will see one; and when he sees bridges worthy of the Thames, he will have faith enough to walk the waters. He will have a government assigned him, when we send out generous and perfectly free colonies; and when he sees West-Indian slaves treated so as not to shock common humanity, he may wash them white.[25]

The matter of 'bridges worthy of the Thames' was in Thomson's mind because only days before this letter was written the parliamentary commissioners appointed to oversee the construction of Westminster Bridge had announced that it would have a cheap wooden superstructure, rather than one of stone. Two months later Thomson's indignant little verse protest against their decision was printed in several journals.[26]

By 9 September Savage had swum back into Thomson's ken along with several other friends; the *Daily Gazetteer* for 13 September 1737 reported:

On Friday Evening last, at Old Man's Coffee-house, Charing Cross, the Hon. William Hawley, Esq; Gentleman Usher to the Prince of Wales, James Thomson, Esq; Author of the Seasons, Dr Armstrong, Author of the Synopsis of the Venereal Disease (abridg'd from Astruc) and of several beautiful Poems, Mr Paterson, of Three King Court, Lombard Street, Author of a Tragedy not yet published, and Mr Sargent, Linnen Draper near Mercers' Chapel, were admitted Free and Accepted Masons. Richard Savage, Esq; Son of the late Earl Rivers, officiated as Master, and Mr Chavine, and Dr Schomberg, Jun. as Wardens; after which the new-made Brethren gave an elegant Entertainment.

The lodge which Thomson had joined was constituted in 1728 at the Red Lion in Richmond; from 1734 it was called Richmond Lodge, though its meeting places from Thomson's admittance to his death were Charing Cross, Great Queen Street, and Suffolk Street.[27] The first initiate in this list was a member of the Prince of Wales's entourage; shortly afterwards, on that significant Protestant day 5 November, the Prince himself was initiated into freemasonary in the presence of other masonic members of his court; he was the first member of the royal family to become a mason.[28] It is not certain exactly why Thomson became a freemason. The author of *Liberty* may have been attracted by a society devoted to tolerance and free discussion. As recently as 16 April 1737 a correspondent in *The Craftsman* had ironically praised 'the wise Governments' of France and Holland for suppressing freemasonry; a year later the Pope would excommunicate all freemasons. The craft's association with charity, deism, and the new science would have been congenial; so too would have been the company of the expatriate Scots who were disproportionately numerous among the officers of London freemasonry in the 1730s. It is most likely that Thomson's motive was not ideological, but was indeed what was described in 1735 as the chief motive of freemasonry, 'good conversation': 'the Basis of our Order is indissoluble Friendship, and the Cement of it Unanimity and Brotherly Love.'[29] His friends Pope, Savage, Quin, Aaron Hill, and Solomon and Moses Mendez were already freemasons; of his fellow-initiates on 9 September Armstrong, Paterson, and John Sargent were also his friends.

On the very same day that the *Daily Gazetteer* carried news of Thomson's masonic initiation some other newspapers printed an ode to the Prince of Wales in which Thomson proclaimed more stridently than ever before his adherence to the Prince's cause. He laments Walpole's pacific foreign policy, which allows Spain and France to take every advantage by their cunning diplomacy, and the corruption at home, which 'eats our Soul away'; he hails the birth of Frederick's first child, a daughter who is the forerunner of new Edwards, Henrys, Annas, and Elizas; finally he prophesies the recovery of Britain and the happy age 'When *France insults*, and *Spain* shall rob no more'.[30] The attitudes and rhetoric of this short poem are very similar to those expressed in *Liberty*, but they are now more partisan in intention and impact, because there has been a change in the Prince's situation, a change partly effected and certainly dramatized by the circumstances surrounding the birth of his daughter, the occasion for Thomson's ode.

The Prince's worsening relations with his parents had reached a crisis in the summer. Retaliating against the King's refusal to increase his allowance, the Prince disobeyed his parents' order that his first child should be born at Hampton Court, where they were in residence. In the middle of the night of 31 July, when the Princess of Wales was almost in labour, he suddenly and secretly removed her to St James's, where she gave birth to a daughter. The Prince subsequently made empty excuses for his conduct. The King replied contemptuously, expelled his son from St James's Palace, and excluded him and all his attendants from his own court. The Prince removed to the White House at Kew, and after that to Norfolk House in St James's Square, which then became the gathering-place for opposition politicians. His popularity increased on account of his father's persecutions. As the coach bearing the evicted Prince and Princess drove out of St James's Palace on 12 September, the mob gathered round, crying out 'God bless you'; on 22 September the Lord Mayor and aldermen waited upon the Prince to offer the City's congratulations on the birth of his daughter and were entertained to dinner. On 4 October 1737 the Prince and Princess of Wales commanded a performance of Addison's *Cato* at Drury Lane; they were clapped and cheered by the audience, and when Cato (played by Quin) spoke the words,

> When vice prevails, and impious men bear sway,
> The port of honour is a private station

'there was another loud huzza, with a great clap, in the latter part of which applause the Prince himself joined in the face of the whole audience'.[31]

By publishing his congratulatory ode less than a week after the King had expelled the Prince from his court, Thomson was nailing his own political colours to the mast. Forthright as it is, the poem as printed was not quite as outspoken as Thomson had intended. On 18 September he wrote to his bookseller Andrew Millar, 'I thank you for getting my Ode printed. In the meantime, who was so very cautious as to advise France & Spain being printed with a Dash? You, I dare say, it was not—You have a superior Spirit to That. I wish you had got or would get it into The Craftsman, or Common Sense'[32] (journals that were more exclusively associated with the opposition than the newspapers which did print the ode). Thomson's poem was sufficiently outspoken to elicit hostile responses in the ministerial *Daily Gazetteer* on 6 and 31 October, in the second of which Thomson is called 'Mr *Manyweathers*'. Bernard Goldgar, commenting on the first of these attacks, notes 'That the *Gazetteer* should have ignored *Liberty* but have devoted an entire issue to assaulting these brief lines can only be indicative of the political significance which panegyric of the prince had now assumed'; on the second attack Goldgar observes that 'Manyweathers' may allude not only to the poet of the *Seasons* but to Thomson's political turnabout. Government supporters denigrated Thomson in private too. When Francesco Algarotti quoted from Thomson's *Poem to Newton* in his *Il Newtonianismo per le Dame* (1737) and asked his friend Lord Hervey to forward a copy of the book to Thomson, Hervey replied that Thomson is 'so little esteem'd, or rather so much decry'd, by all People of good

Taste in this Country, that it will not do credit to any Body that cites him as an authority for any thing; he is an obscure, bombast, laborious, *Diseur des riens*'. Political difference is enough to explain Hervey's antagonism, but there may have been a personal animus, on account of Hervey's epilogue for Thomson's *Sophonisba* not being used when the play was staged.[33]

Murdoch tells us that Thomson's 'chief dependence' for a period of about seven years after the death of the Lord Chancellor was on 'the protection and bounty' of the Prince of Wales, who 'upon the recommendation of Lord *Lyttelton*, then his chief favourite, settled on him a handsome allowance'. Murdoch adds, 'Lord *Lyttelton's* recommendation came altogether unsolicited, and long before Mr *Thomson* was personally known to him'. Johnson's account of the transaction adds some detail:

He now relapsed to his former indigence; but the prince of Wales was at that time struggling for popularity, and by the influence of Mr Lyttelton professed himself the patron of wit: to him Thomson was introduced, and being gaily interrogated about the state of his affairs, said 'that they were in a more poetical posture than formerly', and had a pension allowed him of one hundred pounds a year.[34]

The pension was presumably recommended some time after August 1737, when George Lyttelton was promoted from equerry to secretary to the Prince. Over the previous years the Prince had commanded a performance of *Sophonisba*, praised Thomson's work to the Countess of Hertford, and received the dedication of *Liberty*; but there was no reason why he should have picked out Thomson from the crowd of his would-be pensioners (which included Savage) without Lyttelton's recommendation. There is no reason, either, to doubt Murdoch's story that Lyttelton and Thomson had not met before the recommendation was made; the two men were certainly unacquainted with one another as late as August 1735. Lyttelton was a 28-year-old member of the House of Commons in 1737, when the Prussian ambassador wrote of him: 'Litleton is one of the boldest *frondeurs* in the Parliament. The King hates him so bitterly that he cannot bear to hear his name mentioned ... and he is also the secret author of some of the most ferocious pamphlets against the ministry that have recently been published.' Lyttelton's anti-Walpole *Letters from a Persian* (1735) caught Thomson's attention on their first publication; forty years later Johnson wrote that they 'have something of that indistinct and headstrong ardour for liberty which a man of genius always catches when he enters the world, and always suffers to cool as he passes forward': here the man who wrote *London* and *Marmor Norfolciense* in *his* late twenties spoke from personal experience. Lyttelton was a tall, serious, conscientious young man, but so awkward that the Earl of Chesterfield held him up to his son as an object lesson of the harm that poor deportment might do to a man of real merit and knowledge:

9. George Lyttelton, 1st Baron Lyttelton; artist unknown.

10. Frederick Louis, Prince of Wales, by Philip Mercier.

Wrapped up like a Laputan in intense thought . . . He leaves his hat in one room, his sword in another, and would leave his shoes in a third, if his buckles, though awry, did not save them; . . . his head, always hanging upon one or other of his shoulders, seems to have received the first stroke upon a block. I sincerely value and esteem him for his parts, learning, and virtue; but, for the soul of me, I cannot love him in company.

Thomson was less nice of his company, but then his own 'exterior appearance was not very engaging'; he 'stooped forward rather when he walked, as though he was full of thought' and 'was very careless and negligent about his dress'. Lyttelton was duly numbered among the visitors to Kew Foot Lane and Taylor the intrepid barber took him by his long aristocratic nose, finding him 'tender-faced' and 'devilish difficult to shave'. It was probably through Lyttelton that the young poet James Hammond, one of the Prince of Wales's equerries, became one of Thomson's visitors too. William Robertson recalled: 'Hammond was a gentleman, and a very pleasant man, yet Thomson, I remember, once called him a burnished butterfly.'[35] Hammond would not have shamed Chesterfield in company.

Lyttelton, Hammond, and Thomson were not the only poets on whom Frederick bestowed pensions or places; others included Richard Glover, Henry Brooke, and Gilbert West; David Mallet was appointed under-secretary at £200 a year. The value that the Prince appeared to place upon poets gratified Thomson, not only because he needed money, but because he believed that in a healthy society poets, as teachers of virtue, ought to be in a position which would enable them to influence the men who wielded political power. His belief was shared by others; for instance, Lyttelton wrote to Pope on 25 October 1738, asking him to be with the Prince as much as possible, and to 'Animate him to Virtue, to the Virtue least known to Princes, though most necessary for them, Love of the Publick; and think that the Morals, the Liberty, the whole Happiness of this Country depends on your Success'.[36] The poets who attached themselves to Frederick had what appear in retrospect to be exaggerated expectations of their patriot prince, but he represented perhaps the best hope for enlightened, highly-placed literary patronage at a time when many serious authors were still disinclined to trust themselves to the commercially-determined tastes of booksellers. Aaron Hill seems to have arrived at this conclusion also, to judge by his long poem *The Tears of the Muses*, published in November 1737. It was dedicated to the booksellers' foe, the Society for the Encouragement of Learning, and hailed Frederick as the potential reviver of the languishing, tearful muses. Hill's poem is not overtly controversial, but it has some pro-Elizabethan, anti-Augustan touches, characteristic of opposition writing: the title echoes Spenser; Frederick is called 'Germanicus', after the popular patriot with republican sentiments who came to be hated by his adopted father, the emperor Tiberius. It reflects the political alignments of the poets, as well as Hill's friendships, when Germanicus is shown as finding only two living geniuses, Pope and Thomson, blazing in the general darkness of the age. These two, with Newton, are as it happens the only non-allegorical names in the five hundred lines of Hill's poem.

However poetical the posture of his affairs had been in 1737, Thomson's financial hopes were rising as the following year began, for he now determined to settle a regular allowance on his unmarried sisters Elizabeth and Jean. (The third surviving sister of whom we have record, Mary, was probably married by now to William Craig, a merchant in Edinburgh.[37]) It is not clear whether or not Elizabeth and Jean's millinery business had failed after only one year, but George Ross was still paying out money on Thomson's account in Edinburgh, probably for the sisters, and the account was in the red. Thomson wrote to Ross on 12 January 1738: 'It was kind in you not to draw rashly upon me, which, at present, had put me into Danger: but very soon (That is to say about two Months hence) I shall have a golden Buckler, and you may draw boldly.' This golden buckler may have been the first instalment of Thomson's pension from the Prince of Wales or his expected profits from *Agamemnon*, which was due to come on in that season. The settlement on the sisters was at last arranged in a letter of 18 February from Thomson to Gavin Hamilton, a prominent Edinburgh bookseller and magistrate. Hamilton was asked to pay the two women, on Thomson's account, £8 every Martinmas and every Whitsuntide.[38]

From the letter to Millar in September it is clear that Thomson and Paterson are seeing one another regularly; the letter to Ross in January mentions another college friend, Murdoch:

I have not yet seen the round Man of God, to be. He is to be Parsonifyed, a few Days hence. How a Gown and Cassock will become him! And with what a bold Leer he will edify the devout Females! There is no Doubt of his having a Call; for he is immediately to enter upon a tolerable Living—God grant him more, and as fat as himself. It rejoices me to see one worthy honest excellent Man raised, at least, to an Independency.

Immediately upon his ordination Murdoch was presented by James Vernon (his former travelling pupil's father) to the rectory of Stradishall in Suffolk, where, he wrote to John Forbes, he was well content 'and pleased to find, that so long rambling has not abated my love of study'. Forbes was in Scotland, much missed by his Richmond friends. Murdoch reports that 'Thomson cursed like a heathen' that Forbes did not get himself elected to the seat in the Commons vacated in July 1737 when his father was appointed Lord President of the Court of Session in Edinburgh.[39]

Murdoch's ordination prompted some affectionate advisory couplets from Thomson:

> Thus safely low, my friend, thou can'st not fall:
> Here reigns a deep tranquillity o'er all;

No noise, no care, no vanity, no strife;
Men, woods and fields, all breathe untroubled life.
Then keep each passion down, however dear;
Trust me, the tender are the most severe.
Guard, while 'tis thine, thy philosophic ease,
And ask no joy but that of virtuous peace;
That bids defiance to the storms of fate:
High bliss is only for a higher state.[40]

Thomson's paradox concerning the severity of the tender passions, with its confidential 'Trust me', may point to some episode in the poet's private life about which we have no other hint. Murdoch followed Thomson's advice to the extent of remaining a bachelor to the end of his life.

There was no deep tranquillity for Thomson, because he was awaiting the Lord Chamberlain's verdict on *Agamemnon* and was involving himself in the debate on freedom provoked by the passage of the Licensing Act. Though this Act was defended by government supporters as a restraint upon the licentiousness of the stage, it was widely regarded as a preliminary to censorship of the press. So Millar, making his contribution to the fight against censorship, published in January 1738 a reprint of Milton's *Areopagitica* with a new preface by Thomson.[41] This preface is a rousing defence of 'the best human Rights': 'take away the Liberty of the Press', Thomson declares, 'and we are all at once stript of the Use of our noblest Faculties: our Souls themselves are imprisoned in a dark Dungeon: we may breathe, but we cannot be said to live'. As he had done in *Liberty*, he brings together Gothic and Grecian freedoms, for, he asserts, freedom of thought was cherished alike by the ancient Greeks and Alfred the Great. He does not refer directly to the Licensing Act, but he remarks darkly:

I hope it will never be this Nation's Misfortune to fall into the hands of an Administration, that do not from their Souls abhor any thing that has but the remotest Tendency toward the Erection of a new and arbitrary Jurisdiction over the Press: or can otherwise look upon any Attempt that way, than as the greatest Impiety, the cruellest, the wickedest, the most irreligious thing that can be imagined.

Thomson's preface sharpened what was already provocative; for, though Milton's towering literary reputation had now achieved sufficient respectability in the seats of authority for a monument to be raised to him in the Poets' Corner of Westminster Abbey in 1737, his forthright political views could still serve a purpose in current controversy, particularly if the subject at issue was freedom or Spain. So, even the Oxford Jacobite William King wrote an anti-Walpole, anti- Spanish satire under the name of Milton; this was the once well-known *Miltonis Epistola ad Pollionem*, dedicated to Pope, of which two editions appeared in 1738. In the title of Mark Akenside's *The Voice of Liberty*, 'or a British Philippic: a Poem in Miltonic Verse, occasion'd by the insults of the Spaniards, and the Preparations for War', published in August 1738, the epithet 'Miltonic' refers as much to politics as prosody. Two months after the publication of *Areopagitica* with Thomson's preface, Thomson was associated with Milton again in an attack on the government. On 16 March Millar published *A Manifesto of the Lord Protector*... 'wherein is shown the Reasonableness of the Cause of this Republick against the Depredations of the Spaniards. Written in Latin by John Milton, and first printed in 1655: Now translated into English... To which is added *Britannia*, a Poem. By Mr Thomson'. A second edition of this small, cheap pamphlet was required before the end of the year. The *Manifesto* is a new English translation of a Commonwealth state paper originally published to justify to the world the English punitive expedition to the West Indies that resulted in the capture of Jamaica from Spain; the document was first attributed to Milton by Thomas Birch in his edition of Milton's complete *Historical, Political, and Miscellaneous Works*, published by Millar also in March 1738. This was the collection from which two months earlier Millar had extracted *Areopagitica* for separate publication also as a small, cheap, politically controversial pamphlet.

The text of *Britannia* in the 1738 pamphlet is unchanged from that in the 1730 quarto, perhaps because Thomson, Millar, or Birch (whoever was the prime mover) could argue that the circumstances in which the poem was first written were unchanged. English merchants had long complained about the depredations of Spanish privateers and *garda costas* upon their vessels, trading sometimes legally, sometimes illegally, with the Spanish colonies in America. The government's failure to take vigorous action against Spain had, of course, occasioned the first publication of *Britannia* in 1729. In June 1731 Captain Robert Jenkins returned to England with his famous severed ear and by 1737 public demand for warlike retaliation against Spain was being whipped up clamorously in the pages of *Common Sense* and *The Craftsman*. The campaign was intensified in 1738. As the Licensing Act did not apply to plays written before the Act was passed, Shakespeare's *Richard II*, 'Not acted these forty years', was revived at Covent Garden on 6 February and given nine more performances that season. Its political relevance was not lost upon an audience which loudly cheered such lines as 'The King is not himself, but basely led | By flatterers', and 'The Earl of Wiltshire hath the state in farm', and (referring to the king's treasury),

> War hath not wasted it, for Warr'd he hath not ...
> More hath he spent in peace than they in war.[42]

Lists of merchant ships taken or plundered by the Spaniards were published in journals; at last, on 3 March the House of Commons first debated the Spanish seizure of British ships; on 16 March Captain Jenkins was called before the House of Commons to tell his story, and on the same day Millar published the pamphlet containing Cromwell's warlike *Manifesto* and Thomson's equally bellicose *Britannia*.

Meanwhile *Agamemnon*, Thomson's more substantial contribution to current political debate, went into rehearsal. Though eight years had elapsed since the performance of *Sophonisba*, Thomson's return to the stage was perhaps inevitable. *The Seasons* was becoming quite widely known (and would eventually in the century after Thomson's death become the most popular English long poem apart from *Paradise Lost* and more popular than most novels), but it was still the case in the 1730s that the most popular form of non-religious serious literature was what it long had been: the drama. Its potential profits were attractive to a man of letters and its closeness to a politically highly aware audience made it no less attractive to a poet eager to discuss political ideas.

Thomson had hoped to complete *Agamemnon* in time for the 1736–7 season, but the play was not ready for acting until the beginning of 1738. On 12 January he wrote to Ross, telling him that it had been accepted by the Drury Lane manager Charles Fleetwood, and was about to be submitted to the Lord Chamberlain's Examiner of Plays for approval under the provisions of the new Licensing Act. Shiels tells us that Pope wrote two letters in favour of *Agamemnon* to the theatre management and it was claimed that Quin also helped to promote the play.[43] It is some measure of Thomson's credit in the playhouse, or of his friends' and patrons' influence there, that *Agamemnon* was accepted at all, for the immediate effect of the Licensing Act was to reduce the number of London theatres to the two old patented houses Drury Lane and Covent Garden (together with the King's Opera House, where no plays were performed), and greatly to inhibit the production of new plays. In the season of 1737–8 (a season reduced by six weeks on account of the death of Queen Caroline) the two playhouses between them saw the staging of only four new plays;[44] two of these were disastrous comic pieces which lasted for one night each; the third was John Dalton's adaptation of *Comus*, with Quin in the title role, which had eleven performances at Drury Lane; the fourth was *Agamemnon*. Thomson's play was thus the only new tragedy performed that season and the only new play with any political content. The play's theme was undoubtedly controversial: a chief minister conspiring with a queen to corrupt a kingdom and destroy its king. Its performance, virtually uncut, suggests that in the immediate aftermath of the passage of the Licensing Act, the theatre manager's disinclination to bring on plays was being matched by the Lord Chamberlain's disinclination to censor them; but John Loftis conjectures that 'Queen Caroline's death during the winter prior to the play's production removed its sting, and may have had something to do with the fact that it was licensed.'[45] We shall see that matters were different in the following season.

Agamemnon was received by the Lord Chamberlain's Examiner of Plays on 14 January.[46] It seems that he turned a blind eye to a great deal of material in the play itself concerning evil counsellors, all rather obviously hostile to Walpole, and was content only to censor the last six lines of a prologue which had been written by Mallet to be spoken by Quin. These lines, which were enclosed in inverted commas in the printed edition, contain an allusion to the Licensing Act itself. Mallet declares that Thomson's play had a moral to teach, then he concludes:

> As such our fair Attempt, we hope to see
> Our Judges, — here at least, — from Influence free;
> One Place, — unbias'd yet by Party-Rage, —
> Where only Honour votes, — the *British* Stage.
> We ask for Justice, for Indulgence sue:
> Our last best Licence must proceed from you.

On 2 February Murdoch told John Forbes that 'the Town is in great expectation' of Thomson's tragedy; on 18 February Thomson announced that it would be performed 'about three weeks hence'; on 23 February Thomas Gray told Horace Walpole that it was in rehearsal; Thomas Birch records in his diary that he attended rehearsals on 25 March and 4 April. According to Thomas Davies,

Thomson, in reading his play of Agamemnon to the actors, in the green-room, pronounced every line with such a broad Scotch accent, that they could not restrain themselves from a loud laugh. Upon this, the author good-naturedly said to the manager, 'Do you, Sir, take my play, and go on with it; for, though I can write a tragedy, I find I cannot read one.'[47]

The name part was assigned to Quin, the leading actor of the 1730s, whose roles earlier in this season had included Macbeth, Richard III, Othello, Brutus, Falstaff, Dryden's Antony, and Addison's Cato. Some impression of his style at this time may be derived from Aaron Hill's description of him as Comus, a part which he was playing when *Agamemnon* was in rehearsal: 'there was in all this very little of gesture: the look, the elevated posture, and the brow of Majesty did all.' The same picture emerges from a description of Quin on stage some eight years later: 'with very little variation of cadence, and in a deep full tone, accompanied by a sawing kind of action, which had more of the senate than of the stage in it, he rolled out his heroics with an air of dignified indifference, that seemed to disdain the plaudits that were bestowed upon him.'[48] This account has a less sympathetic tone because Quin's now old-fashioned manner is being contrasted unfavourably with Garrick's new, quicksilver style; in 1738, though, Garrick was still only a wine merchant.

Mrs Mary Porter played Clytemnestra; it would appear that she was specially engaged for the part because there is no record of her appearing in any other play during the 1737–8 season. Her first recorded appearance on the London stage was before Thomson was born; after a carriage accident in 1731 her appearances were relatively infrequent, and she always supported herself on stage with a stick, but her powers were still great. Horace Walpole thought that she surpassed even Garrick in passionate tragedy and he thought so highly of her acting of Clytemnestra in Thomson's *Agamemnon* that he wrote an essay, now lost, on her performance.[49]

Egisthus was played by the company's 'second string' William Milward, whose other parts earlier that season included Hamlet, Cassius, Macduff, and Henry IV. He had made Barton Booth his model, so his style was ponderous; the part of Egisthus gave him the opportunity to display to the full 'the love of ranting' which Thomas Davies though was 'his singular fault'.[50]

The assignment of the attractive role of Melisander is fully documented by the actor himself. Stung by what he took to be a reference in Johnson's *Life of Richard Savage* (1744) to Savage's dislike of him, Theophilus Cibber added a long footnote to Shiels' *Life* of Thomson. It reads, in part, as follows:

I had the pleasure of perusing the play of Agamemnon, before it was introduced to the manager. Mr Thomson was so thoroughly satisfied (I might say more) with my reading of it; he said, he was confirmed in his design of giving to me the part of Melisander. When I expressed my sentiments of the favour, he told me, he thought it none; that my old acquaintance Savage knew, he had not forgot my taste in reading the poem of Winter some years before: he added, that when (before this meeting) he had expressed his doubt, to which of the actors he should give this part (as he had seen but few plays since his return from abroad) Savage warmly urged, I was the fittest person, and, with an oath affirmed, that Theo. Cibber would taste it, feel it, and act it; perhaps he might extravagantly add, 'beyond any one else' ... When I read the play to the manager, Mr Quin, etcetera (at which several gentlemen, intimate friends of the author, were present) I was complimented by them all; Mr Quin particularly declared, he never heard a play done so much justice to, in reading, through all its various parts. Mrs Porter also (who on this occasion was to appear in the character of Clytemnestra) so much approved my entering into the taste, sense, and spirit of the piece, that she was pleased to desire me to repeat a reading of it, which, at her request, and that of other principal performers, I often did; they all confessed their approbation; with thanks. When this play was to come forward into rehearsal, Mr Thomson told me, another actor had been recommended to him for this part in private, by the manager, [but] ... Mr Thomson insisted on my keeping the part. He said, 'Twas his opinion, none but myself, or Mr. Quin, could do it any justice; and, as that excellent actor could not be spared from the part of Agamemnon (in the performance of which character he added to his reputation, though before justly rated as the first actor of that time) he was peremptory for my appearing in it; I did so, and acquitted myself to the satisfaction of the author and his friends (men eminent in rank, in taste, and knowledge) and received testimonies of approbation from the audience, by their attention and applause.[51]

Theophilus Cibber, like his father, was best suited for comic parts but insisted on playing the tragedian. His name continued to appear in the playbills for *Agamemnon* until the end of the run on 25 April, even though it is known that he fled to France on 16 April to escape his creditors and remained there until the summer. Presumably the part of Melisander was played by an understudy from 18 April.

Cassandra was played by Susannah Maria Cibber, second wife of Theophilus and sister of Thomas Arne the composer; in April 1738 she was in the thick of one of the more highly publicized and unsavoury marital separations of eighteenth-century theatrical history. She was to develop into a very fine and expressive player of tragedy, but at the time she appeared in *Agamemnon*, aged 24, she was still rather better known as a singer in opera and oratorio than as an actress. Richard Cumberland writes of her playing Rowe's *Fair Penitent* in 1746, unfavourably contrasting her with Garrick as he had contrasted Quin:

Mrs Cibber in a key, high-pitched but sweet withal, sung or rather recitatived Rowe's harmonious strain, something in the manner of the Improvisatories: it was so extremely wanting in contrast, that, though it did not wound the ear it wearied it; when she had once recited two or three speeches, I could anticipate the manner of every succeeding one; it was like a long old legendary ballad of innumerable stanzas, every one of which is sung to the same tune, eternally chiming in the ear without variation or relief.[52]

Like Quin's, her style was well suited to Thomson's very static tragedies.

Even the tiny part of Talthybius the herald was taken by the experienced William Havard, also a playwright, whose tragedy *King Charles I* had played for twenty nights in 1737 and was one of the plays that the Licensing Act was intended to curb. All in all, it was a strong and well-tried cast, capable of doing the best for Thomson's long, solemn declamations and his emphasis upon oratory at the expense of dramatic action.

Agamemnon opened at Drury Lane on 6 April, rather late in the season for a new play to succeed, and ran for nine nights; the last performance, the author's third benefit, was on 25 April; the play was never revived. Pope 'honoured the representation on the first night with his presence. As he had not been for some time at a play, this was considered as a very great instance of esteem.' Johnson adds that Pope 'was welcomed to the theatre by a general clap'.[53] The performances on the sixth and seventh nights, 18 and 19 April, were by command of the Prince and Princess of Wales, and the play when subsequently printed was dedicated to the Princess.

At the earlier performances all did not go well. Thomas Davies observes:

Agamemnon, though well acted, was not written agreeably to the taste of the critics, who very justly observed, that [Thomson] had not entirely preserved antient manners and

characters: Clytemnestra did not resemble the portrait drawn of her by Aeschylus, which
is more consistent and agreeable to history. The displeasure of the audience shewn to
certain scenes produced a whimsical effect upon the author; he had promised to meet
some friends at a tavern as soon as the play was ended, but he was obliged to defer his
attending them to a very late hour. When he came, they asked him the reason of his stay;
he told them, that the critics had sweated him so terribly by their severe treatment of
certain parts of his tragedy, that the perspiration was so violent, as to render his wig unfit
to wear; and that he had spent a great deal of time amongst the peruke-makers in
procuring a proper cover for his head.

Johnson alludes to this story in his *Life* of Thomson and adds a further anecdote
about *Agamemnon*: 'He so interested himself in his own drama that, if I
remember right, as he sat in the upper gallery he accompanied the players by
audible recitation, till a friendly hint frighted him to silence.' Shiels attaches a
similar tale to the first night of *Sophonisba* (see above, Chapter 4). Thomson's
wig problem is referred to by others. Sir Andrew Mitchell told James Boswell
that 'Thomson used to sweat so much the first nights of his Plays, that when he
came and met his freinds at a tavern in the Piazza, his wig was as if he had been
dip'd in an oil-pot.' The last word on wigs shall be with William Taylor, who
recalled that Thomson always wore a wig and was extravagant with them: 'I
have seen a dozen at a time hanging up in my master's shop, and all of them so
big that nobody else could wear them. I suppose his sweating to such a degree
made him have so many, for I have known him spoil a new one only in walking
from London.'[54]

   Johnson says that *Agamemnon* 'was only endured, but not favoured' and that it
'was much shortened in the representation'. Shiels asserts that the play was
'acted with applause', but confirms Johnson's second statement: 'Mr Thomson
submitted to have this play considerably shortened in the action, as some parts
were too long, others unnecessary, in which not the character but the poet
spoke.' There is a more detailed account in a letter written by Benjamin Victor
during the play's run:

As to Agamemnon, I can promise you an excessive deal of pleasure from the reading it; I
take the first three acts to be equal to any thing that ever was written; they were
excellently performed, and with the loudest, and most universal applause! after this
(such is the uncertainty of human affairs) the two following acts, (particularly the last)
were as deservedly hissed and cat-call'd; and the reason of all this proceeded from a
palpable defect in the plan. — The hero, *Agamemnon*, dies in the fourth act, — and in the
fifth, which, you know, is the act for catastrophe, and should be fullest of business, you
are chiefly entertain'd with the prophetic strains of *Cassandra*, whom *Agamemnon*
brought with him from Troy; and the distresses of young lovers, children to the
depar[t]ed heroes, characters that generally fall into the hands of young, weak actors,
and therefore the consequence of such bad conduct in the author, as well as bad acting,

might have been foretold without the gift of prophecy. But a club of wits, with Mr Pope at the head of them, met at the theatre the next morning, and cut, and slash'd, like dexterous surgeons—the lovers are no more—and they have brought a fine scene, that finish'd the fourth act, into the fifth. If the play is printed, after these necessary alterations, it will be better for the reader, as well as spectator—But the work must for ever remain maim'd and defective.

The club of wits may have included Andrew Mitchell, in view of Boswell's journal-note of a conversation with Mitchell years later: 'He observed that the Drama was not [Thomson's] Province. He was too descriptive. When a sentiment pleased him he used to extend it with rich luxuriance. His freinds used to prune very freely, and poor Thomson used to suffer. Mr Mitchell said now and then, "This is fine, but it is misplaced. *Non est hic locus*".'[55] Though this club met on the morning after the first night, it is unlikely that their revised version could have been acted that evening (Friday). As there were performances on Saturday and Monday, 8 and 10 April, followed by an unusually long gap of four weekdays with no performance, it is likely that the revised text was first acted on Saturday, 15 April.

What these changes were may be discovered by comparing the text printed in April with the manuscript submitted to the Stage Licenser in January. Between the manuscript and the printed text over half the lines following the death of Agamemnon are deleted, three earlier scenes are taken out, and many other smaller cuts and revisions are made. The chief effect is to remove entirely a sub-plot involving a son of Egisthus, named Hemon, who loves Electra, is intended by his father to succeed to Agamemnon's throne, but is killed defending Agamemnon.

Advertisements during the play's run surprisingly make no references to these improvements, but newspaper announcements of the royal command performance of 18 April say that there is to be a new epilogue and a footnote to the epilogue in the printed text explains why: 'Another Epilogue was spoken after the first Representation of the Play, which began with the first six Lines of This: but the rest of that Epilogue, having been very justly disliked by the Audience, This was substituted in its Place.' The first six lines of the printed epilogue, the same as those spoken by Mrs Cibber on the first night, are Thomson's protest against the flippancy of modern epilogues:

> Our Bard, to Modern Epilogue a Foe,
> Thinks such mean Mirth but deadens generous Woe:
> Dispels in idle Air the Moral Sigh,
> And wipes the tender Tear from Pity's Eye:
> No more with social Warmth the Bosom burns;
> But all th' unfeeling, selfish Man returns.

The printed epilogue continues:

> Thus he began: . . . And you approv'd the Strain;
> 'Till the next Couplet sunk to light and vain,
> You check'd him there . . . To You, to Reason just,
> He owns he triumph'd in your kind Disgust.

That light and vain couplet and the rest of the spoken epilogue have not survived, but it is reasonable to surmise that they had something of the archness and innuendo of the epilogue to *Sophonisba*. The rest of the printed epilogue obsequiously owns that the author is 'Charm'd by your Frown, by your Displeasure grac'd', praises the 'rising Virtue' of the audience's taste, and expresses confidence that decent epilogues will henceforth be in fashion.

Ever a moralist, Thomson was conforming to that gradual change of taste that is nicely illuminated four years later in the second part of Richardson's *Pamela*, where there is a criticism of the epilogue to Ambrose Philips's *The Distrest Mother*, in Johnson's opinion 'the most successful Epilogue that was ever yet spoken on the English theatre'. Pamela tells Lady Davers that she was shocked by 'an Epilogue Spoken by Mrs *Oldfield* in the Character of *Andromache*', which 'by lewd, and even senseless *Double Entendre* . . . could be calculated only to efface all the tender, all the virtuous Sentiments, which the Tragedy was design'd to raise'. Pamela was mortified to see a perfect character such as Andromache 'talking Nastiness to an Audience, and setting it out with all the wickedest Graces of Action, and affected Archness of Looks, Attitude, and Emphasis'.[56] She could well speak for Thomson in his revised epilogue to *Agamemnon* and his even more overtly reforming epilogue to *Tancred and Sigismunda* (1745). The epilogue to *Edward and Eleanora* was flippant, but, like the epilogue to *Sophonisba*, it was not written by Thomson, but by an unidentified 'Friend'.

The removal of the sub-plot and the acceleration of events after Agamemnon's death impose a 'classical' unity of action, and the unities of time and place are also rigidly observed, but Thomson's play remains slackly plotted in comparison with the Aeschylean tragedy it all too distantly follows, though it compares not too badly with its structurally closer ancient model, Seneca's *Agamemnon*. It bears out what Francis Gentleman noted of all Thomson's plays:

Thomson seems to have been much better calculated for easy poetry than theatrical composition; yet his plays strongly manifest a knowledge of nature, a moral delicacy of judgment and great strength of expression; but they are wanting in point of business, incidents are too thinly scattered, and his scenes frequently fall from their length, he does not appear to have known, or considered, the effect of representation, and criticism may easily discover that he wrote more for the closet than the stage.[57]

So much could be said of Seneca also.

The revisions to Thomson's *Agamemnon* did not alter the primacy of Clytemnestra, for, like *Sophonisba*, this play is built around a female lead who is on stage more than any other character; nor did the revisions change the characterization of his heroine, who still, as Thomas Davies mildly and correctly observed, did not resemble the portrait drawn of her by Aeschylus. From the outset she is regarded as the victim of Egisthus' seducing wiles. Her first long speech is on the weakness of women, within whom there is a perpetual unequal combat between 'slow Reason and impetuous Passion'. She is perpetually haunted by guilty fear, sharing the wretchedness of all those 'Who feel, yet cannot save, their dying Virtue!' When threatened by her husband's return, she asks her lover to flee with her:

> Excuse my weaker Heart. But how, *Egisthus*,
> How shall I bear an injur'd Husband's Eye?
> The fiercest Foe wears not a Look so dreadful,
> As does the Man we wrong.

After Egisthus has murdered Agamemnon she distractedly upbraids him:

> Yes, Traitor! turn away:
> But, ere you go, give me my Peace again:
> Give me my happy Family around;
> Give me my Virtue, Honour, nay my Glory;
> Or give me Death, tho' Death cannot relieve me.[58]

This softened, domesticated Clytemnestra was apparently to the audience's taste; at least, the playing of it was. We are told:

Mrs Porter gave a striking proof of her great power in expressing the passions. Her action and deportment, through the part of Clytemnestra, marked the consummate actress. In the second act, when in the distress of her mind from conscious guilt, she is torn with conflicting passions at the approach of her injured husband, the force of her action and expression, when she said to her attendant—

> Bring me my children hither, they may perhaps relieve me—

struck the audience with astonishment, who expressed the highest approbation by loud and reiterated applauses.[59]

Such a conception of his chief character accords with Thomson's idea of 'the fair sex' and with the conventions of eighteenth-century sentimental drama, but it also serves Thomson's need to blacken the character of Egisthus for the sake of the play's political message. As in Seneca, but not in Aeschylus, Egisthus is introduced into the action quite early and he re-enters it more frequently and more prominently than he does in either of the ancient plays. Thomson builds him up into a powerful wicked character, the unprincipled pragmatist whose creed is that 'Success . . . makes Villains honest.'[60] In the political allegory he stands for Walpole, so, the more strident the attack upon him, the more muted had to be the criticism of his queen.

The same considerations applied even more strongly to the characterization of Agamemnon. The only faults imputed to him are his long absence and his bad judgement in the choice of a chief minister. He justifies the sacrifice of Iphigenia with an appeal to 'the Public Good' which

> Must bear fond Nature down, in him who dares
> Aspire to worthy Rule;

he cautions against evil ministers, and, like a constitutional monarch, he lectures on the way to rule 'a free People' without 'yielding or usurping Power'. He is a family man, displaying a generous fondness towards Clytemnestra, 'a Love . . . mellow'd into Friendship',[61] and an effusive affection for Orestes and Electra (not at all George II's feelings for the Prince of Wales). The overall effect here, as with Clytemnestra, is to sentimentalize and to substitute the pathetic for the sublime.

Thomson's only attempted excursion into the sublime manner is in Cassandra's prophetic ravings as Agamemnon is about to be murdered, speeches according to Joseph Warton, 'well calculated to fill the audience with alarm, astonishment, and suspense, at an awful event, obscurely hinted at in very strong imagery'.[62] She has the last word, as she does in Seneca's play: she also speaks the epilogue. She is always accompanied by a chorus of Trojan women, who speak, however, only in one scene, where they share in her set-piece lyrical lament.[63] The device of the chorus was virtually obsolete in English drama at this time; Thomson's chorus comes from Seneca, not Aeschylus. So do most of the other minor characters: Electra, Orestes, and Clytemnestra's women attendant (a nurse in Seneca).

The happiest and most creative stroke in Thomson's play is the development of a major character from little more than a hint in the third book of Homer's *Odyssey*, where Nestor relates that an unnamed bard, left by Agamemnon in Mycenae to watch over Clytemnestra's welfare, was abducted by Aegisthus and left to die on a desert island. Thomson gives this bard a suitable name, Melisander, brings him back to Mycenae to reveal Egisthus' villainy, and economically lets him take over the role of a minor character named Strophius, who appears at the end of Seneca's *Agamemnon* to carry Orestes to safety. Thomson also furnishes Melisander with most of the best poetry in his play. His description in Act III, Scene i, of his marooning hardly advances the action, but is a fine piece of scene stealing:

> Next Night—a dreary Night!
> Cast on the wildest of the *Cyclade Isles*,
> Where never human Foot had mark'd the Shore,
> These Ruffians left me—Yet, believe me, *Arcas*,
> Such is the rooted Love we bear Mankind,
> All Ruffians as they were, I never heard
> A Sound so dismal as their parting Oars.—
> Then horrid Silence follow'd, broke alone
> By the low Murmurs of the restless Deep,
> Mixt with the doubtful Breeze, that now and then
> Sigh'd thro' the mournful Woods.[64]

As Lessing pointed out, Melisander's solitary confinement calls Philoctetes to mind;[65] the extended description of his surroundings which follows the words just quoted is as evocative in its way as Sophocles' graphic representation of his hero's desert island, but Thomson's character is an eighteenth-century man of feeling, who makes incidental observations on kindness to animals. Towards the end of the play he addresses Cassandra and the other Trojan women with a copy-book exposition of sentimentalism:

> Sweet Source of every Virtue,
> O sacred Sorrow! He who knows not Thee,
> Knows not the best Emotions of the Heart,
> Those tender Tears that humanize the Soul,
> The Sigh that Charms, the Pang that gives Delight;
> He lives next door to Cruelty and Pride,
> And is a Novice in the School of Virtue.[66]

As the character who most freely asserts the freedom of a virtuous mind to speak the truth even to kings, he is the mouthpiece for much of the political morality of the play; it has been suggested therefore that he represents Bolingbroke, forced into exile by Walpole's threats in 1735, or Carteret, whose term as Lord Lieutenant of Ireland from 1724 to 1730 might be regarded as a kind of exile.[67] He denounces cowards, flatterers, and traitors, and goes so far as to suggest that the king deserves some touch of blame for putting too much power into the hands of a minister. Agamemnon himself remarks that Melisander

> Is none of those dust-licking, reptile, close,
> Insinuating, speckled, smooth Court-Serpents,
> That make it so unsafe, chiefly for Kings,
> To walk this weedy World.

Another loyal public servant is Arcas, who duly enters his bill of complaint against Egisthus/Walpole, and, when asked by Agamemnon whether there yet remain 'A Faithful Few! to save the sinking State', replies with an unmistakable reference to the 'Boy Patriots' led by Lyttelton and Pitt:

> Yes Sir, I know
> A band of generous Youth, whom native Virtue,
> Unbroken yet by Avarice and Meanness,
> Fits for our purpose.

The strongest expression of Thomson's political wishful thinking, though, is in the king's own denunciation of the wicked minister who has betrayed him:

> That Creature of my Power! That Insect! rais'd
> By the warm Beams of my mistaken Bounty! . . .
> One who ne'er saw the glorious Front of War,
> For nothing famous but corrupting Peace,
> And whose sole Merit was my ill-judg'd Favour.

Thomas Davies reports that there was great applause in the theatre when Agamemnon, played by Quin, declared:

> the most fruitful Source
> Of every Evil—O that I, in Thunder,
> Could sound it o'er the listening Earth to Kings!—
> Is Delegating Power to wicked Hands.[68]

At the time *Agamemnon* went into rehearsal Thomson had some thoughts of keeping the copyright and having the play printed on his own account, as he had done, perhaps not very fortunately, with his *Poem to Talbot*, but in the event he sold the copyright to Millar, who published the play on 25 April, the date of its last performance at Drury Lane. The play soon attracted the attention of satirists. There was a mock prologue by 'Tim Birch the second' in the *Literary Courier of Grub Street* on 27 April. It begins:

> As worth, however raggedly distrest,
> 'Scapes not the notice of a gen'rous breast,
> So from a Greek or Trojan threadbare woe,
> Who will not sigh out AGAMEMNON O!
> The long-speech'd Scenes in heavy sadness move,
> Sublimely drawling out unlawful love.

The attribution of authorship and the exclamation in the fourth line indicate that *Sophonisba* is not forgotten. This mock prologue goes on for another ten couplets, comparing Clytemnestra with a celebrated murderess Catherine Hayes, burned at Tyburn in 1726, Cassandra with the probably mythical prophetess Mother Shipton, Melisander with Robinson Crusoe, and Egisthus with the villainous Francis Chartres. On the following day the *Daily Gazetteer*, a government newspaper, sourly commented:

If the Party, with all their Art and Industry have been able to support a dull Play for half a Dozen Nights together, you immediately see Advertisements in all the News Papers, that on such a Day will be published, such a *Tragedy*, or such a Comedy, as it is now acting with *great Applause*, at the Theatre Royal in *Drury Lane*, with a Prologue, an Epilogue, or an Epistle Dedicatory, or perhaps all three, extolling the wonderful Genius of the Author, and the Extraordinary Merit of the Piece.

The printed text of *Agamemnon* indeed included a Prologue, an Epilogue, and a Dedication to the Princess of Wales, written it has to be said, in quite unpartisan terms.

In May the force of opposition satire was greatly augmented by the publication of Pope's *One Thousand Seven Hundred and Thirty Eight, a Dialogue, Something like Horace*, in which, probably under the influence of Thomson's play, Walpole is referred to as Aegisthus.[69] Thomson was not forgotten either in an anonymous satirical reply to Pope's poem, which was published in August under the confusingly similar title, *A Dialogue on One Thousand Seven Hundred and Thirty-Eight*. This poem, written by a supporter of Walpole's ministry paints a frightening picture of what British Government and culture will be should the opposition come to power:

> Then L——tt–n our Government shall mend,
> On F—ld—g our grave Lawyers shall attend:
> Our poets all, from *Agamemnon* write. (71–3)

It insinuates that Pope's associates in opposition are the heirs of seventeenth-century republicans:

> Not to be Mad, will then be held a Crime:
> Not to blaspheme, be Superstition's Note:
> Not *Harrington's Oceana* to promote,
> A Mark of Leaning to the good Old Cause
> Of Monarchy, Religion, Virtue, Laws. (78–82)

One shot from this blunderbuss discharge was on target: Millar, as we have seen, published Birch's edition of Milton's prose in this year (also extracting *Areopagitica* and the anti-Spanish *Manifesto* for separate publication alongside equally controversial writings by Thomson); in 1737 he had published James Harrington's *Oceana*, the great classic of seventeenth-century republicanism: Thomson possessed fine, large-paper copies of both these editions and procured at least one other copy of *Oceana* for another reader.[70]

The ninth performance of *Agamemnon*, on 25 April, was the last night of the regular Drury Lane season, all remaining nights on which the theatre was in use until September being given over to benefits for the players and theatre staff. In the *Daily Post* that day it was announced, 'The Season being so far advanced, and Benefits intervening, we hear that the Tragedy of Agamemnon, which is to be acted this day for the Benefit of the Author, will be acted no more till next Winter.' In the event, Thomson's play was not revived in the following season, but it appears that there was an expectation in some quarters that it would be, for Aaron Hill went to the trouble of proposing revisions, which he sent to Pope on 8 November, asking him to convey them to Thomson as his own. Hill observed, as others had done, that the play fell off towards the end; he suggested in some detail how the last two acts could be rewritten in order to provide a great deal of stage business, by way of plot, counter-plot, deceit, misunderstanding, violent confrontation, and bloodshed. Pope prudently declined to claim that Hill's comments were his own when he communicated them to Thomson.[71] Thomson's reply is not recorded.

Murdoch says that *Agamemnon* 'yielded a good sum'. In addition to the profits of three benefit nights, Thomson must have received something from Andrew Millar for the copyright. Soon after, Millar confirmed his position as Thomson's sole publisher, for on 16 June he bought all Millan's Thomson copyrights (for £105, the same price that Millan had paid in 1729)[72] and published a collected edition of the poet's works. This collection consists largely of reprints; only *Liberty* contains significant substantive revisions and these come to an end two-thirds of the way through Part Two of the poem, just after the insertion of a series of verbal landscapes rather improbably intended to illustrate the history of ancient Greek painting. At the end of Part One there are some changes to sharpen the political edge; of 'Truth' it is said in 1735 that in Britain 'even Kings themselves | Invite her forth', whereas in 1738 she 'dares accost | Even Kings themselves'. The compliment to the King and Queen in 1735 is deleted in 1738, leaving only the praise of the Prince of Wales (the Queen had died in 1737).[73] Possibly Thomson drafted his changes when he was considering buying back the copyright (see his letter of 11 May 1736 to Hill, quoted in Chapter 6 above) but discontinued his revision when he decided not to buy the copyright after all.

Whatever might have been Thomson's hopes for *Liberty* and his plays, *The Seasons* was becoming the work by which he was best known. By 1738 it had risen or descended to the schoolroom, to judge by *The Art of Rhetoric made Easy*, adapted from Longinus on the sublime, 'with Proper Examples, Ancient and Modern', compiled by a Norfolk grammar-school master, John Holmes, and addressed to 'the learned instructors and studious youth of Great Britain and Ireland'. Half of the second volume of this text book is taken up with long quotations from *The Seasons* (and one from the *Poem to Newton*), all lavishly praised by Holmes; it constitutes the fullest non-satirical analysis of a work by Thomson to be published in his lifetime.[74]

8

Censored: *Edward and Eleonora* and *Alfred*,
1738–1742

THE correspondence of Thomas Birch provides some glimpses of Thomson in
the summer of 1738. On 12 August Edward Cave, publisher of *The Gentleman's
Magazine*, wrote to arrange that he and Birch should visit Claremont together
and then dine at Richmond. Cave asks: 'Had I best send Mr Thompson Word,
that we shall be at such an Inn in Richmond by noon his Hour of Rising?'
Birch's diary confirms that the expedition was duly made on 15 August and
notes that those dining with Thomson included also Elizabeth Carter (the
translator of Epictetus) and Richard Savage.[1]

Possibly Thomson dined with Bolingbroke about this time too, for there is an
undated letter from Pope to Mallet, asking him and Thomson to come to
dinner, adding that they will dine with Bolingbroke. George Sherburn assigns
this letter to the period of Bolingbroke's visits to England in 1743 and 1744
because Pope writes also of being ill and it is known that his health was poor in
both those years, but Pope writes in two letters of July 1738 about his own ill
health and Bolingbroke's imminent visit.[2] Thomson was more deeply involved
in party politics in 1738 than in 1743–4; Bolingbroke had fairly recently
associated himself with the Prince of Wales and was helping in the literary
campaign to which Pope, Thomson, and Mallet were major contributors; he
might well have thought that a meeting with Thomson was politically as well as
socially worthwhile.

Another dinner engagement of which we may be sure is mentioned in a letter
from Savage to Birch on 1 September, arranging a visit to Lord Burlington's
house and gardens at Chiswick; Birch's diary records the visit on 7 September
and lists Savage, Thomson, and Mallet at dinner afterwards. Savage's letter
also contained the unhappy news that the pension he had received from the
Queen during the last six years of her life was being discontinued, despite the
King's original instructions, immediately after Caroline's death in November
1737, that all her benefactions were to be maintained;[3] the tone of the letter
bears out, however, Johnson's claim that Savage bore his misfortunes 'not only
with Decency, but with Cheerfulness'. At the time of the outing to Chiswick it

seems that Savage was lodging with Thomson at Richmond. Johnson, who first made Savage's acquaintance in 1737 or 1738, writes that Savage

was sometimes so far compassionated by those who knew both his Merit and his Distresses, that they received him into their Families, but they soon discovered him to be a very incommodious Inmate; for being always accustomed to an irregular Manner of Life, he could not confine himself to any stated Hours, or pay any Regard to the Rules of a Family, but would prolong his Conversation till Midnight, without considering that Business might require his Friend's Application in the Morning; nor when he had persuaded himself to retire to Bed, was he, without Difficulty, called up to Dinner; it was therefore impossible to pay him any Distinction without the entire Subversion of all Oeconomy.[4]

Thomson's lack of a family and dislike of regular hours, together with his love of food, drink, and wit, doubtless made Savage's visits less disruptive than they would have been in the kind of household Johnson describes.

By now both Thomson and Mallet were at work on new tragedies, references to which may be found in the correspondence of Pope and Aaron Hill. From June 1738 onwards Hill had been trying to persuade Pope and Bolingbroke to use their influence to bring on to the stage his new tragedy about the death of Julius Caesar. Hill was in some financial difficulty and had retired to the country; after the middling success of two of his plays on the stage in 1736 his career as a dramatist seemed to be running into the sands. On 29 September Pope courteously refused his request for an epilogue to the new tragedy by appealing to 'an invariable Maxim, which I have held these Twenty Years', not to write such pieces for any of his friends. He added: 'this very Winter, Mr *Thomson* and Mr *Mallet* excuse me, whose Tragedies either are to appear this Season, or the next. I fansy the latter, as I have seen or heard of no more but a *first* Act, yet, of each.' Replying on 4 October, Hill modestly intimated that he would allow the work of those 'two valuable men' to have precedence over his, but asked for further information as to where or when their tragedies would be performed.[5]

It seems that Thomson was not in Richmond at this time, so Pope was unable to discover first-hand what progress had been made. He wrote to Hill on 5 November:

It is near a Month ago that I try'd to see Mr *Thomson*, to know the Time of his Tragedy: He was not within my Reach; and therefore at last I wrote to him, and also to Mr *M———*, to let them both know the Deference you paid them, and the heroic (I will not call it less) Disinterestedness you express'd in regard to them. I have not yet been able to hear where they are, or any way to have an Answer further, than I have learn'd it will be impossible for either of them to bring on their Plays early (a Friend of theirs telling me they are in no Forwardness) till the Middle or End of the Winter; therefore you may have room.

Hill thereupon sent his *Caesar* to Fleetwood, the Drury Lane manager, asking that it should be acted about the beginning of January. Pope's next progress-report to Hill, on 8 December, was that he had 'been confirmed by Mr *Thomson* as to the Retardment of his play, of which he has written but two Acts', that Mallet's play was completed, and that Mallet was 'very willing yours should be first brought on, in *January* as you propose, or after his in *February*, whichsoever may be most agreeable to you'. Hill had still not received from Fleetwood a firm undertaking to stage *Caesar*, so he asked Pope and Mallet to make enquiries on his behalf. As Hill himself disarmingly observed, 'There is a reluctance (I am afraid, it is a *pride*) in my nature, against soliciting any thing, that regards my own interest:— and especially, from the dull and unworthy.' Fleetwood's delay is understandable in view of the fact that there were three other new tragedies under his consideration or known to be in the offing: Mallet's, Thomson's, and one by Henry Brooke. All three were opposition pieces in which the Prince of Wales was taking an interest; it was he who made up Fleetwood's mind for him. There is an undated letter from Lyttelton to Mallet, probably written in December, saying that the Prince had ordered Fleetwood to have Mallet's *Mustapha* acted first, 'to which he agreed with great seeming Readiness, upon my telling him Mr Tomson's Play wou'd not come on this Year'. [6] At this time Lyttelton was trying to draw Pope into the prince's counsels and Pope was willing to be drawn, but it is not known whether Pope was consulted by the Prince in the matter of these opposition plays.

One may easily see why the Prince preferred Mallet's tragedy. It is set at the court of the Turkish emperor Solyman the Magnificent: Solyman's empress and his wicked vizier conspire to alienate Solyman from his virtuous, patriotic son Mustapha, who is at last executed on a false charge of disloyalty to his father. The political application of speeches denouncing an evil chief minister was unmistakeable. The play opened at Drury Lane on 13 February. Thomas Davies reports a, by now, not unfamiliar scene: 'On the first night of its exhibition were assembled all the chiefs in opposition to the court; and many speeches were applied by the audience to the supposed grievances of the times and to persons and characters.'[7] Pope attended the first night and went behind the scenes, 'a place he had not visited for some years', in order to compliment Quin. The play enjoyed a creditable run of fourteen nights, two of them by command of the Prince and Princess of Wales, though the last two perform-ances, on Thursday and Saturday, 1 and 3 March, were eked out by the addition of afterpieces. There was additional drama offstage too, for, on the Friday between, Quin and Theophilus Cibber quarrelled in the Bedford Coffee-House and fought a duel in the Piazza of Covent Garden. The wounds of both men were slight, so that Quin was able to play Solyman in *Mustapha* on the Saturday and both Falstaff and Lear in the week following.[8]

Thomson wrote the fairly uncontentious prologue to Mallet's tragedy; he alludes to the play's political theme of the monarch 'To the false herd of flattering slaves confin'd', but his main concern is with the psychological effect of tragedy; the tragic muse should be a 'Queen of soft sorrows, and of useful fears', for

> Faint is the lesson reason'd rules impart:
> *She* pours it strong and instant thro' the heart.[9]

Ideally, the effect upon the audience is to make the good man better and the bad man repentant; this is an eighteenth-century man of feeling's restatement of Aristotelian pity, terror, and catharsis.

The new tragedy chosen to succeed *Mustapha* at Drury Lane was not Thomson's or Hill's but Henry Brooke's *Gustavus Vasa*, which was put into rehearsal during the run of Mallet's play. Writing to Pope on 26 January, Hill bade 'a hearty farewell to the *stage*', but to Fleetwood a few weeks later he protested that, if during the run of *Gustavus*, 'you do not order mine into rehearsal, it is plain, that you treat it with a contempt, which it will hardly be found to deserve: and in that case, I shall only desire you to redeliver the copy to the bearer'.[10] However, Hill's play was not put into rehearsal and though Brooke's was rehearsed it did not run. On 16 March the acting of *Gustavus Vasa* was forbidden by the Lord Chamberlain: it was thus the first play to be banned under the provisions of the 1737 Licensing Act. Lady Hertford remarked that 'there does not appear to me to be half so much in it liable to objection, as in Mustapha', and Benjamin Victor claimed that both *Mustapha* and *Agamemnon* contained more exceptionable passages: 'party clap-traps *designedly introduced*'.[11] However, Brooke's villain Trollio, vice-regent of the usurping King of Sweden, is plainly meant to represent Walpole; moreover, inasmuch as Trollio's master is a foreign usurper, eventually ejected by Gustavus, 'the Deliverer of his Country' and the man who has the better hereditary right to the crown, the play, whatever Brooke's intention, might be charged with Jacobitism. Brooke complained of harsh treatment, but he earned a very large sum from sales of both trade and subscription editions of the printed text. This text reveals that during rehearsals Gustavus was played by Quin and Trollio by his real-life antagonist Theophilus Cibber.

While *Mustapha* was still in rehearsal Thomson had tired of Fleetwood's delays and taken his play to John Rich, the manager of Covent Garden. On 14 February Pope wrote to Hill that

Mr *Thomson*, after many shameful Tricks from the Manager, is determined to act his Play at the other Theatre, where the Advantage lies as to the Women, and the Success of *his* will depend upon them (I heartily wish you would follow his Example, that we might not be deprived of *Caesar*). I have yet seen but three Acts of Mr *Thomson's*, but I am told, and believe by what I have seen, that it excels in the Pathetic.

When Hill replied on 21 February he agreed that if Thomson's play 'is to depend on his women performers, he has certainly judg'd well, in his choice' of Covent Garden.[12] Though it is true that Drury Lane's company of actresses was at that time depleted by the absence of Susannah Cibber, who made no stage appearances in the 1738–9 season, there was hardly as much difference between the two companies as Hill suggests, so perhaps his comment is flavoured with sour grapes on account of Fleetwood's treatment of *Caesar*.

Thomson had provided two parts for women in his new play, *Edward and Eleonora*. The role of the heroine Eleonora was assigned to Christiana Horton, best known for playing fine ladies in comedy but a celebrated performer of Shakespeare's Cordelia and the title role in *Jane Shore*. The other female role, the Arabian princess Daraxa, was given to Anne Hallam, a famous player of Lady Macbeth. The part of the hero, Edward, Prince of Wales (later Edward I), was given to Dennis Delane, who 'excelled more in the well-bred men',[13] such as Bevil in Steele's *Conscious Lovers*, than in heroic parts. Edward's is the lion's part; he speaks three times as many lines and appears in twice as many scenes as Eleonora, but she is the emotional centre of the play. As in *Sophonisba*, Thomson builds his action round a woman. There are only three other named characters and the play is Thomson's shortest to date, being only 1,500 lines long, three-quarters the length of *Sophonisba*.

The action of *Edward and Eleonora* is based upon an apocryphal story of the last crusade, telling how Prince Edward, at the siege of Jaffa in 1272, was stabbed with a poisoned dagger and how his wife Eleonora sucked the poison from his wound. The play's unserious epilogue (by an unidentified 'Friend') reveals that Thomson's source was Sir Richard Baker's *Chronicle of the Kings of England*, first printed in 1643. Not highly regarded by scholars, it was the favourite reading of Sir Roger de Coverley (*Spectator*, numbers 269 and 329) and was part of the furniture of Squire Booby's country house in *Joseph Andrews*. Thomson completes Baker's story by an episode of his own invention in which Eleonora becomes mortally ill by the poison she has sucked and is cured by a dervish who proves to be Selim, the Sultan of Jaffa and lover of Daraxa, in disguise. Thomson's creation of Selim seems to be modelled upon the humane, tolerant Saladin, the antagonist of Edward's great-uncle Richard I and later the true hero of Scott's *The Talisman*.

In dramatizing a crusading story with an even balance between Christian and Moslem Thomson was following the example of Voltaire's *Zaïre* (Hill's *Zara*); his choice of an oriental setting and a subject from post-classical history is paralleled too in Mallet's *Mustapha*, but his particular choice of hero enables him to add Gothic overtones, particularly when the English national character and love of liberty are under discussion. Curiously enough, Thomson's novel subject is mentioned in a letter written by the Countess of Pomfret in France in February, replying to the Countess of Hertford's news of Brooke's *Gustavus Vasa*. Lady Pomfret praises Brooke for choosing a subject from modern history, and observes:

the world has been so changed by the extirpation of the pagan theology, and the introduction of the Gothic government (from which all the modern nations derive theirs), that we are rendered almost another species; and doubtless the customs, actions, and fortunes, that most resemble our own, must be the most interesting to us. On this account it is that I have often wondered why so many of our English heroes should lie forgotten . . . What instance of conjugal love can exceed that of Edward the First and his queen?[14]

Despite his Gothic material though, Thomson strives as usual for Grecian simplicity—not inappropriately, inasmuch as his theme of a woman sacrificing her life for her husband and then herself being recalled to life is the story of the *Alcestis* of Euripides.

As Pope said, Thomson's play excels in the pathetic. Eleonora's lamentations over the dying Edward in the first half are complemented by Edward's over Eleonora in the second half; the prologue (written, like the epilogue, by an unidentified 'Friend') unashamedly calls upon the audience to weep:

> If these best Passions prompt the pleasing Woe,
> Indulge it freely—Nature bids it flow:
> Where Parent Nature leads, you cannot stray;
> And what she wills, 'tis Virtue to obey.[15]

This is Thomson's most sentimental play, perhaps closer in feeling to Steele's *Conscious Lovers* than to any heroic tragedy. Apart from the fanatical assassin who stabs Edward and speaks only six lines, there is no wicked character.

Selim is the very type of virtuous pagan: he restores Eleonora to life; he teaches lessons of humanity, reason, and religious toleration to the Christians, when, for instance, he refutes the charge of bigotry levelled against his co-religionists and mildly condemns the cruelty of the crusaders as compared with the compassion of Saladin.[16] The last words of the play are Selim's:

> Then let us in this righteous Mean agree:
> Let holy Rage, let Persecution cease;
> Let the Head argue, but the Heart be Peace;
> Let all Mankind in Love of what is right,
> In Virtue and Humanity unite.

The English, with the possible exception of the Archdeacon, are predisposed to accept Selim's lesson. The Earl of Gloster has the religious outlook of an enlightened deist: his God, rather like that of the *Seasons*,

> > pervades, sustains,
> Surrounds and fills this universal Frame;
> And every Land where spreads his vital Presence,
> His all-enlivening Breath, to me is holy.

Eleonora, echoing lines once intended for the opening of *Liberty*, proclaims 'Eternal Goodness reigns' and declares that humanity is 'the Soul of all Religion'.[17]

Thomson's play was put into rehearsal before the end of February. During rehearsals appeared a hastily-prepared anonymous pamphlet, *The History of the Life and Reign of the valiant Prince Edward ... on which ... is founded a Play, written by Mr Thomson ...* This catchpenny work concludes with a puff for the play, which, 'if good Judges may be depended upon, shews his noble Genius in Poetry, his Energy of Stile, his exuberant Fancy, and his noble Sentiments; ... his dramatic Management of this Story, will be equal to any thing exhibited on the Theatre: But I am only saying 'tis broad Day at Noon!'. We cannot tell whether the author of this pamphlet was a simple opportunist working for himself or a puffer in the employ of John Rich, but it would seem that Thomson's name was worth a penny or two in Grub Street.

A transcript of *Edward and Eleonora* was sent to the Stage Licenser on 23 February; rehearsals of the play went on and its opening was announced for 29 March, but on that day several newspapers carried the announcement that on 27 March Thomson had

receiv'd to his great Surprize, a Message from the Lord Chamberlain, absolutely forbidding the acting of the said Play. No Objection having been made to the Whole or any Part of it, we must conclude it was consider'd as *immoral* or *seditious*. If the Author is conscious of not having writ with any such Intention, it is hoped that, for his own Justification, he will print this Play, and so *submit* it to the *Judgment* of his *Country*.[18]

The timing of the ban, over a month after the manuscript was submitted to the Licenser and on the very eve of performance, after actors and management had invested considerable time and money, was doubtless intended to be admonitory and vindictive. It was an exact repeat of the treatment of *Gustavus Vasa* at Drury Lane a fortnight earlier.

Both Shiels and Johnson aver that they were unable to find out why the play was banned; Murdoch too regarded the ban as unreasonable:

The reader may see that this play contains not a line which could justly give offence; but the ministry, still sore from certain pasquinades, which had lately produced the stage-act; and as little satisfied with some parts of the prince's political conduct, as he was with their management of the public affairs; would not risque the representation of a piece written under his eye, and, they might probably think, by his command.[19]

The only marks on the censored manuscript which show passages the Licenser disliked are in Act IV, Scene ii, where Archdeacon Theald assures us that he obtained his clerical preferment 'Without the base Cabal too often practis'd', and in IV. viii, where Edward denounces his father's ministers:

> Is there a Curse on human Kind so fell,
> So pestilent, at once, to Prince and People,
> As the base servile Vermin of a Court,
> Corrupt, corrupting Ministers and Favourites?
> How oft have such eat up the Widow's Morsel,
> The Peasant's Toil, the Merchant's far-sought Gain,
> And wanton'd in the Ruin of a Nation!

These passages are hardly innocent. Neither are the speeches (unmarked by the censor) in the very first scene, where Gloster complains about the state of England:

> Exhausted, sunk; drain'd by ten thousand Arts
> Of ministerial Rapine . . .
> Who knows what evil Counsellors, again,
> Are gather'd round the Throne.

Gloster begs the Prince to return home to save his father from such ministers, for

> Has not the Royal Heir a juster Claim
> To share his Father's inmost Heart and Counsels,
> Than Aliens to his Int'rest, those, who make
> A Property, a Market of his Honour?

(This was written when George II had absolutely forbidden the Prince of Wales to come into his presence.) Gloster's appeal becomes more vehement in the second act, in a speech of over fifty lines which reads in part:

> O save our Country . . .
> Behold it ready to be lost for ever.
> Behold us almost broken to the Yoke,
> Robb'd of our antient Spirit, sunk in Baseness,
> At home corrupted, and despis'd abroad.
> Behold our Wealth consum'd, those Treasures squander'd,
> That might protect and nourish wholesom Peace,
> Or urge a glorious War; on Wretches squander'd,
> A venal Crew that plunder and disgrace us.[20]

Such material was not only provocative; it was so unnecessary to the main plot as even to lend colour to the assertion in the *Gentleman's and London Magazine* (Dublin) for June 1762 that Thomson had deliberately inserted three long speeches after he had finished his play, 'in order to induce the Licenser to prohibit its representation: hoping thereby to render the new Stage-Act, and the Ministry that had procured it, more unpopular'.[21]

It is likely that printing arrangements were in hand before the ban on performance, but the Licenser's decision gave an opportunity to publicize the printed edition; so, following Brooke's example with *Gustavus Vasa*, Thomson issued proposals for a subscription edition 'on a superfine Royal Paper' at five shillings. This was published on 24 May, followed by a larger trade edition (at one shilling and sixpence a copy) published on the following day. Altogether 4,500 copies were printed, a large number and about the same as for *Agamemnon*,[22] but a far higher proportion was on fine paper at five shillings a copy and all were printed for the author, so it is certain that Thomson's profit was higher than for *Agamemnon*.

Edward and Eleonora was dedicated, like *Agamemnon*, to the Princess of Wales, but in this case Thomson took the opportunity in the dedication to draw a parallel between his patrons and the subject of his play:

In the character of ELEONORA I have endeavoured to represent, however faintly, a PRINCESS distinguish'd for all the Virtues that render Greatness amiable. I have aimed, particularly, to do justice to her inviolable Affection and generous Tenderness for a PRINCE, who was the Darling of a great and free People.

Thomson also added to the printed edition a brief 'Advertisement': 'The Representation of this Tragedy, on the Stage, was prohibited in the Year One Thousand Seven Hundred and Thirty-Nine.' The lettering of this date is in Gothic type, to remind readers of ancient Gothic liberties now at risk through the Licensing Act.

Weeks before its publication, *Edward and Eleonora* was under fire in the government press. On 12 April, the day Thomson's subscription proposals were published, the *Daily Gazetteer* printed an attack on Brooke, followed by one on Thomson:

I am sorry in this Place to have Occasion to mention, in a Light little superior to the above Writer, a Gentleman of whom I conceived, on the Publication of his first Poem, a very favourable Idea; and though in *Sophonisba* he greatly erred, it was generally receiv'd as a *tolerable first Attempt*, and the Reception given the *heavy Scenes of Agamemnon* was not thought so bad as to make this Author so entirely despair of his Dramatick Genius, as to prostitute the *Tragick Muse* to the mean Hope of *feeding upon the Depravity* of his Co-temporaries; which attempt is but a melancholy Instance of the Advantages arising from our full Enjoyment of LIBERTY, and what can bring no Benefit to BRITANNIA in any SEASON whatever.

This was remembered by Johnson forty years later in his *Life* of the poet: 'When the publick murmured at the unkind treatment of Thomson, one of the ministerial writers remarked, that "he had taken a *Liberty* which was not agreeable to *Britannia* in any *Season*."'[23] The *Gazetteer* continued its campaign against Brooke and Thomson on 26 April:

I cannot help thinking, that *these two exasperated Bards* must be conscious of their own Deficiency in point of *Poetick Merit*, before they could resolve upon *relying wholly* on the Encouragement they hoped from offering themselves to the Town only as *Party-Writers*; a Light in which even a *good Poet* will be always sure to lose more in his *Character*, than can be made up in his *Purse*.

When *Gustavus Vasa* was published, the *Gazetteer* attacked it again in three essays on 15, 21, and 24 May; then, on 2 June, the newly-published *Edward and Eleonora* received a hostile review, which also damned Thomson's two earlier plays. The reviewer also drew attention to deistical notions in the new play, observing that Thomson puts

into the Mouths of all his Characters, *Christian and Mohometan*, the favourite Phrases that have been invented within these very *few Years*, to avoid the Expressions of *Jehovah, Lord, God, or Jesus*, which savour too strongly of *old Religion*, and too much countenance the Doctrine of *Revelation*, to be used by the Professors of the *new Divinity*, the Friends of the *Essay upon Man*, or the *devout Repeaters* of the *Philosophick Prayer*.

(The 'Philosopher's Prayer' was by the notorious free-thinker Matthew Tindal.) John Henley, 'Orator Henley', also tilted against *Edward and Eleonora* in his absurd weekly broadsheet *The Hyp-Doctor* on 5 June. He declares that the Lord Chamberlain can 'make a *better Tragedy*, than all the *Gustavus's* and *the Eleonora's* put together' because nothing is more distressing than '*Poets*, weeping to see their Heroes *sink* before they *rise* on the Stage'. Henley refers repeatedly to the five-shilling price of the play, claims that it is written in the style of *George Barnwell*, and falls into a kind of free verse as he dwells on the disloyalty of Scotsmen:

> I should be apt to suspect that Mr. *T——n* was a Scot,
> For the *Scots* killed most of their Kings:
> And Captain Porteus was a pretty Fellow in his Time.

Naturally enough, the efforts of the *Gazetteer* and, still less, the *Hyp-Doctor* failed to check the two plays' sales, inflated as they were by the mere fact of the Lord Chamberlain's ban. Thomas Edwards, a critic, observed in a letter of 8 June: 'Such a prohibition alone, as the people are now inclined, is enough to raise their curiosity and pique them into a subscription; and accordingly both these authors have met with very great encouragement'; but the subscribers 'are ashamed of their patronage. I cannot tell how far party prejudice may carry an audience, but I think nothing else could have saved these pieces.'[24] That this was the common opinion of *Edward and Eleonora* is confirmed by Lady Hertford, though she did not share it. On 14 June she wrote to Lady Pomfret: 'I have read Mr Thomson's Edward and Eleonora. I hear, it is the fashion to decry it extremely; but, I own, I am ungenteel enough to prefer it infinitely to Agamemnon.'[25] One can well understand how the more sentimental play would appeal to the soft-hearted Countess. It appealed to John Wesley too, for he wrote of it in his *Journal* on 14 October 1772: 'The sentiments are just and noble, the diction strong, smooth and elegant, and the plot conducted with the utmost art and wrought off in a most surprizing manner. It is quite his masterpiece, and I really think might vie with any modern performance of the kind.'[26] The first stage performance of *Edward and Eleonora* was not until about this time, when an adaptation by Thomas Hull with a sparkling epilogue by Richard Brinsley Sheridan was acted eight times at Covent Garden in 1775–6; there were later performances, including a revival in 1796 with John Philip Kemble and Sarah Siddons in the title roles.

While *Edward and Eleonora* was being printed for subscribers another sub-scription which perhaps involved Thomson was in hand, for Pope was collec-ting money to enable their friend Richard Savage to settle in Wales, where it was hoped he would be able to live prudently and economically, far from his many creditors. The sum required was fifty pounds a year; Pope and Moses Mendez subscribed ten pounds each; Mallet subscribed a smaller amount and it is thought that Thomson was a subscriber also.[27] Savage set off from London in July 1739; by December he had gone no further than Bristol, but he was settled in Swansea at some time in 1741 where, full of resentment against Pope and his other benefactors, he completed his tragedy of *Sir Thomas Overbury*. In 1742 he moved back to Bristol, intending to come to London, despite the danger from his creditors there, in order to arrange for the staging of his play. He was advised by Pope, however, to remain where he was and put his tragedy into the hands of Thomson and Mallet, 'that it might be fitted for the stage, and to allow his friends to receive the profits, out of which an annual pension should be paid him'.[28] Not surprisingly, Savage rejected this advice with contempt. He raised more money from his long-suffering friends, but spent it in the taverns of Bristol; he was arrested for debt there on 10 January 1743 and died in prison on 1 August that year. Thomson's reaction to the death of one of his earliest English literary friends is not known, but the news of it would have reached him when, under the influence of love, he had suddenly been inspired with 'determined good Purposes' to cultivate 'Regularity and Temperance', and had 'resolved upon a more attentive and regular' practice of virtue.[29] Irregularity and imprudence were characteristic faults of Thomson which the life of Savage had displayed in an extreme form; news of Savage's death could have reinforced, at least for a while, Thomson's resolution to amend his own life.

While Savage was on his slow way to exile in the West, Thomson was using the profits from *Edward and Eleonora* to move in 1739 to a larger house, further down the lane from his cottage and next to Richmond Gardens. The new house contained seven rooms on three floors and a kitchen and other offices: it stood on a plot 'by Estimation in front thirty two feet from North to South and one hundred and five feet in depth from East to West abutting West on Kew Lane'; the catalogue of Thomson's effects, sold by auction after his death, indicates that the house was quite roomy and that the poet enjoyed material comfort there. As we have seen, he had a housekeeper named Mrs Hobart; he had a manservant named David; his garden was tended by a young kinsman Andrew Thomson; another young kinsman Gilbert Thomson is mentioned as a dependant, but there is some doubt as to their exact relationship to the poet.[30]

After Thomson's death the house was bought by his friend George Ross, who incorporated some of its rooms into a much grander mansion called Rosedale, which he built on the site. By the end of the eighteenth century, when it was in the hands of the widow of Admiral Boscawen, it had become a place of literary pilgrimage; she made the garden-alcove where Thomson used to write into a sort of shrine, adorned with votive inscriptions. The alcove was mentioned in the reminiscences of Taylor the barber as a place where Thomson 'used to write in summer time. I have known him lie along by himself upon the grass near it, and talk away as though three or four people were along with him.'[31] In the 1860s Rosedale was incorporated into the buildings of Richmond Royal Hospital.[32]

The opposition in Parliament and press continued throughout 1739 to denounce Walpole and call for revenge against Spanish depredations. Thanks to the Licensing Act the public theatre was less outspoken, but in September and October there was a successful revival at Drury Lane of George Sewell's virulently anti-Spanish play *Sir Walter Raleigh*, with Quin playing the part of the hero as he had done in the first production twenty years earlier. The Earl of Egmont wrote of the 1739 revival:

They choose one to represent Count Gundemar the villain, who in all things is like Mr Giraldini, the Spanish minister at our Court lately recalled, and whenever any severe things were said which bore a resemblance to our ministry's transactions, or our backwardness to resent the insults of Spain, the audience clapped all over the house.[33]

The performance on 29 September was by command of the Prince and Princess of Wales.

At last, on the King's insistence against Walpole's advice, war was declared against Spain on 19 October. Patriotic songs were sung in the London theatres; the country was soon cheered by Admiral Vernon's capture in December of the West Indies stronghold of Porto Bello, 'with six ships' as innumerable commemorative medals proclaimed; but Walpole's inability or unwillingness to prosecute the war vigorously ensured that the opposition remained vociferous. Throughout the winter and spring Henry Fielding and James Ralph's new journal *The Champion* whipped up anti-Spanish and anti-ministerial feeling. For instance, it listed the English squadrons and regiments which were doing nothing, or listed names of merchant ships taken by the Spanish and added 'Taken by the English: NONE'.

In January 1740 the Stage Licenser issued his third ban; this was against *Arminius*, by Thomson's friend William Paterson, a play based on the exploits of the first-century German who fought against the Romans, its hero and villain being thinly-disguised portraits of the Prince of Wales and Walpole. According to Murdoch its banning arose from the banning of Thomson's play, because Paterson had acted as Thomson's amanuensis for the copy of *Edward and Eleonora* submitted to the Licenser, so that *Arminius*, 'guiltless as it was, being presented for a licence, no sooner had the *censor* cast his eyes on the handwriting in which he had seen *Edward and Eleonora*, than he cried out, Away with it!'. However, as the Licenser kept the manuscript of *Arminius* for at least three weeks and as the play contained controversial material, Murdoch's story is unlikely.[34]

It was in this climate that Thomson and Mallet jointly wrote *Alfred, a Masque*, which was rehearsed at Drury Lane on 28 July 1740 and first performed on 1 August by command of the Prince of Wales at Cliveden House, the Prince's country retreat on the Thames near Maidenhead. This performance was part of an entertainment to commemorate the anniversary of the accession of George I and the third birthday of the Prince's daughter Augusta. An account in the *London Daily Post and General Advertiser* on 5 August reads as follows:

On Friday last was perform'd at Cliefden (by Comedians from both Theatres) before their Royal Highnesses the Prince and Princess of Wales, and a great Number of Nobility, and others, a Dramatic Masque call'd *Alfred*, written by Mr Thomson; in which was introduc'd Variety of Dancing, very much to the Satisfaction of their Royal Highnesses, and the rest of the Spectators, especially the Performance of Signora Barbarini (lately arriv'd from Paris) whose Grace, Beauty, and suprising Agility, exceeded their Expectations. Also was perform'd a Musical Masque call'd *The Contending Deities* . . . and the humorous Pantomimical Scene of The Skeleton taken from the Entertainment of Merlin's Cave, by Mr Rich and Mr Lalauze. The whole was exhibited upon a Theatre in the Garden compos'd of Vegetables, and decorated with Festoons of Flowers, at the End of which was erected a Pavilion for their Royal

Highnesses the Prince and Princess of Wales, Prince George, and Princess Augusta. The whole concluded with Fireworks made by Dr Desaguliers, which were equal in their kind to the rest of the Performance. Their Royal Highnesses were so well pleas'd with the whole Entertainment, that they commanded the same to be perform'd on Saturday last, with the Addition of some favourite Pantomime Scenes from Mr Rich's Entertainments, which was accordingly began, but the Rain falling very heavy, oblig'd them to break off before it was half over; upon which his Royal Highness commanded them to finish the Masque of *Alfred* in the House.

The Contending Deities is better known as *The Judgement of Paris*, with words by Congreve. The music for both Cliveden masques was by Drury Lane's resident composer Thomas Augustine Arne, whose setting of *Comus*, adapted from Milton by John Dalton, with Quin in the title role, had enjoyed a continuous success since its first production in March 1738. *Comus* provided a model for the form and some of the features of *Alfred*,[35] though the woodland scene and twilight atmosphere of Thomson and Mallet's masque was dictated as much by the setting of its first performance as by any literary model.

We do not know exactly how *Alfred* was divided between its two authors. The earliest newspaper reports of the first performance attribute the words solely to Thomson, but the advertisement to the revised version of the work that was published over Mallet's sole name in 1751 suggests that he contributed the larger share of the 1740 text also. There is general early agreement, at least, that Thomson's contribution included the ode 'Rule Britannia'; it is assigned to him, for instance, in *The Charmer*, volume I (1752), a collection of songs in which all the other attributions to Thomson are accurate.

The printed text of *Alfred* tells us that 'The Scene represents a plain, surrounded with woods. On one side, a cottage: on the other, flocks and herds in distant prospect. A Hermit's cave in full view, overhung with trees, wild and grotesque.' The action is slight. Alfred has been defeated by the Danes and is now hiding, diguised, in the Isle of Athelney, sheltered by the poor, honest shepherd Corin and his wife Emma, who sings of the pastoral delights of peace. Alfred is encouraged by the songs of unseen heavenly spirits, by patriotic and moral advice from the Hermit, and by the love of his queen Eltruda, who bravely comes with their young children to join her husband. The climax of the masque is the Hermit's presentation of a vision of future national glories in which the Genius of England summons up the spirits of Edward III and his queen, Queen Elizabeth, and William III. Meanwhile, offstage, the Earl of Devon has won a great victory and captured the Danes' raven banner. He enters with his soldiers; Alfred's true identity is revealed to the faithful Corin and Emma; a Bard sings 'Rule Britannia', and the piece ends with the Hermit prophesying the rise of Britain's maritime empire.

Most of the principal players came from Drury Lane; the title role was taken by Milward (who played Egisthus in *Agamemnon*), the Earl of Devon by Mills (Syphax in *Sophonisba*), the substantial part of the Hermit by Quin, whose manner was well suited for grand prophetic declamation, and Emma by the famous Kitty Clive. From Covent Garden came Thomas Salway, who played Corin, and Christiana Horton, cast as Eleonora in the previous year and now playing a similar role as Eltruda. Her offstage song was performed by Mrs Arne the composer's wife; the heavenly spirits' duet was sung by Mrs Arne's young sisters and the Genius of England's song was sung by the celebrated Handelian operatic bass Thomas Reinhold; Kitty Clive herself sang the songs assigned to Emma. That information is not in the earliest newspaper announcements, but in a list of songs and singers in the *Daily Advertiser* for 6 August, which concludes: 'after which, a new Ode in Honour of Great Britain, was sung by Mr Salway'. This is the first printed reference to 'Rule Britannia'. Evidently Salway doubled as the Bard, for he was a noted tenor, already known as a singer of patriotic songs. Covent Garden playbills in October and November 1739, during the first weeks of the Spanish war, advertise his singing of 'Britons strike home', 'The Genius of England', and 'To Arms'.

It may be assumed that Mallet and Thomson were in attendance. Possibly this was the occasion of an event which diverted William Shenstone when he was travelling up to London with a tailor of Halesowen whom he employed to carry his portmanteau. They slept at Maidenhead, and the tailor

having walked out to view the Thames, returned staring with astonishment, 'Lord, Sir, what do you think? I have seen the Prince of Wales and all his *nobles* walking by the river's side.' The case was, as his Royal Highness then resided at Clifden, he had walked down to the Thames, it being a fine evening: but the *nobles* that attended him, were only Mallet and Thomson the poets, whom his Highness patronized, and with whom he condescended to converse with great freedom and familiarity.[36]

Most of the actors, apparently, did not approach the Prince so closely. Years later, Thomas Davies wrote: 'the accomodations for the company, I was told, were but scanty, and ill managed; and the players were not treated as persons ought to be who are employed by a prince. Quin, I believe, was admitted amongst those of the higher order; and Mrs Clive might be safely trusted to take care of herself any where.'[37]

Davies also notes that *Alfred* was 'written under the influence of, and by the encouragement, of Lord Bolingbroke, nor do the political maxims insisted upon it differ from those laid down in his idea of the Patriot King'.[38] Bolingbroke was the guest of Pope at various times between July 1738 and April 1739, when he was paying court to the Prince of Wales and writing *The Idea of a Patriot King*, and I have conjectured that Mallet and Thomson dined with him at Pope's table; they could perhaps have seen the *Patriot King* text itself, as Bolingbroke left his manuscript with Pope in April 1739, giving him authority to print a few copies for friends.

Like the other Gothic heroes of the three banned plays, Gustavus Vasa, Prince Edward, and Arminius, Alfred is a royal patriot who is clearly identifiable with the Prince of Wales; but in Alfred's case the identification was made before the play, because in 1735 the Prince had erected in the garden of his London house a statue of Alfred by Rysbrack, with an inscription hailing him as the founder of British constitutional liberty. Heavenly spirits call upon the hero of Thomson and Mallet's masque to

> Arise! and save a sinking land!
> Thy country calls, and heaven inspires;

Alfred duly swears

> to build on an eternal base,
> On liberty and laws, the public weal,

'to humble proud oppressors', and be a father to his people.[39] Alfred on Athelney is, like Frederick, a prince whose power lies in the future. When the Hermit offers advice to Alfred there is, as it were, a dramatization of Lyttelton's wish that Pope and other opposition poets should animate Frederick to virtue; and when the Hermit summons up historic visions he could almost be the poet of *Liberty* addressing his poem to Frederick. Here is an idealized version of what the tailor of Halesowen saw: patriotic poets standing beside a patriot prince.

Patriotism, as so often, implied defiance of some foreign enemy, so the Danes in *Alfred* are equated with modern Spaniards, 'those inhuman pirates', who 'violate the sanctity of leagues'. The Hermit prophesies that Queen Elizabeth

> shall rouse *Britannia*'s naval soul,
> Shall greatly ravish from insulting *Spain*,
> The world-commanding scepter of the deep,[40]

and so sets the context for 'Rule Britannia', the climax of the masque.

Alfred has a political edge hardly less sharp than *Edward and Eleonora*; it has a similar patriotism, but it resembles the earlier play also in its sentimental and domestic tone. Alfred, like Edward, is a tender husband; the scenes between him and Eltruda are a celebration of the moral power of married love:

> There is in love a power,
> There is a soft divinity, that draws
> Even transport from distress; that gives the heart

A certain pang, excelling far the joys
Of gross unfeeling life.[41]

As usual in these years though, the politics aroused most comment. An opposition writer signing himself 'Philomathes' declared in the *London Magazine* for August 1740 that the Prince of Wales's patronage of a masque celebrating the great king to whom we owed our spirit of liberty was a sort of pledge 'that he will endeavour to build the publick Weal on *Liberty and Laws*'. In September 1740 Fielding's *The Champion* included Thomson with Pope, Swift, Young, and Gay as leading poets against Walpole.[42] However, Lady Hertford disliked *Alfred* partly on account of its politics. She wrote in a letter of 10 September:

The clown and his wife are made to speak the dialect of a hero and heroine in a court. The whole conduct of the piece is incorrect. There are two or three fine speeches, several party hints, and one invidious reflection—which did not need the pains that have been taken (by presenting it in a different character) to make it absolutely unpardonable.

It has been suggested that the 'invidious reflection' is praise of Edward III's paternal love of the Black Prince, implicitly contrasted with George II's hatred of his eldest son. The comment on a different character 'would then refer to the italicizing of the words *jealousy* and *filial excellence . . .* and may serve to illustrate how closely contemporary readers looked for political innuendo'.[43] Obviously, Lady Hertford was basing her views on the printed text, which was published by Millar on 19 August.

Their political stage campaign of 1738–40 brought Thomson and Mallet close to the Prince of Wales and also made them acquainted with another poet of the Prince's circle, James Hammond. It was Hammond who, as the Prince's equerry, acted as go-between when Frederick was encouraging the two authors of *Alfred* to bring their masque, suitably enlarged for public performance, on to the London stage in the 1740–1 season.[44] The manuscript sent to Charles Fleetwood, manager of Drury Lane, and submitted by him to the Stage Licenser on 9 February 1741 contains an extra act, inserted between revised versions of the two acts of the 1740 printed text.[45] Even so, Aaron Hill thought the work still lacked action, so he wrote to Mallet on 8 and 23 December, complaining to that effect and offering a lengthy account of all the action he would have included had he been the author. Hill adds, correctly or not, that, as the manuscript is still with the Licenser, his advice comes too late. On 13 June Hill asked Mallet, 'Pray, what became of *Alfred?*—I fear he ran aground upon the *Chamberlain & his Clerks*: or else, it scarce cou'd have been possible we shou'd not, long ago, have heard of his good Voyage.' Mallet then explained, 'Alfred has been long licensed. Why it was not acted last winter, I would tell you without reserve; were it not that I must then descend into some wretched detail of Mr Fleetwood's management.'[46] Fleetwood's deficiencies would come as no surprise to Hill after his transactions with the Drury Lane manager over *Caesar*. Thomson seems to have had little part, perhaps no hand at all, in additions to *Alfred* after 1740. The longest version was published over Mallet's sole name in 1751. Versions with less speech and more songs, described as 'a new Serenata . . . disposed in the Manner of the Oratorios in London' (Dublin, 1744), 'an Opera, alter'd from the Play', 1745, 'a Drama for Music', 1753, and 'an Oratorio', 1754 (these three in London), seem all to have been ventures by Arne, with no new contributions from Mallet or Thomson.[47]

During the early attempts to stage *Alfred* in London, two of Thomson's closest associates, Lyttelton and Pope, set out to celebrate very different ideas of a patriot prince. Lyttelton undertook a huge *History of the Life of Henry the Second*, which was eventually published in 1767–71. It portrays Henry as the greatest English king, not only because he was overlord of England, Scotland, Wales, and much of France, but because he formalized the Gothic system of justice and self-government. On 13 June 1741 Lyttelton told Pope that he wanted his *History* to be 'a Work of some Instruction and Pleasure to my Countrymen, and I hope to the Prince my Master, for whose service I chiefly design it'; then he suggested that Pope could raise out of these 'Gothic Ruins', the old chronicles, 'a new Edifice, that wou'd be fitt to Enshrine the Greatest of our English kings, and Last to Eternity'.[48] This was not the first or last time that Pope's friends pressed him to write elevated national poetry embodying the ideas of patriotism and public virtue, rather than, as they saw it, dissipating his great talent in libels against government ministers of the day and their servants. Pope did not respond to Lyttelton's hint in his letters, but soon afterwards he was at work on a four-book epic poem in blank verse, based on early medieval chronicles, taking Brutus, the great-grandson of Aeneas and legendary founder of the British people, as his hero. In 1742 or 1743 Pope told Spence that 'the matter is already quite digested and prepared'. Surviving records of 'the matter' indicate that Pope conceived his Brutus less as a rounded, shaded character than as the idealization of enlightenment, benevolence, public virtue, and love of country; the idea of his poem 'turns wholly on civil and ecclesiastical government'. It would seem that Pope, still only in his early fifties and at the height of his powers, intended to crown his life's work by becoming the poet of Britannia, no less, attaching himself to the heroic (and blank-verse) line of Milton, and becoming, as he proclaims in some of the few surviving verses of his epic, 'with Britain's Glory fir'd . . . My Country's Poet, to record her Fame'.[49] Had Pope lived to turn his detailed scheme for *Brutus* into poetry he surely would have stolen the Britannic thunder of the author of *Britannia*, *Liberty*, and 'Rule Britannia'.

After *Alfred* Thomson turned to another commission. One of the 'ladies of high rank and distinction' who became his 'declared patronesses' after the publication of *Winter* was Mrs Sarah Stanley, daughter of Sir Hans Sloane and wife of George Stanley of Paulton in Hampshire. The Stanleys' daughter Elizabeth died at the age of 18 in 1738; she was buried in Holyrood Church, Southampton, on 13 December, and plans were made to erect over her grave a monument sculpted by Rysbrack with a long inscription by Thomson, which the poet eventually sent to Mrs Stanley on 25 August 1740. The monument was completed and set in place, but was destroyed, along with most of the church, by German bombs during the Second World War. Transcripts of Thomson's prose and verse inscription may be found, however, in eighteenth-century guidebooks of Southampton and the section in verse was printed in Lyttelton's edition of Thomson's *Poems on Several Occasions* in 1750. Thomson also commemorated Elizabeth Stanley in a passage added to *Summer* for the 1744 edition of the *Seasons*, where the poet imagines the dead girl, now an immortal spirit, still aware of

> A Mother's Love, a Mother's tender Woe:
> Who seeks Thee still, in many a former Scene;
> Seeks thy fair Form, thy lovely-beaming Eyes,
> Thy pleasing Converse, by gay lively Sense
> Inspir'd: where moral Wisdom mildly shone,
> Without the Toil of Art; and Virtue glow'd,
> In all her Smiles, without forbidding Pride.[50]

Elizabeth Stanley thus joins earlier idealizations of female virtue and celebrations of familial piety in the *Seasons*, for instance, those in *Spring*, 1113–76, and *Autumn*, 570–609. Such familial piety, not unmixed with the kindly, good-natured, irritating condescension towards the 'fair sex' that makes Thomson so thoroughly a man of his age, appears in a letter of 1740 to his sister Elizabeth, consenting to her marriage with Robert Bell, the Presbyterian minister of Strathaven, near Hamilton in Lanarkshire:

I must chiefly recommend to you to cultivate, by every method, that union of hearts, that agreement and sympathy of tempers, in which consists the true happiness of the marriage state. The economy and gentle management of a family is a woman's natural province, and from that her best praise arises. You will apply yourself thereto as it becomes a good and virtuous wife. I dare say I need not put you in mind of having a just and grateful sense of, and future confidence in, the goodness of God, who has been to you a 'father to the fatherless'. Tho' you will hereafter be more immediately under the protection of another, yet you may always depend upon the sincere friendship, and tenderest good offices of your most affectionate brother.[51]

The wedding took place on 16 December 1740. It would seem that the unmarried sister Jean moved into the manse along with Elizabeth, for it was to that address that Thomson sent her a letter on 24 April 1742, full of his customary apologies:

I find you are uneasy at my not having writ to you for sometime past. But I have often told you that I am the most irregular Correspondent in the World; when therefore you do not hear from me . . . any longer Time than ordinary, you ought not to deduce any Consequences from it that will give you the least uneasiness. As for my being angry, never let that come into your Head. I am not much given to being angry.

This is a fair self-assessment. The same tenor, though not the same tone, is apparent in Thomson's letter of 10 June 1741 to Solomon Mendez:

Dear, unjust, suspicious Friend,
   Don't be so uncharitable in your accusations. One chief reason why I have not acknowledged yours was, I had many purposes of going to town to see you; and twice or thrice, when I sat down to write, I was interrupted, and so lost the opportunity. Indolence, too, may have had some little share; but want of esteem and friendship I utterly deny. Give me leave to say, that you are vapourish in friendship as well as with regard to health, and imagine what never was, is not, nor ever will be.

Thomson mocks his friend's hypochondria and then expresses astonishment that Solomon's kinsman Isaac has also been reported vapourish:

Isaac! Isaac, vapourish! I should as soon have suspected Mrs——(I cannot think of her name, but it begins with a B, and he knows it well enough) of the green-sickness. If any one had asserted to me, that he heard the Monument sigh, I should not have thought it a greater prodigy. The fall of empires must follow; and I tremble for the Pragmatic Sanction and the House of Austria. He shoot himself? why should he shoot himself? I know but one reason for that, and which, you will say, is an odd one—the want of balls. Pray, bid him take care of himself, for the sake of his friends. I in particular propose yet to spend many a happy hour with him, when the dull world is plunged in sleep and insensibility, and our nocturnal conversations begin.—By all means let us meet some day next week at the Bohemia Head, or where you will; why should we suffer a summer to pass over our heads without such a party? True philosophy is to secure the present, and make the most of it.[52]

   Thomson expects his friends to be indulgent towards what in an earlier letter to Solomon Mendez he calls his 'sweet blood of indolence' if he can delight them with his good humour. Anecdotes about him often lay stress upon his good living, good nature, self-indulgence, indolence, and negligence over money. He lived on very long credit. Taylor the barber recalled: 'he was deucedly long-winded; but when he had money, he would send for his creditors and pay them all round; he has paid my master between twenty and thirty pounds at a time.' A Richmond brewer named Collins said that 'he was so heedless in his money concerns, that in paying him a bill for beer, he gave him two bank notes rolled together instead of one. Mr Collins did not perceive the mistake till he got home, and when he returned the note Thomson appeared perfectly indifferent about the matter, and said he had enough to go on without it.' William Robertson, his Richmond neighbour, recalled Thomson 'being stopped once between London and Richmond, and robbed of his watch, and when I expressed my regret for his loss, Pshaw—damn it, said he, I am glad they took it from me, 'twas never good for any thing'. Johnson's pen-portrait emphasizes good nature, financial negligence, and conscious indolence:

The benevolence of Thomson was fervid, but not active; he would give on all occasions what assistance his purse would supply; but the offices of intervention or solicitation he could not conquer his sluggishness sufficiently to perform. The affairs of others, however, were not more neglected than his own. He had often felt the inconveniences of idleness, but he never cured it; and was so conscious of his own character, that he talked of writing an Eastern Tale of *The Man who loved to be in Distress*.[53]

There are more circumstantial tales about Thomson's indolence. Mrs Piozzi says he 'was once seen lounging round Lord Burlington's garden, with his hands in his waistcoat pockets, biting off the sunny sides of the peaches'. A similar story (located, with greater probability, in Bubb Dodington's garden) is told in the *Public Advertiser* of 16 April 1790, where it is also recorded that Charles Burney found him one day in bed 'at two o'clock at noon, and asked him, Why he was in bed at that hour? "Mon", replied he, in his Scotch accent, "I had no motive to rise." ' This encounter could be no earlier than 1744, when Burney first came to London in the employment of Dr Arne. William Robertson, being asked whether the poet kept late hours, replied: 'No sir,— very early.—He was always up at sunrise.—But then he had never been in bed.' Robertson agreed with his interlocutor that Thomson was governed by the 'vis inertiae' to a great degree.[54]

There is an unattributed story intended to show that if any force could overcome Thomson's *vis inertiae* it was his love of the table: 'Quin one day telling him, that he believed him so completely idle, that he supposed he would let him chew his meat for him. "That indeed I would not, my good friend", replied Thomson; "for I should be afraid that you would afterwards swallow it".' Andrew Mitchell told Boswell that, notwithstanding Thomson's 'fine imitation of Ovid on the Pythagorean system, he was an egregious gormandiser of Beefsteaks'. Writing to Mitchell in 1742 about Thomson's prospects of patronage, Paterson said, 'I wish to God he were in some way of getting a Beef Stake and of going to the Golden Ball on a certain footing.'[55] The Golden Ball was a coffee-house in Drury Lane. Boswell's *Journal*, under 1 January 1763, records an overheard dialogue at Child's Coffee-House:

1 Citizen. [Joseph Warton] is fond of Thomson. He says
    he has great force.
2 Citizen. He has great faults.
1 Citizen. Ay, but great force, too.
2 Citizen. I have eat beefsteaks with him.
3 Citizen. So have I.

In a conversation of 1768, recorded by Boswell, Johnson accused Thomson of 'gross sensuality and licentiousness of manners',[56] but the worst he has to say in his *Lives of the Poets* is to report that

Savage, who lived much with Thomson, once told me how he heard a lady remarking that she could gather from his works three parts of his character, that he was 'a great lover, a great swimmer, and rigorously abstinent'; but, said Savage, he knows not any love but that of the sex; he was perhaps never in cold water in his life; and he indulges himself in all the luxury that comes within his reach.

Johnson adds, 'Yet Savage always spoke with the most eager praise of his social qualities, his warmth and constancy of friendship, and his adherence to his first acquaintance when the advancement of his reputation had left them behind him.'[57] Answering Boswell's charge of coarseness, Robertson said, 'Thomson was neither a petit maitre, nor a boor; he had simplicity without rudeness, and a cultivated manner without being courtly.' Thomson described himself in *The Castle of Indolence* as a bard 'more fat than Bard beseems'. Johnson quotes this line, adding that Thomson had 'a dull countenance, and a gross, unanimated, uninviting appearance'. Murdoch conceded

that his exterior was not the most promising; his make being rather robust than graceful: though it is known that in his youth he had been thought handsome. His worst appearance was, when you saw him walking alone, in a thoughtful mood: but let a friend accost him, and enter into conversation, he would instantly brighten into a most amiable aspect, his features no longer the same, and his eye darting a peculiar animated fire.[58]

    As the misunderstandings of the lady who spoke to Savage indicate, Thomson's social qualities were those of a man's man. The story told by Johnson (probably from Savage) that Thomson lost the Countess of Hertford's favour because he 'took more delight in carousing with Lord Hertford and his friends than assisting her ladyship's poetical operations'[59] is not true in fact, but perhaps truthfully bears witness to Thomson's greater ease in congenial and convivial male company, drinking and talking about women, rather than talking to them. Such are the glimpses we have of him in a letter by Stephen Duck on 24 September 1740 to Dr Oliver at Bath, 'Thomson and I have drank plentifully to Miss Robbison's health', in Lyttelton's invitation to Mallet earlier in 1740, saying that a party which was also to include Thomson, Andrew Mitchell, James Hammond, and Viscount Barrington, would comprise 'Learning, Witt, Honest Politicks, and much Bawdy' (with, one hopes, each guest bringing more than one item), and in hasty notes in which Thomson arranges dinner and drinking engagements with his friends. There is, for instance, an undated note from Thomson to 'Messrs Forbes, Warrender, and Gray':

Chers Messieurs,

I did not get Millar's Note till after three; so cannot pretend to be at Brentford time enough to dine with you. Besides, my own Dinner will be ready at four. So soon as I have dined, I will walk down the Lane, either to find you at the three Pidgeons, or meet you by the way, and so conduct you hither.[60]

Ensign John Forbes and the Revd Hugh Warrender (Rector of Aston All-Saints, near Sheffield, since 1740) were visitors, but Thomson's old friend John Gray lived on Richmond Hill and Andrew Millar was a neighbour too. According to Robertson, 'he took a box near Thomson's in Kew-lane, to keep in with an author that was very profitable to him. — Andrew was a good natured fellow, and not an unpleasant companion, but he was a little contracted by his business; had the dross of a bookseller about him.' Mallet took a house close by, at Strand-on-the-Green, near the site of Kew Bridge; Thomson visited him there often and used to walk back 'at all hours in the night'. The Three Pigeons mentioned in the note to the other Scots cronies was the best-known inn in Brentford; Thomson's drinking with Quin at the Castle has already been noted; it was also reported that he associated with his convivials at the Orange-Tree in Kew Lane. There appears to have been no shortage of local inns ready to claim Thomson as one of their regular drinkers, nor any lack of stories about his drinking at home. At one of his dinner parties 'there was a general stipulation agreed on by the whole company, that there should be no hard drinking. Thomson acquiesced, only requiring that each man should drink his bottle. The terms were accepted unconditionally; and when the cloth was removed, a three-quart bottle was set before each of his guests.' It was reported that 'when he was writing in his own house, he frequently sat with a bowl of punch before him, and that a good large one too'.[61] In such stories we have the impression that Thomson is acting up to the image that his friends had formed of him.

It was an image that earned public comment, to judge by an anonymous verse libel published in December 1739 under the title *The Satirists, a Satire*:

> Should I say T———for a Ven'son Pye,
> Wou'd Sacrifice his darling Liberty;
> Wou'd he the plump delicious Haunch refrain?
> And sink the Epicure to humble *Spain*?

Or shou'd I add full thrice a Week he's Drunk,
Lolls out his Tongue and all besmears his Punk,
Wou'd he for this forswear old *Shakespear*'s Head?
And reel no more at six a Clock to Bed?
Wou'd he if I shou'd bid him be sincere?
And his Friend M——praise without a Sneer?
Bid him the Dinners he's in Debt repay,
Wou'd he remember the long trusted Day?

This lampoon confirms the familiar charges of gluttony, drunkenness, and debt, but it adds to them the unfamiliar accusations of whoring ('besmears his Punk') and ingratitude towards Mallet. The Shakespear's Head in line 7 was a tavern under the piazza in Covent Garden; it was in use for masonic meetings by 1738. Its mention in this satire suggests that it was a disreputable place, and it had certainly gained a very unsavoury reputation by the 1750s.[62]

Lady Hertford was not amused by reports she heard. Replying in September 1742 to an enquiry about the poet, she wrote:

I have not seen Thomson almost these three Years he keeps Company with scarce any Body but Mallet & one or two of the Players, & indeed hardly any body else will keep Company with him, He turns Day into Night, & Night into Day & is (as I am told) never awake till after Midnight & I doubt has quite drown'd his Genius.[63]

His genius was not altogether drowned. At least he had plans to make creative use of his indolence and self-indulgence at this time, for 1742 is the date attached to a Spenserian parody by the Revd Thomas Morell, 'To Mr Tomson. On his unfinish'd Plan of a Poem call'd *the Castle of Indolence*':

As when the Silkworm, erst the tender Care
    Of *Syrian* Maidens, 'gins for to unfold
From his Sleek Sides, that now much Sleeker are,
    The glossy Treasure, & soft Threads of Gold;
    In Various Turns, & many a winding Fold,
He spins his Web; &, as he spins, decays;
    Till within Circles infinite enroll'd,
    He rests supine, imprison'd in the Maze;
The Which himself did make, the Gathering of his Days.

So Thou, they say, from thy prolific Brain,
    A Castle, hight, of Indolence, didst raise:
Where listless Sprites, withouten Care, & Pain,
    In idle Plesaunce spend their jocund Days,
Nor heed rewardfull Toil, nor seeken Praise.
    Thither thou didst repair in luckless Hour,
    And lulled with thine own enchanting Lays

Didst lie adown; entranced in the Bow'r,
The which thyself didst make, the Gathering of thy Pow'r.

But Venus suffring not her fav'rite Worm,
    For aye to slepen in his silky Tomb;
Instructs him to throw off his pristine Form,
    And the gay Features of a Fly assume.
    When lo! eftsons from the surrounding Gloom,
He vigorous breaks, forth issuing from the Wound,
    His horny Beak had made; & finding Room
On new-plum'd Wings he flutters all around,
And buzzing speaks his Joy in most expressive Sound.

So may the God of Science, and of Wit,
    With pitying Eye ken Thee his darling Son;
Shake from thy fatty Sides the slumbrous Fit,
    In which alas! Thou are so Woe-begone!
    Or with his pointed Arrows goad Thee on,
Till Thou refeelest Life in all thy Veins;
    And on the Wings of Resolution,
Like thine own Hero dight, fliest o'er the Plains,
Chaunting his peerless Praise in never-dying Strains.[64]

Morell (1703–84) was curate at Kew Chapel and Twickenham in the 1730s and 1740s; he was a botanist and historian; he edited Chaucer's *Canterbury Tales*, compiled notes on Locke for Queen Caroline, and revised Hogarth's *Analysis of Beauty*; he was a friend of Handel, for several of whose oratorios he wrote libretti. He shared Thomson's interest in Greek drama, for he edited or translated plays by Aeschylus and Euripides, and he seems to have had some temperamental resemblances to Thomson:

He was warm in his attachments; and was a cheerful and entertaining companion. He loved a jest, told a good story, was fond of musick, and would occasionally indulge his friends with a song. In his exterior appearance, however, he never condescended to study the Graces; and, unfortunately for himself, he was a total stranger to oeconomy.[65]

Morell's lines confirm Murdoch's statement that *The Castle of Indolence* 'was, at first, little more than a few detached stanzas, in way of raillery on himself, and on some of his friends, who would reproach him with indolence; while he thought them, at least, as indolent as himself'.[66] By 1742 it was evidently a joke among Thomson's friends that he was too indolent to finish the poem.

Whatever the current state of progress on *The Castle of Indolence*, there is reference to a definite work-in-hand in an exchange of letters between Hill and Mallet in August 1742. Hill had heard playhouse gossip that Thomson was writing a tragedy about the Black Prince, a plausible possibility in view of the fact that Frederick had erected alongside his statue of Alfred one of the Black Prince, with an inscription promising to make that prince's conduct the model of his own.[67] Mallet replies that Thomson is not writing about the Black Prince, but he 'is indeed going upon the subject of Coriolanus'.[68]

With such a hero, Thomson's *Coriolanus* could hardly fail to have a political theme, but, when it eventually appeared, this play's political sentiments were not those of *Agamemnon*, *Edward and Eleonora*, or *Alfred*. Circumstances changed with the resignation of Walpole on 2 February 1742. The Prince of Wales was received again at his father's court on 17 February and soon afterwards was given the increased allowance which his supporters had long called for in Parliament, whereupon the dispossessed Prime Minister's son Horace wrote ironically: 'We may indeed hope a little better to the declining arts. The reconciliation between the royalties is finished, and £50,000 a year more added to the Heir Apparent's revenue. He will have money now to tune up Glover, and Thomson, and Dodsley again.'[69] It would be two years, though, before Thomson would sing again, and then only in revisions to the *Seasons*. He was still the Prince's man, but those years saw him paying court elsewhere, as the next chapter will reveal.

9

Courtship: Revised *Seasons* and *Tancred and Sigismunda*, 1742–1745

THOMSON had not drowned his genius, nor did he keep company only with Mallet and one or two of the players. Among his Richmond neighbours at the time when Lady Hertford was shaking her head over his condition was William Robertson, one of Thomson's younger Scottish friends during his earliest years in London; Robertson had subsequently spent some years abroad with the East India Company, but by 1742 was a physician to the royal court at Kew. He had married a Scotswoman named Mary Young; she was in Bath in November 1742, accompanied by her sister Elizabeth and a certain Miss Berry. On 27 November Thomson wrote a long letter, addressed to Mrs Robertson, but, in view of subsequent events, almost certainly intended for the eyes of Elizabeth Young also.

Thomson's tone is unremittingly gallant; his witty account of the physical dangers of the ladies' journey and the moral perils they may be exposed to at Bath is intended to amuse, but it is not altogether lighthearted. His condemnation of the vanities of the Bath season hints at some unstated personal anxieties: 'When the head is full of nothing but dress, and scandal, and dice, and cards, and rowly powly, can the heart be sensible to those fine emotions, those tender, humane, generous passions that form the soul of all virtue and happiness? Ah! then, ye lovers, never think to make any impression on the hearts of the dissipated fair.' He flatters himself with the hope of hearing from the ladies: 'If you send me but your three names, and above them—"We are well", I shall be glad even of that', and he signs himself 'Your, and Miss Young's, And Miss Berry's, Devoted humble servant'.[1]

On 7 December Thomson wrote a jocular letter, as from his dog Buff to another dog named Marquis, who belongs to a good family in Richmond and is now at a watering-place. A. D. McKillop conjectures that the letter was addressed to Andrew Millar, but there is an equal possibility that it was in fact directed to the gentlemen accompanying the three ladies at Bath. In it Buff approvingly quotes Pope's doggy epistle from Bounce to Fop and asserts his own Bounce-like, country-dog independence from the cold flattery and self-interest of dogs at court: 'For me, it is always a maxim with me,

> To honour humble worth, and scorning state,
> Piss on the proud inhospitable gate.

For which reason I go scattering my water every where about Richmond.' Buff's letter ends: 'Pray lick for me, you happy dog you, the hands of the fair ladies you have the honour to attend. I remember to have had that happiness once, when one who shall be nameless, looked with an envious eye upon me.' No doubt, the nameless friend was Buff's owner. An undated subsequent letter by Thomson begins 'Buff is quite disconsolate that Marquis will not answer his Letter.'[2]

Evidently the humans in her party were as uncommunicative as Marquis, for on Christmas Day 1742 Thomson wrote another letter to Mrs Robertson, beginning:

I believe I am in love with some one or all of you; for though you will not favour me with the scrape of a pen, yet I cannot forbear writing to you again. Is it not however barbarous, not to send me a few soft characters, one pretty name to cheer my eyes withal? How easily some people might make others happy if they would! But it is no small comfort to me, since you will not write, that I shall soon have the pleasure of being in your company. And then, though I were downright picqued, I shall forget it all in a moment.

His pretext for writing is that he has recently kissed Mrs Robertson's six-months-old son, whose eyes 'put me in mind of a certain near relation of his, whom I need not name'. Thomson declares that he now pities 'the joyless inmates of Bachelor's Hall', and he repeats what he calls 'Milton's divine Hymn on Marriage', that is the lines from *Paradise Lost* (IV. 750–8) beginning 'Hail, wedded Love!' The letter continues:

Now that I have been transcribing some lines of poetry, I think I once engaged myself while walking in Kew-lane to write two or three songs. The following is one of them, which I have stolen from the Song of Solomon; from that beautiful expression of Love, 'Turn away thine eyes from me, for they have overcome me.'

Then follows a love-song addressed to 'Myra', which begins:

> O thou, whose tender serious eyes
> Expressive speak the mind I love;
> The gentle azure of the skies,
> The pensive shadows of the grove:
>
> O mix their beauteous beams with mine,
> And let us interchange our hearts;

> Let all their sweetness on me shine,
> Pour'd thro' my soul be all their darts.[3]

The next surviving letter by Thomson makes explicit what was implicit in this poem and hinted at in the letters already quoted. It is dated 10 March 1743 and is addressed to Elizabeth Young; it would appear to be the first letter by the poet to that lady, because it addresses her in the formal style of 'Madam' and it is numbered '1' in the contemporary numbering of the whole series of love letters, which were carefully preserved by their recipient and are now in the Pierpont Morgan Library. The letter begins:

Madam,

As I have not an Opportunity of speaking, I can no longer forbear writing to you. And now that I am sit down to write, my Heart is so full and Words so weak to express it, I am at a Loss where to begin and what to say. What shall I say but that I love you, love you with the utmost Ardor, the most perfect Esteem, and inexpressible Tenderness. Imagination, Reason and the Heart, all conspire to love you. I may venture to say, without Extravagance, I love you better than my own Soul. My Happiness is only a secondary Consideration to yours, can alone consist in making you happy: there is no Happiness for me but in passing my Life with you, in devoting it to please you.

He asks for the opportunity to make his declaration in person, so that he may know whether to hope or despair:

The first will awaken to me to the Pursuit of whatever can be agreeable to you, of whatever can recommend to your Esteem and Friendship—I would fain also add, Love and Tenderness . . . The last will plunge me in a gloomy careless Indolence . . . Not even Friendship and the Study of Nature will be able to maintain any Charms for me. I care not where I am if I am not with you.

After more pathetic appeals Thomson breaks into verse:

> Ah wise too late! from Beauty's Bondage free,
> Why did I trust my Liberty with thee?
> And thou, why didst thou with inhuman Art,
> If not resolv'd to take, seduce my Heart?
> Yes, yes, you saw (for Lovers' Eyes speak true)
> You must have seen how fast my Passion grew;
> And when your Glances chanc'd on me to shine,
> How my fond Soul extatic sprung to thine.
> But mark me, fair-one what I now declare
> Thy deep Attention claims, and serious Care.
> It is no common Passion fires my Breast;
> I must be wretched, or I must be blest:
> My Woes all other Remedy deny;
> Or pitying give me Hope, or bid me dy.

He concludes, 'Pardon me if I only add, Whatever Reception you give to this, you can never be so sincerely, so ardently, so tenderly beloved, as by him who is with unalterable Truth, and the most cordial Friendship and Affection yours James Thomson.'[4] The care that the poet took in composing this declaration of love is evidenced by the existence of his corrected earlier draft, now in the Scottish Record Office.

Though he once sheepishly admitted his susceptibility to woman's beauty in a letter of 1729 to Mallet, and though he composed some tender love lyrics, wrote eloquently and at length on the delights and pains of love in *Spring* (1728), praised an unidentified 'Melinda' in *Autumn* (1730),[5] created a Princess Eleonora, and flirted platonically with Lady Hertford, his own regular companions, by all accounts, were hard-drinking men. Suddenly, it seems this good-natured, easy-going, self-indulgent, fat, sweaty, sentimental confirmed bachelor was desperately set upon matrimony. Conceivably, he was partly impelled by the marriage of his sister, or the more recent engagement of Murdoch to a 17-year-old girl, or his other close friend Mallet's even more recent marriage (his second) to a woman with a dowry of ten thousand pounds;[6] but perhaps his head was turned solely by a pair of tender, serious eyes.

There is no accounting for love; the case of Thomson is particularly difficult because hardly anything is known about Elizabeth Young. All that William Robertson, her brother-in-law, says of her character is, 'She was a fine sensible woman; and poor Thomson was desperately in love with her.'[7] Mrs Robertson is said to have reported that 'she was not a striking beauty, but a gentle-mannered, elegant-minded woman, worthy of the love of a man of taste and virtue. She surely derived none of her gentleness from [her] mother, who was a coarse, vulgar woman.'[8] Other accounts, though, lend support to Oscar Wilde's generalization that the tragedy of all women is to become like their mothers. A late writer, claiming reliance upon family tradition, calls her 'as regular a red-haired, "rump-fed ronyon" as ever startled the passing traveller into wondering whether she were man or woman'.[9] A human creature very different from the idealization in Thomson's letters and love poems emerges from the following marginalia by Lady Philippina Knight (d. 1799) in her copy of Boswell's *Life of Johnson*:

Thomson was a very passionate man. It has been told me that his amiable Amanda, who was his relation, and him one evening disagreeing, she pulled off his wig and threw it on the ground, and he threw a glass of punch at her; that she was a woman of great natural sense and quick repartee, and, though violent and harsh in expression, yet had as strong humanity as any woman I ever was acquainted with. He wanted to have married her, and she refused by saying: 'Prove to me that you can maintain me before you offer to court my consent.' . . . Her dialect was as strong as if she had never quitted her country. I loved her for her good qualities, and I lamented her harshness of expression, which having never, I suppose, been corrected for her in her youth she was not sensible of it.[10]

The poet's letters give no hint of horseplay with wig and punch; they are all rapture, despair, and high-minded resolve. On 18 April, five weeks after his proposal, he contrived to meet her, when, it seems, she drew attention in a kindly manner to his irregular habits and he took her reproofs for encouragement. On the following day he wrote,

Miss Young, my Love, my Soul! it is impossible to speak the Agitation of my Heart ever since I parted from you. All that an absent Lover can feel I feel in it's most exquisite and charming Distress. I would not wish you had a better and more affecting Picture of my Love than to have been conscious to what passed in my Mind as I returned. Then you could never doubt it more; never tell me again that it will be transitory, and that there is no such thing as undecaying Love in the World. Mine will not only last but grow forever.

After more such outpourings in prose and poetry he assures Miss Young that she has inspired him with virtue and moral resolution:

Were not those Hints with Regard to Regularity and Temperance, which you now and then so prettily insinuated, meant for me? Yes, I will interpret them so; for it most exquisitely flatters my Heart to think that you would wish all Objections removed that may ly betwixt us. And shall such low, such vile, such false Pleasures ever stand in the least Competition with that Happiness, that darling Happiness, I shall enjoy with You?

At their interview she had been too courteous to refer to his lack of fortune:

But Heaven has constituted Things so graciously, that Happiness does not consist of Fortune, or those external Advantages that are out of our own Power. Competency with Contentment, a virtuous improved well-ordered Mind, right Affections, Friendship and Love, these give the truest Happiness, and these we may command.[11]

This recipe for happiness finds its way into the revisions of *Spring* which Thomson was making just at this time, revisions which also included praise of 'Amanda', the poetical name he now bestowed upon Elizabeth Young, though it had been employed in his lyric poetry at least as early as 1732. It was probably at this time that he addressed to her the song beginning 'Come, dear Eliza, quit the Town', because it is optimistic in tone and refers to Spring; it echoes the Song of Solomon, like Thomson's first, indirect love-song to Miss Young, and it ends:

> Too soon our Spring will take it's Flight:
> Arise, my Love, and come away.

A revised version of this song was printed in *The Gentleman's Magazine* in 1744, with 'Eliza' altered to 'Amanda'.[12]

His letter continues to appeal for encouragement from her, which will, he declares, 'inform me with a new Soul, will inspirit me to the Pursuit of all that can be agreeable to you'. He took whatever she had said at their meeting as qualified encouragement, but 'The Hope you permitted me to indulge is not enough. There are Remains of Doubt and Anxiety that still distract my Mind, that render me incapable of performing what I have promised my Friends, the Public, and above all my own Heart upon your Account.' He begs for a letter, for a meeting, for a few kind words, apparently with no success, because his next letter, on 28 April, begins

My dearest Miss Young! it is now ten long days since I saw you, since I was blest with a Look from those Eyes where all Beauty all Sweetness and all Excellence shine. Pardon me then if I cannot resist writing. My Heart o'erflows, and can find no Consolation but in pouring itself forth to Her who has confirmed it in right Sentiments, and Virtues, which I have often felt but never truly possessed before. I wish you was conscious to whatever has passed in my Mind since I saw you last: You would find the Whole but one fond Letter, one continued Effusion of Soul devoted to you and Virtue ...

He continues in this now familiar vein, concluding with a reference to his revisions of *Spring*:

I am going, if I can, to put a finishing Hand to the Description of a Season now in high Song and Beauty, but to which I am dead. You alone I hear, You alone I see: all Harmony and Beauty are comprised in You. Those Parts, however, will be obliged to You which attempt a Picture of virtuous happy Love. O Miss Young! thou loveliest of thy Sex, and the most beloved! as you have taught me the Virtue, so teach me the Happiness of this best Passion! O let the Picture be ours![13]

Shortly afterwards Thomson met Elizabeth Young again. She asked him not to write to her; she was evidently giving no positive encouragement to his addresses, but he was determined to be hopeful. On 14 May he wrote

My dearest Miss Young! let me pour forth my Soul in Gratitude to you, for the Peace and Harmony of Mind you have at last given me. Yes, I will now exert myself, and perform the Promises I have made my own Heart; I will keep your enlivening Image ever in my View, and endeavour to render myself worthy not only of your Esteem but of your Love and Tenderness. Virtue was always my determined Choice; I always loved it with my warmest Approbation, and resolved upon a more attentive and regular Practice of it: but now I love it doubly, it is doubly beautiful, as proceeding from you. Should my Name live, and I be mentioned hereafter, I shall be ambitious to have it said of me, that when seduced by that most fatal Syren Indolence and false Pleasure, to the very Brink of Ruin, the Angel of Love came in your Form and saved me.

He begs again for a letter from her, but to no purpose.[14]
On 26 May he sent her a song beginning

> How long, Eliza, must I languish
> And waste my Soul in tender Anguish,
> How long thus drag out Life in vain?

It appeals:

> O let no Pride and foolish Fashion,
> And too much Prudence starve my Passion,
> Consult sometimes the generous Breast.

The song is enclosed in the now usual sort of letter, where the poet attempts to make building-blocks of hope out of the wispiest straws of encouragement:

Do you know, Madam, that I shall begin to put a vain Interpretation on your obstinately refusing to write? 'You think it improper to write kindly, and your Heart will not permit you to write indifferently.' Thus will I turn your very Silence into a Love-Letter. I remember you threatened me with a Letter, which, you said, perhaps I would not like, and I rashly dared you to it. Upon second Thoughts my Courage fails me. No, dont write unless the Spirit of the Letter be kind; however you season it with those pretty Piquancies with which you can agreeably vex a Lover. Remember the Condition upon which I gave you full Freedom to plague me. Let all the little Darts of Raillery be thrown by Love, and they will please. You may plague, but do take Care of hurting me. I am infinitely tender, and the least Shadow of a real Unkindness would kill me, would make me more miserable than I have ever yet been, for I hope more.[15]

From the words attributed to her one has the impression that Elizabeth Young was trying to deal firmly but gently with this self-pitying, eloquent, lovesick, and importunate friend of her brother-in-law.

Thomson's immediate purpose in the letter of 26 May was to ask if he might join her party in a walk to Chelsea that he had heard was planned for the next weekend. He went to Chelsea on the following Sunday, only to discover that she was walking at that very time close to his own cottage in Kew Foot Lane. On the next day, 30 May, he wrote in great agitation:

Unkind, yet ever dearest Miss Young! did you but know what I suffered yesterday, and still suffer, you must pity me even from common Humanity. Indifference itself would pity me. To one who loves as I do every Disappointment pierces the Heart, but when it carries a Look of Unkindness it is Torture, it is Agony. If your good Sense (which is excellent) told you that as you was circumstanced it was improper to come, could you not have contrived how to prevent my miserable Walk?

She was about to leave for London and her lover was in despair:

If you do not give me an Opportunity of talking with you before you go to Town, if you will not settle my Mind into some Peace and Harmony, I am the most miserable Man alive, as the most in Love. I shall see I shall converse with no Body, I shall do nothing—but break my Heart . . . As you do not go to Town this Day (a Circumstance you attempted cruelly to conceal from me) may not I flatter myself with the Hopes of walking with you this Evening? O then, if you have any the least Regard for me, let me know when and where I may have an half Hours Conversation with you! Cannot you put it down on Paper, in case you have not an Opportunity of telling me by Word of Mouth? I live in Hopes of it—If you neglect to do it you will kill him who is fondly and unalterably your's, however you use him, James Thomson.[16]

A letter dated 'Wednesday Morning' may be conjecturally assigned to 1 June; it continues in the same agitated manner as the 30 May letter to ask for some mark of kindness before Miss Young leaves Richmond:

My lovely dearest Miss Young! I have only Time at present to tell you, that unless you alter your Conduct towards me, unless you treat me with more friendly Confidence, more frank Generosity and undisguised Tenderness, I am unhappy, unable to improve my Time to any good Purpose, in a Word undone—and all because you will not abate a little of false Pride, of mistaken Prudence . . .
Nothing can save me but the Knowledge I have your Heart, and a well-grounded Hope I shall have your Hand soon. Give me This, and I will undertake to answer soon for all other Considerations of Prudence and Fortune—But without it I shall go on in the Way I have been for many Months, be miserable and useless. O think what I shall be in a few Hours, when you, the Life of my Life, the Soul of my Soul, are gone; think what I shall suffer till I see you again, and do something for the Relief of him who loves you more than ever Woman was beloved, who is, with the warmest Truth and Tenderness unexpressible all all yours.[17]

As usual Thomson asks for a line of acknowledgement, but received none.

Though he complained of his inability to improve his time to any good purpose, he was working on a full revision of *The Seasons* and had written parts of *The Castle of Indolence* and *Coriolanus*. Another project may also have been under way at this time if A. D. McKillop is correct in assigning to 1743 a letter from Lyttelton to Mallet, dated 11 July. Lyttelton writes to dissuade Mallet from undertaking a tragedy on the death of Socrates because he doubts whether an interesting play can be written on that subject and because, despite Lyttelton's expressed objections, Thomson is already determined to write a tragedy on it: 'he is so full of the Plan that was sent him by the Bishop of Derry (in which however he made some Corrections) that I apprehend he will go on with it, and have it ready against next Winter.'[18]

Thomson's *Socrates* was never written, but when Voltaire published his own *Socrate* (Amsterdam, 1759) he claimed in the preface that his play was a translation from a manuscript by Thomson given to Voltaire by Lyttelton. The improbability of this assertion appears all the plainer in some corroborative detail that Voltaire adds, in the interest, no doubt, of artistic verisimilitude: for instance that Thomson wrote his play in three acts in prose, that Dodington and Lyttelton revised it in collaboration, and that the work was based upon an outline given by Addison to Thomson, 'son élévè'. It is true that, according to Thomas Tickell, Addison once intended to write a tragedy on the death of Socrates, but his own death occurred in 1719, years before Thomson went to England. After seeing Voltaire's preface Lyttelton wrote to the *Monthly Review* in 1760 firmly denying Thomson's authorship of any play on Socrates.[19]

The main labour of 1743 though was a full-scale revision of *The Seasons* for publication in the following year, a substantial task carried through despite love-sickness or perhaps because the poet wanted to show his mistress that he could resist the fatal siren indolence. The timing of this revision might appear to have been influenced by the 1710 Copyright Act, inasmuch as clause xi of the Act provided that, after the expiration of a term of fourteen years from first publication, copyright was to return to the author, if still living, for another fourteen years. If the Act applied, the first term of fourteen years after publication of *The Seasons* entire would have expired in June 1744, but there is no other indication that either Thomson or his booksellers thought that the Act had any bearing upon their dealings, since Thomson's copyright assignments in 1729–30 and Millan's to Millar in 1738 had been 'for ever' and had covered all revisions as well as the original texts. Whether or not Thomson legally recovered copyright in 1744 and sold it again to Millar, one would hope that he received at least an *ex gratia* payment from his publisher, similar, say, to the one later made by Millar to Fielding on the success of *Tom Jones*.

The revised edition of *The Seasons* was to be dedicated to the Prince of Wales, so the Prince's secretary Lyttelton took a considerable interest in it, and in the summer he invited the poet to stay at his father's country seat, Hagley Hall in Worcestershire. Replying to this invitation on 14 July, Thomson explained that 'some Reasons' prevented him from going down to the country immediately, but he hoped to make his visit in the autumn:

for I think that season of the year the most pleasing, and the most poetical. The spirits are not then dissipated with the gaiety of Spring and the glaring light of Summer, but composed into a serious and tempered joy—The Year is perfect. In the mean time I will go on with correcting and printing the Seasons, and hope to carry down more than one of them with me. The Muses, whom you obligingly say I will bring along with me, I shall find with you; the Muses of the great simple country, not the little fine-lady Muses of Richmond-hill.[20]

The reasons which prevented Thomson from going down to the country immediately arose from his plans to meet Miss Young. They met on 15 August, probably in the company of others, for Thomson complains in a letter to her two days later that she took pains to pique him and make him uneasy. Nevertheless he begs for another meeting and reproaches her cruelty in refusing to walk with him:

it was a most miserable Day to me. Think seriously, consult your Heart, does Love like mine deserve such usage? Not to say generous, is it just to use me so? Remember that your Conduct towards me must determine of my Welfare, and the future Happiness of my Life. Can you neglect the Happiness of him whose only Wish is to make you happy? Yet I must always be, however you treat me, with unshaken Friendship and the most affectionate Tenderness all yours J. Thomson.[21]

On 19 August Thomson took the Worcester stage-coach from London and, after a disagreeable journey, came to Hagley. Ten days later he described the place in a letter to Elizabeth Young:

The Park, where we pass a great Part of our Time, is thoroughly delightful, quite enchanting. It consists of several little Hills, finely tufted with Wood and rising softly one above another; from which are seen a great Variety of at once beautiful and grand extensive Prospects: but I am most charmed with it's sweet embowered Retirements, and particularly with a winding Dale that runs thro' the Middle of it. This Dale is overhung with deep Woods, and enlivened by a Stream, that, now gushing from mossy Rocks, now falling in Cascades, and now spreading into a calm Length of Water, forms the most natural and pleasing Scene imaginable. At the Source of this Water, composed of some pretty Rills, that purl from beneath the Roots of Oaks, there is as fine a retired Seat as a Lover's Heart could wish.

His enumeration of landscape beauties here is either a draft for or an echo of the description of Lyttelton's home added to *Spring* in the revised edition of 1744.[22] At this date Hagley was still owned by George Lyttelton's father Sir Thomas, but George had begun the improvement of its landscape and had already formed the cascades to which Thomson refers and a 'Seat of Contemplation'.

The remainder of this letter from Hagley develops Thomson's obsessive theme of anguished, languishing love. On the retired seat at the head of the cascades,

I often sit, and with a dear exquisite Mixture of Pleasure and Pain, of all that Love can boast of excellent and tender, think of you. But what do I talk of sitting and thinking of you There? Wherever I am, and however employed, I can never cease to think of my loveliest Miss Young. You are Part of my Being; you mix with all my Thoughts, even the most studious, and instead of disturbing give them greater Harmony and Spirit. Ah tell me, do I not now and then steal a tender Thought from you? I may claim that Distinction from the Merit of my Love. Yes I love you to that Degree as must inspire into the coldest Breast a mutual Passion. So look to your Heart, for you will scarce be able to defend it against my Tenderness.

The household at Hagley provides 'the truly happy Life', a 'Union of Retirement and choice Society' which 'gives an Idea of that which the Patriarchal or Golden Age is supposed to have been; when every Family was a little State by itself, governed by the mild Laws of Reason, Benevolence, and Love'; but, remembering Elizabeth Young's taste for the town, Thomson adds:

Dont however imagine me so madly rural as not to think those who have the Powers of Happiness in their own Minds happy everywhere. The Mind is it's own Place, the genuine Source of it's own Happiness; and, amidst all my Raptures with Regard to the Country, I would rather live in the most London Corner of London with you, than in the finest Country Retirement, and that too enlivened by the best Society, without you. You so fill my Mind with all Ideas of Beauty, so satisfy my Soul with the purest and most sincere Delight, I should feel the Want of little else. Yet still the Country Life with You, diversifyed now and then by the Contrast of the Town, is the Wish of my Heart. May Heaven grant me that favourite Happiness, and I shall be the happiest of men. And so much the happier as the Possession of you will excite me to deserve my Happiness, by whatever is virtuous and Praise-worthy.[23]

At Hagley Thomson continued his revisions of *The Seasons*, entering them on the interleaved copy of the first volume of the 1738 edition of his *Works*. This copy, now in the British Library, also contains many revisions in Lyttelton's hand. His corrections, made generally in the interests of decorum or metrical regularity, appear in all four *Seasons* and affect about a hundred and fifty lines of text; they are particularly extensive and sweeping in the Palemon and Lavinia story in *Autumn* and the lists of worthies in *Summer* and *Winter*. In nearly every case Thomson accepts the need for a correction, even if he does not take Lyttelton's emendation word for word into his own text. His compliance was remembered twenty years later when James Grainger sent a manuscript of *The Sugar-Cane* to two of his friends for correction: 'You will please let Mr Shenstone know, that I can bear to have my verses butchered, as Thomson used to call it, so that they need not stand on ceremony with me.'[24]

The relationship between patron and poet troubled Smollett, who admired Thomson but hated Lyttelton, partly on account of his unwillingness to further Smollett's ill-considered career as a dramatist, but perhaps partly on account of the natural resentment that a proud, irascible man of genius might feel towards his own need for patronage. So Lyttelton is excoriated in chapter 102 of the first edition of *Peregrine Pickle* (1751) under the character of Gosling Scrag, 'the universal patron', whose 'arrogance and self-conceit' call for authors who will humble themselves, 'meanly beg his protection', and 'scratch' themselves into his favour:

Never did he befriend a man of poetical merit, who did not court and retain his favour by such slavish prostitution, except one author, lately deceased; and even he extended his complaisance too far, in complimental lines, which the warmth of his gratitude inspired, though he would never submit to the tame criticism of his patron, or offer such an outrage to his own judgment, as to adopt the alterations which he proposed.

The 'author, lately deceased' when Smollett's novel was written is Thomson; the complimental lines are those added to the revised edition of *Spring* (1744). Smollett was misinformed or deceived himself in his belief that Thomson never adopted Lyttelton's alterations: evidently he preferred not to admit that his friend and fellow-Scotsman could be levelled with Fielding and other clients of Lyttelton, who are ridiculed in the continuation of the passage just quoted:

Let a scribbler (for example) creep into his notice by the most abject veneration, implore his judgment upon some performance, . . . receive and read his emendations with pretended extasy . . . bawl for him on all occasions in common conversation, prose and rhime, . . . feed him with the soft pap of dedication, . . . the friendship of Mr Scrag will be sooner or later manifested in some warm sine-cure, ample subscription, post or reversion.[25]

Smollett speaks, not for the first or last time, out of his own rich store of resentments, but he speaks also on Thomson's behalf. A correspondent describing Lyttelton's son to Smollett in 1771 said that his character reminded him of what Thomson had once told Smollett about Lyttelton himself: 'His mind is the most susceptible of delusive flattery of any that ever I met with; and should others be silent, he will trumpet forth his own excellencies. If one desired to lead him, the grossest adulation would intoxicate him, and render him obedient as a lamb.'[26] If truly reported, his evidence gives another aspect to 'the Patriarchal or Golden Age' at Hagley, 'governed by the mild Laws of Reason, Benevolence, and Love'. Those two views of patronage could easily co-exist, for it is possible to be at once grateful and open-eyed.

Back in Richmond, away from whatever delights and irritations his patron's hospitality and literary co-operation may have afforded, Thomson wrote to Miss Young on 28 September, sending her a copy of John Gay's comedy *The Distress'd Wife*, printed earlier that year, and making his criticism of the play the pretext for an attack on 'the dull, tiresome, vain, tattling, impertinent, unfeeling, and utterly worthless gay World' of the town.[27] This outburst, like his agitated comments on the moral dangers of Bath society in his November letter to Mrs Robertson, or the submissiveness of his remarks on 'the most London Corner of London' in the letter from Hagley, suggests that Thomson feared Miss Young might prefer the company of wits in a drawing-room to that of a poet on a rural walk. Her birthday, which fell on 1 January, was celebrated in verse by the lovelorn and still hopeful poet:[28]

> Hail to the Day! hail to the smiling Skies!
> That first unseal'd my lov'd Amanda's Eyes . . . (1–2)

> Come, Source of Joy! come from thy Southern Goal,
> O Phoebus come! and chear my drooping Soul!
> Come, with the Loves and Graces in thy Train,

Whate'er inspires the Bard or charms the Swain:
The dancing Hours, the rosy-finger'd Dews,
The gentle Zephirs, and the vernal Muse.... (11–16)

Father of Love, come on! and, as along
Thy Pomp proceeds, I first begin the Song.
Soon will th' awaken'd Groves their Chorus join,
And amorous Nature mix her Joy with Mine;
The Blackbird soon will, from the Hawthorn Bush,
Chaunt his gay Notes, and soon the mellow Thrush;
Thro the soft Gleamings of a milder Day,
Soon will the Woodlark tune his various Lay.
Then fast they follow: *Valentine* will rise;
They chuse their Mates; rous'd by the genial Skies,
They sing what Beauty and what Love inspire,
Till Philomel compleats the charming Quire,
Till his unrival'd Song enchants the Grove,
And Heaven and Earth are Harmony and Love.

Wilt thou, Amanda, *then*, give up thy Charms,
And yield thee to a faithful Lover's Arms?
Wilt thou forsake the City-Throng for me,
Whose Heart so long has imag'd None but thee? ... (23–40)

It matters not, my Dearest! where we be,
In Town or Country; 'tis the same with thee:
Thy powerful Presence Time and Place beguiles,
And everlasting Eden round thee smiles.

What tho by Friends forgot? tho Fortune frown?
Great Love can make a Fortune of his own.
Love bade Heaven-breath'd Ambition first aspire,
And thro the Bosom pour'd a generous Fire;
Love first to Labour rous'd the quicken'd Heart,
The lively Source of every Human Art;
By Love first Cities rose, and Nations throve,
And Wealth and Fame the Bounty are of Love.... (51–62)

Come then! let no cold Fear thy Kindness curb,
No poor desponding Thought our Love disturb;
To Trust in Heaven yield an unbounded Scope:
'Tis nobler far to give a Loose to Hope.
Enough for me, if sacred Hymen join
Our Fates in One, and I can call thee Mine. (73–8)

As these extracts reveal, this substantial lover's address (86 lines long) draws heavily upon the themes and phrasing of *Spring*, but Thomson makes prudent use also of the 'progress of arts' passage at the beginning of *Autumn*.[29]

The unheaded, undated manuscript of this poem was preserved by Elizabeth Young among Thomson's love-letters and other poems. It is the only one among them in which she is called 'Amanda': in all the others she is addressed as 'Eliza' or 'Thou', except in the first of the series, that is 'O thou whose tender serious Eyes' in the Christmas Day 1743 letter to Mrs Robertson, intended, one imagines, primarily for the eyes of Miss Young; this poem is addressed to 'Myra'.[30] As we have seen, when 'Come dear Eliza, quit the Town' was printed in *The Gentlemen's Magazine* for March 1744 'Eliza' because 'Amanda';[31] the identification of 'Amanda' with Elizabeth Young in additions to the 1744 *Seasons* (*Spring* 483 and *Summer* 1401) is confirmed by the verses accompanying Thomson's presentation copy 'To Miss Young, my dearest Amanda'.[32] His other 'Amanda' poems must have been written for an earlier love if they had any specific addressee. 'For ever, Fortune', printed in 1732, ends:

> All other Blessings I resign,
> Make but the dear Amanda mine!

Neither this nor the equally conventional song beginning

> Unless with my *Amanda* blest,
> In vain I twine the woodbine bower,

was sent to Elizabeth Young. Another song of probably about the same date as those two, 'Come gentle Power of soft Desire', was printed in 1736 in a version ending

> And wouldst thou me for ever gain?
> Put on *Amanda's* winning form.

When Thomson revised this poem to send to Miss Young he changed 'Amanda' to 'Eliza'.[33]

The love-songs written as much as ten years before Thomson proposed to Elizabeth Young and those written during his courtship are similar in tone and feeling. Many of them dwell with gentle plaintiveness on love frustrated by inequalities in fortune; all of them breathe tender, refined, and virtuous sentiments. The letters to Miss Young are expansive repetitions of these sentiments. 'Come gentle Power of soft Desire' (1736) speaks of the 'tender Spirit' in the beloved's eye; 'Hard is the Fate of Him who loves', addressed to the Countess of Hertford, probably in 1735 or earlier, has the poet drinking virtues from his beloved's eye:

> And where her Eyes, sweet-beaming shine,
> Heaven on th'extatic Gazer breaks,
> Inspiring Something all-divine.

Thomson writes in similar terms to Elizabeth Young on 26 May 1743:

I long more to see you than ever, to lose my Soul again, with unspeakable Pleasure, in your beauteous Eyes. What sensible Softness, what lively Sweetness do they contain! The last Time I saw them they looked with a particular Loveliness, for they looked kinder. To gaze upon, or rather to look into, the tender Eyes of those we love is a pure and exalted Pleasure; it resembles the Love of Angels, which Milton calls—mixing Irradiance—There is a Light shines from them that charms refines and nourishes the Soul.

His proposal of marriage on 10 March and the letter conjecturally dated 1 June repeat the unusual phrase 'Life of Life' from his song 'For ever Fortune', printed in 1732, where Thomson laments the fact that mercenary interests too often prevent the union of mutual hearts.[34] It is as if that other Thomson (not the fat, coarse, hard-drinking, convivial friend of Quin and the actors) had long rehearsed the part of a timid, despairing, pitiable lover. The pain of his frustration in 1743 was no doubt real enough, but his unrequited love for Elizabeth Young was in some sense a work of the literary imagination; at least, she embodied an 'Amanda' idea long present in his mind and heart.

Shortly after her sister's birthday Mrs Robertson died. On 21 January 1744 Thomson wrote a letter of condolence to Miss Young, for

I claim it as one of the sweetest Priviledges of Love, to mix my Tears with yours. Why am I not now with you? By what cruel Considerations of Prudence am I thus debarred free Access to your Company? That I might, by all which my Reason can suggest, by all the Arts of Tenderness in my Power share and lighten your Affliction.

He addresses her humanely and rationally on the benefit of mourning and the hope of futurity:

Grief is it's own best Consolation. Nature has given Tears as a Balm to heal the Wounds of Sorrow. Then weep, my dearest Love, weep a gentle and amiable Sister; your chearful Companion, and tender Friend, from infant Years . . . But after the first Sallies of Grief are past, consider, that when we lament upon these Occasions, it is ourselves we lament. Consider, that the dark and dreadful Passage from this to a higher and more exalted State, which yet abides us, is over with Her . . .
There is no real Evil in the whole general System of Things; it is only our Ignorance that makes it appear so, and Pain and Death but serve to unfold his gracious Purposes of Love. The Dead, whom we lament, may be supposed to address us thus.

> Grieve not like Those
> Who have no Hope: we yet shall meet again;
> We still are in a kind Creator's Hand:
> Eternal Goodness reigns.

(from Eleonora's dying speech in *Edward and Eleonora*, Act III, Scene v)

Thomson cannot avoid turning his letter of condolence into a lover's appeal:

Permit me here, upon this serious Occasion, to mention to you another Source of Comfort, if I may fondly flatter myself it can be of any. Think, my dearest Miss Young, that there is one alive, who loves you with unequalled Tenderness, who loves you more greatly more, than all Friends, all Relations, all the World besides can do; who lives alone, and could dy, for you. Oh come to my Soul, and let me hush your Fears with everlasting Fondness! Alas, that Fortune should put it so much out of my Power to prove, by more than Words, what a boundless Desire I have to make you happy.

He encloses a copy of the epitaph he had written four years earlier on Elizabeth Stanley and concludes with the customary appeal for a letter from his beloved.[35] She, as usual, did not write in reply; Thomson did not write to her again for nearly two years.

During the early months of 1744 Pope was plainly dying, still turning over in his mind the project for a patriotic blank-verse epic on Brutus. Edward Young recalled that he 'heard the dying Swan talk over an epic plan a few weeks before his decease'. Pope died on 30 May, with Mallet in attendance towards the end.[36] Thomson continued his revisions of *The Seasons*;[37] little is known of his movements at this time, but he was at Hagley in May, when a fellow guest was George Lyttelton's cousin Gilbert West, the translator of Pindar and author of works on piety. It would appear that Thomson had laid aside *Coriolanus* in favour of *Tancred and Sigismunda*, a sentimental tragedy about unhappy love perhaps more congenial to the feelings of an unhappy lover. In the early months of the year however his principal task must have been to complete his thoroughgoing revisions of *The Seasons*, the effect of which was to enlarge the 1730 version of the poem by over a quarter.

The incidence of revision in the 1744 version is uneven. Though many short passages are rewritten in *Spring* and *Autumn*, these two books are enlarged overall by only about a hundred lines each. To the all-British nature descriptions of *Spring* is now added a lively and finely-observed account of trout fishing in the georgic mode. Here Thomson is returning to his native country and to the sports of his youth as he had first described them in 'Of a Country Life' in 1720. Immediately following the fishing piece is another new passage, addressing the nature-lover, who, resting in a shady place on the river bank at noon, can

> catch thy self the Landskip, gliding swift
> Athwart Imagination's vivid Eye:
> Or by the vocal Woods and Waters lull'd,
> And lost in lonely Musing, in a Dream,
> Confus'd, of careless Solitude, where mix
> Ten thousand wandering Images of Things,
> Soothe every Gust of Passion into Peace.[38]

Thomson implies the possibility of an interpenetration of object and subject in an act of the projective imagination. The other substantial addition to *Spring* is an inserted 'local poem' on Hagley Park, where, though Thomson speaks of the eye being 'snatched' by a wide prospect, the stance is rather that of the disengaged observer whose aesthetic sensibility organizes the view into a landscape painting.

> Meantime you gain the Height, from whose fair Brow
> The bursting Prospect spreads immense around;
> And snatch'd o'er Hill and Dale, and Wood and Lawn,
> And verdant Field, and darkening Heath between,
> And Villages embosom'd soft in Trees,
> And spiry Towns by surging Columns mark'd
> Of houshold Smoak, your Eye excursive roams:
> Wide-stretching from the *Hall*, in whose kind Haunt
> The *Hospitable Genius* lingers still,
> To Where the broken Landskip, by Degrees,
> Ascending, roughens into rigid Hills;
> O'er which the *Cambrian* Mountains, like far Clouds
> That skirt the blue Horizon, dusky, rise.[39]

The more famous and much-admired landscape of Stowe, the estate of Lyttelton's uncle and political mentor Viscount Cobham, is praised in a passage added to *Autumn*, but the most considerable addition to this Season is a dissertation upon the origin of springs and rivers which supplies a new theory to correct the one offered in the 1730 text. This is the most scientific and also one of the most heroic of the added passages.[40] Thomson calls upon man's scientific intelligence to uncover hidden strata of pervious and impervious rocks which form subterranean reservoirs and conduits:

> O thou pervading *Genius*, given to Man,
> To trace the Secrets of the dark Abyss,
> O lay the Mountains bare! and wide display
> Their hidden Structure to th' astonish'd View!
> Strip from the branching *Alps* their piny Load,
> The huge Incumbrance of horrific Woods
> From *Asian Taurus*, from *Imaüs* stretch'd
> Athwart the roving *Tartar's* sullen Bounds!
> Give opening *Hemus* to my searching Eye.

(His roll-call of mountains continues in this sonorous manner for another twenty lines down to the Andes, the highest peaks then known.) In the passage just quoted there is a conspicuous and challenging echo of Milton's simile describing Satan wandering upon the outer crust of the universe:

As when a vulture on Imaus bred
Whose snowy ridge the roving Tartar bounds
(*Paradise Lost*, III. 431–2)

Thomson is cavalierly appropriating Milton's sublime manner, but whereas in Milton sublimity is related to Satan's (questionable) heroism and greatness, in Thomson it belongs merely to a huge object. In the Miltonic simile, as everywhere in *Paradise Lost*, we are aware of Milton's own heroic effect of mind which has risen to the highth of his great argument; Thomson's description is offered to us explicitly as an effort of the scientific intelligence and such a mental activity which moves mountains has something of an heroic quality. There is a visionary power, albeit of a sublunary kind.

One of the happiest revisions to *Autumn* is a short passage added to the mock-heroic drinking episode following the hunt. In 1730 this episode ends with all the company in a drunken sleep under the table, but in 1744 it ends with a hero who contains within himself the Miltonic abyss:

> Perhaps some Doctor, of tremendous Paunch,
> Awful and deep, a black Abyss of Drink,
> Out-lives them all; and from his bury'd Flock
> Retiring, full of Rumination sad,
> Laments the Weakness of these latter Times.[41]

Thomson's own well-reported habits in the early 1740s may have enabled him to draw this clerical portrait from the life.

Winter and *Summer* are far more considerably rewritten than *Spring* and *Autumn*. *Winter* is lengthened overall by nearly three hundred lines and *Summer* by nearly six hundred, the additions in both books serving mostly to extend the historical and geographical excursions of the 1730 text. In *Winter*, acting on hints from Lyttelton, Thomson doubles the number of heroes in his catalogue of ancient worthies and adds enough detail to make it five times as long as it was in 1730. The additional names now make the Romans nearly as numerous as the Greeks, but the greater importance of the Greeks is recognized by their being given twice as many lines. (Their importance is recognized in *Spring* too, where in 1730 Thomson mentioned the elegance and taste of ancient Rome, but in 1744 adds 'by *Greece* refin'd'.) In *Winter*, though, the 1744 text now invites the shades of heroic ancient Romans and Greeks alike to look upon a modern exemplary hero. This is Peter the Great, who is shown gathering abroad 'the Seeds of Trade, of useful Arts, | Of Civil Wisdom, and of Martial Skill', then returning to Russia to exert a reforming vigour, before which '*Sloth* flies the Land':[42] in his nature and progressive activities he foreshadows the Knight of Arts and Industry in *The Castle of Indolence*.

The panegyric upon Peter the Great follows a mental journey through the

Arctic winter expanded threefold from 1730. Thomson introduces a state felon
exiled to Siberia, which is paradoxically a 'Prison of unbounded Wilds'; he
refers to the nomads of Tartary, whose restless, warlike ancestors migrated to
Europe and overthrew the Roman empire, as narrated in *Liberty*; but he devotes
far more space to the peaceable Lapps, who enjoy a frugal, contented life in a
landscape that seems enchanted. In the long night of winter a blue crust of ice
reflects the waving blaze of the aurora borealis, and vivid moons 'light the
Chace, | Or guide their daring Steps to *Finland*-Fairs'. Summer reveals

> Lakes and Floods,
> Where pure *Niemi's* fairy Mountains rise,
> And fring'd with Roses *Tenglio* rolls his Stream.

Turning from the beautiful to the sublime,

> Still pressing on, beyond *Tornea's Lake*,
> And *Helca* flaming thro' a Waste of Snow,
> And farthest *Greenland*, to the Pole itself,
> Where failing gradual Life at length goes out,
> The Muse expands her solitary Flight;
> And, hovering o'er the wild stupendous Scene,
> Beholds new Seas beneath another Sky.[43]

It is as if Thomson is trying the stamina of 'Imagination's vivid Eye'.

A similar trial is made in *Summer*, when Thomson sets out upon a mental
journey, now extended to three times its 1730 length, with the exhortion:

> Now come, bold *Fancy*, spread a daring Flight,
> And view the Wonders of the *torrid* Zone.

Corresponding lines in the earlier text had promised a recital of

> The various Summer-Horrors, which infest
> Kingdoms that scorch below severer Suns,

but in the 1744 tropical excursion, as too in the arctic excursion in *Winter*,
pleasures and pains, horrors and delights, are more evenly balanced than in
1730. In the earlier text Thomson drew attention to the fortunate paradox that
tropical fruits contain cooling juices; in 1744 he enlarges that earlier brief
reference into an ecstasy of innocent sensuous delight. 'Bear me *Pomona*', he
exclaims, as in imagination he enjoys the lemon, lime, orange, coconut, and
pomegranate, or reclines beneath 'the spreading Tamarind that shakes |
Fann'd by the Breeze, its Fever-cooling Fruit', or seizes a pineapple:

> Quick let me strip thee of thy tufty Coat,
> Spread thy ambrosial Stores, and feast with *Jove*.

There is a feast too which delights and satiates the wandering eye in 'Plains immense . . . interminable Meads . . . vast Savannahs . . . Prodigious Rivers' and all the scenes 'where retir'd, | From little Scenes of Art, great *Nature* dwells'.[44]

Most of the mental travel in *Summer* 1730 was restricted to the north African desert, but in 1744 Thomson calls upon his Muse to 'burst' the 'Desart-Barrier', to view the earthly paradise of Abyssinia and trace the course of the Nile; his imaginative eye then darts over the world's great rivers from Siam to South America, in each case picking out some small, strange picturesque or societal detail:

> From *Menam*'s orient Stream, that nightly shines
> With Insect-Lamps, to where Aurora sheds
> On *Indus*' smiling Banks the rosy Shower . . .
> Wide o'er his Isles, the branching *Oronoque*
> Rolls a brown Deluge; and the Native drives
> To dwell aloft on Life-sufficing Trees,
> At once his Dome, his Robe, his Food, and Arms.

As in the earlier flight over 'vast Savannahs', the eye of fancy tires as it takes in the immensity of rivers such as the Amazon or 'Sea-like *Plata*':

> In silent Dignity they sweep along,
> And traverse Realms unknown, and blooming Wilds,
> And fruitful Desarts, Worlds of Solitude,
> Where the Sun smiles and Seasons teem in vain.

The endless pouring of mighty rivers is in *Autumn* evidence of the Providential 'full-adjusted Harmony of Things', [45] but in *Summer* it is regarded in a more limited, political aspect as a 'wondrous Waste of Wealth'. Like the prolific vegetation and precious minerals of the tropics it cannot benefit the natives, whose political institutions are as tyrannical as the sun itself.

The rest of the tropical excursion in 1744 is mostly a catalogue of horrors, beginning with the serpent and other dreadful desert beasts and the fearful solitary, all carried over from *Summer* (1727), with some additional lurid circumstances. Two of the most extravagant desert horrors of earlier versions, the story of the two tombs (1727) and the petrified city (1730) are now omitted, possibly because Thomson now thought they were fabulous. In their place are a sandstorm and a typhoon. The conclusion of the passage, when, after a caravan is buried, and,

> In *Cairo*'s crouded Streets,
> Th 'Impatient Merchant, wondering, waits in vain,
> And *Mecca* saddens at the long Delay,

was praised by Wordsworth as a 'beautiful instance of the modifying and *investive* power of the imagination'.[46] The conclusion of the typhoon passage, when sharks devour the human cargo of a sinking slave-ship, inspired Turner's famous painting of that subject. The last of the summer-horrors here, as in earlier texts, is plague, the description of which is now greatly elaborated in order to incorporate a scientific explanation.[47]

The English scenes of *Summer* are not enlarged nearly as much as the tropical ones, but Thomson now adds an idyllic-georgic sheep-shearing episode and the description of an evening walk and the prospect from Richmond Hill, with an address to 'Amanda'. The habits from which he wanted Elizabeth Young to save him may have guiltily crossed his mind when he only slightly revised his exhortation to early rising at the beginning of *Summer* and reproached the man who lies upon 'the Bed of Sloth . . . losing Half | The fleeting moments of too short a Life'. He rewrites a passage on microscopic nature transferred from *Spring* and alters the sex of personified 'Ignorance' from male to female (a change that might just possibly glance at Elizabeth Young's mother). He alters the story of Damon and Musidora, removing what little moral import it might have had in 1730. His last considerable revision to *Summer* is the elaboration of detail in the catalogue of English worthies and the addition to it of Alfred ('the best of *Kings*'), the warlike Edwards and Henrys, Chaucer and Spenser.[48]

Though praise of Alfred at this date could not of itself be described as a political act, it is in keeping with the clear political bias brought into the *Seasons* as a result of the 1744 revisions, for Thomson now introduces several lengthy commendations of leading opposition politicians: Chesterfield, a man of 'Patriot-Virtues', who 'Rejects the Allurements of corrupted Power'; Lyttelton, 'unwarp'd by Party-Rage', who plans to raise Britannia 'from the venal Gulph'; Pitt, whose eloquence

> Of honest Zeal th' indignant Lightning throws,
> And shakes Corruption on her venal Throne;

James Hammond, the Prince of Wales's equerry, who died young after 'glowing in the Band | Of *youthful Patriots*'; and Cobham, the Nestor of them all, whose case prompts a little bellicose outburst, characteristic of the poet of *Britannia*. Thomson complains that Cobham's military skills are not being employed by the government even though Britain and France are now at war, or, as he puts it,

> the proud Foe
> The faithless vain Disturber of Mankind,
> Insulting *Gaul*, has rous'd the World to War,

and British youth are eager to press 'Those polish'd Robbers, those ambitious Slaves' within their bounds. To complement all this added praise of the opposition Thomson deleted a reference to the 'patriot-band' in his earlier account of the Jail Committee in *Winter*, presumably because the epithet 'patriot' was now so fully appropriated by the opposition that it could no longer be applied to a body set up by the government.[49] The opposition credentials of the revised complete *Seasons* were confirmed when it was dedicated to the Prince of Wales, though the individual dedications of its four books still stand virtually unaltered from 1730.

When this new edition was published by Millar in July Thomson presented a copy to Aaron Hill, sending it not direct but by way of their common acquaintance the printer and novelist Samuel Richardson. Hill had helped Thomson in his early literary career and resented Thomson's recent neglect of him. He now felt slighted by the use of an intermediary in the matter of the presentation copy, so his reply to Richardson on 24 July carries a not-unjustified whiff of sarcasm:

To the Author of the Seasons will you be so good as to return my thanks, for his remembering an old friend; who though he had still been forgotten, would, not withstanding that, have yearly traced him round with new delight, from Spring quite down to Winter. And, because I find myself obliged to another writer for his present, through such a hand as your's, pray please to let him know, I thank him for the favour. But, indeed, the more I read these blank verse eruptions, the more beautifully necessary I perceive the yoke of rhyming.[50]

Although, as I conjecture, Thomson may have been paid for his very considerable labour in revising the *Seasons*, he was so pinched at this time that he was obliged to ask his friend and fellow freemason John Sargent to lend him twenty guineas. The letter containing his request is dated from Richmond on 24 July; it also expresses the hope that the fortunes of their common friend John Armstrong will improve, presumably as a result of the publication of his poem *The Art of Preserving Health* by Millar three months before. There is a glimpse of the Scottish friends also in a letter of 10 October from Millar to John Forbes, then on the Continent with his regiment: 'Our Freind Peter [Murdoch] is well in Suffolk, Mr Mitchell, Thomson, and Armstrong are all in good health and frequently join with me in remembring you.' Sargent was an acquaintance of the Edinburgh days with whom Thomson re-established a firmer friendship in the last years of his life. In April 1748 Thomson wrote to his old friend William Paterson of Sargent, 'who in verity turns out one of the Best men of our youthful Acquaintance, honest, honourable, friendly, and generous', and who 'is so happily married, that I could almost say—The same Case happen to us all.' Thomson borrowed from Sargent for 'five or six months', but within less than four months he was receiving money from his London friend Solomon Mendez. On 8 November he wrote to Mendez from Richmond, 'I received yours, and thank you for this kind Instance of your Friendship. If it is in a Bank-Bill, inclose it and bid Mr Foster the Waterman take care of it, as being of value; but should it be in Money, even give it him to bring to me: he is a very honest Man.' Thomson also asks Mendez to send two books by way of the honest waterman; Robert James's *Medicinal Dictionary* and a natural history of Barbadoes (probably the one by Sir Hans Sloane).[51]

Thomson's long-continued reading of travel literature is borne out by the *Seasons* and by the contents of his library, but McKillop conjectures that Thomson's particular interest in the natural history of Barbadoes at this time was stimulated by his appointment as Surveyor-General of the Leeward Islands.[52] It is uncertain, however, exactly when between 1744 and 1746 this appointment was made. Murdoch and Smollett say that Thomson obtained this post through the influence of Lord Lyttelton.[53] This influence could perhaps have been exerted as early as November 1744, by which time some of Lyttelton's political allies had joined the government now headed by Henry Pelham; Lyttelton himself did not desert the Prince of Wales and join the government until 25 December 1744, when he was appointed a Lord of the Treasury in the 'Broad Bottom' ministry. Thomson's interest in the *Medicinal Dictionary* is explained by the remainder of his November letter to Mendez which is given over to a wry, half-humorous description of his state of health:

I have really been very ill for some Days past of a Cold and sore Throat, the Swelling of the Glands behind the Ear that truly torment me. My Throat is so sore that I cannot eat, nay, which is worse, I cannot drink—only gulp something even with immense Pain. I had a sharp-pointed little Knife directed by a skilful Surgeon's Hand, in my Throat today, but with little Ease. The Worst of it is the Muses, those Daughters of continual Delight, abhor such a State.[54]

He could not, however, have been abhorrent to the Muses for long, because he was able to finish his new tragedy *Tancred and Sigismunda* by the end of the year.

On 29 December 1744 David Garrick wrote to John Hoadley, 'Thompson has a Tragedy ready for Us, upon the Tapestry story in the Second Vol. of Gilblas.'[55] The 'Us' of this letter referred to the new management at Drury Lane, from which Charles Fleetwood had recently departed; he had sold his patent to a pair of bankers, who installed the actor James Lacy (1696–1774) as manager. Fleetwood's unreliability was the likely reason why *Edward and Eleonora* had been submitted to the other house, Covent Garden: now he was gone it was natural that Thomson would return to the theatre where *Sophonisba* and *Agamemnon* had been acted. Covent Garden now possessed one attraction, in as much as his close friend Quin had transferred his talents there in 1742, but it seems that John Rich, the manager, was at this time unsympathetic to new plays. No entirely new play had been presented there in the four theatrical seasons since the banning of *Edward and Eleonora*, in which time a dozen had been seen at Drury Lane. Perhaps Thomson's patron Lyttelton and Lyttelton's friend William Pitt influenced the choice of theatre, as it was said they took a hand in directing the play. Thomas Davies recalls that the two young states-men 'had taken upon themselves the patronage of Thomson's Tancred and Sigismunda; under their direction and influence it was acted at Drury-Lane'. They attended the rehearsal 'with great assiduity; they had a sincere value for the amiable author. Their instructions were heard by the players with great respect, and embraced with implicit confidence.'[56]

It was quite common for members of the aristocracy to approach managers on behalf of playwrights. About the time that Lacy agreed to take *Tancred and Sigismunda* he was asked by Mallet's old pupil Lord George Graham (Montrose's son) to stage Smollett's play *The Regicide*. Smollett's preface to the printed edition of 1749 quotes a letter in which Lord George tells Smollett, 'I have received Mr L——'s Answer; who says, he thinks your Play has indubi-table Merit, but has prior Promises to Mr T——n, as an honest Man, cannot be evaded.'[57] No doubt Pitt and Lyttelton were as bent upon improving *Tancred and Sigismunda* aesthetically, as Lyttelton was in his revisions to the *Seasons* eighteen months earlier, but it is possible that they were making political signals by approving and improving a play that was much less controversial than *Agamemnon* or *Edward and Eleonora*.

Tancred and Sigismunda is set in twelfth-century Sicily, so it completes with *Edward and Eleonora* and *Alfred* a trio of dramatic pieces on Gothic subjects. It is longer and has a far more complicated plot than any other play by Thomson. The hero Tancred, an offspring of the old, now dispossessed, royal line of Sicily has been kept in ignorance of his high birth during his education in the household of Siffredi, Lord High Chancellor of Sicily, whose daughter Sigismunda loves and is loved by Tancred. At the beginning of the play the King of Sicily ('William the Good') dies, whereupon Siffredi reveals to Tancred the secret of his birth and urges him to marry the late King's sister Constantia, the rival claimant to the throne. It soon transpires that such a marriage is enjoined in King William's will as a condition for Tancred's succession. Loving Sigismunda as he does, Tancred refuses Siffredi's proposal; he gives Siffredi a blank paper with his signature, ordering that a marriage contract between himself and Sigismunda should be drawn up on it. Siffredi, though, writes a marriage contract between Tancred and Constantia on the paper; he also promises Sigismunda's hand to Count Osmond, High Constable of Sicily and leader of Constantia's faction. Siffredi, in the presence of Tancred, Constantia, and the Sicilian Senate, produces both King William's will and the contract he has just fabricated: both documents are received by the Senate and people with joy, as the means of reconciliation between the rival royal lines. Though indignant, Tancred is too amazed to disavow the forged contract immediately and publicly; meanwhile Sigismunda, believing that Tancred has betrayed her, obeys her father and is hastily married to Osmond, immediately after which she receives a letter from Tancred, explaining what has happened and vowing fidelity to her. Tancred, now king, tyrannically resolves to annul Sigismunda's marriage and orders the imprisonment of Osmond, who is promptly released on parole by the justifiably sympathetic commander of the castle and comes into Sigismunda's apartment late at night, where she is alone with Tancred who is vainly trying to persuade her to renounce her marriage. Osmond draws his sword upon Tancred, but is mortally wounded by him; Sigismunda throws herself down beside her husband to assure him that she is a faithful wife but he stabs her to death. Tancred is prevented by his friend Rodolpho from killing himself. The play ends with Siffredi regretting the deceit that he had practised with such good intentions.

This plot is based upon 'Le mariage de Vengeance', a nouvelle in Le Sage's *Gil Blas* (1715), book iv, chapter 4. It is thus an unusually modern source for a Thomson play; Le Sage was still alive when it was first acted. Thomson takes his story-line and its principal episode from *Gil Blas*, but compresses the action in time and space to observe the unities as usual; he takes hints for dialogue from his source, and, like Le Sage, he makes much of the struggle between passion and reason, but he renames the lovers, who are called Henriques and Blanche in *Gil Blas*. The name Sigismunda may have been suggested by the story in the *Decameron* that is imitated in Dryden's *Sigismunda and Guiscardo*; Boccaccio's tale also has a Tancred, but he is Sigismunda's tyrannical father. Their tragic history does not resemble the plot of Le Sage's nouvelle or Thomson's play.[58]

Thomson's Tancred more significantly is a historical figure, for Thomson provides his play with a far more specific historical context than Le Sage's story. William the Good, who dies at the opening of the action, leaving the fatal will, in fact ruled Sicily from 1166 to 1189 and deserved his surname so fully that he is praised in Dante's *Paradiso* (xx. 61–6). He died childless, leaving his kingdom to Constance, his aunt (not his sister as in the play); she was wife of Henry VI, King of the Romans, son of Frederick Barbarossa. In Act V, Scene ii, Thomson refers to the will and names all these historical figures, but he departs from fact by redrawing the will to make Constantia/Constance succeed to the throne only if Tancred refuses to marry her. The historical Count Tancred of Lucca was the natural son of William the Good's uncle, and descended, as in the play, from 'our famous Heroe, Roger the First',[59] the man who refounded the Norman Kingdom of Sicily after its recovery from the Saracens. Under

Norman law, Constance was not barred from succession by her sex, nor was Tancred barred by his illegitimacy. With his Sicilian connections Tancred was popular, with her German connections Constance was not. On William's death Tancred disputed the succession with Constance and there was a civil war. Thomson could have found all this in Maimbourg's *History of the Crusades*, the 1685 English translation of which was in his own library.[60]

Thomson's addition of authentic and invented historical material to his source in Le Sage testifies less to an antiquarian interest in twelfth-century Sicily then to his continuing involvement in contemporary English politics, though we shall see that the political message of *Tancred and Sigismunda* is very different from that of *Agamemnon* and *Edward and Eleonora*. Walpole had fallen in 1742; by the end of 1744 Henry Pelham was emerging as clear victor in the struggle for power among Walpole's former associates and opponents. Pelham formed a 'Broad Bottom' government in November, which Lyttelton joined a month later as a Lord of the Treasury, thereupon losing his post at the Prince of Wales's court. Pitt resigned his office in the Prince's household, but found it difficult to earn the King's forgiveness for his earlier attacks on pro-Hanover policies; nevertheless he supported Pelham's ministry, commending, for instance, its 'moderate and healing' measures.[61]

This reconciliation between former Whig opposition and post-Walpole Whig administration is the political context of *Tancred and Sigismunda*. It is surely alluded to in Osmond's speech about the projected union of Tancred and Constantia:

> We meet to-day with open Hearts and Looks,
> Not gloom'd by Party, scouling on each other,
> But all the children of one happy Isle,
> The social Sons of Liberty. No Pride,
> No Passion now, no thwarting Views divide us.

Osmond could almost be Lyttelton making his peace with Pelham when he declares:

> I here renounce those Errors and Divisions
> That have so long disturb'd our Peace, and seem'd,
> Fermenting still, to threaten new Commotions —
> By time instructed, let us not disdain
> To quit Mistakes.[62]

There was no doubt concerning such a contemporary political application in the mind of Benjamin Victor, a former friend of Thomson now resentful of his success, when he wrote sarcastically in the *Daily Post* on 26 April 1745:

We all plainly saw by what Interest the Author of *Tancred and Sigismunda* was supported. A very remarkable new Lord of the Treasury was proud of appearing its Foster Father, and attended at the Publick Rehearsals; the first Night of the Performance this celebrated Person, and his Friends in the Box with him (all very lately most flaming Patriots!) were seen clapping their Hands at the following remarkable Speech.

Victor here quotes the lines beginning 'I here renounce', adds that in his opinion the right reading of the fourth line is 'by *Place* instructed, etc.', continues with a denunciation of Lyttelton and Pitt as turncoats, and concludes with dismissive satire of Thomson's play.[63]

A very different kind of political context for the play was suggested in a gossipy late-Victorian compilation, John Doran's *London in the Jacobite Times* (1877). Doran asserts: 'Whigs and Jacobites sat in judgement [on *Tancred and Sigismunda*]. Thomson's cunning, however, enabled him to please both parties.' Doran then quotes some passages from the play which he claims were applauded in the theatre, being taken by one party to be pro-Whig and the other party to be pro-Jacobite. Doran's unsupported assertions are the basis for John Loftis's argument that some speeches in *Tancred and Sigismunda* covertly support the Jacobite cause,[64] but Doran finds covert Jacobitism in all Thomson's earlier plays and he shows very little understanding of the politics of the 1730s and 1740s, evidently believing that Jacobites formed the sole opposition to the government; so he is hardly an authoritative witness. There is no evidence from Thomson's own century to indicate that he had any Jacobite sympathies; all the political statements in his writings show him to be a typical anti-Papist, lowland Scotch Whig. If there are any Jacobite references at all in *Tancred and Sigismunda* they are likely to be hostile: for instance, French-assisted Jacobitism could conceivably be the implicit danger against which Osmond counsels political unity in the passages quoted above. The printed play was dedicated to the Prince of Wales and it contains a now-familiar Thomsonian description of the ideal patriot king, who loves his people, exalts the good, depresses the bad, spurns flatterers and slanderers, and is faithful to the spirit of 1688, so deserving the gratitude of

> a People in their Rights
> And Industry protected; living safe
> Beneath the sacred Shelter of the Laws.[65]

This paragon, like other such in Thomson's plays may have been sketched with Frederick in mind. Here, though, he is not the hero or even a character in the action, but dead King William: an indication perhaps that politics are not as central to this play as to Thomson's earlier efforts for the stage.

Tancred and Sigismunda is the termination of a steady development from

Sophonisba, through *Agamemnon* and *Edward and Eleonora*, away from the historical and heroic towards the melodramatic, sentimental, and domestic. The more inward nature of the later play is evidenced by the fact that in it there are over ten times as many lines spoken in soliloquy as in *Sophonisba*. This said, Tancred is the typical protagonist of heroic tragedy in that he is placed in a situation where love and honour are in conflict, but he is tricked into that situation and he seeks to escape from it by unhesitatingly giving way to his passions; he will risk civil war to win back Sigismunda. There is no villain, for Osmond is justified in his fear of Siffredi's and Tancred's designs and he displays a sounder awareness of the rights and responsibilities of kingship than Tancred does. When he interrupts the lovers in Act IV and defies his new king he is not only defending his honour as a husband but asserting the right of a subject to rebel against a tyrant.

The primary conflict of the play is between 'the cold Prudence of remorseless Age' and the instinctive and dangerous passions of youth. Siffredi is the embodiment of public duty and reason; he articulates the moral wisdom which Thomson approves of in other contexts, when, for instance, he warns Tancred not to allow his sense of honour to be blinded by passion:

> Nothing so easy as in Speculation,
> And at a distance seen, the Course of Honour,
> A fair delightful Champian strew'd with Flowers.
> But when the Practice comes; when our fond Passions,
> Pleasure and Pride and Self-Indulgence throw
> Their magic Dust around, the Prospect roughens:
> Then dreadful Passes, craggy Mountains rise,
> Cliffs to be scal'd, and Torrents to be stem'd:
> Then toil ensues, and Perseverance stern;
> And endless Combats with our grosser Sense,
> Oft lost, and oft renew'd; and generous Pain
> For others felt; and, harder Lesson still!
> Our honest Bliss for others sacrific'd;
> And all the rugged Task of Virtue quails
> The stoutest Heart of common Resolution.
> Few get above this turbid Scene of Strife
> Few gain the Summit, breathe that purer Air,
> That heavenly Ether, which untroubled sees
> The Storm of Vice and Passion rage below.

This is the same magic dust that the wicked enchanter of *The Castle of Indolence* throws into the eyes of his victims when he tries to seduce them into a life of self-indulgence. Siffredi, like the Knight of Arts and Industry in Thomson's *Castle*, is the spokesman for reason and virtue, who, like the Knight, uses a (metaphorical) net to good purpose, for he speaks of setting an 'honest Snare' for Tancred. Siffredi is a moral preceptor with correct views; he acts from the highest and most disinterested motives when he parts the lovers, incidentally sacrificing the 'honest Bliss' he would feel if his daughter were both a queen and happy. The effects of well-meaning deceit in his trick upon Tancred are compounded by his exercise of parental authority upon his daughter in the name of 'Honour, Duty, and determin'd Reason', and by Sigismunda's obedience, 'Sweet filial Piety', and desire to make her father happy.[66] With Sigismunda bound by her wifely honour and Tancred and Osmond roused by jealous sexual rage, not unmixed with political rivalry, there is a situation which, we feel, can be resolved only in tragedy. It need hardly be said that we are not in the loaded allegorical world of *The Castle of Indolence*. Every character in *Tancred and Sigismunda* has some right on his side, and, to that degree at least, may command some of our sympathies.

It has been argued further that the situation of the hero and heroine had a particular poignancy for Thomson because he was drawing upon private emotional experience. Douglas Grant claims:

The conclusion is unavoidable that the poet was dramatizing his own love-affair with Elizabeth Young, who he believed, or persuaded himself to believe, would have married him, as Sigismunda would have married Tancred, had a parent not interposed her authority. Siffredi's concluding address to the audience is, in effect, Thomson's warning appeal to Mrs Young. Siffredi, looking towards the dead Sigismunda, says:

> Behold the fatal Work of my dark Hand,
> That by rude Force the Passions would command, . . .
> They may be rul'd, but will not be opprest.
> Taught hence, Ye Parents, who from Nature stray,
> And the great Ties of social Life betray;
> Ne'er with your Children act a Tyrant's Part:
> 'Tis yours to guide, not violate the Heart.[67]

This may be so, though the very last words of Siffredi's summing-up are addressed to men in public life, the 'vainly wise, who o'er Mankind preside', warning them not to believe that 'from Evil Good can ever rise'.[68]

Tancred and Sigismunda opened at Drury Lane on 18 March 1745 and ran for nine nights to 2 April. As with his previously staged plays, the author enjoyed three benefit performances, the third being on the eighth night of acting, because of a rearrangement of Peg Woffington's benefit. The Prince and Princess of Wales attended Thomson's second benefit, on 26 March. The first author's benefit was, as usual, on the third night, but Thomson did not unduly bestir himself to ensure its success, to judge by a letter from Viscount Barrington to Mallet:

There is but one Man in England more Indolent than myself and that is Thompson. Would you believe it, he has never sent me a single Tickett to dispose of. I got some from Millar without his Knowledge, so he will as it happens lose nothing by forgeting that I wish him well, but I dare swear many others whom his lazyness or modesty has made him neglect take it ill, and what is worse take no Ticketts.[69]

Thomson was as fortunate in his actors as his friends. Thomas Davies recalled:

The play was well acted in all its parts; but its success depended chiefly upon the two principal characters, acted by Mr Garrick and Mrs Cibber, who were formed by nature for the illustration of each other's talents. In their persons they were both somewhat below the middle size: he was, though short, well made; she, though in her form not graceful, and scarcely genteel, was, by the elegance of her manner and symmetry of her features, rendered very attractive. From similarity of complexion, size and countenance, they could have been easily supposed to be brother and sister; but in the powerful expression of the passions, they still approached to a nearer resemblance. He was master of all the passions but more particularly happy in the exhibition of parts where anger, resentment, disdain, horror, despair and madness, predominated. In love, grief and tenderness, she greatly excelled all competitors; and was also unrivalled in the more ardent emotions of jealous love and frantic rage, which she expressed with a degree of sensibility in voice, look, and action, that never failed to draw tears from the most unfeeling.[70]

Garrick, now rapidly rising to pre-eminence on the English stage, was the leading actor at Drury Lane after Quin had decamped to Covent Garden in 1742; his lighter, spontaneous, natural style was gradually proving more acceptable to theatre audiences than Quin's weightier, deliberate, formal style. The contrast between the two actors at this period is vividly brought out by Richard Cumberland, then a Westminster schoolboy, in his account of a performance of Rowe's *The Fair Penitent* at Covent Garden on 14 November 1746. His account of *The Fair Penitent* also included a portrait of Susannah Cibber, which is quoted above in relation to her portrayal of Cassandra in Thomson's *Agamemnon*. Cumberland tells how Quin, playing Horatio, presented himself upon the rising of the curtain in a green velvet coat embroidered down the seams, an enormous full bottomed periwig, rolled stockings and high-heeled square-toe shoes. Cumberland then describes his style as already quoted in my account of Quin's performance as Thomson's Agamemnon. Cumberland continues

but when after long and eager expectation I first beheld little Garrick [playing Lothario], then young and light and alive in every muscle and in every feature, come bounding on the stage . . . it seemed as if a whole century had been stept over in the transition of a single scene; old things were done away, and a new order at once brought forward, bright and luminous, and clearly destined to dispel the barbarisms and bigotry of custom, and superstitiously devoted to the illusions of imposing declamation.[71]

As in *Edward and Eleonora*, Thomson works economically with a cast of four men and two women, though the action of this play is far more complicated than the earlier one. Garrick and Mrs Cibber were brilliant, but by all accounts the remainder of the small cast were very good. Siffredi was played by Thomas Sheridan, the youngest man in the cast, later a noted writer on elocution and father of Richard Brinsley Sheridan. Osmond was played by Denis Delane, and Rodolpho, Tancred's friend, by William Havard, both of whom had been in the casts of earlier Thomson plays (Delane in *Edward and Eleonora* and Havard in *Agamemnon*). One of the audience, Catherine Talbot declared: 'Everybody agrees that no play was so much improved in acting, at least not since the Booths and Bettertons. That first scene especially, where Siffredi discovers to Tancred who he is, pleased one almost beyond any thing I ever saw, indeed even before I saw it, that scene was my favourite.' She also said that it is 'fashionable to run mad about' *Tancred and Sigismunda*. Her correspondent, Elizabeth Carter replied: 'I have really so much pleasure in the beauties of Mr Thomson's writings, and so great a veneration for the morality of them, that it hurts me to find any faults; but yet I cannot help thinking that all the characters in this play (except Osmond's) are unnatural and inconsistent.'[72] Horace Walpole testifies to the play's popularity, but, as always, he writes disparagingly of Thomson:

The town flocks to a new play of Thomson's called *Tancred and Sigismunda*: it is very dull; I have read it. I cannot bear modern poetry; these refiners of the purity of the stage and of the incorrectness of English verse, are most woefully insipid. I had rather have written the most absurd lines in Lee, than *Leonidas* or *The Seasons*; as I had rather be put into the roundhouse for a wrong-headed quarrel, than sup quietly at eight o'clock with my grandmother.[73]

Thomson wrote both the Prologue and the Epilogue. His undistinguished Prologue affirms, not for the first time, that the author will appeal to the hearts of his audience. His Epilogue is less commonplace. Its first lines are normal enough; they are spoken by Anne Budgell (who played Sigismunda's confidante Laura) and they ironically lament Sigismunda's fate:

> Was ever Woman so by Love beytray'd?
> Match'd with two Husbands, and yet—die a Maid.

As she speaks, though,

The Back-Scene opens; and discovers a romantic Silvan Landskip; from which Mrs CIBBER, in the Character of the TRAGIC MUSE, advances slowly to Music, and speaks the following Lines.

> Hence with your flippant Epilogue, that tries
> To wipe the virtuous Tear from BRITISH Eyes:
> That dares my Moral Tragic Scene profane,
> With Strains—at best, unsuiting, light and vain.
> Hence from the pure unsully'd Beams that play
> In yon fair Eyes, where Virtue shines—Away!

She reminds the audience that Greek, Roman, and French tragedies were not sullied by low epilogues, and concludes:

> When thro' five Acts your Hearts have learnt to glow,
> Touch'd with the sacred Force of honest Woe;
> O keep the dear Impression on your Breast,
> Nor idly lose it for a wretched Jest![74]

As we have seen, the Prince of Wales attended the second benefit on 26 March, which was also the day on which the printed text of *Tancred and Sigismunda* was published by Millar. The play was dedicated to the Prince, who was apparently still prepared to be Thomson's patron, even though the poet's chief friend at the Prince's court, Lyttelton, had now left Frederick's service and joined the government. In the dedication Thomson praises the Prince for favouring and protecting letters, as great princes have in all ages. Alluding to his patronage of the drama Thomson makes out familiar claims for the moral and social importance of the theatre and hits in passing at the Licensing Act of 1737:

of all the different Species of Writing, none has such an Effect upon the Lives and Manners of Men, as the Dramatick; and therefore that of all others most deserves the Attention of Princes, who, by a judicious Approbation of such Pieces as tend to promote all Publick and Private Virtue, may more than by any coercive Methods secure the Purity of the Stage, and in consequence thereof greatly advance the Morals and Politeness of their People.'[75]

The preliminary pages of the 1745 edition also included the following advertisement: 'This play is considerably shortened in the Performance; but I hope it will not be disagreeable to the Reader to see it as it was at first written; there being a great Difference betwixt a Play in the Closet, and upon the Stage.' In his satirical letter to the *Daily Post* on the politics of the play, quoted above, Benjamin Victor says that three hundred lines were cut on the morning after the first night. The nineteenth-century theatrical biographer Richard Ryan adds some detail, without specifying his source:

When the famous Thomson...had his tragedy, called 'Tancred and Sigismunda', performed at Drury-Lane Theatre, several friends joined Mr Sheridan to entreat Thomson to shorten speeches, which they foresaw would weary the audience: but they offended the poet, without effecting their purpose. Garrick, who played the part of *Tancred*, listened, and said nothing: but at rehearsals, though apparently perfect in his part, continued, occasionally, to take the prompter's copy, and read. The first night, however, without a whisper of his intention, he curtailed his own part, wherever his judgment directed, and the applause he received was great; while Mr Sheridan, and other actors, who had long and tedious parts, laboured on with great difficulty. The conduct of Garrick saved the piece; and Thomson, though enraged when he heard the first omissions, returned Garrick, in the end, his hearty thanks.[76]

No cut lines are marked in the 1745 edition, perhaps because copy for all but the preliminary pages had gone to the printer before the stage run began. *Tancred and Sigismunda* was published only eight days after the first night, whereas the first printed text of *Agamemnon*, in which stage revisions are incorporated, did not appear until nearly three weeks after the first night. The next printed edition of the play, in 1752, adds the following note to the advertisement just quoted: 'What is omitted in the Acting, is marked with inverted Commas.' However, collation of the 1745 and 1752 editions reveals that some lines and one entire scene of the earlier text are omitted from the later text without comment. When these are added to lines marked with inverted commas they make a total of about six hundred, that is a quarter of the entire play, and twice as many as Victor states were cut on the morning after the first night. Though the printed text of *Tancred and Sigismunda* makes it far and away the longest of Thomson's plays, its eventual acting length was about the same as *Agamemnon* (about 1,800 lines). Probably the acting version of 1752 (often reprinted) is the outcome not only of the cuts reported by Victor but also of further cuts for one or more of the revivals of the play in 1747, 1749, and 1752. This might account for the fact that the deleted scene is Act II, Scene iv, the one containing the lines beginning 'I here renounce those Errors and Divisions', for though the scene was applauded in 1745 its sentiments would have been less timely when the play was revived.

Most of the cuts are in the first two acts.[77] Very nearly half of Act II disappears, having the effect of hurrying the action from the announcement of Tancred's engagement to Constantia towards its fatal consequences. Some cuts are made for the sake of decorum: thus the words 'devoutly shave | My holy Scalp' are cut from a characteristic exclamation by Osmond, responding to Siffredi's well-meaning suggestion that Sigismunda should enter a convent to prevent Osmond and Tancred fighting over her:

> Ere Then, by Heavens! I would devoutly shave
> My holy Scalp, turn whining Monk myself.[78]

Verbal flowers, similar to those in *Sophonisba* which irritated Barton Booth are plucked out; for instance the whole of Siffredi's fine speech on the 'Course of

Honour' in Act I, Scene iv, is cut. Apart from the politically significant deletion of Act II, Scene iv, the substantial cuts are generally to shorten long speeches, especially soliloquies. For instance Sigismunda's 56-line speech in Act III, Scene i, 'alone, sitting in a disconsolate Posture',[79] is cut to 19 lines. The parts of the two principal male characters are cut even more overall. In the full-length version printed in 1745 Tancred has the largest number of lines, nearly a hundred more than Sigismunda, who has fewer even than Siffredi, but in the acting version of 1752 hers becomes the longest part of all and Tancred's the third longest (after Siffredi's); Sigismunda also appears in more scenes than any other character. Thus the acting version emphasizes a little more the importance that Thomson always gives to his leading woman.

In its shortened version *Tancred and Sigismunda* was far and away Thomson's most successful play. In addition to the revivals already mentioned, it was revived in 1755 and thereafter played on the London stage in most seasons down to the 1790s. It was played also in Dublin, the English provinces, and America. It was translated into French and German in the 1760s. Murdoch noted in 1762 that the play 'from the deep romantic distresses of the lovers, continues to draw crowded houses'.[80] By this date Mrs Cibber had chosen the play for her benefit night on no fewer than four occasions,[81] for she was as famous in the role of Sigismunda as Garrick was in that of Tancred—so much so that in 1746, believing that neither of them was to be re-engaged at Covent Garden that season, she wrote to Garrick, 'as there is no Tancred, I am resolved they shall have no Sigismunda'.[82] Garrick played this part in altogether seven seasons; one of the best-known engravings of him shows him costumed as Tancred in the 1752 revival.[83] It may be that Garrick's illness from 4 April 1745 was the only reason that the original run of the play did not extend beyond its ninth night on 2 April.

10

Last Years: *The Castle of Indolence* and *Coriolanus*, 1746–1748

During the original run of *Tancred and Sigismunda*, *Alfred* was revived, also at Drury Lane, where it was played on 20 March, for Mrs Arne's benefit; on 3 April, a version that was edited by Thomas Arne was put on, incorporating more music, more elaborate scenic effects, and less spoken dialogue than the 1740 masque. The title was now *Alfred the Great, King of England*, 'An Historical Musical Drama'; advertisements note 'The Musick composed by Command of his Royal Highness the Prince of Wales, and never perform'd in England, but at his Royal Highnesses Palace at Cliefdon. The Poem was written by Mr Thompson and Mr Mallet. The musick by Mr Arne. To conclude with a Celebrated *Ode in Honour of Great Britain* in imitation of those formerly sung at Banquets of Kings and Heroes.'[1] This *Ode* is 'Rule Britannia', now the grand finale of the work. The libretto was published by Millar on 20 April as *Alfred. An opera. Alter'd from the Play written by Mr Thomson and Mr Mallet.* Thomson was not directly concerned with this revival.

He now had the agreeable task of collecting his profits from *Tancred and Sigismunda*. On 31 May he wrote to a lady, probably the Dowager Viscountess Barrington, mother of the viscount who had complained to Mallet in March that Thomson was too indolent to send him tickets to dispose of:

I did not receive your Pacquet, left for me at Mr Lyttelton's, till Wedensday last. In it I received, along with the returned Tickets, three Pounds six and sixpence in Money, and a Bank Note of fifty Pounds; which makes your whole Collection for Tancred and Sigismunda amount to one hundred and seventy two Pounds sixteen Shillings, and exactly agrees with the Account you sent me Inclosed. This Account, by the Bye (give me Leave to say) you need not have given yourself the Trouble of writing out. Only, it affords a very proper Lesson to one like me, to teach me to be exact even when it is not in the least necessary.

After thanking his correspondent, he continues:

I have undertaken again the terrible Task of writing a new Play; for, not intirely trusting to the Broad Bottom, I will try to subsist upon the narrow but sure one of Self-

Independency, The subject is Titus Marcius Coriolanus, to which my two Friends (whom I will not name least by any Chance the Author of the Daily Post should hear of it) are now reconciled. They are to give me their Advice upon it on Sunday next, when I am to dine with them at Petersham.[2]

The *Daily Post* author is of course Benjamin Victor. Petersham was the seat of the Earl of Harrington; it is praised in a passage added to *Summer* in the 1744 edition (lines 1418–19). Harrington was secretary of state and an important member of Pelham's Broad-Bottom administration which Lyttelton had joined in the previous December. Thomson's reference to the 'Broad Bottom' indicates that he has at least half a hope for a sinecure or pension now that more of his friends and patrons have joined the government.

Nor had he entirely given up hope of securing the love of Elizabeth Young. On 23 October he wrote to her:

You will very likely be surprized to see this Hand, after so long a Silence. Perhaps too your Heart may be moved at the Sight of it, as Mine is in the Writing; the Occasion whereof was This. A little While ago I happened to light upon some imperfect Scrawls of Letters I formerly wrote to You. What Effect they had upon me the following Lines will shew.

> O thou, for whom these Letters speak a Flame,
> Than which from Heaven a purer never came;
> Where every Line with genuine Passion glows,
> While from the Heart the full Effusion flows;
> Where endless Proofs of Love unequal'd reign,
> That cordial Spirit Falsehood cannot feign;
> Where highest Friendship holds the smallest Part,
> Lost in the tender Transports of the Heart,
> The restless Wish that sought thy Good alone,
> And center'd in thy Happiness my own:
> How couldst thou ever form so fell a Thought,
> To lose the Lover who these Letters wrote?

There are eleven more couplets, ending:

> Then let—once dear! oh dearest still!—a Line
> Revive the Heart that ever must be thine!

On 4 November Thomson wrote again:

My dearest charming Miss Young!—but Words cannot express how dear you are to me—have Pity on me, have Pity on a Heart that feels for you every thing that is good and tender in Love and Friendship. Think what I suffer during this Neglect and Silence of yours. I muse forever on You, not with that pleasing Joy as formerly, but with a Dejection that could not but move your Compassion if you knew it. O if you saw the Tears that often rush into my Eyes at the Thought of your Unkindness, That would be instead of all I can write to you! Is there any thing in Nature so prevailing as the Tears and Intreaties of Love like mine? You surely cannot be so barbarous as to reject them. Give me Leave to cite two Lines of a Work I am at present engaged in.

> Art thou above the Gods, who joy to shower
> Their doubled Goodness on repenting Mortals?

The quotation is from Act III, Scene ii, of *Coriolanus*. Thomson begs for a meeting, if only for half an hour; he flatters himself with the hope that he will be the happiest, kindest, and best of husbands before next spring: 'Without you I cannot live. You are truly the Life of my Life, the Soul of whatever is excellent good and desireable to me. I wish to live only to live with you; I wish for the Goods of Fortune only to bestow them on You.'[3]

Thomson intermittently enjoyed pensions and sinecures, his plays were moderately profitable, but his management of his erratic income was more poetical than prudent, so he never secured a regular or substantial supply of the goods of fortune. William Robertson says that he was never wealthy enough to marry. His lack of wealth was certainly the objection vigorously urged by Elizabeth's widowed mother, who 'constantly opposed the poet's pretensions to Amanda, saying to her one day, "What! would you marry Thomson? He will make ballads and you will sing them."' A version of this story was printed in the *Universal Magazine* in 1780, with the added claim that Elizabeth herself encouraged the poet's addresses, but Lady Philippina Knight's testimony is that Elizabeth shared her mother's objections to Thomson's lack of fortune. On the evidence of Thomson's own letters we may doubt if Miss Young really encouraged him. For all his poetic sensibility, Thomson gormandized and drank heavily; he carried himself awkwardly, had run to fat, was negligent in his dress, and sweated copiously. His appearance, to judge by the portrait painted in 1746 by John Patoun, was unprepossessing: see Plates 11 and 12. Douglas Grant wisely observes that Miss Young 'must have seen many objections to Thomson in his age, habits, impecuniosity, and perhaps in his manner of courtship; his letters, and probably his conversation, were too self-pitying, hesitant, and gauche to win a woman's heart.'[4] The fact that she carefully preserved Thomson's letters probably indicates, however, some tenderness on her part towards the poet.

The man who did eventually win her heart was a naval officer named John Campbell; he talked broad Scots like Thomson but was otherwise as different from the poet as can be imagined. At the time Thomson was courting Miss Young to no avail Campbell was in his early twenties, sailing the western Pacific, serving as master's mate, subsequently as sailing master, under Commodore Anson, aboard the *Centurion* on that famous four-year circumnaviga-

11. James Thomson, engraving by Basire, 1761, after John Patoun, 1746.

12. James Thomson, after John Patoun.

tion when Anson lost most of his ships and their crews but captured more treasure than any English naval expedition had ever brought home before or would ever bring home again. On that very Sunday when Thomson was cruising near Chelsea in the hope of intercepting *his* great prize the sea-worn and battle-hardened crew of the *Centurion* were at gunnery practice as they waited off the Philippine Islands to intercept a rich plate galleon from Acapulco. The galleon was captured, the *Centurion* returned safely to England a year later, and thirty-two wagons were needed to carry the treasure chests from Portsmouth to the Tower of London. After legal wrangles over the prize money were settled in 1747, Captain Campbell, as he had then become, was worth several thousand pounds and well able to support a wife. Able to win one too, if we may judge by the very fine physical presence displayed in a surviving portrait of Campbell.[5] We do not know when or how he met Elizabeth Young or when they married, but, in the light of William Robertson's remarks on Thomson's death, the marriage must have been before August 1748; she died before 1780; he was Governor of Newfoundland for four years from 1782; he died in 1790, having reached the high naval rank of Vice-Admiral of the Red. Lady Philippina Knight's recollections suggest that the two were well matched: 'though very few mixed more in the general world than they both did, yet they both retained the behavior of those Scotch who have not taken up the task of outdoing the French in ceremony and servility'. Campbell's obituarist in *The Gentleman's Magazine* wrote:

He preserved his original simplicity of manners till his death, notwithstanding he lived among and mixed with the first people in the Kingdom; but he had withal a dry sarcastic mode of expression as well as manner, which approached so near to that in which Mr Macklin played the character of Sir Archy McSarcasm, that I have often thought that excellent actor must have seen and copied him.

There is a story to confirm that Campbell had the kind of downright, practical, no-sentimental-nonsense character that one might expect of a sailor who had been a petty officer and had 'come up through the hawse-hole' to commissioned rank. At the battle of Quiberon Bay in 1759, England's greatest naval victory since the Armada, he was captain of Admiral Hawke's flagship, proving himself to be, in Hawke's words, 'an honest, brave and good officer in all respects, and fully answered the good opinion I had ever conceived of him'. Campbell was given the honour of taking the despatches giving news of the victory to the King. Anson rode in the coach with him and, it is said, intimated to him that a knighthood was his if he wanted it: 'Campbell—widely regarded as a very decided Scotch character—replied: "Throth, my Lord, I ken nae use that will be to me." Anson murmured that his wife might like it. "Well then", Campbell swiftly replied, "His Majesty may knight her if he pleases!".'[6]

Though Thomson's matrimonial hopes had been shipwrecked, his poetical reputation was set fair. The 1744 edition of *The Seasons* sold so rapidly that Millar published new editions in June 1745 and May 1746, both editions containing revisions by Thomson. The poet's work was becoming known in Germany, for a translation of *The Seasons* by Barthold Heinrich Brockes (1680–1747) was printed with parallel English text in 1745, and the English text of *Agamemnon* was reprinted for the benefit of German students of English in John Tompson's *English Miscellanies*, 'collected out of the most approved authors of the English tongue' (Gottingen, 1746). That his name could be included among possible identifications of the unnamed editor of a new weekly journal *The True Patriot*, launched in November 1745, suggests that Thomson's writings were still thought to have political force in England: the names are Bolingbroke, Bishop Hoadly, Chesterfield, Warburton, Dodington, Lyttelton, Fielding (the actual editor and the compiler of this list), Thomson 'or indeed any other Person who hath distinguished himself in the Republic of Letters'.[7]

Thomson completed *Coriolanus* at some time in 1746. He would have been working on it at the time when the Young Pretender, like Coriolanus, was invading his ancestral home, but there is nothing that can be construed as a reference to the '45 in the play or, indeed, in any other surviving public or private utterance by the poet. All we know is that Thomson, like a true lowland Whig, regarded the Highland clans as barbarous. In *Liberty*, he includes among various forms of moral and social degeneration in the Middle Ages the transformation of

> Brave antient *Freedom* to the *Rage of Slaves*,
> Proud of their State, and fighting for their chains.

A footnote indentifies this Rage as 'Vassalage, whence the Attachment of Clans to their Chief'; the context of the passage associates clansmen with superstitious monks, 'banditti' crusaders, duellists, and other embodiments of anarchy or social backwardness.[8]

By 1746 too the Broad Bottom ministry had provided Thomson with a sinecure. Through the influence of Lyttelton he was appointed, jointly with his friend William Paterson, to the office of Surveyor-General of Customs for the Leeward Islands. It was Paterson who travelled out to Barbados and carried out the duties of the post; his warrant to commence duty is dated 29 May 1746. The place was worth £400 a year for Paterson, and, it was claimed, £300 for Thomson.[9] Paterson had lost his employment in Lord Tweeddale's office when the Secretaryship of State for Scotland was abolished in 1746.

There is a glimpse of Thomson about this time in the reminiscences of a young Scotsman Alexander Carlyle, who met him in London, 'at the Ducie

Tavern at Temple Bar', in the early part of 1746, when the company included Armstrong, Murdoch (recently elected FRS in recognition of his mathematical writings), Millar, and a young Scots physician named Thomas Dickson. Carlyle writes, 'Thomson came last and Disappointed me both by his Appearance and Conversation. Armstrong bore him Down, having Got into his Sarcastical Vein, by the Wine he had Drank before Thomson Join'd us.' Murdoch asserts that in mixed or very numerous company Thomson 'made but an indifferent figure: but with a few select friends, he was open, sprightly, and entertaining. His wit flowed freely, but pertinently, and at due intervals, leaving room for every one to contribute his share.'[10]

Smollett was a member of the tavern-haunting Scottish circle by this time, for he had returned from the excitements of naval service in the West Indies and was settled in London as a surgeon; he was in a coffee-house with Carlyle in April 1746, 'when news of the battle of Culloden arrived, and when London all over was in a perfect uproar of joy'.[11] One of Thomson's closest friends, Andrew Mitchell, was Smollett's kinsman, and references in Smollett's writings indicate personal acquaintance with as well as respect for Thomson. Possibly Thomson was losing his taste for London taverns when Carlyle was disappointed in him, for on 31 March 1747 we find him writing to Mallet from Richmond in order to decline an invitation to come to London and read the manuscript of Mallet's *Amyntor and Theodora* (published April 1747): 'Your offer is very kind and friendly; but I shall relish the Pleasure, which I know I must have in reading your Poem infinitely better here than in a damned London Tavern.' Richmond was where the finest poet among the new generation of young literary adventurers cultivated Thomson's acquaintance. Murdoch writes that, by 1748, William Collins 'had lived some time at *Richmond*, but forsook it when Mr *Thomson* died'. William Robertson confirms that Collins visited Thomson in Richmond. On at least one occasion Collins brought along an old schoolmate and promising young poet, for Joseph Warton recalled, 'Thomson was well acquainted with the Greek Tragedies, on which I heard him talk learnedly, when I was once introduced to him by my friend Mr W. Collins.'[12] Joseph and his brother Thomas took the *Seasons* as a model for their romantic nature descriptions in blank verse (Joseph's *The Enthusiast*, 1744–8, and Thomas's *The Pleasures of Melancholy* 1747). The far more original odes of Collins owe something to Thomson too; Collins, like Smollett, also wished to follow Thomson as a writer of tragedies.

Another poetic disciple acquired at this time was William Shenstone, for it was in August 1746, during a stay at Hagley Park, that Thomson was taken by William Lyttelton, the youngest brother of his patron, to visit Shenstone at his nearby *ferme ornée*, The Leasowes. Shenstone described Thomson's reaction to the beauties of his estate and its surrounding landscape:

'You have nothing to do (says he) but to dress Nature. Her robe is ready made; you have only to caress her, love her; kiss her; and then—descend into the valley.' Coming out into the court before the house, he mentioned Clent and Waw-ton Hill as the two bubbies of Nature: then Mr L. observed the nipple, and then Thomson the fringe of Uphmore wood; till the double entendre was workt up to a point, and produced a laugh. Thomson observed the little stream running across my gate, and hinted that *he* should avail him self of that also. We now passed into Virgil's Grove. What a delightful place, says he, is this for a person of a poetical genius. I don't wonder you're a devotee to the Muses.—This place, says Mr L. will *improve* a poetical genius.—Aye, replied Mr T. and a poetical genius will improve this place ... He denominated my Virgil's Grove there Le Vallon occlus.—Sombre, says Mr L.—No, not sombre occlus.—This must evidently be the idea of Petrarch's Valclusa ... Thomson asked if I had seen many places laid out in the modern way? No.—Asked if I had seen Chiswick? Yes. He mentioned it as a sublime thing in the true Venetian taste. He supposed me to come often to town; and desired to wait on me at Richmond, Mr L. commending Richmond prospects, he said they were only too rich in villas. He begged a pinch of snuff; and, on passing by the Abetes [Abeles], near the Mill Pool, mentioned that Pope had a scheme in his head of planting trees to resemble a Gothic Cathedral. Hearing the Dam there was made by the Monks, O! says he, this is God-dam the wit of which I could not see.

One can visualize the slightly prim young host adapting quite well to the unbuttoned manner of his famous visitor, though Shenstone himself was not altogether satisfied with the impression the had given: 'My behaviour was a little awkward, and better calculated to express the satisfaction I took in the honour he did me, than to give him any idea either of my understanding or politeness.' Summing up Thomson's manner, Shenstone observed, 'He had nothing of the Gentleman in his person or address. But he made amends for the deficiency by his refined sense and spirited expression; and, as I remember, a manner of speaking not unlike his friend Quin. He did not talk a great deal or fluently; but, after pauses of reflection, produced something or other that accounted for his delay.' This confirms Murdoch's observation that Thomson's wit flowed at due intervals. Shenstone was so flattered by the 1746 visit that he resolved to commemorate it in a Latin inscription upon a seat in the area of his garden he called Virgil's Grove. On 30 June 1747 he asked the opinion of his friend Richard Graves on the alternative inscriptions he has in mind while uneasily admitting 'I fancy you will imagine I lay too much stress on Mr Thomson's visit.' We can infer that Shenstone made much of Thomson's visit to his friend Lady Luxborough (Bolingbroke's half-sister), because after Thomson died she wrote to Lady Hertford that Thomson approved the taste of Shenstone and contracted a friendship with him: 'Mr Shenstone hoped he'd have continued it, and have criticized or corrected what he writes, which would have been an advantage to a young poet.'[13]

Coriolanus was completed in time for the 1746–7 theatrical season. Thomson had the temerity to take a Shakespearian subject, albeit the subject of one of the most rarely performed of all Shakespeare's plays. It was not acted on the London stage during Thomson's lifetime, except between 1718 and 1722. There were then in all ten performances of the play, either more or less as Shakespeare wrote it or in a very free adaptation by John Dennis, entitled *The Invader of his Country, or the Fatal Resentment*, where Coriolanus was intended to call to mind the Old Pretender. Another adaptation, Nahum Tate's *The Ingratitude of a Common-Wealth* was acted twice in 1681. Thus the field was fairly open for Thomson.

As one might expect from his other plays, Thomson unifies and abbreviates his plot. The scene is the Volscian camp outside Rome; the action begins with Coriolanus's defection to the Volscians and ends with his death. Thomson's play is less than half as long as Shakespeare's, and his five acts have less action than Shakespeare's last two. It seems that he is attempting to classicize Shakespeare's play as Dryden had classicized *Antony and Cleopatra* in *All for Love*.

Thomson takes the names of his characters from Livy and Dionysius of Halicarnassus, rather than from Plutarch and Shakespeare, so his Volumnia is Coriolanus' wife, Coriolanus' mother is called Veturia, and the Volscian general is called Attius Tullus. The female parts are smaller than in any other play by Thomson, for the two women appear in only one scene. This, the famous supplication, is the most important scene in Thomson's play as it arguably is in Shakespeare's but Thomson makes it something of an isolated set piece. His play is built about the developing and shifting attitudes of Tullus towards Coriolanus. Tullus appears in nineteen of the play's twenty-two scenes; Coriolanus appears in twelve, ten of them with Tullus. Though Coriolanus has the most sonorous long speeches and dominates most of the longest scenes, Tullus is prominent enough to make a not ill-matched partner and rival; he is more credibly motivated than his Shakespearian counterpart Tullus Aufidius.

Thomson invents a new character, a Pythagorean philosopher and pacifist named Galesus, who preaches a Thomsonian natural religion in which 'Each Bird each Insect, flitting thro' the Sky' teaches that

> There is a Power,
> Unseen that rules th' illimitable World,
> That guides its Motions, from the brightest Star,
> To the least Dust of this sin-tainted Mold.

He speaks the last words of the play, advocating reason and patriotism:

> . . . private Views and Passions . . .
> May darken Reason, and her Course controul;
> But when the Prospect clears, her startled Eye

Must from the treacherous Gulph with Horror fly,
On whose wild Wave, by stormy Passions tost,
So many hapless Wretches have been lost.
Then be this Truth the Star by which we steer;
Above Ourselves *our* COUNTRY *should be dear.*[14]

Johnson said of Shakespeare's *Coriolanus*, 'There is, perhaps, too much bustle in the first Act, and too little in the last.' Thomson's play is quite without bustle throughout. For the most part it is a series of cerebral debates upon the just war, the legitimacy of revenge, the individual person's duty to the community, and other such politico-moral questions. Though its subject, is on the face of it, more political than those of any other plays by Thomson, there is no obvious reference to contemporary politics. It was written between 1742 and 1746, but Thomson avoids drawing any parallel between Coriolanus and the Young Pretender. 'Faction' comes under attack as usual in Thomson, but despite the echo of the lines in *Tancred and Sigismunda* satirized by Benjamin Victor in his letter to the *Daily Post*, it would probably be over-ingenious to argue that the Roman consul Minucius' address to Coriolanus contains a reference to Lyttelton's joining the government at the end of 1744:

we have felt our Error,
And now invite thee back to aid the Senate,
With thy heroic Spirit to restrain
The giddy Rage of Faction, and to hold
The Reins of Government more firm hereafter.[15]

Even so, this play's generalized appeals for national unity could hardly not be written or read without some awareness of the Jacobite rebellion and the internal strains of Pelham's administration under the stresses of that rebellion and the war with France.

Thomson hoped to have his new play staged in the 1746–7 theatrical season. On 18 October 1746 his friend Thomas Birch reported that 'Thomson has a new Tragedy for us this Season, the Subject of which is Coriolanus. It is to be exhibited at Covent Garden where Garrick, Quin, Mrs Cibber, and Mrs Pritchard have fram'd themselves into one Body; and the first three are to be Managers of the Stage.' The 1746–7 season was the only one when Garrick and Quin were in the same company; they were both at Covent Garden, the patentee of which was John Rich. It appears that Thomson had written the part of Coriolanus with Quin in mind and hoped that Garrick would play Tullus. The reason that the play was not acted in the 1746–7 season is not clear, but Smollett blamed Garrick. Writing to Alexander Carlyle in the spring of 1747 he complains that Garrick had persuaded Rich to reject his own tragedy *The Regicide* and adds 'he has served Thomson in the selfsame Manner'.[16] A year or so later Thomson also blames Garrick's 'little dirty Jealousy' of Quin, though by then Garrick and Quin were once again playing in different houses. Thomson naturally takes Quin's side over the well-publicized rivalry between the two actors, and perhaps he is attributing to Garrick the envious nature of the character Tullus which he wished him to play. During the frustrations of the 1746–7 season, in March 1747, Thomson told Mallet that he was 'pretty much indifferent whether' *Coriolanus* should ever appear upon the stage or not.[17]

Lyttelton's wife Lucy, to whom he had been married only four years, died in January 1747, and Thomson sent him a copy of the 1746 *Seasons* inscribed with some sympathetic verses with a conventional Spenserian echo. They begin:

> Go, little book, and find our Friend,
> Who Nature and the Muses loves.

The devout Lyttelton found comfort in religion. On 21 May he wrote to Thomson:

My refuge and consolation is in philosophy—Christian philosophy, which I heartily wish you may be a disciple of, as well as myself. Indeed, my dear friend, it is far above the platonick. I have sent you a pamphlet upon a subject relative to it, which we have formerly talkt of. I writt it in Kew Lane last year, and I writt it with a particular view to your satisfaction. You have therefore, a double right to it, and I wish to God it may appear to you as convincing as it does to me, and bring you to add the faith to the heart of a Christian.[18]

The pamphlet was the newly published *Observations on the Conversion and Apostleship of St Paul*, intended to prove that St Paul's career is 'of itself a demonstration sufficient to prove Christianity to be divine revelation', and 'to convince those unbelievers that will not attend to a longer series of arguments'. Though written in Thomson's house and with Thomson in mind, the pamphlet is addressed to Lyttelton's cousin Gilbert West, author of a recently published complementary work, *Observations on the Resurrection*. Both were frequently reprinted, often together, and became widely popular. Thomson's immediate response to his friend's evangelical effort is not known, but Lyttelton claimed after the poet's death that his pamphlet had had the desired effect:

Thomson, I hope and believe died a Christian. Had he lived longer I dont doubt but he would have openly profest his Faith, for he wanted no Courage in what he thought right, but his Mind had been much perplex'd with doubts which I have the pleasure to think my book on St Paul had almost entirely Removed. He told me so himself, and in his Sickness declared so to Others. This is my best Consolation in the Loss of him, for as to the Heart of a Christian he always had that, in a degree of perfection beyond most Men I have known.[19]

Lyttelton's letter of 21 May was concerned also with more earthly matters. He asks for the return of the key to the royal gardens at Richmond of which Thomson has for a while enjoyed the use. He arranges to meet Thomson in a week's time at Hounslow so that they can travel down to Hampshire together by post-chaise to spend a weekend at Mrs Stanley's place. He adds, 'I have sent you a small present of claret in return for your rum, of which my Father will send me back a good part, having more than he has occasion for. He has also disposed of some to Frank Clare in your name, that he may receive you more graciously when you come into Worcestershire.'[20] Was the rum, one wonders, a perquisite of the Surveyor-Generalship of the Leeward Islands?

Thomson made his visit to Hagley in September and October. Shenstone wrote to Richard Graves on 21 September,

As I was returning last Sunday from Church, whom should I meet in my way, but that sweet-souled bard Mr James Thomson, in a chaise drawn by two horses lengthways. I welcomed him into the country, and asked him to accompany Mr Lyttelton to the Leasows ... which he promised to do. So I am in daily expectation of them and all the world this week. I fancy they will lavish all their praises upon nature, reserving none for poor *art* and *me*.

Shenstone was particularly eager for a visit because he had just dedicated the seat to Thomson in his 'Virgil's Grove', but in the event Thomson did not visit The Leasowes. This was perhaps because Lyttelton enjoyed his company so much, for, also on 21 September, he asked his cousin and fellow Lord of the Treasury George Grenville to arrange for him to be absent for another three weeks from Treasury Board meetings so that he could keep company with Thomson, who 'is just come to us' and 'is very unwilling to leave this place soon'.[21] In due course Lyttelton and Thomson, accompanied by the Scots historian Archibald Bower (1686–1766), returned to London by way of Ebrington in Gloucestershire, where they had gone to visit Mrs Fortescue, the mother of Lyttelton's dead wife. Their journey is described by Bower ('Jammy' is of course Thomson):

From Ebrington we were attended to Oxford by Mrs Fortescue's coach and six. We got to our inn before it was dark, and immediately from thence went to see the Ratcliffe Library. As we were then near the Coffee House, which is chiefly frequented by the Fellows of Queen's, I proposed their going to see there the daughter of the house, who is reckoned the greatest beauty in Oxford. I did not doubt but I should meet some of my acquaintance there, and was very sure that they would invite us all to pass the evening with them in the Common room; and so it happened ... As for the Beauty, they both agreed that she had a just claim to that title. I had said great things of her, and Jammy no sooner saw her than he cried out in a kind of extacy, 'Je m'accorde avec vous!' As she sat opposite to him in the bar, he continued staring at her as in a trance, as long as we stayed. At 8 o'clock we went all three to Queen's and there found Dr Shaw, with whose company as well as with that of the gentlemen of Queen's, Mr Lyttelton was so taken that he did not think of coming away till past twelve; nay he would fain have persuaded Mr Tomson and me to stay the next day. As we had taken our places in the Flying Coach we did not chuse to stay.

Jammy and I set out at three in the morning and reached London about seven [in the evening]. We had one very agreeable young gentlewoman with us, but the rest, a carpenter, his sister, near twice as big as Tomson, and a she-stroller going with her taber and pipe to a fair, were downright *bestia balezzata*. The fat woman, taking Tomson for a Scotch rebel, and me for a Frenchman, was very reserved, lookt sour, and would speak to neither the whole morning. But in the afternoon, understanding from our talk that we came from Hagley, she all at once changed her countenance and behaviour, saying that if we had been at Hagley she was sure we were of the good sort; which neither of us understood till she herself explained it. There had been all the morning a constant contest between her and me. Our quarrel was about the window, she pulling it down as fast as I pulled it up, and I pulling it up as fast as she pulled it down. [She also made some unprintable remarks about Thomson's corpulent figure.] But after she knew that we had been at Hagley, she never offered to pull down the window, 'for fear the gentleman should catch cold' [and withdrew her remarks about Thomson]. This honest Lytteltonian Whig is of Worcestershire, but I have forgot and never shall remember the name of the place she came from. I would fain have treated her and her brother with a pint of wine, but they would not accept of my offer.[22]

While at Hagley Thomson wrote to his sister Jean. Their sister Elizabeth Bell was now dead; her widower, a man of evident delicacy, asked for Thomson's approval of his remarrying, which was readily given and which prompted further reflections on matrimony:

As I approve intirely of his marrying again, you may readily ask me why I dont marry at all. My Circumstances have hitherto been so variable and uncertain in this fluctuating World, as in Prudence to keep me from engaging in such a State and now, tho they are more settled, and of late (which you will be glad to hear) considerably improved, I begin to think Myself too far advanced in Life for such youthful Undertakings. Not to mention some other petty Reasons, that are apt to startle the Delicacy of difficult old Batchelors. I am however not a little suspicious, that was I to pay a Visit to Scotland (which I have some Thoughts of doing soon) I might possibly be tempted.

Thomson had not been back to his native land since he had first run abroad over twenty years before: there is perhaps more Farfrae-like sentimentality than serious resolve in his thought of visiting Scotland soon. Nevertheless his emotions were easily stirred by recollections of Scotland. When the son of William Gusthart called at Thomson's cottage in Richmond the poet

came forward to receive him, and looking stedfastly at him (for they had not seen one another for many years) said, Troth Sir, I cannot say I ken your countenance well—Let me therefore crave your name. Which the gentleman no sooner mentioned but the tears gushed from Mr Thomson's eyes. He could only reply, good God! are you the son of my dear friend, my old benefactor; and then rushing to his arms, he tenderly embraced him; rejoicing at so unexpected a meeting.

Thomson retained a Scots accent to his death, unlike Mallet, who Anglicized his speech soon after coming to London; Johnson was able to declare, 'I never catched Mallet in a Scotch accent'.[23]

Marriage and remarriage are the subject of an exchange of letters between Thomson and Lyttelton later this year. In a letter now lost Lyttelton urges his friend to marry a woman whose identify is not now known. Thomson replied on 14 December:

I should have answered your kind, and truly friendly Letter sometime ago. My not having answered it hitherto proceeded from my giving it a mature and deep Consideration. I have considered it in all Lights, and in all Humours; by Night, by Day, and even during these long Evenings. But the Result of my Consideration is not such as you would wish. My Judgment agrees with you: you know, I first impressed yours in her Favour. She deserves a Better than me and has as many good and worthy Qualities as any Woman: nay to others and those too men of Taste, she has charming and piquant ones. But every Man has a singular and uncontroulable Imagination of his own: now, as I told you before, She does not pique mine. I wonder you should treat that Objection so lightly, as you seem to do in your last. To strike ones Fancy is the same in Love that Charity is in Religion: Tho a Woman had the Form, and spoke, with the Tongue of Angels; tho all divine Gifts and Graces were her's; yet, without striking the Fancy, she does nothing. I am too much advanced in Life to venture to marry, without feeling myself invigorated, and made as it were young again, with a great Flame of Imagination. But we shall discuss this Matter more fully, when I have the Happiness of seeing you at full Leisure. What betwixt Judgment and Fancy, I shall run a great Risque of never entering into the holy State. In the meantime, I wish to see you once more happy in it. Forgive me if I say, it would be an ungrateful Frowardness, to refuse the Bounty of Providence, because you have been deprived of former Enjoyments. If you cannot again love so exquisitely as you have done, so much the better; you will not then risque being so miserable. To say that one cannot love twice, is utterly unphilosophical, and give me Leave to say contrary to my own Experience.

One of Thomson's loves was Elizabeth Young; the other referred to here has not been identified. It might be the fair neighbour of Mallet's mentioned in a letter in 1729, or the Melinda of *Autumn* (1730), or the Amanda addressed in love-songs printed in 1732 and 1736.[24]

Perhaps it was also in December 1747 that Thomson wrote 'An Ode, on the Winter Solstice', where he hails the sun's turning which will bring back the spring; but, he adds, his 'downward Age' cannot hope for many visits more of that season, whose 'blest Poet' he is.[25] This ode remained unpublished until the present century, but in January 1748 two of Thomson's other short poems found a place in what would become the most influential anthology of the century, Dodsley's *Collection of Poems*. The two were 'Hymn on Solitude' and 'The Happy Man', reprinted in texts so close to the printings of 1729–30 that it is quite likely that Thomson had no direct hand in preparing them for Dodsley's press. The 'Hymn on Solitude' was reprinted in all later editions of the *Collection*, but 'The Happy Man' was deleted. Thomson was reading *Clarissa*, four volumes of which had appeared by April 1748; he was one of those who entreated Richardson to give the novel a happy ending.[26]

In addition to finding him a possible wife Lyttelton was attempting to provide for Thomson's more mundane needs. When, in early 1748, Chesterfield approached the Prime Minister in search of government patronage for Mallet, Pelham told him 'that he had been exceedingly pressed by Lyttelton in favour of Thomson and West'.[27] Thomson already had his surveyorship but he had lost his pension from the Prince of Wales. He writes of this and of his expectations from Lyttelton ('our Friend in Argyll Street') in a letter of April 1748 to his friend and Deputy Surveyor William Paterson in the West Indies. Peace of mind and moderation of desires, he tells Paterson,

are the Treasures, dug from an inexhaustible Mine in our own Breasts; Which, like Those in the Kingdom of Heaven the Rust of Time cannot corrupt, nor Thieves break thro and steal. I must learn to work at this Mine a little more, being struck off from a certain hundred Pounds of Year which you know I had. West, Mallet, and I were all routed in one day. If you would know why—out of Resentment to our Friend in Argyll Street. Yet I have Hopes given me of having it restored with Interest, some Time or other.

He recommends the Corycius senex of Virgil's Fourth Georgic 'as a perfect Model of the truest happy life' for Paterson and himself. His own way of life is comfortable enough:

Retirement, and Nature, are more and more my Passion every Day. And now, even now, the charming Time comes on: Heaven is just upon the Point, or rather in the very Act, of giving Earth a green Gown. The Voice of the Nightingale is heard in our Lane. You must know, that I have inlarged my Rural Domain much to the same Dimensions you have done yours. The two Fields next to me; from the First of which I have walled—no, no,—paled in about as much as my Garden consisted of before: so that the Walk runs around the Hedge, where you may figure me walking any Time of the Day, and sometimes under Night. For you, I image you reclining under Cedars, and Palmettoes; and there enjoying more magnificent Slumbers than are known to the pale Climates of the North; Slumbers rendered awful, and divine, by the solemn Stillness, and deep Fervors, of the Torrid Noon! At other Times, I image you drinking Punch in Groves of Lime or Orange Trees, gathering Pine-Apples from Hedges as commonly as we may Black-Berries, Poetizing under lofty Laurels, or making Love under full-spred Myrtles.

But to lower my Stile a little—As I am such a genuine Lover of Gardening, why dont you remember me in that Instance, and send me some Seeds of Things that might succeed here during the Summer, tho they cannot perfect their Seeds sufficiently, in this to them ungenial Climate, to propagate. In the which Case is Calliloo; that, from the Seed it bore here produc'd, came up puny, ricketty, and good for Nothing. There are other Things certainly with you, not yet brought over hither, that might flourish here in the Summer Time, and live tolerably well, provided they be sheltered in an hospitable Stove or Green-House during the Winter. You will give me no small Pleasure by sending me, from Time to Time, some of these Seeds, if it were no more but to amuse me in making the Tryal. With Regard to the Brother-Gardiners; you ought to know, that, as they are half Vegetables, the Animal Part of them will never have Spirit enough to consent to the Transplanting of the Vegetable into distant dangerous Climates. They, happily for themselves, have no other Idea, but to dig on here, eat, drink, sleep, and mow their wives.[28]

The brother-gardeners were said by William Robertson to be Thomson's nephews: 'they did not live *with* him, but they lived *upon* him. He was so generous a man, that if he had but two eggs, he would have given them both away.' Taylor the barber gave the names of the gardener-nephews as Andrew and Gilbert Thomson; the Earl of Buchan, ever alert for Thomson's family honour, claimed, however, that the two parasites spoken of were not Thomson's nephews.[29]

Thomson's letter to Paterson also gives news of their less earthy acquaintance, beginning with the widowed Lyttelton, who 'has had the severest Tryal an humane tender Heart can have'. He mentions Mitchell, elected MP for Aberdeenshire in 1747, Gray, and Symmer, who, one infers, has given up his tutorship in the Earl of Warwick's household, for he 'is at last tired of Quality, and is going to take a semi-country House at Hammersmith'. Warrender is 'stunted in church Preferment', because he is still in the Yorkshire rectory to which he was preferred in 1740; he is currently in town, as too is Murdoch, 'Tutor to Admiral Vernon's Son, and is in good Hopes of another Living in Suffolk, that Country of Tranquillity, where he will then burrow himself in a Wife and be happy. Good-natured obliging Millar is as usual.' Finally, though Armstrong 'increases in his Business, he does not decrease in Spleen; but there is a certain Kind of Spleen that is both humane and agreeable, like Jacque's in the Play. I sometimes have a Touch of it.'[30] One close friend not mentioned here is John Forbes, though he had come to London on the death of his father, Thomson's old patron, on 10 December 1747. The family estate was greatly encumbered by the personal debts incurred by Duncan Forbes while he defended the Hanoverian cause in the Scottish Highlands during the 1745 rebellion; John Forbes was still in London dealing with his late father's affairs on 30 April, when he was taken by Lyttelton to see Henry Pelham.[31]

As it was mid-April the end of another London theatre season was approaching, but *Coriolanus* had still not been staged. Thomson explains to Paterson that this is because of 'the little dirty Jealousy of Tullus—I mean of him who was desired to act Tullus, towards him who alone can act Coriolanus. Indeed, the First has intirely jockyed the Last off the Stage for this Season; but, I believe, he will return on him next Season, like a Gyant in his Wrath.' Thomson wanted Garrick to take the part of Attius Tullus in his play and Quin to take the title role. No love was lost between the two players; Quin was still much respected but he resented being overshadowed by the wildly popular younger actor. In friendship Thomson would always side with Quin. During the 1746–7 season, when *Coriolanus* was ready for the stage, both actors were in the Covent Garden company under John Rich, and it is quite possible that the jealousy complained of by Thomson could have prevented Garrick from playing second fiddle to Quin. By the opening of the 1747–8 season Garrick was joint manager of Drury Lane and Quin had retreated to Bath where he was waiting for Rich to renew his own engagement, perhaps on more advantageous terms now that his great rival Garrick had gone. Rich was content to manage without him, so Quin made only four stage appearances that season, all at Covent Garden in April and May: all but one of these were in benefit performances including, remarkably, his own benefit. In these circumstances Garrick could hardly be expected to persuade Quin to play Coriolanus at either theatre, and it was perhaps unjust to blame him for Quin's recent absence from the stage; Thomson is merely venting his frustration over the continued non-appearance of *Coriolanus*. Garrick probably saw little merit in what is generally accepted to be Thomson's weakest play. Shiels reports that *Coriolanus* 'was first offered to Mr Garrick, but he did not think proper to accept it'.[32]

Thomson has a happier fate to report to Paterson concerning an even longer-gestated work:

know that, after fourteen or fifteen Years, the Castle of Indolence comes abroad in a Fortnight. It will certainly travel as far as Barbadoes. You have an Apartment in it, as a Night-Pensioner; which, you may remember, I fitted up for you during our delightful Party at North-Haw. Will ever these Days return again? Dont you remember your eating the raw Fish that were never catched.

The holiday mood of this reference confirms Murdoch's account of the original conception of *The Castle of Indolence, an Allegorical Poem, written in Imitation of Spenser*: 'It was, at first, little more than a few detached stanzas, in the way of raillery on himself, and on some of his friends, who would reproach him with indolence, while he thought them, at least, as indolent as himself.'[33] (As it happens, one of the stanzas on himself and some of the stanzas on his friends which are in the published poem must date from some years later, after

Thomson had come to know Quin and Lyttelton; even the friendly raillery on the 'little, round oily Man of God' must have been written after 1738, when Murdoch was ordained.)

Murdoch continues his account of the poem's genesis: 'But he saw very soon, that the subject deserved to be treated more seriously, and in a form fitted to convey one of the most important moral lessons.' As fourteen or fifteen years elapsed between conception and publication we have no means of telling how soon was 'very soon', but it would appear that the moral lesson and at least the outline of the fable had been worked out by 1742, when Thomas Morell wrote his Spenserian stanzas calling upon Thomson to finish his poem. Between 1734 and 1748 Thomson wrote four plays and his share of *Alfred*, he wrote *Liberty* and the *Poem to Talbot*, and he also largely rewrote the *Seasons*; however, five of the years saw no new publication of any length by him, so one could not press the case that Thomson was just too busy to find time to sing about his own indolence.

Perhaps he thought that the subject of *The Castle of Indolence* and/or the Spenserian stanza and quaint, obsolete diction were suitable for a private poem to be shown to friends, but were inappropriate for the public utterances of the bard whose reputation was built largely upon politically or morally elevating sentiments in blank verse. Thomson admired *The Faerie Queene*. Even though he made no published reference to Spenser earlier than the revised *Seasons* of 1744, we have no reason to disbelieve Shiels' claim, made apparently from first-hand acquaintance, that Thomson 'has often confessed that if he had anything excellent in his poetry, he owed it to the inspiration he first received from reading the Fairy Queen, in the very early part of his life', and that, as a descriptive poet, 'he form'd his Taste upon *Spenser*'. Shiels writes of the descriptive, not the moral Spenser. Similarly, when, in the 1744 *Seasons*, Thomson couples the names of Chaucer and Spenser, it is Chaucer's verse that is described as 'Well-moraliz'd', whereas Spenser is

> Fancy's pleasing Son;
> Who, like a copious River, pour'd his Song
> O'er all the Mazes of enchanted Ground.[34]

Despite the unimpeachable moral of *The Castle of Indolence* Thomson may have believed that its character as a burlesque, even a private joke, or as a romantic fantasy, even an indulgence in romantic introspection, made it too private for public consumption.

His decision to complete and publish might then have been influenced by the publication of other imitations of Spenser by younger poets during the time he was brooding upon his. Those others included Shenstone's *School-Mistress*, (in *Poems upon Various Occasions*, 1737, then expanded and sentimentalized for separate publication in 1742), Gilbert West's *A Canto of the Fairy Queen* (1739), William Thompson's *Sickness* (1745–6), and John Upton's *A New Canto of Spencer's Fairy Queen* (1747). Shenstone, West, and Upton were all acquaintances of Thomson by 1746. Shenstone's and West's Spenserian imitations were brought to wide public notice when they were republished in January 1748 in Dodsley's *Collection of Poems*, which also contained Gloster Ridley's *Psyche, or the Great Metamorphosis, a Poem written in Imitation of Spenser*, and shorter Spenserian imitations by Edward Bedingfield, Robert Lowth, and William Mason. Thomson's *The Castle of Indolence* was published five months later.

The text eventually published in quarto by Millar on 7 May 1748 consists of two cantos, each containing about eighty Spenserian stanzas, prefaced by a somewhat defensive Advertisement, excusing 'the obsolete Words and a Simplicity of Diction . . . which borders on the Ludicrous', which 'were necessary to make the Imitation more perfect'. The prefatory material also includes a small glossary of obsolete words,[35] though the poem itself contains really very little archaic diction.

The first canto describes an imaginary castle which is an amalgam of tempting earthly paradises in Spenser's *Faerie Queene* (such as the Bower of Bliss, Phaedria's Bower, and Castle Joyeuse) with Armida's palace in Tasso's *Gerusalemme Liberata*. It also draws features from the *Arabian Nights*, where luxury, self-indulgence, and the cultivation of pleasure are not condemned, and from the Abbey of Thélème in Rabelais, where freedom reigns, the only rule is 'Do what thou wilt', and the wickedness and ugliness of the world are excluded. This castle is set in a delightful secluded pastoral valley, sheltered by woods, with quiet lawns, glittering streamlets, 'And vacant Shepherds piping in the Dale'. It is provided with beautiful works of art, abundant food, drink, music, and every creature comfort, such as 'Caps, Slippers, Gowns', and (with a hint of mock epic) 'Soft Quilts on Quilts, on Carpets Carpets spread'.[36]

The castle belongs to a wizard who draws men into it with an enchanting song and charms them with deep draughts of Nepenthe, the drink described in *The Faerie Queene* as a reward bestowed by the gods upon fortunate men, to dispel anguish and rage, and confer 'sweet Peace and quiet Age'. Thomson's Wizard sings of the moral benefits of Epicureanism, 'joining Bliss to Virtue' (as Thomson claimed in *Liberty*) and linked with the Horatian ideal of virtuous philosophic retirement praised in, for instance, Thomson's 'Hymn on Solitude'. The Wizard asks:

> 'What, what, is Virtue, but Repose of Mind?
> 'A pure ethereal Calm! that knows no Storm;
> 'Above the Reach of wild Ambition's Wind,
> 'Above those Passions that this World deform,
> 'And torture Man, a proud malignant Worm!

'But here, instead, soft Gales of Passion play,
'And gently stir the Heart, thereby to form
'A quicker Sense of Joy; as Breezes stray
'Across th' enliven'd Skies, and make them still more gay.

He evokes Lucretius's ideal of calm mind above the storm of passion and concludes his stanza with a simile which points to that ideal harmony between man and nature presented in the *Seasons*. In the next stanza, 'the Best of Men have ever lov'd Repose', he proffers the example of Scipio, praised in *Winter*, 517–20 and *Liberty*, V. 419–21, and introduced as an admirable character in *Sophonisba*; and he might have added not only other virtuous Romans praised in the *Seasons* but Lyttelton as he appears in *Spring*, 909–22, pensive and soothed by the murmuring stream. Virtuous retirement is repeatedly applauded in the *Seasons*, as too is good nature. Addison, as a popularizer of Shaftesbury, wrote in *Spectator*, number 243:

The two great Ornaments of Virtue, which shew her in the most advantageous Views, and make her altogether lovely, are Chearfulness and Good-nature. These generally go together, as a Man cannot be agreeable to others who is not easie with himself. They are both very requisite in a Virtuous Mind, to keep out Melancholy from the many serious Thoughts it is engaged in, and to hinder its natural Hatred of Vice from sowering into Severity and Censoriousness.

The Wizard argues in similar terms:

'Here nought but Candour reigns, indulgent Ease,
'Good-natur'd Lounging, Sauntering up and down:
'They who are pleas'd themselves must always please;
'On Others' Ways they never squint a Frown,
'Nor heed what haps in Hamlet or in Town.
'Thus, from the Source of tender Indolence,
'With milky Blood the Heart is overflown,
'Is sooth'd and sweeten'd by the social Sense;
'For Interest, Envy, Pride, and Strife are banish'd hence.[37]

Behind this part of the Wizard's appeal lies one of the chief moral ideas of the *Seasons*, where Creative Bounty is reflected in man's social feeling.

Canto I makes indolence attractive, but we have been told at the outset that the Wizard is a false enchanter, with the implication that his castle is a false paradise, so it is no surprise to discover at the end of the canto that this castle conceals a dungeon into which its carefree dwellers will eventually be thrown. This is described in four burlesque stanzas contributed by Thomson's friend, the physician John Armstrong, author of *The Art of Preserving Health* (1744) and, like Thomson himself, a dweller in the castle. Armstrong represents the dungeon as a den of grotesque personifications, such as Gout, Apoplexy, and Lethargy, 'a mighty Lubbard . . . Stretch'd on his Back', snoring night and day; also Hypochondria, 'Mother of Spleen' or melancholy. Long before this point is reached, the morally alert reader has detected false notes in the Wizard's song. The Wizard tells his victims that in his castle they need no longer go through the city,

> 'To cheat, and dun, and lye, and Visit pay,
> 'Now flattering base, now giving secret Wounds;
> 'Or proul in Courts of Law for human Prey,
> 'In venal Senate thieve, or rob on broad High-way.

Nor, he adds, will they 'heed what haps in Hamlet or in Town'.[38] Ludicrous alliteration emphasizes the message, which is really a call for indifference, not virtue. Elsewhere, the Wizard undermines his own claims for the 'virtue' of a quiet life by a facetious pragmatism, for instance in the implied decibel scale of 'No Dogs, no Babes, no Wives, to stun your Ear'.[39]

The second canto of Thomson's poem introduces a heroic Knight of Arts and Industry, modelled upon Spenser's Satyrane in his birth and upbringing and upon Guyon at the Bower of Bliss in his rescue of the captives. His allegorical career echoes the histories of social progess in *Liberty* and the opening of *Autumn*; he resembles the patriot king described by Siffredi in *Tancred and Sigismunda*, I. iv. 11–28, or Peter the Great in the 1744 additions to *Winter*. He also resembles the ideal of an English landed gentleman, when, after a life encouraging industry, commerce, the arts, and representative government, he retires to improve his rural estate:

> Gay Plains extend where Marshes slept before;
> O'er recent Meads th'exulting Streamlets fly;
> Dark frowning Heaths grow bright with *Ceres'* Store,
> And Woods imbrown the Steep, or wave along the Shore.[40]

It is as if the landscape around the Castle of Indolence, as described at the opening of the poem, has now been turned to use; the literary mode is georgic, as against pastoral. Like Scipio, the prime exhibit in the Wizard's case, the Knight has earned repose by earlier toil and his 'repose' is useful activity. The same might be said of Lyttelton, for the passage in *Spring*, referred to above, which tells of him straying in the peace and quiet of Hagley Park, goes on to allude to his active moral life as historian, politician, and landlord. As it happens, Lyttelton is mentioned in *The Castle of Indolence*, but as an occasional visitor, who cannot be persuaded to take up residence with the Wizard.[41]

The Knight of Arts and Industry is accompanied in his attack on the Wizard's castle by a Druid bard, who, countering the Wizard's tempting song, summons the indolent dwellers in the castle to a life of useful activity. Some are called 'to Courts, and Some to Camps; To Senate Some . . . To high Discovery Some . . . Some to the thriving Mart; Some to the Rural Reign . . . To the sweet Muses Some, who raise the Heart'. His song restates the true and complete moral philosophy of the *Seasons*, based on the georgic concept of work as divinely ordained to beautify the earth and exalt humankind, and on Thomson's distinctive notion of spiritual ascent. Though the Wizard cites scripture it is the Bard of Canto II who is the true religious poet, as Druids reputedly were. He proclaims the immanence of God in the terms that Thomson had already employed in his *Poem to Newton*, *Spring*, and *Edward and Eleonora*:

> 'What is TH' ADOR'D SUPREME PERFECTION, say?
> 'What, but eternal never-resting Soul,
> 'Almighty Power, and all-directing Day;
> 'By whom each Atom stirs, the Planets roll;
> 'Who fills, surrounds, informs, and agitates the Whole?

God sanctifies morally strenuous industry, which draws humankind up towards perfection as well as giving pleasure. The Bard appeals:

> 'Toil, and be glad! Let Industry inspire
> 'Into your quicken'd Limbs her buoyant Breath!
> 'Who does not act is dead; absorpt intire
> 'In miry Sloth, no Pride, no Joy he hath.[42]

Some of the castle-dwellers are convinced by this argument, but most are not; so it is necessary for the Knight to wave an anti-magic wand which transforms the delightful landscape around the castle into a hideous morass, and which exposes the dungeon of lethargic misery. Thereupon, nearly everyone embraces a life of useful toil, and the few who do not are harried by fiends called Beggary and Scorn. The canto ends with a joke at the expense of muddy, insalubrious Brentford, in a burlesque stanza which, for style and topographical detail, could easily have found a place in Pope's Spenserian imitation, 'The Alley'. Thus Thomson concludes his poem in the mood of raillery in which, according to Murdoch, it was conceived.

On Thomson's dating, *The Castle of Indolence* was begun in 1733–4, when he was writing *Liberty*. The spectacle of indolence, luxury, slavery, and human decay in modern Rome which prompted him to write *Liberty* is described in a letter to Lady Hertford from Paris, 10 October 1732 (p. 117 above); and this same letter contains also perhaps another germ of *The Castle of Indolence*, unrelated to Murdoch's account:

As for their Music, it is a sort of charming malady that quite disolves them in softness, and greatly heightens in them that universal Indolence men naturally (I had almost said reasonably) fall into when they can receive little or no advantage from their Industry.

Indolence and Industry are the opposites personified in the two cantos of Thomson's poem, while through the first canto flows, as the accompaniment to the enchanter's 'enfeebling Lute' and 'Syren Melody', a music that inclines to languishment.[43] A link with *Liberty* suggests that *The Castle of Indolence, an Allegorical Poem* might contain a political allegory; political meanings have duly been discovered by a number of readers in the 1980s.

John MacQueen, while conceding that it 'would be an oversimplification to suggest that the domain of Sir Industry is England, that of Indolence, Scotland', nevertheless relates the poem to the theme of Scottish economic improvement after the Union, thus casting Thomson into his familiar role as the poet of Britannia.[44] Mary Jane W. Scott develops this notion and overlays it with a more specific political interpretation in which the Wizard is the Stuart cause, the inhabitants of the castle are Scotsmen who remain inactive under the Jacobite threat, and the Knight represents Whig Hanoverian leadership which at last calls these Scotsmen to their true patriotic duty, which is to serve a united Britain.[45] For John Barrell the castle is really an eighteenth-century country house, where men of the upper orders retreat to avoid the labours appropriate to their station (law, politics, commerce, etc.); the Knight, a retired gentleman, restores them to their proper duties in camps and courts and public life. Thomson refers repeatedly to 'toil', but he avoids the reality of labour as experienced by the lower orders; the ambiguities of his poem 'proceed from the nature of the task that Thomson has set himself, of justifying the fruits of social division, while denying at the same time that any serious social divisions exist'.[46] Christine Gerrard, picking up Barrell's hint that the poem's political context is opposition to Walpole, regards indolence as a national problem: it is what opponents to Walpole in the 1730s saw as 'a malaise of inertia, self-interest, hedonism, corruption, and loss of public spirit'. The wicked enchanter is Walpole himself, the Knight of Arts and Industry is perhaps Bolingbroke, and the Druid bard who accompanies him is, as Joseph Warton first conjectured, Alexander Pope. So, like the *Dunciad* and Pope's Horatian satires, Thomson's poem tells of Britain falling into decadence for lack of public virtue; but, unlike Pope, Thomson imagines the defeat of corruption and a revival of public spirit.[47]

Dr Gerrard's argument is persuasive, particularly when she quotes such passages as the following description of the spread of the 'soul-enfeebling Wizard' Indolence's power:

> Spred far and wide was his curs'd Influence;
> Of Public Virtue much he dull'd the Sense,
> Even much of Private; eat our Spirit out,
> And fed our rank luxurious Vices: whence
> The Land was overlaid with many a Lout;
> Not, as old Fame reports, wise, generous, bold, and stout.

> A Rage of Pleasure madden'd every Breast,
> Down to the lowest Lees the Ferment ran:
> To his licentious Wish Each must be blest,
> With Joy be fever'd; snatch it as he can.
> Thus *Vice* the Standard rear'd; her Arrier-Ban
> *Corruption* call'd, and loud she gave the Word.[48]

This said, it has to be admitted that no evidence has been found that Thomson's contemporaries read the poem as a political allegory. They merely associate it with the author's own indolence, or praise in general terms its imaginative power, or artfully laid plan, or beautiful succession of descriptions. Even a long and favourable review by the politically-alert Henry Fielding in his political periodical, *The Jacobite's Journal* (4 June 1748), does not hint at any political allegory in *The Castle of Indolence*.[49]

Whatever the politics of this poem, Thomson's *moral* allegory has all the palpability of a sore thumb, and, like a sore thumb, it feelingly arises from particular circumstances in the author's life. This moral is spelt out unequivocally in the first stanza of the first canto:

> O MORTAL MAN, who livest here by Toil,
> Do not complain of this thy hard Estate;
> That like an Emmet thou must ever moil,
> Is a sad Sentence of an ancient Date:
> And, certes, there is for it Reason great;
> For, though sometimes it makes thee weep and wail,
> And curse thy Stars, and early drudge and late,
> Withouten That would come an heavier Bale,
> Loose Life, unruly Passions, and Diseases pale.[50]

The penalty of Adam is hard, but its alternative would be worse. Donald Greene observes that 'Thomson knew what he was talking about; it is a poem of personal experience'. Its power perhaps 'comes from the fact that Thomson— the fat, lazy, complaisant Jemmy Thomson, who never quite realized the potential his friends saw in him—knew something of' the suffering that arises from somnolence, lethargy, and paralysis of the will in a man of sensitivity and genius.[51] We have seen that Thomson's self-indulgence and idleness were a stock joke among his friends, and that he hoped Elizabeth Young's love would rescue him from 'that most fatal Syren Indolence and false Pleasure', make him a new man, and spur him to virtue and industry.[52] His courtship failed; he was unable to summon up the resolution to change his own character and habits, but the allegory of his own escape from the castle of indolence is not altogether a wish-fulfilment fantasy.

Describing this escape at the beginning of the second canto, Thomson discusses, not for the first time in this poem, his role as a poet. He complains that there is no effective copyright act, so booksellers take the rewards due to authors:

> a fell Tribe *th'Aonian Hive* despoil,
> As ruthless Wasps oft rob the painful Bee.[53]

Later in this canto, echoing Spenser's lament over the decay of enlightened patronage, Thomson condemns the 'Poor Sons of puft-up Vanity' who now appropriate the title of Maecenas.[54] He regrets the lack of patrons who can provide the Muses with 'the Sun-shine of uncumber'd Ease', but in the next stanza he claims that Liberty is his eternal patron and 'The best, and sweetest far, are Toil-created Gains'.[55]

The poet is reflecting upon his own status. Though Millar treated him generously by booksellers' standards of the day and was a personal friend, Thomson distrusted the market; he believed that high art should not be subject to commercial considerations. Patronage could be a better guarantee of good poetry, but the servility that patronage often entailed at this period must sometimes have irritated a man of even Thomson's easy-going nature. By 1748 he was disillusioned with the Prince of Wales, to whom he had dedicated most of his writings since 1735, and who for a while may have seemed an approximation to the ideal of disinterested royal support for the arts. According to Smollett, Thomson intended to retract his flattery of at least some patrons, 'a laudable scheme of poetical justice, the execution of which was fatally prevented by untimely death'.[56] To judge by the revised *Seasons* this laudable scheme was formed later than 1744. *The Castle of Indolence*, however, bears out Smollett's claim, to the extent that it has no dedication and the encomiums in it are all of close friends, among whom the patron Lyttelton may fairly be numbered.

In speaking out more directly than ever before about his own poetic role Thomson finds what a modern critic hears as 'a new note, a different pace, ... a vigour and an ease, almost one would say a lordly Byronic assumption of careless power':

> I care not, Fortune, what you me deny:
> You cannot rob me of free Nature's Grace;
> You cannot shut the Windows of the Sky,
> Through which *Aurora* shews her brightening Face:

You cannot bar my constant Feet to trace
The Woods and Lawns, by living Stream, at Eve:
Let Health my Nerves and finer Fibres brace,
And I their Toys to the *great Children* leave;
Of Fancy, Reason, Virtue, nought can me bereave.[57]

Spenserian fancy dress and allegory are blown away by a fresh, open-air, 'cheerful Morn of Life' manner, like that of the early *Seasons*, as Thomson offers a personal testimony of his integrity as a poet. Poetic integrity consists in the trinity of Fancy, Reason, and Virtue, but in *The Castle of Indolence* as a whole it is recognized that Fancy sometimes conflicts with Reason and Virtue.

The description of the castle in the first canto is conspicuously a work of the fancy or imagination. The castle is set among 'soothing Groves' and 'quiet Lawns', 'Half prankt with Spring, with Summer half imbrown'd', where

unnumber'd glittering Streamlets play'd,
And hurled every-where their Waters sheen;
That, as they bicker'd through the sunny Glade,
Though restless still themselves, a lulling Murmur made.

It is overshadowed by a 'sable, silent, solemn Forest',

Where nought but shadowy Forms were seen to move,
As *Idless* fancy'd in her dreaming Mood . . .
And where this Valley winded out, below,
The murmuring Main was heard, and scarcely heard, to flow.

This is the natural world of the *Seasons* viewed through a dreamy haze:

A pleasing Land of Drowsyhed it was:
Of Dreams that wave before the half-shut Eye;
And of gay Castles in the Clouds that pass,
For ever flushing round a Summer-Sky.

It is a world under the view of what Thomson, in *Spring*, line 459, called 'Imagination's vivid Eye'. As when the seduced pilgrims slip into the castle,

In silent Ease: as when beneath the Beam
Of Summer-Moons, the distant Woods among,
Or by some Flood all silver'd with the Gleam,
The soft-embodied Fays through airy Portal stream.

The castle is a 'Fairy-Land' of 'fair Illusions' and 'artful Phantoms', but these illusions often reproduce the visual delights of the *Seasons*, for instance the play of light over the natural scene:

And hither *Morpheus* sent his kindest Dreams,
Raising a World of gayer Tinct and Grace;

> O'er which were shadowy cast Elysian Gleams,
> That play'd, in waving Lights, from Place to Place,
> And shed a roseate Smile on Nature's Face.
> Not *Titian's* Pencil e'er could so array,
> So fleece with Clouds the pure Etherial Space.[58]

Within the castle there are tapestries depicting the pastoral patriarchal age of Abraham, and also paintings:

> Whate'er *Lorrain* light-touch'd with softening Hue,
> Or savage *Rosa* dash'd, or learned *Poussin* drew.

These tapestries and paintings make up a receding vista of imaginary landscapes, thronged with shadowy forms. At the centre is a blank, walled area, where 'solitude and perfect silence reign', and where one is constrained to dream:

> As when a Shepherd of the *Hebrid-Isles,*
> Plac'd far amid the melancholy Main,
> (Whether it be, lone Fancy him beguiles;
> Or that aerial Beings sometimes deign
> To stand, embodied, to our Senses plain)
> Sees on the naked Hill, or Valley low,
> The whilst in Ocean *Phœbus* dips his Wain,
> A vast Assembly moving to and fro:
> Then all at once in Air dissolves the wondrous Show.[59]

Joseph Warton wrote of this stanza: 'I cannot recollect any solitude so romantic ... The mind naturally loves to lose itself in one of these wildernesses.'[60] But this wilderness is itself within the mind: the castle of indolence is a Chinese box of dreams within dreams; movement through it has the characteristic of movement in mental space in that it can be at the same time inwards and outwards. In one aspect the castle represents the poet's own self-absorbed, self-justifying, capricious, insatiable, irresponsible, creative imagination. It is the art and sensibility which created the more inward parts of the *Seasons*. The pleasures of indolence are the pleasures of enhanced self-awareness and of contemplation; they are the pleasures of the imagination, or, as Thomson's contemporaries sometimes called them, the pleasures of melancholy, for, according to classical and Renaissance tradition, melancholy marked the temperament of the creative artist.

Thomson's castle of indolence reveals, however, a darker face of melancholy, which is seen in the dungeon described at the end of canto I. Delightful visions are offset by nightmares: the creative imagination which, in pleasant indolence, can charm itself with romantic visions, is also, in its self-absorption, a prey to sinister, fearful eruptions of boredom, despair, and madness. Thomson knows that the imagination can be a dangerous pleasure ground, the melancholy main can be a perilous sea, and the romantic wilderness within the mind can be a hostile country.

Of course, well before we learn about the dungeon we have been warned about the enchanter's wickedness and have perhaps detected moral irresponsibilities in his siren melody. At the very point where the romantic dream is most seductive, the moment of the Hebridean shepherd's vision, Thomson appears in his own person for the first time in his poem to assert the higher values of socially responsible art. Calling on the Muse, he proclaims:

> Thou yet shalt sing of War, and Actions fair,
> Which the bold Sons of BRITAIN will inspire . . .
> Thou yet shalt tread in Tragic Pall the Stage,
> Paint Love's enchanting Woes, the Heroe's Ire,
> The Sage's Calm, the Patriot's noble Rage,
> Dashing Corruption down through every worthless Age.

Like Spenser, speaking through the mouth of Piers in *The Shepheardes Calender* ('October'), he proclaims that he will rise to higher kinds of poetry.[61] Implicitly, he vindicates *Liberty* and the patriot plays published between the conception and the printing of *The Castle of Indolence*.

Thomson in the second canto rejects the sweet dwelling of the romantic imagination, that whole world of romantic images, from Arabia to the Hebrides by way of fairyland, which he took from Spenser and Milton, and was to have some part in handing on to the nineteenth century. He aspires to be a moralist, not a self-indulgent, self-absorbed dreamer, and he insists that reason and virtue must be linked with fancy, that is, imagination. True virtue is not repose of mind, but selfless activity, as appears in the Bard's song. The greatest poetry of the past was that which fired the breast 'To Thirst of Glory, and heroic Deeds',[62] and the task of the present-day poet is to serve the cause of public virtue. The characters of the Wizard and the Bard, the castle and its destroyer, articulate very clearly and bring into head-on collision the two poets inside Thomson, the poets who coexist easily in the *Seasons*: they are the retired dreamer whose object is pleasure and the active teacher whose object is moral instruction. Victory goes to the latter: to the Bard of *Liberty* rather than the Hymner of Solitude. Thomson gives unequivocal answers to the questions he raises concerning the role of the poet and the value and status of dreaming. The achievement of his poem is to make us feel the power of romanticism and respond with delight to its appeal, while at the same time we judge it, and know the dangers of its rejection of responsibility and reality.

Thomson's intentions may well have been unequivocal, but, as Johnson observed of *Liberty*, 'an author and his reader are not always of a mind'; from the beginning, most readers found the first canto more appealing than the second. In a letter of 15 May 1748 Lady Hertford wrote, 'I think the *Wizard's Song* deserves a preference; 'He needs no Muse who dictates from his heart'. Lady Luxborough agreed that it was no wonder that the Wizard's song was the most engaging, for 'Thomson's heart was ever devoted to that Archimage'. Shelley said that 'the Enchanter in the first canto was a true philanthropist, and the Knight in the second an oligarchical imposter, overthrowing truth by power'. Douglas Grant and Earl Wasserman speak for the majority of twentieth-century readers on both sides of the Atlantic when the first declares that the first canto 'is by far the finer of the two', and the second says that the 'dull didactic' second canto 'is an artistic failure'.[63]

The first canto contains, at stanza xl, what is apparently the earliest published reference in English to what would become a prime symbol of the poetic imagination: the Aeolian harp.[64] This device is also mentioned in 'An Ode, on the Winter Solstice' and is the subject of Thomson's last-published poem, his 'Ode on Aeolus's Harp', printed (together with 'On the Report of a Wooden Bridge') in the second edition of Dodsley's *Collection of Poems* in June 1748 and in subsequent editions. A footnote to the 'Ode on Aeolus's Harp' describes the harp as 'a musical Instrument, which plays with the wind, invented by Mr Oswald', but strictly it was the rediscovery of an invention described in a Latin treatise of 1650 by the German Jesuit Athanasius Kircher. James Oswald, 'the Scotch Orpheus', was a dancing-master, singer, cello player, and composer who came from Scotland to London in 1741, where he prospered as a music publisher; he composed musical settings for at least three of Thomson's love lyrics.[65] According to Charles Burney, who knew both men quite well, Thomson translated the 1650 description of the Aeolian Harp for Oswald, who could not read Latin 'and let it pass for his invention, in order to give him a better title to the sale of the instrument at his music-shop in St Martin's Church-yard'. It is not known whether Thomson possessed an Aeolian harp (none is mentioned in the sale catalogue of his goods after his death), but Shenstone's friend Lady Luxborough certainly had one before November 1748.[66]

Thomson's last writing was the few corrections and revisions to a second edition of *The Castle of Indolence* published in octavo by Millar on 22 September, by which time the poet himself was dead. Murdoch recounts:

He had always been a timorous horse-man; and more so, in a road where numbers of giddy or unskilful riders are continually passing: so that when the weather did not invite him to go by water, he would commonly walk the distance between *London* and *Richmond*, with any acquaintance that offered; with whom he might chat and rest himself, or perhaps dine, by the way. One summer evening, being alone, in his walk from town to *Hammersmith*, he had overheated himself, and in that condition, imprudently took a boat to carry him to *Kew*; apprehending no bad consequence from the chill air on the river, which his walk to his house, at the upper end of *Kew-lane*, had always hitherto prevented. But, now, the cold had so seized him, that next day he found himself in a high fever, so much the more to be dreaded that he was of a full habit. This however, by the use of proper medicines, was removed, so that he was thought to be out of danger: till the fine weather having tempted him to expose himself once more to the evening dews, his fever returned with violence, and with such symptoms as left no hopes of a cure. Two days had passed before his relapse was known in town; at last Mr *Mitchell* and Mr *Reid*,[67] with Dr *Armstrong*, being informed of it, posted out at mid-night to his assistance: but alas! came only to endure a sight of all others the most shocking to nature, the last agonies of their beloved friend. This lamented death happened on the 27th day of *August*, 1748.

Shenstone said that he had heard that Thomson 'waited too long for the return of his friend Dr Armstrong, and did not chuse to employ any other physician'; but Thomson was attended at the end also by Robertson, who recalled:

Armstrong and myself were with him till the last moment. I was in the room with him when he died. A putrid fever carried him off in less than a week. He seemed to me to be desirous not to live; and I had reason to think that my sister-in-law [Elizabeth Young] was the occasion of this—He could not bear the thoughts of her being married to another.

Taylor the barber associated Thomson's death with drink: 'having had a batch of drinking with Quin, he took a quantity of cream of tartar, as he frequently did on such occasions, which, with a fever before, carried him off'. Robertson disagreed with this diagnosis, though he was glad to call upon Taylor in his proper professional capacity to shave Thomson, 'as a refreshment to his friend'. Taylor recalled: 'I shaved him the very day before his death: he was very weak, but made a shift to sit up in bed. I asked him how he found himself that morning. "*Ah* WULL," he replied, "I am very bad indeed".'[68]

On the day of the death itself, Mitchell, 'almost sunk', wrote a sad note to Murdoch. Mitchell immediately took responsibility for sealing up the dead poet's belongings and arranging his funeral; he asked William Gusthart in Edinburgh to notify Thomson's kin in Scotland of his death. Armstrong described the fatal illness in a letter to Murdoch on 30 August:

Poor Thomson died last Saturday morning of a fever, which at first appeared to be an intermittent; but in a short time degenerated from a fever, which I hoped would do him a great piece of service, by scouring his habit, into the nervous malignant one which soon proved fatal to him, as it has to many. This blow makes a hideous gap; and . . . I question whether I shall ever be able to see Richmond again without sorrow and mortification.

He gave further details and reflections in a letter to John Forbes on 3 September:

The loss of such an agreeable friend as poor Thomson is so much the more shocking, that it was unexpected by every body. He died of a malignant nervous fever, that came upon the back of a tertian; and I had no notice of his being in any danger till I saw it in the most formidable shapes. It is certain, nature was oppressed in him with a great load of materials for a disease, not to be easily thrown off by a constitution so much worn as his was; and if he had struggled thro' that Fever, there are many reasons to believe, that it must almost unavoidably have been followed by some lingering disease, much worse than a speedy death: this is the most comfortable light in which I can view this shocking loss. Besides, I think him greatly to be envied, to have got fairly rid of this rascally world, and to have left it so universally regretted.

Forbes had already received the miserable news from Murdoch, who confessed 'that nothing in life has ever more shocked and afflicted me'. Murdoch wrote to Forbes again on 8 September,

Although I wrote you but two posts ago, I cannot let pass any opportunity of conversing with you; now, that I know you to be oppressed with the deepest melancholy, and in need of all the consolation your friends can lend. But, alas! what can I say? who myself as much stand in need of a comforter. We have lost, my dear F., our old, tryed, amiable, open, and honest-hearted Thomson, whom we never parted from but unwillingly; and never met but with fresh transport; whom we found ever the same delightful Companion, the same faithful depository of our inmost thoughts, and the same sensible sympathising adviser.

Murdoch urges Forbes to seek the same consolation in Heaven that Thomson had found when he lost Charles Richard Talbot: 'Think likewise, that if any thing earthly could disturb the happiness of our departed friend, it would be to see an unbecoming excess of grief in those whom he loved. I think I hear him kindly chide us, and point to a passage in his *Seasons*, that admirably suits our case.'[69] (The *Seasons* reference is probably to the passage on resurrection at the end of *Winter*.)

The affectionate tone of these private tributes is heard also in the obituary printed in Fielding's *Jacobite's Journal* for 27 August and reprinted in other newspapers:

This Morning at Four o'clock died of a violent Fever, at his House in Kew Lane, the celebrated Mr James Thompson, Author of the Seasons, &c. an honest Man, who has not left one Enemy behind him. His Abilities as a Writer, his Works sufficiently witness to all the World; but the Goodness of his Heart, which overflowed with Benevolence, Humanity, universal Charity, and every amiable Virtue, was best known to those who had the Happiness of his Acquaintance; by every one of whom he was most tenderly beloved, and now most sincerely and most deservedly lamented.

News of the poet's death reached the Midlands the very week that he was to have arrived on a visit to Hagley. Lady Luxborough described the scene: 'at

Hagley we learned the death of Mr Thomson, which Mr Lyttelton was grieving at under one tree, and Mr Shenstone under another, as we walked in the gloomy part of the Park'. Shenstone 'was as much shocked to hear of his death, as if [he] had known and loved him for a number of years'; he mourned the loss of one who might have proved a disinterested critic of his verse if the friendship had been allowed by fate or the Lytteltons to ripen: 'I valu'd Mr Thomson as he was the only Person of Figure that ever the Hagley Family introduc'd to me ... Had he liv'd he might have found *some* satisfaction here [The Leasowes] notwithstanding the vicinity and the Table of Hagley.' Lyttelton was in great grief, but his reaction was characteristically religious:

God's will be done! it has pleas'd his Providence to afflict me lately with a new stroke in the sudden death of poor Mr Thomson, one of the best and most beloved of my friends. He loved my Lucy too, and was loved by her. I hope and trust in the Divine goodness that they are now together in a much happier state. That is my consolation, that is my support.

His further consolation was that his own book on the conversion of St Paul might have helped Thomson to die a Christian.[70] Lyttelton commemorated Thomson at Hagley by building a half-octagonal stone temple. Shenstone promised an urn at The Leasowes, but apparently erected nothing more than the seat in Virgil's Grove which he dedicated to Thomson in 1747;[71] he also mourned the poet in *Verses written towards the end of 1748*, addressed to William Lyttelton, the man who first brought Thomson to The Leasowes. Short verse epitaphs in Latin and English appeared in the journals,[72] but the earliest substantial verse tribute to be printed was Robert Shiels's blank-verse *Musidorus: a Poem sacred to the Memory of Mr James Thomson*, of October, 1748.

Thomson's remains were buried under a plain stone in the north-west corner of St Mary's Church, Richmond, on 29 August. Among the mourners at the funeral were Mitchell, Millar, Quin, Robertson, and 'another friend patronised by the Earl of Warwick' (probably Symmer). The exact site of Thomson's grave is uncertain, but is thought not to be close to the brass tablet inscribed to Thomson and placed in the church in 1792 by the Earl of Buchan.[73] The enthusiastic earl was responsible also for the raising in 1819 of a commemorative obelisk on the hillside overlooking Thomson's birthplace at Ednam. Earlier, in 1762, a monument to Thomson was set up between those to Shakespeare and Rowe in the 'Poet's Corner' of Westminister Abbey. This was paid for by the young George III (subscribing a hundred pounds) and the other royal, noble, and wealthy subscribers to a fine quarto edition of Thomson's *Works*, on which Millar, 'for the honour of the booksellers ... sacrificed his interest, by giving up the advantages of his copy'. The description in a contemporary report of the monument's unveiling shows how its designer,

Robert Adam, contrived to allude to Thomson's status as tragedian and bard, and the poet of *Liberty* as well as the *Seasons:*

It is . . . executed by Michael Henry Spang, Statuary, after a design of Mr Adam, Architect to his Majesty. There is a figure of Mr Thomson sitting, who leans his left arm upon a pedestal, and holds a book with the cap of Liberty in his other hand. Upon the pedestal is carved a bas-relief of the Seasons, to which a boy points, offering him a laurel crown as the reward of his genius. At the feet of the figure, is the tragick mask, and ancient harp.[74]

Thomson died intestate, but on 25 October 1748 the Prerogative Court of Canterbury granted administration of his estate to George Lyttelton and Andrew Mitchell, 'the lawfull Attorneys of Mary Craig the natural and lawfull Sister and next of Kin of the said deceased for the use and benefit of the said Mary Craig now residing at Edinburgh'.[75] Mary was the eldest of Thomson's two surviving sisters; the other sister was Jean, who was married to Robert Thomson, master of Lanark Grammar School. Presumably Lyttelton and Mitchell acted effectively as executors throughout the winding-up of the debt-laden estate, though the notice for the auction of Thomson's household furniture, his pictures, and his considerable library, says that the sale is 'By Order of the Executrix' (that is, Mary Craig).[76] The sale took place at Kew-Foot Lane on 15, 16 and 17 May, 1749, after which the house was bought by Thomson's old friend, George Ross.

Even before they were granted administration, Lyttelton and Mitchell started to arrange for the performance of *Coriolanus* in order to clear the poet's debts and provide for his sisters. Thomas Birch wrote to Lord Chancellor Harwicke on 17 September,

Thomson the poet, tho' he had till lately a pension from the prince,—and a good Place from the Crown of Joint-Patentee with one Paterson, the Author of Arminius, a prohibited Tragedy, in the Office of Surveyor of the Leeward Islands, yet thro' Luxury and ill Oeconomy has died many hundred pounds in debt to his Friends as well as to Tradesmen. But Mr Lyttelton has the Generosity to administer to him and order'd the Bills of the latter, which are no less than thirty at Richmond and in the Neighbourhood only, to be collected, in order to their Discharge; for which purpose his *Coriolanus* will be brought on the Stage early this Season.

On 30 September Birch wrote in similar terms to John Boyle, fifth Earl of Orrery (the friend of Swift and Pope), to whom he also recommended *The Castle of Indolence.*[77]

Coriolanus was staged at Covent Garden, where Quin was the leading actor; Garrick acted generously by undertaking not to bring on any new play at Drury Lane while Thomson's play was running at the other house. Aaron Hill, who shared the belief, not uncommon among dramatists, that theatre managers were hostile towards him, complained towards the end of 1748 that Garrick was acting maliciously in delaying the production of Hill's tragedy *Merope* in favour of Johnson's *Irene*, but Richardson explained in a letter to him on 12 January 1749:

As to Mr Garrick, give me leave to say what I know: which is, That he was actually long ago ingaged in Irene. The Author was his Tutor; and it was expected to come on last Season. Mr Garrick had also engaged to Mr Lyttelton, that no new Play should be acted during the run of Coriolanus. There was Ill-will between Mr Thomson and Mr Garrick on the score of Mr Quin, and of that Play, and Mr Garrick was glad of an Opportunity to regain Mr Lyttelton's Opinion by such a Promise. So these were not mere Pretenses.[78]

Thomson's orphan play opened on 13 January and played for ten nights; its three benefit performances were advertized as for 'the Sisters of the Deceased Author'. One of the author's former patrons was conspicuous by his absence: *Coriolanus* was the only play by Thomson acted in the lifetime of Frederick, Prince of Wales, that did not receive the benefit of a performance commanded by the Prince. The printed text was published by Millar on 19 January in the unusually large edition of 4,500 copies. From the profits of the stage benefits and the sale of Thomson's remaining copyrights (for which Millar paid the sisters two hundred pounds in 1751) and his more solid property, the creditors were satisfied and 'a handsome sum' was remitted to Mary and Jean.[79] *Coriolanus* was never revived in the form in which Thomson left it, but Thomas Sheridan's *Coriolanus or the Roman Matron* is a conflation of Shakespeare's and Thomson's plays, both very heavily cut. Sheridan's first two acts are from Shakespeare, his last three from Thomson with a few Shakespearian inter-polations; there are also some new linking passages. This version was first acted in 1752 and proved popular, as did another combination of Shakespeare and Thomson by John Philip Kemble in 1789. A version of *Coriolanus* containing passages of Thomson was played in London as late as 1838.

The original version, acted in 1749, had a strong cast, even though Garrick and Quin, now in different companies, could not appear together. The part of Tullus, which Thomson had written for Garrick, was played by Lacy Ryan, who had been cast as Selim in *Edward and Eleonora*; he was about the same age as his friend Quin and an actor of the same school. Galesus was played by Denis Delane, Osmond in *Tancred and Sigismunda* and cast as Edward in *Edward and Eleonora*, when he had been the rising young star not yet eclipsed by Garrick. Miss George Anne Bellamy, then in the early stages of a colourful career, played Volumnia. Veturia was played by Peg Woffington, said to be the handsomest woman who ever appeared on the stage, then at the height of her powers and appearing for the first time in a play by Thomson. She painted her face with wrinkles for the part, but reverted to her normal complexion to speak the epilogue, where she also reverted to the usual archness of stage epilogues spoken by women, and made an irresistible appeal to the audience:

> If with my grave Discourse, and wrinkled Face,
> I thus could bring a Hero to Disgrace,
> How absolutely may I hope to reign
> Now I am turn'd to my own Shape again! . . .
> It is my Sovereign Will,—Hear, and obey,—
> That you with Candour treat this *Orphan Play*.

Shiels says that the epilogue was spoken 'with an exquisite humour' and that it 'greatly pleased'.[80] In view of the complaint against flippant epilogues in the epilogue to *Tancred and Sigismunda*, it is unlikely that Thomson wrote the epilogue to *Coriolanus*.

Quin took the title-role, as Thomson intended. There is an engraving of him as Thomson's Coriolanus, in a helmet with a huge plume of feathers, an embroidered tunic with a stiff, wide, flared skirt or *tonnelet*, and buskins; he carries a sword at his side and a general's baton in his hand.[81] Smollett probably saw him in this part because the hostile discussion of Quin's heavily exaggerated acting style in chapter 102 of *Peregrine Pickle* (1751) includes ridicule of his delivery of a speech in *Coriolanus*.[82] George Anne Bellamy recalled a comic error brought about during rehearsals by Quin's old-fashioned pronunciation of 'a', so that when he ordered the centurions to lower their fasces, they imagined he said 'faces' and duly bowed their heads. Fortunately it was all right on the night.[83] Quin's speaking of the prologue, written by Lyttelton, provided a moving and memorable experience for the first-night audience. Shiels recalled:

when he spoke the following lines, which are in themselves very tender, all the endearments of a long acquaintance, rose at once to his imagination, while the tears gushed from his eyes.

> He lov'd his friends (forgive this gushing tear:
> Alas! I feel I am no actor here)
> He lov'd his friends with such a warmth of heart,
> So clear of int'rest, so devoid of art,
> Such generous freedom, such unshaken zeal,
> No words can speak it, but our tears may tell.

The beautiful break in these lines had a fine effect in speaking. Mr Quin here excelled himself; he never appeared a greater actor than at this instant, when he declared himself none: 'twas an exquisite stroke to nature; art alone could hardly reach it . . . A deep-fetch'd sigh filled up the heart felt pause; grief spread o'er all the countenance; the tear started to the eye, the muscles fell, and,

The whiteness of his cheek
Was apter than his tongue to speak his tale.

They all expressed the tender feelings of a manly heart, becoming a Thomson's friend.
His pause, his recovery were masterly; and he delivered the whole with an emphasis and
pathos, worthy the excellent lines he spoke; worthy the great poet and goood man, whose
merits they painted, and whose loss they deplored.[84]

1749 saw the publication of a more durable tribute to the dead poet in the
shape of William Collins's *Ode occasion'd by the Death of Mr Thomson*. Murdoch
said that Collins 'had lived for some time at *Richmond*, but forsook it when Mr
Thomson died'; his *Ode*, like the prologue to *Coriolanus*, is both a public
performance and an intimate expression of friendship. It is dedicated to George
Lyttelton; its scene is the Thames near Richmond; one of its prefatory mottoes
from Virgil's *Eclogues* is *Amavit nos quoque Daphnis*: 'me, too, Daphnis loved'.
Murdoch praised the ode 'for the dirge-like melancholy it breathes, and the
warmth of affection that seems to have dictated it',[85] and reprinted it at the
conclusion of his *Life* of Thomson. It is the best memorial, other than
Thomson's own poetry.

I

In yonder Grave a DRUID lies
  Where slowly winds the stealing Wave!
The *Year's* best Sweets shall duteous rise
  To deck *it's* POET'*s* sylvan Grave!

II

In yon deep Bed of whisp'ring Reeds
  His airy Harp shall now be laid,
That He, whose Heart in Sorrow bleeds
  May love thro' Life the soothing Shade.

III

Then Maids and Youths shall linger here,
  And while it's Sounds at distance swell,
Shall sadly seem in Pity's Ear
  To hear the WOODLAND PILGRIM's Knell.

IV

REMEMBRANCE oft shall haunt the Shore
  When THAMES in Summer-wreaths is drest,
And oft suspend the dashing Oar
  To bid his gentle Spirit rest!

V

And oft as EASE and HEALTH retire
  To breezy Lawn, or Forest deep,
The Friend shall view yon whit'ning Spire,
  And 'mid the varied Landschape weep.

VI

But Thou, who own'st that Earthy Bed,
  Ah! what will ev'ry Dirge avail?
Or Tears, which LOVE and PITY shed
  That mourn beneath the gliding Sail!

VII

Yet lives there one, whose heedless Eye
  Shall scorn thy pale Shrine glimm'ring near?
With Him, Sweet Bard, may FANCY die,
  And JOY desert the blooming Year.

VIII

But thou, lorn STREAM, whose sullen Tide
  No sedge-crown'd SISTERS now attend,
Now waft me from the green Hill's Side
  Whose cold Turf hides the buried FRIEND!

IX

And see, the Fairy Valleys fade,
  Dun *Night* has veil'd the solemn View!
—Yet once again, Dear parted SHADE
  Meek NATURE's CHILD again adieu!

X

The genial Meads assign'd to bless
  Thy Life, shall mourn thy early Doom,
Their Hinds, and Shepherd-Girls shall dress
  With simple Hands thy rural Tomb.

XI

Long, long, thy Stone and pointed Clay
  Shall melt the musing BRITON's Eyes,
O! VALES, and WILD WOODS, shall HE say
  In yonder Grave YOUR DRUID lies!

Appendix: Portraits of Thomson

The earliest authentic likeness of Thomson is in the engraving of 1761 by Basire, which was used as the frontispiece of Thomson's *Works* (1762), volume i. It is inscribed 'James Thomson/Aetatis XXV' and 'Aikman pinxit'. See Plate 1. This engraving was copied in smaller sizes by several engravers for later eighteenth- and early nineteenth-century editions of Thomson's poems. The original portrait by William Aikman of which the Basire engraving was a copy seems now to be lost. There is an unsigned undated eighteenth-century oil copy of the Basire engraving at the Huntington Library, no. 20.23: see Plate 3. This portrait has not been cleaned, but the bust seen dimly to the left of the sitter's head is undoubtedly Janus, an appropriate accessory for the poet of the seasons.

There are two other early portraits to which the names of Thomson and Aikman are linked. One is a signed chalk drawing in Edinburgh University Library, attached to which is an inscription by Aikman's grand-daughter: 'A sketch of Mr James Thomson the Poet done about the year 1720, by William Aikman, Painter. Anne Forbes.' This drawing is reproduced as a likeness of Thomson in Grant (frontispiece), but the identification of the sitter has been questioned: see a correspondence in the *Times Literary Supplement* (1942), 421, 429, 469, 547, and 583. John Kerslake, in *Early Georgian Portraits* (1977), i. 278, declares that 'the sitter's features are not easily reconciled with Thomson's as they appear in any reasonably well-authenticated likeness'. I agree.

A less improbable likeness is the oval oil portrait in the Scottish National Portrait Gallery, no. 331. See Plate 2. This has been cut down from a larger canvas; according to the gallery's catalogues it was once signed by Aikman and dated 1720 on the reverse, but I learn from Dr Iain G. Brown of the National Library of Scotland, where the painting is on long-term loan, that it has been relined and laid down on board, so that no trace of any old inscription is now visible. Kerslake (*loc. cit.*) says that it 'derives probably from the [Aikman/Basire] engraving' of 1761, but James Holloway, author of the only monograph on Aikman, tells me that the portrait seems to him to have been painted much earlier than 1761, 'possibly in 1720 as the inscription suggests'. It should be added that Mr Holloway is by no means sure that this painting is by Aikman. The pose and costume of the sitter are conventional, so a general similarity in these respects cannot be taken as proof of a direct relationship between this oval and the, so-far unlocated, Aikman original from which Plates 1 and 3 are derived. The features of the sitters, however, have enough resemblance to allow at least the possibility that the oval represents Thomson a few years younger than he appears in the engraving.

A second painting in the Scottish National Portrait Gallery (no. 642) is a possible likeness of Thomson in his twenties: see Plate 4. This is an oil, signed and dated 1726 by John Vanderbank, which could perhaps represent the same sitter as the Aikman/Basire engraving. Another oil portrait, signed and dated 1730 by Vanderbank, is said to be of

Thomson. It turned up in a catalogue of Charles J. Sawyer, Ltd., booksellers, in February 1937, and at Christies forty years later; I do not know its present whereabouts. To judge by the catalogue reproduction is bears very little resemblance to any authentic likeness of Thomson.

The first Thomson portrait concerning which we have a contemporary reference is the one by Stephen Slaughter that is the subject of verses by G. W. (probably Gilbert West) in the *Gentleman's Magazine*, December 1736, p. 743: 'On Mr *Thomson's* Picture drawn by Mr *Slaughter*, with the Figure of Liberty in his Hand, as described by him in his Poem on that Subject'. No drawing has been traced, but there is in the collection of Mr and Mrs Paul Mellon an oil painting of this subject, signed by Slaughter and dated 1736: see Plate 5. 'G. W.' s' poem and the paper in the sitter's hand are strong enough evidence that the Mellon oil is a likeness of Thomson. There is a small eighteenth-century stipple-engraved print of Thomson with the figure of Liberty, evidently derived from this Slaughter portrait-type, in the British Museum Department of Prints and Drawings (Anderton Collection, volume 98). In this print the head, facing the same way as in the Slaughter oil, is set in an oval frame with an ornamental surround. The inscription reads 'Painted by Wilson. Ornamented by Craig. Engraved by Chapman'. This trio might perhaps be Benjamin Wilson, William Marshall Craig, and John Chapman, all of whom were active in the 1780s.

The 'Wilson–Craig–Chapman' print is reproduced by McKillop in *Letters*, facing p. 68, accompanied by the puzzling note, on p. x, that it is 'said to be engraved from a painting by Hudson'. It has been claimed that James Craig, Thomson's nephew, who died in 1795, had in his possession Thomson's 'original portrait painted by Hudson, for Mr Millar, the bookseller, which was presented to him by Lady Grant [Millar's widow]' (*The Seasons*, with an Original Life of the Author by Robert Heron, Perth (1793), p. xlix, note). This assertion, made nearly fifty years after Thomson's death, may well be correct about the commission but wrong about the artist. Millar invested a large sum of money in Thomson and *Liberty*, so it is quite possible that he would commission a painting of his investment, but by Slaughter, not Hudson. No further references to a Hudson portrait of Thomson have come my way and no such portrait has been traced.

Stephen Slaughter may have painted Thomson's likeness twice, for there is in Leicester City Art Gallery another oil portrait said to be of Thomson and attributed to Slaughter. See plate 6. On the back of the canvas is an inscription by the eleventh Earl of Buchan: 'Portrait of Thomson, the Poet, by Slaughter. Procured for the Earl of Buchan by his friend Richard Cooper, Esqr. Engraver.' This Cooper could have been either of the engravers of that name: the father, who died in 1764, or the son, who was born about 1740 and died in 1814. One of the later eighteenth-century small versions of the Basire engraving after Aikman was engraved by R. Cooper. The portrait in Leicester Art Gallery bears hardly any resemblance to the painting in the Mellon Collection, but its attribution seems fairly sound (see A. C. Sewter 'Stephen Slaughter', *The Connoisseur*, 121 (1948), 12) and the general cast of the sitter's features can just be reconciled with authentic likenesses of Thomson.

The latest of those authentic likenesses, like the earliest, is a Basire engraving of 1761. This one was used as the frontispiece of volume ii of Thomson's *Works* (1762): it is inscribed 'James Thomson/Aetatis XLVI' and is after a lost painting by John Patoun.

See Plate 11. There are oil copies in the Scottish National Portrait Gallery, no. 794 (see Plate 12) and the National Portrait Gallery, no. 11, this second one presented to the gallery in 1857 by Thomson's 'grandneice, Miss Bell'. Another copy, dated 1774, by John Medina the younger, is at Edinburgh University: see Dr Talbot Rice, *The University Portraits* (Edinburgh, 1957), p. 202.

A version of the Patoun portrait in which the sitter is wearing a necktie was once at Hagley. It was presumably painted for George Lyttelton, and, according to one of Lyttelton's descendants was said by William Pitt, Earl of Chatham, to be 'beastly like': see Peter Cunningham's edition of Johnson's *Lives of the English Poets* (1854), iii, 235, n. 39. (Cunningham writes Aikman in error for Patoun.) This portrait was destroyed in the Hagley fire of 1925, but a photograph of it is reproduced in Kerslake, *op. cit.*, plate 796. Peter Cunningham (*loc. cit.*) refers to Patoun's original 'drawing' at Culloden House, but the present whereabouts of any such drawing are not known.

The Patoun portrait type may have served as the model for a marble oval bas-relief head and shoulders in the National Portrait Gallery, no. 4896. It is incised: 'Scotland gave me birth / England a Grave / I Sung the Seasons'. It was carved by an unidentified sculptor after Thomson's death, for an outdoor setting: see Kerslake, *op. cit.*, i. 278 and plate 797. The only other surviving sculpture said to represent Thomson is the seated figure in Roman dress on the monument to the poet carved by Michael Henry Spang after a design by Robert Adam, set up in Westminster Abbey in 1762.

Abbreviations

Bee	*The Bee, or Literary Weekly Intelligence*, ed. James Anderson, vols. 6 and 7 (Edinburgh, 1791–2).
Boswell's Johnson	*Boswell's Life of Johnson*, ed. G. B. Hill, rev. L. F. Powell, (6 vols., Oxford, 1934–50).
Grant	Douglas Grant, *James Thomson, Poet of 'The Seasons'* (London, 1951).
Hertford Correspondence	*Correspondence between the Countess of Hertford and the Countess of Pomfret* (2 vols., 1805).
Johnson	'Thomson', in *Johnson's Lives of the English Poets*, ed. G. B. Hill (Oxford, 1905), vol. iii, 281–301.
Letters	*James Thomson (1700–1748): Letters and Documents*, ed. A. D. McKillop (Lawrence, Kan., 1958).
London Stage	Arthur H. Scouten (ed.), *The London Stage, 1660–1800: Part 3, 1729–1747* (2 vols., Carbondale, Ill., 1961).
Murdoch	Patrick Murdoch, 'An Account of the Life and Writings of Mr. James Thomson', in *The Works of James Thomson* (1762), vol. i, pp. i–xx.
OET Liberty	James Thomson, *Liberty, The Castle of Indolence, and Other Poems*, ed. James Sambrook (Oxford, 1986).
OET Seasons	James Thomson, *The Seasons*, ed. James Sambrook (Oxford, 1981).
Plays	*The Plays of James Thomson, 1700–1748: a Critical Edition*, ed. John C. Greene (2 vols., New York and London, 1987).
Pope Correspondence	*The Correspondence of Alexander Pope*, ed. George Sherburn, (5 vols., Oxford, 1956).
Rundle Letters	*Letters of the late Thomas Rundle, LLD, Lord Bishop of Derry in Ireland, to Mrs Barbara Sandys*, with 'Memoirs' by James Dallaway (2 vols., Gloucester, 1789).
Shiels	Robert Shiels, 'Mr James Thomson' in 'Theophilus Cibber', *Lives of the Poets of Great-Britain and Ireland* (1753), vol. v, 190–218.
Twickenham Pope	*The Twickenham Edition of the Poems of Alexander Pope*, general ed., John Butt (11 vols., London and New Haven, Conn., 1939–69).
Walpole Correspondence	*The Yale Edition of Horace Walpole's Correspondence*, ed. W. S. Lewis et al. (48 vols., London and New Haven, Conn., 1937–83).
Weekly Entertainer	'Memorandum of Thomson, the Poet, collected from Mr. William Taylor . . . at Richmond, September 1791', in *The Weekly Entertainer* (Sherborne), 13 January 1800, vol. 35, 22–6.

Notes

CHAPTER I

1. Hew Scott, *Fasti Ecclesiae Scoticanae*, ii (Edinburgh, 1917), 139.
2. Murdoch, p. ii. An unattributed anecdote illustrating the mingled kindness and severity of Thomas Thomson towards a parishioner is recounted by James Logie Robertson ('Hugh Haliburton') in *Furth in Field* (1895), p. 185:

   > He had lent his pony to a parishioner of the name of Muir, and the rascal had so overworked or ill-used it that it died under his charge. Thereupon the minister charged him with cruelty, greed, and ingratitude. Muir retorted, declaring that 'he would not be hectored by him, for he was but the offscourings of the earth', and proceeded to curse the minister, For his ill-will and evil words Muir was sisted [summoned] before the Session, and tholed [suffered] rebuke; but it does not appear from the Session Records that he made good to the minister the loss of the pony.

3. See *DNB* under Baillie, Lady Grizel (1665–1746); Baillie, Robert (d. 1684); Hume, Patrick (1641–1724); and Campbell, Alexander (1675–1740).
4. Murdoch, p. iv.
5. Scott, *Fasti*, ii. 139.
6. Grant, 10.
7. *OET Seasons*, 42: lines 840–8.
8. John Sinclair, *The Statistical Account of Scotland*, xii (Edinburgh, 1794), 72: 'Southdean' by Revd William Scott.
9. Daniel Defoe, *A Tour thro' the Whole Island of Great Britain*, ed. G. D. H. Cole (1927), ii. 700.
10. Thomas Somerville, *My Own Life and Times, 1741–1804* (Edinburgh, 1861), 305.
11. Henry Grey Graham, *The Social Life of Scotland in the Eighteenth Century*, 5th edn. (1969), i. 151.
12. Defoe, *Tour*, ed. Cole ii. 730.
13. *OET Seasons*, 214–18, 22–4: *Winter*, lines 223–321, *Spring*, lines 379–442, 446.
14. *OET Seasons*, 260: *Winter* (1726), lines 6–16.
15. John More, *Strictures, Critical and Sentimental on Thomson's Seasons* (1777), 172–3.
16. George Watson, *The History of Jedburgh Grammar School* (Jedburgh, 1909), 7.
17. Shiels, 190.
18. James Thomson, *Poetical Works*, ed. Robert Bell (1855), i. 7 n.
19. David Steuart Erskine, Earl of Buchan, *Essays on the Lives and Writings of Fletcher of Saltoun and the Poet Thomson* (1792), 184.
20. Shiels, 190.
21. See *OET Seasons*, p. xxviii and n.
22. Murdoch, p. ii.
23. Letter from Riccaltoun to William Hogg, 30 April 1759, in *Gentleman's Magazine*, NS 40 (1853), 369. It has been argued that some of the philosophical and theological ideas expounded in Riccaltoun's prose *Works* (1771–2) may, in their germinal state, have influenced the young Thomson; see Mary Jane W. Scott, *James Thomson, Anglo-Scot* (Athens, Ga., 1988), 30–4.

24. Murdoch, p. iii.
25. See *OET Liberty*, 224-76.
26. Shiels, 217-18; Murdoch, pp. ii-iii.
27. Scott, *Fasti*, i. 124, ii. 108.
28. *Letters*, 108, 116, 119, 132, 213.
29. Scott, *Fasti*, ii. 101.
30. See *Letters*, 14; *OET Liberty*, 224.
31. Revd John Richmond of Southdean, *To the Memory of Thomson, in the Temple of the Muses at Dryburgh Abbey* (1818).
32. *OET Seasons*, p. xxxvi.
33. *The Seasons and the Castle of Indolence* (1841), p. xiv; James Thomson, *Poetical Works* (Aldine edn., 1847), i. p. xvii.
34. Buchan, *Lives of Fletcher and Thomson*, 184.
35. Murdoch, p. iii.
36. A. S. Bell, 'Three new letters of James Thomson', *Notes and Queries*, 217 (October 1972), 369.
37. Alexander Allardyce (ed.), *Scotland and Scotsmen in the Eighteenth Century* (1888), i. 39 n.
38. *OET Liberty*, 238-9, 240, 249-52.
39. Bell, 'Three new letters', 368.
40. Robert Chambers, *A Biographical Dictionary of Eminent Scotsmen*, iv (1835), 346-7 (story communicated by Revd John Richmond, minister of Southdean); William Howitt, *Homes and Haunts of the most eminent British Poets* (1847), i. 215.
41. Bruce Lenman, *The Jacobite Risings in Britain, 1689-1746* (1980), 154.
42. *OET Seasons*, 42, 180-2: *Spring*, lines 844-8, *Autumn*, lines 929-43.
43. Defoe, *Tour*, ed. Cole, ii. 708, 710.
44. Quoted in Robert Chambers, *Traditions of Edinburgh* (Edinburgh, 1868), 4.
45. William Ferguson, *Scotland: 1689 to the Present* (Edinburgh, 1978), 85-6.
46. John Macky, *A Journey through Scotland* (1723), 69.
47. Henny Mackenzie, *Anecdotes and Egotisms*, ed. H. W. Thompson (1927), 39.
48. Chambers, *Traditions of Edinburgh*, 201, 200.
49. *OET Liberty*: 'Upon the Hoop', (p. 241), 'Upon Beauty' (pp. 229-32), 'Upon Mrs Elizabeth Bennet', (pp. 249-52), 'Ten a-clock of night', (p. 248).
50. *The Hibernian Magazine, or Compendium of Entertaining Knowledge* (Dublin, 1773), 591-2; Robert Heron, *The Seasons, with an Original Life of the Author* (Perth, 1793), p. ix; Hester Lynch Piozzi, *Autobiography, Letters, and Literary Remains*, ed. A. Hayward, 2nd edn. (1861), ii. 159-60; *Thraliana: The Diary of . . . Mrs Piozzi*, ed. K. C. Balderston (Oxford, 1942), ii. 956-7.
51. Thomson, *Poetical Works* (Aldine ed., 1847), i. p. xii.
52. *Letters*, 5.
53. Murdoch, p. iii.
54. *OET Seasons*, pp. 296-7: *Summer*, lines 1044-57. See also *OET Seasons*, pp. 190-2, 379: *Autumn*, lines 1108-21.
55. Murdoch, pp. iii-iv.
56. *OET Liberty*, 275-6.
57. Alexander Bower, *The History of the University of Edinburgh* (Edinburgh, 1817), ii. 37.
58. Robert Wodrow, *Analecta, or Materials for a History of Remarkable Providences, mostly relating to Scotch Ministers and Christians*, iii (Edinburgh, 1843), 515.
59. Alexander Grant, *The Story of the University of Edinburgh during its first Three Hundred Years* (1884), ii. 328; i. 8 n.

60. Ibid. i. 263.
61. Eric S. Taylor, 'James Thomson: Poet of Nature and Reason' (University of Edinburgh thesis, 1943), 10 n.
62. Wodrow, *Analecta*, iii. 204.
63. Ibid. 203.
64. Shiels, 192.
65. Wodrow, *Analecta*, iv (1843), 139–40.
66. Ibid. iii. 302, 514.
67. Shiels, 192; Murdoch, p. v.
68. Murdoch, p. iv.
69. A. F. Tytler, *Memoirs of the Life and Writings of Henry Home of Kames* (Edinburgh, 1807), i. 164–5.
70. Wodrow, *Analecta*, iii. 514.
71. Allardyce (ed.), *Scotland and Scotsmen in the Eighteenth Century*, i. 9.
72. e.g. *OET Seasons*, pp. 330, 333, 336–8: *Spring*, lines 321, 625, 868, 915, 1023.
73. *Edinburgh Magazine*, 1 (1793), 4.
74. Ibid. ii. 338, in *Letters*, p. 34.
75. Johnson, *Lives of the English Poets*, ed. G. B. Hill (Oxford, 1905), iii. 403. Johnson's accusation receives some support from Thomson's Scottish friend William Robertson, who, many years after the deaths of both poets, said of Mallet: 'that person's name was properly "Malloch"; but I used to call him "Moloch" in our festive moments, and Thomson enjoyed the jest. Sir, he had not Thomson's heart; he was not sound at the core; he made a cat's-paw of Thomson, and I did not like the man on that account' (*Bee*, 6, 284). Cf. Ch. I, n. 103.
76. Shiels, 194 n.
77. *Edinburgh Magazine*, 1 (1793), 5.
78. 'To Mr Thomson, the Author of Winter', in Joseph Mitchell, *Poems on Several Occasions* (1729), ii. 283.
79. *Edinburgh Magazine*, 1 (1793), 4.
80. Murdoch, p. v.
81. Herbert Drennon, 'James Thomson and John Norris', *PMLA* 53 (1938), 1094–1101; *OET Liberty*, 268.
82. 'The Hawk and the Nightingale' by John Callendar, in the *Edinburgh Miscellany* (1720).
83. *OET Liberty*, 246.
84. *European Magazine*, 23 (1793), 338.
85. *Edinburgh Miscellany* (1720), p. ii. Some of the authors however (e.g. Ayton and Montrose) were long dead.
86. *OET Liberty*, 271, line 65: cf. *OET Seasons*, 24, line 435.
87. Scott, *Fasti*, iv, 519; Grant, 27–8, 34, 282. The parish of Ancrum also contributed to this bursary; see *Letters*, 14.
88. Murdoch, pp. v–vi; Shiels, 192–3.
89. Grant, p. 34, referring to Hamilton's note that Thomson performed an exercise on Psalm 98 on 2 March 1723. David Laing in Thomson, *Poetical Works* (Aldine edn., 1830), i, p. xcviii. William Goodhugh, *The Observer*, 19 September 1818.
90. *OET Liberty*, 234–7.
91. Shiels, 194.
92. See *OET Liberty*, 406, for a discussion of this attribution.
93. See Herbert Drennon, 'The Source of James Thomson's "The Works and Wonders of Almighty Power"', *Modern Philology*, 32 (1934–5), 33–6.

94. *OET Liberty*, 277: lines 23–8.

95. *Letters*, 1–2.

96. Ibid. 4–6.

97. Ibid. 6.

98. Murdoch, p. v; Shiels, 193–4. When Thomson's sister Jean told Boswell in 1778 that she 'never heard' that her brother 'had any intention of going into holy orders', she was probably referring to Anglican orders; see *Boswell's Johnson*, iii. 360.

99. *Letters*, 5–6.

100. Murdoch, p. vi.

101. Grant, 37.

102. Bell, 'Three new letters', 368–9; *Letters*, 15 n.

103. *Edinburgh Magazine*, 2 (1793), 2, 171: letters of 15 September and 29 December 1725 (dates corrected in *Papers of the Bibliographical Society of America* 72 (1978), 230). A discreditable reason for Malloch's name change is given by John Almon in his edition of *The Correspondence of the late John Wilkes* (1805), i. 77 n.: on 'his arrival from the north, he became a great declaimer at the London coffee-houses against the Christian religion. Old surly [John] Dennis was highly offended at his conduct, and always called him Moloch. He then changed his name to Mallet.' Cf. Ch. I, n. 75.

CHAPTER 2

1. E. A. Wrigley, 'London and the Great Leap Forward', *The Listener*, 6 July 1967, 7–8.

2. Daniel Defoe, *A Tour thro' the Whole Island of Great Britain*, ed. G. D. H. Cole (1927), i. 326, 316.

3. Act I, Scene i, lines 135–6: *Plays of Richard Steele*, ed. S. S. Kenny (Oxford, 1971), p. 221. The idea of the several nations of London is elaborated by Addison and Steele in *Spectator*, 403 and 454 (12 June, 11 August 1712).

4. A. S. Bell, 'Three new letters of James Thomson', *Notes and Queries*, 217 (October 1972), 368. See Bryant Lillywhite, *London Coffee-Houses* (1963), 211; Thomson's letter antedates the earliest reference to Forest's noted by Lillywhite.

5. *Boswell's Johnson*, ii. 337.

6. *Spectator*, 49 (16 April 1711); *Boswell's Johnson*. i. 105.

7. *A Trip through London* 5th edn. (1728), 6.

8. Shiels, 195.

9. Sir Harris Nicolas says, in James Thomson, *Poetical Works* (Aldine edn., 1847), i. p. xvii, that Mr Elliot is probably a brother of Sir Gilbert Elliot of Minto, but neither of the Sir Gilberts alive in Thomson's lifetime had a brother living in London. The Elliots of Stobs were connected by marriage with the Scotts of Ancrum, Cranstoun's parish; William Elliot of this branch of the family was a merchant in London, probably at this date. Other Elliots certainly in London at this time were George Elliot 'of Princes Square', son of the minister of Hownam, near Kelso, and Robert Elliot, Clerk to Sir John Barnard, MP and future Lord Mayor. See G. F. S. Elliot, *The Border Elliots and the Family of Minto* (Edinburgh, 1897), 263, 294, 297, 520, 234–5.

10. *Letters*, 7.

11. Bell, 'Three new letters', 368.

12. *Letters*, 7–9 and n.

13. Ibid. 12.

14. Murdoch, p. vii.

15. Bell, 'Three new letters', 368.
16. Johnson, 297–8.
17. Ibid. 283.
18. *Letters*, 8.
19. Alexander Allardyce (ed.), *Scotland and Scotsmen in the Eighteenth Century* (Edinburgh and London, 1888), ii. 547.
20. *Letters*, 7–9.
21. Bell, 'Three new letters', 369. Mallet writes about his own tutorship in July 1723: 'My encouragement is £30' (*European Magazine*, 24 (1793), 24).
22. Joseph Spence, *Observations, Anecdotes, and Characters of Books and Men*, ed. J. M. Osborn (Oxford, 1966), i. 370.
23. *Letters*, 10–11.
24. *OET Liberty*, 280–3, 409–10.
25. Ibid. 279.
26. See *DNB* under Hamilton, Charles (1697–1733) and Hamilton, Thomas (1680–1735).
27. Murdoch, p. vi.
28. University of Edinburgh, MS Laing II. 330, fo. 1: letter of 14 June 1791.
29. See *DNB* under Forbes, Duncan (1685–1747); *OET Seasons*, 182 (*Autumn*, lines 944–9).
30. *OET Liberty*, 193 (*Castle of Indolence*, canto 1, line 551); *Letters*, 108 n.
31. Murdoch, p. vi. *The Bee*, 18 (Edinburgh, 1793), 4.
32. See Appendix: Portraits of Thomson.
33. *Letters*, 8.
34. Ibid. 34.
35. Spence, *Observations*, i. 370.
36. *Letters*, 16–18.
37. See *OET Seasons*, 260–4: lines 33–79, 133–85, 5–6, 19.
38. V. & A., Forster Collection MS F. 48 E. 2.
39. *Gentleman's Magazine*, NS 40 (1853), 369.
40. This letter came to light when, in 1797, a housemaid in the manse at Ancrum used it as packing round some candlesticks being sent to Kelso for exchange, and the recipient of the parcel realized its value (*Kelso Mail*, 13 April 1797; *Scots Magazine*, 49 (1797), 222–5). It is very likely that other letters were similarly treated as waste-paper and were destroyed.
41. *Letters*, 20–1; *OET Liberty*, 283–4.
42. Shiels, 195 n.; Spence, *Observations*, i. 370.
43. *OET Seasons*, 260–7: lines 19, 101–3, 135–6, 221–3, 307. William Hazlitt, *Complete Works*, ed. P. P. Howe (1930), v. 88; Johnson, 299.
44. *OET Seasons*, 260: line 10. Allan Ramsay, *Works*, ed. A. M. Kinghorn and A. Law (Edinburgh, 1970), iv. 236.
45. *OET Seasons*, 268: lines 338, 340, 355.
46. Ibid. 261–70: lines 66–73, 143–54, 210–15, 363–405, 253–300, 143–7.
47. Johnson, 298.
48. Geoffrey Tillotson, 'The Methods of Description in Eighteenth- and Nineteenth-Century Poetry', in C. Camden (ed.), *Restoration and Eighteenth-Century Literature*, (Chicago, 1963), 235.
49. *OET Seasons*, 264–5: lines 190–4.
50. George Saintsbury, *A History of English Prosody* (1923), ii. 479.
51. *OET Seasons*, 261–5: lines 39, 73, 96, 172, 201.
52. Ibid. 263–4: lines 136, 180.

53. *The Seasons* is the most modern poem quoted frequently in Johnson's *Dictionary* (1755); it is cited over six hundred times.

54. *OET Seasons*, 261–5: lines 47, 193.

55. Johnson, 300–1.

56. *OET Seasons*, 263: line 122; cf. John Arthos, *The Language of Natural Description in Eighteenth-Century Poetry* (Ann Arbor, Mich., 1949), 394–404.

57. Benjamin Victor, *Original Letters, Dramatic Pieces, and Poems* (1776), iii. 27.

58. Shiels, 196; Spence, *Observations*, i. 370.

59. *Weekly Entertainer*. A garbled version of this account appeared in John Evans, *Richmond and its Vicinity* (1825), giving rise to the erroneous impression that Park Egerton was a bookseller in 1730; see C. H. Timperley, *Encyclopaedia of Literary and Typographical Anecdote* (1842), 676, and H. R. Plomer et al., *A Dictionary of Printers and Booksellers, 1726–1775* (1932), 83.

60. *Bee*, 6 (1791), 281.

61. *Letters*, 10–11; *Edinburgh Magazine*, 2 (1793), 171, 89, (dates corrected in *Papers of the Bibliographical Society of America*, 72 (1978), 230). One of Mallet's letters to Hill is probably that dated 19 June, printed in the *European Magazine*, 6 (1784), 280: see *Notes and Queries* (September 1954), 390–1.

62. *Letters*, 22–4; Johnson, 284.

63. *Letters*, 24–7.

64. Ibid. 27. The warm tone of Thomson's reference to Savage by name in this letter seems to rule out the conjecture by Douglas Grant and others that Savage is also the subject of references elsewhere in the same letter to an 'unimprovable', 'unhappy Creature', who has given Hill 'barbarous Provocation' (Grant, 68). Though such terms could reasonably be applied to Savage at that time, it is more likely that Thomson alludes here to some other, now unrecognized, ungrateful recipient of Hill's kindness.

65. John Dyer, *Grongar Hill*, ed. R. C. Boys (Baltimore, 1941), 51–2.

66. Ralph M. Williams, *Poet, Painter, and Parson: The Life of John Dyer* (New York, 1956), 41–3. The most notorious of the abuse and scandal referred to was in *Memoirs of a Certain Island Adjacent to the Kingdom of Utopia* by Eliza Haywood, a former member of the Hill circle.

67. Benjamin Victor, *Original Letters, Dramatic Pieces, and Poems* (1776), i. 68.

68. Thomson wrote a song to 'Myra' in the latter part of 1742, evidently addressed to Elizabeth Young, the woman to whom he would propose marriage; see *OET Liberty*, 306–7, 431. The words of the poem, as well as his own account of its composition, seem to rule out the damaging possibility that he was re-using an earlier address to Mrs Sansom.

69. Shiels, 196–7; *Rundle Letters*, i. pp. xli–xlii; Alexander Pope, *Works*, ed. Joseph Warton (1797), i. 288 n; William Goodhugh, *The English Gentleman's Library Manual* (1827), 294. Goodhugh was probably accepting Mitchell's claim in his verse address to Thomson in 1729. Warton impossibly claims that Spence's *Essay on Homer's Odyssey* first made *Winter* known, though the Second Part of Spence's *Essay*, where *Winter* is praised, was not published until August 1727, after Thomson had brought out *Summer*, the *Poem to Newton*, and two editions of *Winter*.

70. Murdoch, pp. vii–viii.

71. Spence, *Observations*, i. 370; *OET Seasons*, 302.

72. *Pope Correspondence*, iv. 458–9.

73. *Letters*, 28, 32; Johnson, 285.

74. *Letters*, 32-3.

75. Ibid. 36, 38.

76. See *OET Seasons*, pp. xxxviii-xxxix.

77. *Letters*, 36. Dyer wrote a verse address to Thomson, probably in 1727, but it was never printed in his lifetime: see H. S. Hughes, 'John Dyer and the Countess of Hertford', *Modern Philology*, 27 (1929-30), 319.

78. *OET Seasons*, 221-3, 214-16; lines 388 + (*260*, 267-78), 389-413, 245-56.

79. Ibid. 303-5: lines 34-9, 52-5, 75-80, 6-12. See John Dennis, *Critical Works* ed. E. N. Hooker (Baltimore, 1939), i. 329-30; Aaron Hill, *The Creation* (1720), 5.

80. *OET Seasons*, pp. xxxix-xl.

81. *Letters*, 30.

82. Ibid. 34.

83. John Stow, *Survey of the Cities of London and Westminster, brought down to the present time by John Strype* (1720), ii. 41, 170, 173.

84. See Pat Rogers, *Grub Street: Studies in a Subculture* (1972).

85. *OET Seasons*, 283, 148: lines 513-22, 118-33. In both passages Thomson regrettably defines the 'sheets' of a ship like a landlubber.

86. *Post-Boy*, 2-4 June 1726.

87. See *DNB*, under Bland, John (1702-50); Lens, Bernard (1682-1740); and Stirling, James (1692-1770); see also E. G. R. Taylor, *The Mathematical Practitioners of Hanoverian England, 1714-1840* (Cambridge, 1966), 7, 113, 144-6, 166-7, for Stirling, the Watts brothers, William Vream, instrument-maker to the Academy, and Peter Brown and Archibald Patoun, who taught mathematics there.

88. Grant, 57; *London Evening-Post*, 18-21 January 1729.

CHAPTER 3

1. *Letters*, 36.

2. Ibid. 39: the first edition of *Summer* is reprinted in *OET Seasons*, 270-99.

3. *Letters*, 40.

4. Ibid. 45.

5. Ibid. 48.

6. Ibid. 40, 46.

7. Ibid. 40, 48-9.

8. Ibid. 47, 50.

9. Ibid. 50, 40; for the dunces see *DNB* under Beckingham, Charles (1699-1731); Cooke, Thomas (1703-56); and Mitchell, Joseph (1684-1738); for Bezaleel Morrice (1675?-1749) see *Twickenham Pope*, v. 449; John Rooke appears in Millan's advertisements and in the British Library *Catalogue of Printed Books* as the translator of Xenophon's *Ephesian History* (1726), and in D. F. Foxon, *English Verse, 1701-1750*, as the author of *Select Translations* (1726).

10. Shiels, 197-8.

11. *Letters*, 50.

12. Léon Morel, *James Thomson: sa vie et ses oeuvres* (Paris, 1895), 66-7 n.

13. *Letters*, 54. Incidentally, Thomson addresses this letter from the Academy in Little Tower Street. George G. Williams, in his *Guide to Literary London* (1973), asserts, without citing his authority, that Thomson wrote *Summer* in lodgings at the upper end of Whitehall, on the east side, 'seven or eight doors down from' the entrance to Craig's

Court and opposite to the Admiralty (p. 14). Mrs Piozzi more improbably claims that Thomson wrote *Summer* in 'his lodgings at a milliner's in Bond-street' (Hester Lynch Piozzi, *Observations and Reflections made in the Course of a Journey through France, Italy and Germany* (1789), 416).

14. *OET Seasons*, 271–4, 293–6, 288, 292, 294: lines 127, 154, 1026, 1042, 147, 36, 1038–9, 916–17, 725, 875, 939.

15. *OET Seasons*, 274, 277, 281, 289, 292: lines 172–5, 284, 268–89, 425–50, 739–60, 860–9, 871–6.

16. Ibid. 297, line 1071.

17. John MacQueen, *The Enlightenment and Scottish Literature*, vol. i: *Progress and Poetry* (Edinburgh, 1982), 57.

18. *OET Seasons*, 270–4, 296, 283–4: lines 89–93, 21–3, 103–4, 126–44, 1026, 535–57.

19. Ibid. 282–3, 285: lines 498–501, 610, 585–91, 606–9, 611.

20. Ibid. 286–8: lines 657–62 and n., 706–31, 632–42, 669–97, 651–6, 663–9, 698–705, 616–31.

21. Ibid. 273, 275, 277–8, 295: lines 107, 189, 267, 323, 976–80.

22. Ralph M. Williams, 'Thomson and Dyer: Poet and Painter', in *The Age of Johnson: Essays presented to Chauncey Brewster Tinker*, ed. F. W. Hilles (New Haven, Conn., 1949), 209–16.

23. Joseph Warton, *Essay on the Genius and Writings of Pope*, [i] (1756), 46.

24. *OET Seasons*, 274, 285: lines 152–5, 595–609.

25. Ibid. 271, 294–5: lines 39–47, 964–74.

26. Ibid. 297–8: lines 1078–82, 1090–8.

27. *OET Seasons*, 299: lines 1141–6.

28. Alexander Pope, *Works*, ed. Joseph Warton (1797), ix. 121 n.

29. Joseph Spence, *Observations, Anecdotes, and Characters of Books and Men*, ed. J. M. Osborn (Oxford, 1966), i. 370.

30. Johnson, 297; see also Johnson's *Lives of the English Poets*, ed. Peter Cunningham (1854), iii. 229.

31. Robert Wodrow, *Analecta*, iii. (Edinburgh, 1843), 432.

32. Murdoch, p. viii.

33. E. G. Vining, *Flora MacDonald* (1967), 69; William King, *Political and Literary Anecdotes* (1818), 196–7.

34. See *DNB* under Sloane, Sir Hans (1660–1753); Stanley, Hans (1720?–1780); Seymour, Algernon (1684–1750); Rundle, Thomas (1688–1743); and Talbot, Charles (1685–1737).

35. *Letters*, 56.

36. Murdoch, p. ix: another friend, Robert Symmer, thought that Murdoch exaggerates Gray's help (British Library, Add. MS 6839, fo. 214). See *DNB* under Reid, Andrew (d. 1767). John Gray was elected FRS in 1733.

37. *Spectator*, 543 (22 November 1712).

38. Colin Maclaurin, *An Account of Sir Isaac Newton's Philosophical Discoveries* (1748), 391. Maclaurin's book was edited by Thomson's close friend Patrick Murdoch.

39. *OET Liberty*, 8, 11: lines 46–56, 119–24.

40. Ibid. 9: lines 68–72, 82–5 n.

41. Ibid. 13–14: lines 190–204; 'jarring' was substituted for 'frantic' in the press.

42. Ibid. 6.

43. *Pope Correspondence*, ii. 426–7; Jonathan Swift, *Correspondence*, ed. H. Williams (Oxford, 1963), iii. 207.

44. Quoted in A. D. McKillop, *The Background of Thomson's* Seasons (Minneapolis, 1942), 176.
45. *Letters*, 41, 50.
46. B. A. Goldgar, *Walpole and the Wits* (Lincoln, Nebr., 1976), 219, 14, 34, 47.
47. See *OET Liberty*, 1–2.
48. Wodrow, *Analecta*, iii. 432.
49. Clerk of Penicuik Papers, quoted in Grant, 73.
50. *Edinburgh Magazine*, 2 (1793), 258.
51. Molyneux relinquished his secretaryship in 1727 and died in 1728.
52. H. S. Hughes, 'Thomson and the Countess of Hertford', *Modern Philology*, 25 (1927–8), 443. The passage is lines 64–73 (*OET Seasons*, 261–2).
53. H. S. Hughes, 'John Dyer and the Countess of Hertford', *Modern Philology*, 27 (1930), 318–19; R. M. Williams, *Poet, Painter, and Parson: The Life of John Dyer* (New York, 1956), 71.
54. Johnson, 287. It has been assumed that Savage was Johnson's source for this story, but there is no hard evidence; see C. Tracy, *The Artificial Bastard, a Biography of Richard Savage* (Toronto, 1953), 107–8.
55. *OET Liberty*, 294–6, 298–9, 420–5. See H. H. Campbell, 'Thomson and the Countess of Hertford yet again', *Modern Philology*, 67 (1970), 367–9.
56. *OET Liberty*, 280–3, 409–11.
57. *OET Seasons*, 300, 2.
58. Richard Cumberland, *Memoirs* (1806), 140–1, 146.
59. Johnson, 297.
60. *Letters*, 47; Edward Young, *Correspondence* ed. E. L. Pettit (Oxford, 1971), 58.
61. John Carswell, *The Old Cause* (1954), 164 n. Voltaire, *Correspondence*, ed. T. Besterman (Geneva, 1968–77), liv. 137; xviii. 67.
62. Ruth T. Murdoch, 'Voltaire, James Thomson, and a Poem for the Marquise du Châtelet', *Studies on Voltaire and the Eighteenth Century*, 6 (1958), 147–53.
63. *Letters*, 57–8.
64. Samuel Johnson, *Life of Savage*, ed. C. Tracy (Oxford, 1971), 38.
65. *OET Seasons*, pp. xliii–xliv.
66. Bryant Lillywhite, *London Coffee-Houses* (1963), 535; *Tatler*, 78 (8 October 1709), see also Addison's *Spectator*, 457 (14 August 1714); *Letters*, 59–60.
67. *Letters*, 58–9.
68. Ibid. 60–1.
69. *OET Seasons*, pp. xliv–xlv.
70. Ibid., p. xlv. I conjecture that there was a large printing because I have traced many more copies of *Spring* than of any other book by Thomson printed in the years from 1726 to 1729.
71. Pope, *Works*, ed. Warton, ix. 121 n. Warton's note reads '*Summer*', not '*Spring*', but it is clear from the context that this is a printer's error.
72. Johnson, 298–9.
73. *OET Seasons*, 34, 37–8, 32: lines 654–6, 740–6, 629–30. The first of these passages was improved in 1744, when 'Ingeniously' was deleted.
74. John Keats, *Letters*, ed. H. E. Rollins (Cambridge, 1958), ii. 186.
75. *OET Seasons*, 10: lines 155–68. Martin Price, *To the Palace of Wisdom* (New York, 1964), 357.
76. *OET Seasons*, pp. 30, 52–3, 18, 9–11, 12, 26–30: lines 566, 1053–73, 314–16, 136ff., 203–17, 516–71.

77. Ibid. 43–5: lines 861–4 n. These allusions to wrath and justice are deleted in 1744, when Thomson tones down all his references to God in *The Seasons*.
78. Ibid. 14, 44–6: lines 258, 867–903; *Letters*, 26.
79. Ibid. 47–9; 904–64 n: cf. Locke, *Essay concerning Human Understanding*, Book ii, ch. 8.
80. *OET Seasons*, 42, 4–6: lines 842–8, 32–77.
81. *Letters*, 61.
82. *OET Seasons*, 170: lines 652–706.
83. Christopher Pitt, *An Epistle to Dr Edward Young. Written at Eastbury* (1722), lines 1–2.
84. *Boswell's Johnson*, ii. 63.
85. *OET Liberty*, 284–6, 411–12.
86. Michael Treadwell, 'London Trade Publishers, 1675–1750', *The Library*, 6th series, 4 (1982), 113, 120–3.
87. *OET Liberty*, 21: line 17.
88. Ibid. 21, 30: lines 11–13, 295–9.
89. Ibid. 24, 27–8, 22–3: lines 107, 228–32, 34–46, 63–89.
90. James Thomson, *The Castle of Indolence and Other Poems*, ed. A. D. McKillop (Lawrence, Kan., 1961), 159–60.
91. John Carswell, *The Old Cause* (1954), 172. *OET Liberty*, 24: line 126.
92. *Letters*, 61. Edinburgh University, MS Laing II. 330, fo. 1.
93. *Letters*, 62–3.
94. Hughes, 'Thomson and the Countess of Hertford', 445. *Letters*, 63. Pope, *Works*, ed. Warton, i. 288.
95. A. S. Bell, 'Three new letters of James Thomson', *Notes and Queries*, 217 (October 1972), 369.
96. *Letters*, 64. *London Journal*, 26 April 1729.
97. *Letters*, 64–5.
98. *Factotum: Newsletter of the XVIIIth Century S. T. C.*, 22 (October 1986), 13–14; 23 (February 1987), 9–10. *Joseph Andrews*, book iii, ch. 3.
99. *Letters*, 65–6. There is a story that Thomson married early in life, but took his wife 'merely for her person' and concealed her from his friends. (J. Taylor, *Records of my Life* (1832), i. 185–8.) This story is unconfirmed and improbable, but it is repeated in Robert Chambers, *A Biographical Dictionary of Eminent Scotsmen*, iv (1835). Chambers adds that Mr George Chalmers, who heard the story, found in Marylebone Church Register the entry 'Died Mary Thomson, a stranger', but a correspondent in *Notes and Queries*, 16 July 1881, 46, asserted that no such entry was to be found, nor has it been found since.

CHAPTER 4

1. *Letters*, 29.
2. Mallet's letters to John Ker in *Edinburgh Magazine*, 2 (1793), 89, 338. Savage's first tragedy, *Sir Thomas Overbury*, was acted in 1723.
3. *Letters*, 46.
4. *Letters*, 64, 68. Mallet's play, retitled *Eurydice*, was first acted in February 1731.
5. *London Stage Part 3*, vol. i. p. cxxxviii.
6. *OET Seasons*, 304.
7. Livy, xxx. 12–15; Diodorus Siculus, xxvii. 7; Appian, *Punic Wars*, 10, 28.
8. A. N. L. Munby (ed.), *Sale Catalogues of the Libraries of Eminent Persons*, (1971), i. 57, items 80 and 94.
9. 11 April, 18 May 1726; 5 July 1728.

10. *Plays*, i, 64: (Act IV, Scene ii).
11. Ibid. i. 36: (I.v). Corrected from the first edition.
12. *OET Seasons*, 266: lines 260–1.
13. *Plays*, i. 40, 69: (II. i; IV. iv).
14. *OET Seasons*, 231, 146, 148, 186: *Winter*, line 589; *Autumn*, lines 43–7, 111–14, 1020–9.
15. *Plays*, i. 73, 76: (V. ii).
16. Johnson, 288.
17. *Plays*, i. 87, 24: (V. ix), Prologue.
18. Johnson, 288.
19. *Twickenham Pope*, vi. 310–11. Johnson echoes the first three lines of the *Sophonisba* Prologue in the opening couplet of his Drury Lane Prologue (1747); in his substitution of Shakespeare for Sophonisba, with reference to the revival of drama, Johnson perhaps ridicules Pope's lines.
20. Hervey's epilogue was printed in Robert Dodsley's *A Collection of Poems*, iv (1755), 107–8.
21. *Plays*, i. 88.
22. Johnson, *Lives of the English Poets*, ed. G. B. Hill (3 vols., Oxford, 1905), ii. 132; Alexander Pope, *Works*, ed. Joseph Warton (1797), i. 390.
23. Benjamin Victor, *Original Letters, Dramatic Pieces, and Poems* (1776), i. 316.
24. The printed text reads 'Stands', not 'Sits'.
25. See *OET Liberty*, 286–7, 412–13.
26. *Pope Correspondence*, iii. 86.
27. *Letters*, 68–9.
28. Johnson, 288.
29. *Letters*, 70.
30. *Daily Journal*, 29 January 1730; *Fog's Weekly Journal*, 7 and 14 February 1730; *Timoleon* (1730), Preface.
31. *Daily Journal*, 29 January 1730.
32. In some press-variant copies of *Timoleon* the Preface is greatly shortened, to remove all hostile references to the managers.
33. *Morning Post* and *Fog's Weekly Journal*.
34. Evidently Thomson took note of this attack. In the complete *Seasons*, published in June 1730, the offending lines are emended decorously to 'and round the rocking dome, | For entrance eager, howls the savage blast'. See *OET Seasons*, 212–13: *Winter*, lines 189–90.
35. *London Stage Part 3*, vol. i. pp. xxxiii, 40–3.
36. *Letters*, 7–8.
37. Thomas Davies, *Dramatic Miscellanies* (1784), iii. 436.
38. W. R. Chetwood, *A General History of the Stage* (1749), 202–3.
39. She was buried in Westminster Abbey, in fine cerements, which prompted Pope's lines on Narcissa in his *Epistle to Cobham*. Among her pallbearers were George Bubb Dodington and Lord Hervey.
40. There is an analysis of his well-known performance of Hamlet in Aaron Hill's *The Prompter*, 100 (24 October 1735).
41. *Plays*, i. 23.
42. Quoted in Philip H. Highfill *et al.*, *A Biographical Dictionary of Actors, Actresses*, etc. (Carbondale, Ill.), x (1984), 249.

43. Davies, *Dramatic Miscellanies*, iii. 441.

44. She was the first wife of Colley's son Theophilus, and so was not (*pace* Grant) the Mrs Cibber who acted in Thomson's later plays.

45. Murdoch, p. ix; Shiels, 210. Johnson retells Shiels's anecdote, but attaches it to the first night of *Agamemnon* (Johnson, 291).

46. Mrs Pendarves to Mrs Ann Granville, 4 April 1730, in Mary Granville, *The Autobiography and Correspondence of Mary Granville, Mrs Delany* (1861), i. 251; Mrs Rowe to Lady Hertford, H. S. Hughes, 'Thomson and the Countess of Hertford', *Modern Philology*, 25 (1928), 452; *Rundle Letters*, ii. 108–9.

47. Information privately provided by Professor Arthur H. Scouten.

48. *Daily Post*, 7 March; *London Stage Part 3*, vol. i. p. cxii.

49. D. F. Foxon, 'Oh! Sophonisba! Sophonisba! Oh!', *Studies in Bibliography*, 12 (1959), 204–13.

50. *Daily Post* and *Daily Post-Boy*, 13 March 1730; Joseph Spence, *Observations, Anecdotes, and Characters of Books and Men*, ed. J. M. Osborn (Oxford, 1966), i. 371. Spence's anecdote is dated 1729–30; it could refer either to the dedication of *Sophonisba* or to praise of the queen in *Autumn* (see *OET Seasons*, 175: lines 304, 773–4), along with any of the several patriotic passages in the 1730 text of *The Seasons*.

51. *Letters*, 74: letter of 24 October 1730.

52. *A Criticism of the New Sophonisba* (1730), 13, 3, 4, 30–1, 22.

53. Shiels, 209–10.

54. *London Evening-Post*, 17 March 1730.

55. Grant, 92.

56. *Defence of Sophonisba* (1730), 20, 15.

57. Henry Fielding, *Tom Thumb and The Tragedy of Tragedies*, ed. L. J. Morrissey (Edinburgh, 1970), 20: Prologue 18–20, 28–9. Cf. Prologue to *Sophonisba* 9–14, 19–20.

58. Ibid. 43.

59. D. E. Baker, *Biographia Dramatica*, with additions by I. Reed and S. Jones (1812), ii. 125–6. See also *Private Correspondence of Garrick with Celebrated Persons*, i (1831), 542.

60. *Works of the British Poets*, ed. Robert Anderson, x (Edinburgh, 1795), 347–8.

61. Thomson was so little moved by the satires of 'Tim Birch' and Fielding that he allowed his derided verse to stand in all editions of *Sophonisba* printed in his lifetime. He did not alter it even when he was making manuscript corrections to the play in the interleaved copy of his *Works* (1738), now in the British Library; this is the copy which contains important revisions to *The Seasons* (see *OET Seasons*, p. lxvi n.). It was Lyttelton who emended the line to 'Oh, *Sophonisba*! I am wholly thine', in his thoroughgoing rewriting of this and other plays and poems for the 1750 edition of Thomson's *Works*. Lyttelton's revised texts are reprinted in all editions of Thomson's plays from 1750 to 1979.

62. *OET Liberty*, 280, 287–8.

63. Ibid. p. 287. The attribution to Thomson was made by Pat Rogers in 'James Thomson: an unnoted Contribution', *American Notes and Queries*, 9 (1970), 3–6. The 1732 reprint by Savage was not noted in *OET Liberty*; it confirms the attribution to Thomson.

64. *Twickenham Pope*, vi. 324–7.

65. Welsted to Dodington, 14 November 1730, in *HMC Var. Coll. from the Mss of Mrs Eyre Matcham* (Dublin, 1909), vi. 9. Thomson is ridiculed twice (once alongside Mitchell and once alongside Hill) in an anonymous, obscene *Sequel to the Dunciad* (1729), a tedious catalogue of poetical excrement from Chaucer to the eighteenth century.

66. Beinecke Rare Book and Manuscript Library, Yale University: Osborn File. The dating of the letter is James Osborn's.

67. D. F. Foxon, *Pope and the Early Eighteenth-Century Book Trade*, rev. and ed. James McLaverty (Oxford, 1991), pp. 182–4. See also *OET Seasons*, pp. xlviii–xlix, xci–xciii.

68. *OET Seasons*, 78, 99, 120–1, 127–9: lines 352–70, 628ff., 1269–1370 n., 1494–1531 and nn.

69. Ibid. 216–20, 232–8, 245–6, 71: lines 276–388, 617–52, 691–759, 904–46, 206.

70. Ibid. 146–50, 168–72, 196–201: lines 28–150, 610–706, 1235–1373; 145–6, 164–70: lines 25, 38, 522, 686: also 67, 234, 296: lines 130–9 n., 643, 1038 (the one occurrence before 1730).

71. Ibid. 150–6, 166: lines 177–310, 554–61; pp. lxxiv–lxxix, 321–2.

72. Ibid; 178–80: lines 927–8, 880, 862–70.

73. Ibid. 186–7: 1004–29 and nn.

74. Ibid. 220: line 1352.

75. Ibid. 258–9: lines 113–16 and n.

76. Shiels, 202. Johnson, 299.

77. *OET Seasons*, 249, lines 1004–6; 7, lines 101–13; 193, lines 1151–6; 104, line 946; 112–13, lines 1150–1a; 12, lines 189–97: cf. *Paradise Lost*, I. 204–8; IX. 445, 634–42; II. 636–7; I. 612–15; II. 492–5.

78. 'Liberty' and 'freedom' occur twice in *Summer* (1727), once in *Spring* (1728), and seven more times in the 1730 additions to the *Seasons*; 'patriot' twice in *Summer* (1727) and eleven more time in the 1730 *Seasons*; 'Britain' and 'Britannia' twice in *Summer* (1727), once in *Spring* (1728), and five more times in the 1730 *Seasons*; these words are not used in the early versions of *Winter*. The word 'England' appears only once, in the mouth of the boorish squire during the burlesque drinking episode in *Autumn*.

79. *OET Seasons*, 278–85: lines 301, 515, 603; 146–9, 180: lines 43, 72, 141, 914; 260–5: lines 8, 66, 199. Compare *Autumn*, lines 43–150, with *The Castle of Indolence*, canto II, stanzas vii–xxii.

80. Johnson, 298–9.

81. *OET Seasons*, 138, line 1689; 82, line 477; 6, line 89; 81, line 309; 146, line 41; 26, lines 518–19; 231, line 582; 28, line 543; 7, line 111; 170, line 661; 201, line 1365; 13, line 210; 297, line 1071; 42, line 859; 269, line 383.

82. Ibid. 186: line 1016; Wordsworth, *Prose Works*, ed. W. J. B. Owen and J. W. Smyser (Oxford, 1974), iii. 72, 74. *OET Seasons*, 145, line 22.

83. *OET Seasons*, 144–5: lines 13, 16–17. John, Lord Hervey, *Memoirs of the Reign of George II*, ed. R. Sedgwick (1931), i. 74–5.

84. *Boswell's Johnson*, iii. 37.

85. An advertisement in John Toland, *The Life of John Milton, with Amyntor*, edited by Thomas Hollis, published by Millar over the date 1761, reads 'The *Works* of Mr. *Thomson*, in 2 Vols. The second Vol. may be had alone, to complete those Gentlemen's Sets who subscribed to the Author for the Seasons, being the first. Quarto.' The first volume of this advertised set can only be the 'subscription quarto'. The Toland *Milton* was issued in late 1760, because Hollis's presentation copy to the British Museum is dated 1 January 1761.

86. *OET Seasons*, pp. xlvi–lii.

87. Foxon, *Pope and the Early Eighteenth-Century Book Trade*, p. 63.

88. *OET Seasons*, pp. lii–lx.

89. B. Lenman, *The Jacobite Risings in Britain, 1689–1746* (1980), 189–95.

90. Spence, *Observations*, i. 370.

91. Murdoch, p. viii.
92. *Rundle Letters*, ii. 126–134.

CHAPTER 5

1. Joseph Addison, *Miscellaneous Works*, ed. A. C. Guthkelch, (1914), ii. 17. *Boswell's Johnson*, iii. 36.
2. *Letters*, 72–3. *Twickenham Pope*, v. 124, line 195.
3. *Letters*, 73. *OET Seasons*, 20–2, 330: lines 336–78.
4. *Letters*, 75.
5. *Pope Correspondence*, iii. 158, 226. Johnson 291. Alexander Pope, *Works*, ed. Joseph Warton (1797), iv. 10 n.
6. *Rundle Letters*, ii. 153.
7. *Pope Correspondence*, iii. 128. *Twickenham Pope*, vi. 318–19.
8. *Letters*, 77.
9. Ibid. 73–4.
10. Murdoch, p. x. Shiels, 203.
11. *Letters*, 79. Joseph Spence, *Letters from the Grand Tour*, ed. Slava Klima (1975), 54, 419–20. *Hertford Correspondence*, i. 104.
12. *Letters*, 77–8.
13. John Carswell, *The Old Cause* (1954), 166, 173.
14. *Rundle Letters*, ii. 164–5.
15. *OET Liberty*, 140–1: Part V. lines 468–523.
16. Spence, *Letters from the Grand Tour*, 52.
17. Richard Colt Hoare, *Recollections Abroad, during the Years 1785, 1786, 1787* (Bath, 1815), 16. *OET Liberty*, 318.
18. Spence, *Letters from the Grand Tour*, 53–4. The verses may be a convivial recollection. Another of Spence's anecdotes, attributed to 'Thomson?' bears a convivial interpretation: 'Which d'ye love best, ale or wine?—Wine. Which d'ye love best, wine or ale?—Ale. The last word strongest on his mind. He'll come again—he's gone to catch the other.' Joseph Spence, *Observations, Anecdotes, and Characters of Books and Men*, ed. J. M. Osborn (Oxford, 1966), i. 371–2.
19. *Letters*, 108.
20. *Hertford Correspondence*, i. 104.
21. *Letters*, 79.
22. Spence, *Letters from the Grand Tour*, 419–20. *Letters*, 80. R. Scott-Moncrieff (ed.), *Household Book of Lady Grisell Baillie, 1692–1733*, (Edinburgh, 1911), 327–9.
23. Spence, *Letters from the Grand Tour*, 139.
24. *Letters*, 79–80.
25. Johnson, 288–9.
26. A. N. L. Munby (ed.), *Sale Catalogues of the Libraries of Eminent Persons*, (1971), i. 47–66.
27. Hester Lynch Piozzi, *Observations and Reflections made in the Course of a Journey through France, Italy, and Germany* (1789), i. 413–16. See also Jean Hagstrum, *The Sister Arts* (Chicago, 1958), 259–61.
28. *OET Liberty*, 47: Part I, lines 134–43. Spence, *Letters from the Grand Tour*, 117: letter of 23 August 1732.
29. *OET Liberty*, 48–9: Part I, lines 213–16, 222–5, 177–9.
30. Ibid. 93–7: Part IV, lines 134–214, 269 n.
31. Ibid. 100: Part IV. lines 348–62.

32. *Letters*, 81–3.

33. Ibid. 81–2.

34. Ibid. 197, 82.

35. *Pope Correspondence*, iii. 222. *OET Liberty*, 288–90, 415–17.

36. *OET Liberty*, 290, 417–18.

37. *Letters*, 83.

38. H. S. Hughes, 'Thomson and the Countess of Hertford', *Modern Philology*, 25 (1927–8), 459.

39. Carswell, *The Old Cause*, 167–8.

40. A. S. Foord, *His Majesty's Opposition, 1714–1830* (Oxford, 1964), 32.

41. Carswell, *The Old Cause*, 167.

42. Ibid. 174–5.

43. James Ralph, *Critical History of the Administration of Sir Robert Walpole* (1743), 256, quoted in Paul Langford, *The Excise Crisis* (Oxford, 1975), 1.

44. John, Lord Hervey, *Memoirs of the Reign of George II*, ed. R. Sedgwick (1931), i. 138, 176.

45. *Letters*, 86.

46. *Rundle Letters*, ii. 180–1. Thomson recalls such a scene in his *Poem to Talbot* (1737); see *OET Liberty*, 157: lines 254–8.

47. *Universal Spectator*, 29 September 1733.

48. *Letters*, 207, 101. *OET Liberty*, 42: Part I, lines 1–14 and n.

49. *Letters*, 85. *Pope Correspondence*, iii. 392–3.

50. *Letters*, 86–7, 213. Voltaire thought so well of Thomson's tragedies that he published his own *Socrate* (1759) under the pretence that it was a translation from the English of Thomson; see Ch. 9.

51. *Pope Correspondence*, iii. 171, 357–8. Norman Ault, *New Light on Pope* (1949), 286–97.

52. Ault, *New Light on Pope*, 290.

53. Hervey, *Memoirs*, i. 242–3.

54. John Campbell, *Lives of the Lord Chancellors*, 4th edn. (1857), vi. 140.

55. *Journals of the House of Commons*, xxi (1803), 893: 18 April 1732.

56. J. E. Smith, *Bygone Briefs* (1896), 28.

57. William Holdsworth, *A History of English Law*, 7th edn. (1956), i. 612–13.

58. *Journals of the House of Commons*, xxi. 892–3.

59. *Critical Review*, 19 (1765), 141.

60. Murdoch, p. xi.

CHAPTER 6

1. *Letters*, 83.

2. Letter to Henry Fox, 7 October 1734, quoted in John Carswell, *The Old Cause* (1954), 178.

3. John, Lord Hervey, *Memoirs of the Reign of George II*, ed. R. Sedgwick (1931), ii. 399–401.

4. *OET Liberty*, 156: lines 245–6.

5. Hervey, *Memoirs*, ii. 405.

6. K. Thomson, *Memoirs of Viscountess Sundon* (1847), ii. 248–9.

7. *Rundle Letters*, ii. 241–5.

8. J. H. Plumb, *Sir Robert Walpole: The King's Minister* (1960), 330–2.

9. G. W. Cooke, *Memoirs of Lord Bolingbroke* (1835), ii. 276–7.

10. *Letters*, 88–9.

11. *OET Liberty*, 32–3.

12. Ibid. 41, 55, 72.

13. Ibid. 40, 54 and n.

14. Murdoch, pp. xii. *Critical Review*, 19 (1765), 142. William Talbot's younger brother George had also joined the opposition by now, to judge from the anonymous verses, *A View of the Town, a Satire* (1735), where he is one

> Who dares chastise the vices of a court,
> Tho' arbitrary laws their pow'r support.

15. Aaron Hill, *Works*, (1753), i. 210–15.

16. Ibid. i. 222.

17. The poems published between January 1734 and February 1735 are *Epistle to Cobham; An Essay on Man, Epistle IV; Second Satire of the Second Book of Horace Paraphrased; Sober Advice from Horace* (anon.); *Epistle to Arbuthnot*; and *Of the Characters of Women*.

18. *OET Liberty*, 297–8.

19. Ibid. 295–9, 316–17, 421–5.

20. *Letters*, 94, 93.

21. Ibid. 94–5: John Thomson had gone to Kelso in 1725 to set up as a saddler (see Ch. 2 above), but in the mid–1730s was apparently back in London.

22. William Holdsworth, *A History of English Law*, 7th edn. (1956), i. 436, 441.

23. *Critical Review*, 19 (1765), 141–2.

24. *Letters*, 95.

25. *Craftsman*, 6 September 1735. *Twickenham Pope*, vi. 369, 372. Jonathan Swift, *Complete Poems*, ed. Pat Rogers (Harmondsworth, 1983), 556–9.

26. *OET Liberty*, 76: lines 106–9.

27. Aaron Hill, *Advice to the Poets* (1731). pp. xii, xiii. *The Prompter*, 38 and 42, (21 March and 4 April 1735).

28. *Letters*, 98. Hill, *Works*, ii. 128–9.

29. *Letters*, 99–101. *OET Seasons*, 232, 389: lines 603–8 and n. *OET Liberty*, 42: line 14 and n. Nothing is recorded of Thomson's two older brothers Andrew and Alexander beyond their baptismal dates (see Ch. 1 above) and the fact that, like John, they did not outlive the poet (*Bee*, 7 (1792), 235). James asked his sister Jean on 12 January 1738 to remember him 'to sisters, and all friends' (*Letters*, 116), and he did not refer to any living brothers when he disposed of John's effects; it may be presumed that Andrew and Alexander died young.

30. *OET Liberty*, 33–4.

31. Ibid. 91–2, 112–13, 124–5: Part IV, lines 1135–6, 48–83, 1105–7, 775–7, 783–9, 1145–6, 1188–91.

32. Ibid. 141, 147: Part V, lines 528–9, 717–20

33. A. D. McKillop, *The Background of Thomson's* Liberty, *Rice Institute Pamphlet* 38, no. 2 (July 1951), 11. This is the best and fullest account of the poem.

34. *OET Liberty*, 293, 419–20; 44 (Part I, lines 56–9).

35. R. M. Williams, 'The Publication of Dyer's *Ruins of Rome*', *Modern Philology*, 44 (1946), 97–101.

36. *OET Liberty*, 93–5, 65–7: Part IV, lines 134–206, 157–61; Part II, lines 291–349. *OET Seasons*, 116, 121: lines 1217–22, 1019–21 (cf. 122, lines 1344–9).

37. *OET Liberty*, 76: Part III, lines 106–9 (see also 133–4: Part V, lines 221–76).

38. J. W. Johnson, *The Formation of English Neo-Classical Thought* (Princeton, NJ, 1967), 48–9.

39. *OET Liberty*, 87, 110: Part III, lines 516-18, 529-33; Part IV, lines 689-97.

40. Lyttelton, *Epistle to Mr Pope*, lines 61-3. Alexander Pope, *Works*, ed. J. Warton (1797), i. 90-1.

41. *OET Liberty*, 35, 323-37.

42. Ibid. e.g. 44, 79-80, 81, 87, 100: Part I, lines 53-66; Part III, lines 226-56, 320-7, 512-26; Part IV, lines 348-62.

43. Murdoch, p. x. Johnson 289.

44. These parodies and others were reprinted in Browne's *A Pipe of Tobacco* (1736); this may have been where Thomson first read them.

45. Joseph Spence, *Observations, Anecdotes, and Characters of Books and Men*, ed. J. M. Osborn (Oxford, 1966), ii. 214.

46. *OET Liberty*, 299-300.

47. Perhaps Francis Blyth, who issued proposals for 'Poems on various subjects', 16 November [174 ?]: 'a reference to previous proposals suggests a chronic state of impending publication' (D. F. Foxon, *English Verse, 1701-1750: A Catalogue* (Cambridge, 1975), i. 67).

48. *OET Liberty*, 290-2, 417-19.

49. *Gentleman's Magazine*, 6 (1736), 479, 741, 743.

50. No drawing has been traced, but an oil painting and an engraving of this subject survive. See Appendix: Portraits of Thomson. Though the couplet quoted is common enough opposition rhetoric one wonders whether it contains some reference to Thomson's offer to resign his Secretaryship of the Briefs and his not receiving its income after this offer.

51. *Letters*, 104-6. D. Cornu, 'Swift, Motte, and the Copyright Struggle', *Modern Language Notes*, 54 (1939), 114-24.

52. Hill, *Works*, i. 230, 235.

53. Clayton Atto, 'The Society for the Encouragement of Learning', *The Library*, 4th s. 19 (1938-9), 263-88. *Gentleman's Magazine*, 6 (1736), 353. BM Sloane MS 4478 C.

54. James Ralph, *The Case of Authors by Profession or Trade* (1758), 59-60.

55. *Letters*, 107.

56. Ibid. 108-9, 161-2. Thomas Warton implies that the Prince of Wales was responsible for Thomson's return to play-writing: in his *Elegy on the Death of the late Frederic Prince of Wales* (written in 1751), Warton says that the Prince

> bade sweet Thomson share the friendly Board,
> Soothing with verse divine the toil of state!
> Hence fir'd, the Bard forsook the flowery plain,
> And deck'd the regal mask, and tried the tragic strain. (33-6)

57. *Letters*, 197.

58. *Letters*, 102-3. M. Smith is described in the diary of another Scots traveller passing through Boulogne in the summer of 1736 as 'Mr Smith, the great Scotch wine merchant there' who had been formerly in the 1715 Jacobite rebellion. (A. Forbes (ed.), *Curiosities of a Scots Charter Chest, 1600-1800*, (Edinburgh, 1897), 100). 'Peter' is Patrick Murdoch.

59. *OET Liberty*, 193-4: canto I, lines 550-6, 559-65.

60. Andrew Bissett, *Memoirs and Papers of Sir Andrew Mitchell* (1850), I. 66; letter of 21 September 1747.

61. Ibid. 42-3. Letter of 16 May 1754; British Library Add. MS 6861, fo. 118.

62. See *DNB* under Mitchell, Sir Andrew (1708-71); Scott, George Lewis (1708-80); Armstrong, John (1709-79).

63. *Culloden Papers* (1815), 310–11.
64. British Library Add MS 6839 and 6861.
65. See *DNB* under Dick, Sir Alexander (1703–85).
66. E. C. Mossner, *The Life of David Hume* (Edinburgh and London 1954), 107 n.
67. James McCosh, *The Scottish Philosophy from Hutcheson to Hamilton* (New York, 1875), 95–9; James Thomson, *The Castle of Indolence and Other Poems*, ed. A. D. McKillop, (Lawrence, Kan. 1961), 190. Mary Jane W. Scott suggests that the inhabitant of the Castle of Indolence commonly thought to represent William Paterson may represent Turnbull instead: see her *James Thomson, Anglo-Scot* (Athens, Ga., 1988), 245–6.
68. *Walpole Correspondence*, ii, 186. *Boswell's Johnson*, v, 255.
69. C. Tracy, *The Artificial Bastard, a Biography of Richard Savage* (Toronto, 1953,) 120–2.
70. *Letters*, 106.
71. Samuel Johnson, *Life of Savage*, ed. C. Tracy (Oxford, 1971), 83.
72. Hill, *Works*, i. 230, 337.
73. Tracy, *Artificial Bastard*, 129.

CHAPTER 7

1. *Letters*, 90, 95, 101, 103, 107; Aaron Hill, *Works* (1753), i. 238.
2. *OET Seasons*, 125: lines 1433–7.
3. H. M. Cundall, *Bygone Richmond* (1925), 7–8, 45. *The Craftsman*, 11 June 1730. Richard Crisp, *Richmond and its Inhabitants from the Olden Time* (1866), 361. Grant, 156.
4. *Gentleman's Magazine* (1735), frontispiece. E. P. Thompson, *Whigs and Hunters* (1975), 181–9. Cundall, *Bygone Richmond*, 8, 34, 69–70.
5. *Letters*, 106. *Weekly Entertainer. Bee*, 6 (1791), 284.
6. William Cobbett, *Parliamentary History of England*, ix (1811), 1223, 1375–84, 1426–7. John Carswell, *The Old Cause* (1954), 183.
7. R. A. Roberts (ed.), *HMC: Diary of the Earl of Egmont*, (1920–3), ii, 390. *London Stage*, ii. 675.
8. George, Lord Lyttelton, *Works*, ed. G. E. Ayscough, 2nd edn, (1775), 731, 734. See also Lyttelton's verse epistle *To Mr Glover; on his Poem of Leonidas*, ibid. 632–3.
9. *Letters*, 111. Alexander Pope, *Works*, ed. Joseph Warton (1797), vii. 307 n.
10. Murdoch, p. xi. Shiels, 205. *Critical Review*, 19 (1765), 142.
11. *Letters*, 110; *OET Liberty*, 148–9.
12. *OET Liberty*, 151–2, 159: lines 25–9, 51, 92, 56, 358–62.
13. John Barrell, *English Literature in History, 1730–1780: An Equal Wide Survey* (1983), 52.
14. *OET Liberty*, 156, 151: lines 244–6, 39–45.
15. *Walpole Correspondence*, xvii, 452–3, 486; xviii, 185; also (for another woman) xx, 507 n. Charles Churchill, *The Ghost* (1762), Book I, lines 201–320; *The Duellist* (1764), lines 431–40.
16. Mary Granville, *The Autobiography and Correspondence of Mary Granville, Mrs. Delany* (1861), i. 609.
17. Murdoch, pp. xi, xii.
18. Anon., *The Life of Mr James Quin, Comedian* (1766), 82–3.
19. Anon., *The Tell-Tale* (1756), i. 152–4.
20. Francis Gentleman, *The Dramatic Censor* (1770), 463–4.
21. *Bee*, 6 (1791), 286. *Weekly Entertainer*.

22. Thomas Davies, *Memoirs of the Life of David Garrick* (new edn., 1780), ii. 113. The 'gentleman' is identified as William Warburton by Horace Walpole: see *Walpole Correspondence*, x, 150.

23. *Letters*, 110, 112, 113. Moses Mendez, or Mendes (d. 1758, see *DNB*), the poet and dramatist, was a member of this family. His *The Seasons* (1751), which consists of four short descriptive poems in Spenserian stanzas, opens with an elegiac tribute to Thomson.

24. *OET Liberty*, 304; other poems to members of the Mendez family are on 304–5.

25. *Letters*, 112–13. Savage's poem is a revised version of a birthday address to the Prince of Wales, first published in January 1736: see Richard Savage, *Poetical Works*, ed. C. Tracy (Cambridge, 1962), 219–34.

26. *OET Liberty*, 300–1, 426–7.

27. *Letters*, 114. John Lane, *Masonic Records, 1717–1886* (1886), 24.

28. James Anderson, *Constitutions of Masons*, new edn., by John Noorthouck (1784), 234–5.

29. 'Masonic address by Martin Clare' (December 1735), reprinted in D. Knoop *et al.* (eds.), *Early Masonic Pamphlets* (Manchester, 1945), 327.

30. *OET Liberty*, 301–2, 427–8.

31. A. Edwards, *Frederick Louis, Prince of Wales, 1707–1751* (1947), 120. John, Lord Hervey, *Memoirs of the Reign of George II*, ed. R. Sedgwick (1931), iii. 839.

32. *Letters*, 114.

33. B. A. Goldgar, *Walpole and the Wits* (Lincoln, Nebr., 1976), 146–7. Hervey's letter is dated 28 December 1738; a copy of Algarotti's book reached Thomson, because one was in his library at his death; Algarotti was friendly with Andrew Mitchell, Thomson's friend, as well as with Hervey; see Thomson's *The Castle of Indolence and Other Poems*, ed. A. D. McKillop (Lawrence, Kan., 1961), 146. For Hervey's epilogue to *Sophonisba* see Robert Dodsley, *A Collection of Poems*, iv (1755), 107–8.

34. Murdoch, p. xii. Johnson, 291.

35. R. M. Davis, *The Good Lord Lyttelton* (Bethlehem, Pa., 1939), 78. *Letters*, 95. Samuel Johnson, *Lives of the English Poets*, ed. G. B. Hill (Oxford, 1905), iii. 446. Earl of Chesterfield, *Letters*, ed. B. Dobrée (1932), iv. 1402–3. Shiels, 217. *Weekly Entertainer. Bee*, 6 (1791), 286.

36. *Pope Correspondence*, iv. 138.

37. A. J. Youngson, *The Making of Classical Edinburgh* (Edinburgh, 1966), 288, 295; William and Mary Craig's son designed the New Town of Edinburgh. William is called 'merchant' in Hew Scott, *Fasti Ecclesia Scoticanae* (Edinburgh, 1917), ii. 139, but Shiels said in 1753 that Mary was married 'to a man of low circumstances' in Edinburgh (Shiels, 215). There is no record of Thomson's sisters Isobel and Margaret after their baptisms; they are not mentioned in the account of the poet's siblings in *The Bee*, 7 (1792), 235–6; perhaps they died in infancy.

38. *Letters*, 116–19.

39. Ibid. 117. *Culloden Papers* (1815), 148–9.

40. *OET Liberty*, 302.

41. Pope, *Works*, ed. Warton, iv. 315 n.; *Letters of Sir William Jones*, ed. G. Cannon (Oxford, 1970), i. 423.

42. Thomas Davies, *Dramatic Miscellanies* (1784), i. 151–4.

43. *Letters*, 117. Shiels, 210; anonymous 'Life of Quin' in *European Magazine*, 21 (1792), 52.

44. *London Stage*, i, p. cxlviii.

45. John Loftis, *The Politics of Drama in Augustan England* (Oxford, 1963), 151.

46. L. W. Connolly, *The Censorship of English Drama, 1737–1827* (San Marino, Calif., 1976), 49–50. The manuscript sent to the Examiner is entitled *The Death of Agamemnon*;

it is now in the Larpent Collection of the Huntington Library: it is discussed in J. B. Kern, 'James Thomson's Revisions of *Agamemnon*', *Philological Quarterly*, 45 (1966), 289–303.

47. *Culloden Papers* (1815), 143; *Letters*, 119; *Walpole Correspondence*, xiii 151; British Library Sloane MS 4478c. Davies, *Dramatic Miscellanies*, iii. 498 n.

48. Aaron Hill, *The Actor* (1755), 235. Richard Cumberland, *Memoirs* (1806), 59.

49. *Walpole Correspondence*, xxxviii, 524; xiii, 151–2; xl, 27.

50. Davies, *Dramatic Miscellanies*, iii. 117.

51. Shiels, 211–12 n. The list of actors in the printed text of *Agamemnon* includes Cibber, but the list of characters there excludes Hemon, who was cut from the play as a result of revisions during its run. Hemon was presumably played by 'Hill', whose name disappears after 10 April from the lists of actors in newspaper advertisements for the play. If my conjecture earlier in this chapter about the date of these revisions is correct, the cast list in the printed text could be accurate only for the performance on Saturday, 15 April. See *London Stage*, ii. 710–15.

52. Cumberland, *Memoirs*, 59.

53. Shiels, 210. Johnson, 291.

54. Davies, *Memoirs of Garrick*, ii. 33, Johnson, 291. James Boswell, *Private Papers*, ed. Geoffrey Scott (1928), iii. 37, *Weekly Entertainer*.

55. Johnson, 291. Shiels, 210, Benjamin Victor, *Original Letters, Dramatic Pieces, and Poems* (1776), i. 10–11. Boswell, *Private Papers*, iii. 37.

56. Johnson, *Lives of the Poets*, iii. 315, Samuel Richardson, *Pamela* (3rd edn., 1742) iv. 85–6.

57. Gentleman, *The Dramatic Censor*, i. 463.

58. *Plays*, i. 126, 133, 132, 185 (I. i. 65, I. iv. 137, 87–90, V. viii, 7–11).

59. Davies, *Dramatic Miscellanies*, iii. 499. The manuscript and printed text read: 'Go bring my Children hither: | They may relieve me' (II. i. 17–18).

60. *Plays*, i. 177 (V. i. 94). This statement occurs in a speech 76 lines long. Shiels (p. 211) says that Thomson's 'speeches are often too long, especially for an English audience'.

61. *Plays* i. 139, 144, 141 (II. ii. 32–4, 108–9; II. v. 35–6).

62. Pope, *Works*, ed. Warton, iv, 10 n.

63. IV. iii in the printed version; V. iii in the Larpent MS (*Plays*, i. 165–7, 198–202).

64. *Plays*, i. 153 (III. i. 44–54).

65. G. E. Lessing, *Laokoön* (1766) ch. 4. Lessing is perhaps the most distinguished champion of Thomson's abilities as a dramatist; he translated Shiels's *Life* of Thomson, wrote a commendatory preface to a German translation of Thomson's plays in 1756, and partially translated *Agamemnon* himself.

66. *Plays*, i. 179 (V. iii. 7–13).

67. D. C. Tovey, 'Memoir', in James Thomson, *Poetical Works*, ed. D. C. Tovey (1897), i, p. lxi; *Plays*, i. p. cxxvii.

68. *Plays*, i. 155, 146, 161, 157–8 (III. i. 144–54; II. v. 99–102; III. ii. 225–8, 67–8, 91–3, 207–10). Davies, *Memoirs of Garrick*, ii. 32.

69. *Dialogue* I. line 51: Pope changed the name to Sejanus in 1740. See *Twickenham Pope*, iv. 301.

70. A. N. L. Munby (ed.), *Sale Catalogues of the Libraries of Eminent Persons*, (1971), i. 47–66, items 230, 231. *Letters*, 114.

71. Aaron Hill, *Works* (1753), i. 308–19; Hill sent an identical letter to Mallet (see *Letters*, 125–6). *Pope Correspondence*, iv. 152.

72. Murdoch, p. xii. *Letters*, 120–2.

73. *OET Liberty*, 67, 54: Part II, lines 349–63, Part I, lines 364–78.

74. Holmes's presentation copy to Thomson is in the Bodleian Library, shelfmark 3809 l. 185.

CHAPTER 8

1. *Letters*, 123, British Library Add. MS 4478c fo. 34r.
2. *Pope Correspondence*, iv. 453, 108, 110.
3. *Letters*, 124, British Library Add. MS 4478c fo. 36r.
4. Samuel Johnson, *Life of Savage*, ed. C. Tracy (Oxford, 1971), 109, 98.
5. *Pope Correspondence*, iv. 105–12, 120–3, 126–9, 132. The only violation of Pope's maxim in those twenty years were his contribution to the Prologue to *Sophonisba*, and his 'Prologue for the benefit of Mr Dennis,' 1733 (see Chs. 4 and 5 above).
6. *Pope Correspondence*, iv. 145, 146, 151, 152, *Letters*, 127.
7. Thomas Davies, *Memoirs of the Life of David Garrick* (1780), ii. 34.
8. *Political State of Great Britain*, 49 (March 1739), 232.
9. *OET Liberty*, 303.
10. *Pope Correspondence*, iv. 162; Aaron Hill, *Works* (1753), ii. 13–14.
11. *Hertford Correspondence*, i. 103–4; Benjamin Victor, *Original Letters, Dramatic Pieces, and Poems* (1776), i. 33.
12. *Pope Correspondence*, iv. 166–7.
13. Davies, *Memoirs of Garrick*, i. 27.
14. *Hertford Correspondence*, i. 89–90.
15. *Plays*, ii. 235.
16. In *Liberty*, Part IV, line 86, Thomson calls the crusaders 'Banditti Saints'.
17. *Plays*, ii. 288, 241, 265, 268 (V. iv. 72–6; I. iii. 67–70; III. v. 62; III. vi. 10).
18. *London Evening-Post*, 29 March 1739.
19. Shiels, 214; Johnson, 292; Murdoch, pp. xii–xiii.
20. *Plays*, ii. 269, 279, 238–9, 252 (IV. ii. 4, viii. 70–6; I. i. 45–6, 51–2, 80–3; II. ii. 121–42).
21. Quoted in L. W. Connolly, *The Censorship of English Drama 1737–1827* (San Marino, Calif., 1976), 58–9.
22. *Notes and Queries* (September 1855), 218.
23. Johnson, 292.
24. *Letters*, 129; for Thomas Edwards (1699–1757), see *DNB*.
25. *Hertford Correspondence*, i. 126.
26. John Wesley, *Journal*, ed. F. W. Macdonald (1906), iii. 488.
27. C. Tracy, *The Artificial Bastard, a Biography of Richard Savage* (Toronto, 1953), 137–8; *Pope Correspondence*, iv. 180–1, 210.
28. *Pope Correspondence*, iv. 331, 392, 417.
29. *Letters*, 151, 155.
30. Grant, 157. A. N. L. Munby (ed.), *Sale Catalogues of the Libraries of Eminent Persons*, (1971), i. 47–66. *Letters*, 138, 161; *Bee* 6 (1791), 284; 7 (1792), 235–6.
31. C. Aspinall-Oglander, *Admiral's Widow* (1942), 120–1, 125. *Weekly Entertainer*.
32. There are engravings and a description of Rosedale in John Evans, *Richmond and its Vicinity* (Richmond, 1825), 138–45.
33. R. A. Roberts (ed.), *Diary of the First Earl of Egmont* (1923), iii. 83.
34. Murdoch, p. xiii. Connolly, *Censorship of English Drama*, 60.
35. A. D. McKillop, 'The Early History of *Alfred*', *Philological Quarterly*, 41 (1962), 316–19.
36. Richard Graves, *Recollections of William Shenstone* (1788), 93–4.
37. Davies, *Memoirs of Garrick*, ii. 36.

38. Ibid. ii. 39.
39. *Plays*, ii. 326, 329 (I. iii. 8–9, v. 91–3).
40. Ibid. ii. 339 (II. iii. 216–18).
41. Ibid. ii. 331 (I. vi. 34–8).
42. *London Magazine* (1740), 393. *The Champion*, 8 July 1740, quoted in B. A. Goldgar, *Walpole and the Wits* (Lincoln, Nebr., 1976), 191.
43. *Hertford Correspondence*, ii. 62. A. D. McKillop, 'The Early History of *Alfred*', *Philological Quarterly*, 41 (1962), 313 n.
44. *Letters*, 131.
45. *Plays*, ii. 353–81.
46. Hill, *Works* (1753), ii. 162–7, 197–213. Quoted in A. D. McKillop, 'Thomson and the Licensers of the Stage', *Philological Quarterly*, 37 (1958), 453.
47. A. D. McKillop, 'The Early History of *Alfred*', *Philological Quarterly*, 41 (1962), 320–4; Alexander Scott, 'Arne's Alfred', *Music and Letters*, 55 (1974), 390–1.
48. *Pope Correspondence*, iv. 348–9.
49. Joseph Spence, *Observations, Anecdotes, and Characters of Books and Men*, ed. J. M. Osborn (Oxford, 1966), i. 153. *Twickenham Pope*, vi. 404. The prose notes for *Brutus* are conveniently printed in *Alexander Pope, Selected Prose*, ed. Paul Hammond (Cambridge, 1987), 290–6.
50. Murdoch, p. viii. *Letters*, 130. OET *Liberty*, 303–4, 429–30. OET *Seasons*, 87, lines 569–75.
51. OET *Seasons*, 54–6, 166–8. *Letters*, 132.
52. *Letters*, 134, 132–3.
53. *Letters*, 112. *Weekly Entertainer*. *Bee*, 6 (1791), 282. Johnson, 297.
54. Hester Lynch Piozzi, *Autobiography, Letters, and Literary Remains*, ed. A. Hayward (2nd edn., 1861), i. 87. *Bee*, 6 (1791), 282.
55. William Seward, *Supplement to the Anecdotes of some Distinguished Persons* (1797), 137–8. James Boswell, *Private Papers*, ed. Geoffrey Scott (1928), iii. 37. Boswell heard this remark when he dined with Mitchell on 24 July 1764; Mitchell's reference is to *Spring*, lines 336–78; British Library, Add. MS 6861, fo. 120.
56. *Boswell's Johnson*, ii. 63.
57. Johnson, 297–8.
58. *Bee*, 6 (1791), 286. OET *Liberty*, 195: i. 604; Johnson, 294. Murdoch, p. xvi.
59. Johnson, 287.
60. *Letters*, 115, 129–30, 104.
61. *Bee*, 6 (1791), 285, 284, 283, 287. *Weekly Entertainer*. Evans, *Richmond and its Vicinity*, 51.
62. Bryant Lillywhite, *London Coffee-Houses* (1963), 525.
63. *Letters*, 153.
64. Ibid. 135–6.
65. John Nichols, *Literary Anecdotes of the Eighteenth Century*, i (1812), 655–6.
66. Murdoch, p. xiv.
67. *London Magazine*, July, September 1735, 390, 485.
68. *Letters*, 136–7 (letters of 4, 12 August 1742).
69. *Walpole, Correspondence*, xiii, 249 (letter of 4 May 1742).

CHAPTER 9

1. *Letters*, 139.
2. Ibid. 142–3.

3. Ibid. 144–5. *OET Liberty*, 306–7, 431.
4. *Letters*, 146–9. *OET Liberty*, 307, 432.
5. *Letters*, 65–6 (see pp. 79–80 above); *OET Liberty*, 290–6, 304–9; *OET Seasons*, 47–56: lines 963–1176; 168, lines 620–4.
6. *Culloden Papers* (1815), 178; Thomas Davies, *Memoirs of the life of David Garrick* (1780), iii. 48.
7. *Bee*, 6 (1791), 282.
8. Recollections of John Ramsay of Ochtertyre, who was friendly with the Robertsons when he was in England in 1758 and 1763, in Alexander Allardyce (ed.), *Scotland and Scotsmen in the Eighteenth Century* (Edinburgh and London, 1888), i. 23 n.
9. Charles Knight (ed.), *London*, [1842], iii. 331.
10. C. G. Osgood, 'Lady Philippina Knight and her Boswell', *Princeton University Library Chronicle*, 4 (1943), 48–9. Nowhere else is it claimed that Thomson and Elizabeth Young were related. For the name 'Amanda', see p. 148.
11. *Letters*, 150–2.
12. *OET Seasons*, 56: lines 1161–5; 25: lines 483–93; *OET Liberty*, 308–9, 432–3.
13. *Letters*, 152–5.
14. Ibid. 155.
15. *OET Liberty*, 308–9, 433. *Letters*, 158.
16. *Letters*, 160–1.
17. A. D. McKillop, 'Two More Thomson Letters', *Modern Philology*, 60 (1962), 128. The conjectural dating is McKillop's.
18. *Letters*, 161–2. The assignment to 1743 is a conjecture based on the fact that Aaron Hill wrote to Mallet on 24 May 1743, welcoming Mallet's 'resurrection' of *Socrates*, pointing out some difficulties in treating that subject on the tragic stage, but expressing confidence that Mallet could make it shine (Hill, *Works* (1753), ii. 14–20). Thomas Rundle, Bishop of Derry, died 14 April 1743.
19. *Letters*, 163.
20. Ibid.
21. Ibid. 165.
22. Ibid. 165. *OET Seasons*, 46, lines 909–22.
23. *Letters*, 165–6.
24. Grainger to Thomas Percy, 5 July 1762, in John Bowyer Nichols, *Illustrations of the Literary History of the Eighteenth Century*, vii (1848), 279.
25. Tobias Smollett, *Peregrine Pickle*, ed. J. L. Clifford, rev. P.-G. Boucé (Oxford, 1983), 658–9. The passages quoted above were deleted in the second edition of *Peregrine Pickle* (1758). The unreliable patron, Lord Rattle, in *Roderick Random* (1748), ch. 63, is modelled in part upon Lyttelton also.
26. 'Lewis Melville', *Life and Letters of Tobias Smollett* (1926), 244–5.
27. *Letters*, 168.
28. *OET Liberty*, 309–11. Grant and McKillop both conjecture that the birthday celebrated here was 1 January 1745, but in my view 1744 is the more likely date. Of the twelve surviving letters from Thomson to Elizabeth Young, ten can be firmly dated between 10 March 1743 and 21 January 1744, and two 'after so long a Silence' (*Letters*, 182) are dated 23 October and 4 November 1745; Thomson also sent a copy of *The Seasons* to her about July 1744. It is more likely that the birthday poem formed part of the earlier sequence of letters, when Thomson was urging his love with more eagerness than despair, than that it was an isolated communication nearly half-way through a silence of fifteen months.

29. *OET Seasons*, 3, unadopted revisions to lines 3-4; 31, 146-8, 151; lines 598-604, 680-4, 72-6, 109-14, 186-91.

30. The poems sent in or with letters to Elizabeth Young are numbers 18, 39, 40, 41, 42, 43, 44, 45, and 47; see *OET Liberty*, 292, 305-8, 312, 419, 431-5.

31. Another poem of the series, 'How long Eliza, must I languish', was printed about this time with the name Eliza unaltered. The printing is on a single sheet of music dated '1745?' in the BL Catalogue; see *OET Liberty*, 433.

32. See *OET Liberty*, 434-5.

33. Ibid. 290-2, 417-19.

34. Ibid. 292, 295, 290. *Letters*, 157-8, 148.

35. *Letters*, 169-70. *OET Liberty*, 303-4.

36. Edward Young, *Conjectures on Original Composition*, ed. E. J. Morley (Manchester and London, 1918), 30. *Pope Correspondence*, iv. 522-4.

37. Perhaps some of this revision was done in the Doves Coffee-House at Hammersmith in view of a local tradition that 'he wrote part of' *Winter* there. It was also said, plausibly enough, that the same coffee-house was one of Thomson's favourite resting-places on his long walks between London and his house in Richmond. See T. Faulkner, *Historical and Topographical Account of Fulham* (1813), 359, and W. Thornbury and E. Walford, *Old and New London*, vi (1885-6), 544.

38. *OET Seasons*, 22-4, lines 379-442, 458-64. *OET Liberty*, 271, lines 53-66.

39. See John Barrell, *The Idea of Landscape and the Sense of Place, 1730-1840* (Cambridge, 1972), 13-20. *OET Seasons*, 47; lines 950-62.

40. *OET Seasons*, 188-9, 174-7; lines 1037-81, 743-835.

41. Ibid. 166; lines 565-9.

42. Ibid. 224-8, 5, 247-8; lines 439-526, 57, 950-87.

43. Ibid. 240-4; lines 799-893.

44. Ibid. 90-4; lines 631-2, (27) 614-5, 663-702.

45. Ibid. 95-101, 177; *Summer*, lines 747-897; *Autumn*, line 865.

46. Ibid. 104: lines 977-90. William Wordsworth, *Prose Works*, ed. W. J. B. Owen and J. W. Smyser (Oxford, 1974), iii. 74.

47. *OET Seasons*, 105-8: lines 980-1091.

48. Ibid. 78-80, 123-5, 62, 76, 118-23, 126-7; lines 371-431, 1371-1437, 67-8, 321-3, 1259-1370, 1479-87.

49. Ibid. 234-5, 46, 188, 230, 188-9, 220-1; lines 656-90, 906-35, 1048-69, 555-71, 1071-81, 376-81.

50. Samuel Richardson, *Correspondence*, ed. A. L. Barbauld (1804), i. 103.

51. *Letters*, 174, 194-5, 172, 174-5. McKillop conjectures that the natural history was Sir Hans Sloane, *A Voyage to the Islands Madeira, Barbados, Nieves, S. Christophers, and Jamaica, with the Natural History . . . of the last of those Islands* (2 vols., 1707-25).

52. Ibid. 175.

53. Murdoch, p. xi; Tobias Smollett, *Continuation of the Complete History of England* (1761), iv. 129.

54. *Letters*, 174.

55. David Garrick, *Letters*, ed. D. M. Little and E. M. Kahrl (Cambridge, Mass., 1963), i. 46.

56. Davies, *Memoirs of Garrick* (1780), i. 78-9.

57. Tobias Smollett, *The Regicide* (1749), p. iv.

58. Pace F. S. Boas, *An Introduction to Eighteenth-Century Drama* (Oxford, 1953), 162-3. *Plays*, ii. 394, cites two plays, Robert Wilmot's *Tancred and Gismunda* (1591) and

Susannah Centlivre's *The Cruel Gift* (1716), based on Boccaccio, neither of which resembles Thomson's play except in coincidence of names.

59. *Plays*, ii. 453, 406 (V. ii. 29–33, I. iv. 70–1).
60. A. N. L. Munby (ed.), *Sale Catalogues of the Libraries of Eminent Persons* (1971), i. 47–66, item 245. One of the relevant passages reads: '*William*, King of *Sicily*, being dead without Issue, the *Sicilians*, who were resolved to have a King of the Race of their *Norman* Princes, placed his Cousin *Tancred*, the Natural Son of *Roger*, Duke of *Pavia*, upon the Throne, notwithstanding that, before his Death, *William* had caused Queen *Constance*, his Aunt, the Wife of the Emperor *Henry* VI to be acknowledged their Queen.' (*Maimbourg's History of the Crusades*, trans. John Nalson (1685), Part II, Book iii, 193.) As it happens this historical Tancred played a part in English history subsequent to the period referred to in Thomson's play. He was an ally of Richard I of England, who supported his claim to the Sicilian throne; this antagonized Henry VI (Constance's husband), who threw Richard into prison when he was returning from the crusades and held him there for ransom.
61. Speech of 23 January 1745, quoted in *DNB*, 45 (1896), 356.
62. *Plays*, ii. 418–19 (II. iv. 3–7, 13–17).
63. *Letters*, 178–80. The letter was printed over a pseudonym in the *Daily Post*, but it was reprinted in Benjamin Victor's *Original Letters, Dramatic Pieces, and Poems* (1776), i. 101–2, where the satire on Thomson is sharpened and a second 'remarkable speech' is added to illustrate the kind of material that drew applause from the quondam Patriots:

> With what impartial care
> Ought we to watch o'er prejudice and passion,
> Nor trust too much the jaundic'd eye of party,
> Henceforth its vain delusions I renounce,
> Its hot determinations. (*Plays*, ii. 417; II. ii. 40–4)

Victor admired Thomson's early work; he tells us that he helped to find a publisher for *Winter* (see Ch. 2 above). He gave qualified approval to *Agamemnon*, but had evidently turned against Thomson by the time of *Tancred and Sigismunda*. It seems likely that he was envious of the success of Thomson and other Scots poets, probably including Mallet. When the stage success of *Mustapha* was fresh and *Edward and Eleanora* was selling very well Victor wrote in a letter, 'I have just read *Mr. Glover's* poem, call'd *London*; and have congratulated the author, and his friends in the city, on this second defeat of the vainglorious bards of the North!' (Victor, *Original Letters*, i. 45). Presumably the first 'defeat' of the Scots was Glover's *Leonidas*.

64. 'Thomson's *Tancred and Sigismunda* and the Demise of the Drama of Political Opposition', in G. W. Stone (ed.), *The Stage and the Page*, (Berkeley, Los Angales and London, 1981), 34–54.
65. *Plays*, ii. 405 (I. iv. 20–2).
66. Ibid. ii. 444, 409, 416, 436, 440 (IV. i. 72, iv. 152–70; II. i. 53; II. ii. 156; III. iii. 113).
67. Grant, 237–8.
68. *Plays*, ii. 466 (V. viii. 105–8).
69. *Letters*, 178. McKillop adds the following note: 'Barrington may be speaking of tickets for the opening night, or very possibly the reference is to tickets for the author's benefit on the third night, March 21. Advertisements announced that tickets for the benefit performance could be had from the booksellers Millar, Strahan, and Dodsley, as well as from the "Stage Door-Keeper" Hobson (*General Advertiser*, March 21), but an author was expected to help in the distribution.'

70. Davies *Memoirs of Garrick*, i. 79.

71. Richard Cumberland, *Memoirs* (1806), 59–60.

72. Elizabeth Carter, *Letters between Elizabeth Carter and Catherine Talbot* (1809), i. 90–1, 93. Catherine Talbot's letter is misdated 2 March 1745; Elizabeth Carter's reply is dated 26 April 1745.

73. *Walpole Correspondence*, xix, 27–8 (letter of 29 March 1745).

74. *Plays*, ii. 467.

75. Ibid. ii. 399.

76. Richard Ryan, *Dramatic Table-Talk* (1825), iii. 221–2.

77. John Brownsmith, *The Dramatic Time-Piece* (1767), 15, quoted in *Plays*, ii. 389, says that *Tancred and Sigismunda* took one hour and forty-nine minutes to perform at that period; he timed the five acts, in order, at 27, 17, 19, 15, and 31 minutes respectively. These times are roughly proportional to the pages of printed text in the last three acts, but are not remotely proportional in the first two acts.

78. *Plays*, ii. 454 (V. ii. 72–3).

79. Ibid. 431–2.

80. Ibid. 391–3. Murdoch, pp. xiii–xiv. What is probably the earliest provincial revival was in 1746 at Richmond, with Havard, the original Rodolpho, promoted to the role of Tancred; see Philip H. Highfill *et al.*, *A Biographical Dictionary of Actors*, (Carbondale, Ill.), vii (1982), 186.

81. 7 March 1749, 22 March 1756, 7 April 1758, 18 March 1762; see G. W. Stone (ed.), *London Stage 1660–1800: Part 4, 1747–1776*, (Carbondale, Ill., 1960).

82. David Garrick, *Private Correspondence with celebrated Persons*, i (1831), 47.

83. The costume is discussed in Allardyce Nicoll, *The Garrick Stage* (Manchester, 1980), 152–4. This same costume appears in an engraving on the title page of a 32-page pamphlet, *The History on which is founded the Tragedy of Tancred and Sigismunda*. This undated, anonymous prose narrative is based on Thomson's play; one assumes that it was, like *The History of the valiant Prince Edward* (see Ch. 8 above), a catchpenny piece intended to take advantage of the play's anticipated or actual success on the atage.

CHAPTER 10

1. *London Stage*, ii. 1161.

2. A. D. McKillop, 'Two More Thomson Letters', *Modern Philology*, 60 (1962), 129.

3. *Letters*, 182–4.

4. *Bee* 6 (1791), 282. Alexander Allardyce (ed.), *Scotland and Scotsmen in the Eighteenth Century* (Edinburgh and London, 1888), i. 23 n. *Universal Magazine*, 67 (1780), 368; *Princeton University Library Chronicle*, 4 (1943), 48–9. See Appendix: Portraits of Thomson. Grant, 210.

5. Leo Heaps (ed.), *The Log of the Centurion* (1973), 253–5; S. W. C. Pack, *Admiral Lord Anson* (1960), 145–52; see also *DNB* under Campbell, John (1720?–1790), and E. G. R. Taylor, *The Mathematical Practitioners of Hanoverian England, 1714–1840* (Cambridge, 1966), 32, 45, 69, 199, plate IV.

6. *Princeton University Library Chronicle*, 4 (1943), 48–9. *Universal Magazine*, 67 (1780), 368. *Gentleman's Magazine*, 61 (1791), i. 100. R. F. Mackay, *Admiral Hawke* (Oxford, 1965), 256–7.

7. *OET Seasons*, pp. lxxi–lxxiii. Henry Fielding, *The True Patriot and Related Writings*, ed. W. B. Coley (Oxford, 1987), 108–10.

8. *OET Liberty*, 92: Part IV. lines 84–96.

9. Samuel Johnson, *Lives of the English Poets*, ed. G. B. Hill (Oxford, 1905), iii. 460. G. B. Hill argues that Thomson never held the post, even as a sinecure, but Thomson's close friend Murdoch declares quite unequivocally that he did (see Murdoch, p. xi). Two other friends, writing close to the event, agree that Lyttelton obtained a comfortable government place for Thomson in 1746: Birch in a letter of 30 September 1748 (*Letters*, 208) and Smollett in his *Continuation of the Complete History of England* (1761), iv. 129. The figure for Thomson's income is from Robert Phillimore, *Memoirs and Correspondence of George, Lord Lyttelton* (1845), i. 113. The government in London subsequently had some difficulty with Paterson. On 3 September 1748 George Grenville wrote to Pelham, the Prime Minister, 'as poor Thomson for whose sake he was appointed is dead I suppose Mr Lyttelton will be less concerned for Patterson than he otherwise would be'; see Lewis M. Wiggin, *The Faction of Cousins* (New Haven, Conn., 1958), 135 n. Paterson was still in office in 1758; see Richard Pares, *War and Trade in the West Indies, 1739–63* (Oxford, 1936), 399 n.

10. Alexander Carlyle, *Anecdotes and Characters of the Times*, ed. James Kinsley (London, New York, and Toronto, 1973), 101. Murdoch, p. xvii.

11. Carlyle, *Anecdotes and Characters*, 198–9.

12. *Letters*, p. 188. Murdoch, p. xvi. *Bee* 6 (1791), 286. *Works of Pope*, ed. J. Warton (1797), iv. 10 n.

13. *Letters*, pp. 185–6, 204. William Shenstone, *Letters*, ed. Marjorie Williams (Oxford, 1939), 106, 152. H. S. Hughes, *The Gentle Hertford* (New York, 1940), 168.

14. *Coriolanus* (1749), 17, 61–2: cf. *Plays* 514, 553–4 (II. v. 18–21, V. iv. 31, 34–40); Greene prints a variant text taken from the Larpent manuscript.

15. *Coriolanus* (1749), 33: cf. *Plays*, 527 (III. iii. 112–16).

16. Tobias Smollett, *Letters*, ed. L. M. Knapp (Oxford, 1970), 40.

17. *Letters*, 196–7, 188.

18. *OET Liberty*, 313. *Letters*, 189.

19. George, Lord Lyttelton *Works*, (2nd edn., 1775), 253; *Letters*, 210.

20. *Letters*, 188–9.

21. Shenstone, *Letters*, ed. Williams, 116, 152 (letter of 30 June 1742, *pace* Williams). *Letters*, 192, n 1. W. J. Smith (ed.), *The Grenville Papers*, (1852), i. 69.

22. Maud Wyndham, *Chronicles of the Eighteenth Century* (1924), i. 230–1.

23. *Letters*, 190–1. Shiels, 218. *Boswell's Johnson*, ii. 159.

24. *Letters*, 192–3, 65. *OET Seasons*, 168, lines 619–24. *OET Liberty*, 290, 292.

25. *OET Liberty*, 313–14.

26. Samuel Richardson, *Selected Letters*, ed. J. Carroll (Oxford, 1964), 99–100.

27. Philip Dormer Stanhope, Earl of Chesterfield, *Letters*, ed. Bonamy Dobrée (1932). iii. 1119.

28. *Letters*, 195–6.

29. *Bee* 6 (1791), 284; 7 (1792), 235. *Weekly Entertainer*.

30. *Letters*, 197–8.

31. George Menary, *The Life and Letters of Duncan Forbes of Culloden* (1936), 341.

32. *Letters*, 197. Shiels, 215.

33. *Letters*, 197. Murdoch, p. xiv.

34. Shiels, 217; *Musidorus: A Poem sacred to the Memory of Mr James Thomson* (1748), 23. *OET Seasons*, 132: lines 1572–9.

35. *OET Liberty*, 173–4.
36. Ibid. 176, 182, 184: canto I, lines 31, 227, 294.
37. Ibid. 179: canto I, stanzas xvi, xv.
38. Ibid. 177, 197, 178–9: canto I, lines 69, 660, 673, 114–17, 131.
39. Ibid. 179: line 121. The significance of negative statements in canto I is discussed in P. M. Spacks, *The Poetry of Vision* (Cambridge, Mass., 1967), 54–9.
40. *OET Liberty*, 207: canto II, lines 240–3.
41. *OET Seasons*, 46–7: lines 922–62: *OET Liberty*, 194–5: canto I, lines 577–94.
42. *OET Liberty*, 217, 213, 215: canto II, lines 532–40, 419–23, 482–5.
43. *Letters*, 82: cf. *OET Liberty*, 48: Part I, lines 190–2.
44. John MacQueen, *The Enlightenment and Scottish Literature*, vol. i: *Progress and Poetry* (Edinburgh, 1982), 64–5.
45. Mary Jane W. Scott, *James Thomson, Anglo-Scot* (Athens, Ga., 1988), 278–9.
46. John Barrell, *English Literature in History, 1730–80: An Equal, Wide Survey* (1983), 89.
47. Christine Gerrard, '*The Castle of Indolence* and the Opposition to Walpole', *Review of English Studies*, NS 41 (1990), 45–64.
48. *OET Liberty*, 207: canto II, lines 256–67.
49. *Letters*, 209; Johnson, 294; Shiels, 205; Henry Fielding, *The Jacobite's Journal and Related Writings*, ed. W. B. Coley (Oxford, 1974), 300–2.
50. *OET Liberty*, 175: canto I, stanza i.
51. Donald Greene, 'From Accidie to Neurosis: The Castle of Indolence revisited', in M. E. Novak (ed.) *English Literature in the Age of Disguise* (Los Angeles, 1978), 135–6.
52. *Letters*, 155.
53. *OET Liberty*, 199: canto II, lines 14–15. 'Aonian' is conventional, but in this context it is perhaps a recollection of the *Poem to Talbot*, lines 39–46, where, faced with the example of Talbot's busy life of public service, Thomson anticipates the theme and some of the phrasing of *The Castle of Indolence*: see *OET Liberty*, 151.
54. *OET Liberty*, 205: canto II, lines 202–3; cf. Spenser, *The Shepheardes Calender*, 'October', line 61.
55. *OET Liberty*, 205: canto II, lines 195–207.
56. Tobias Smollett, *The Adventures of Ferdinand Count Fathom* (1753), 'Dedication'. Voltaire disparages Thomson's dedications in the entry headed 'Flatterie' in his *Dictionnaire philosophique* (1764).
57. Bonamy Dobrée, *English Literature in the Early Eighteenth Century, 1700–1740* (Oxford, 1959), 498; *OET Liberty*, 199; canto II, stanza iii.
58. *OET Liberty*, 175–6, 180, 188: canto I, lines 16–49, 177–80, 388–94.
59. Ibid. 186, 183: canto I, lines 341–2, 262–70.
60. Joseph Warton, *An Essay on the Genius and Writings of Pope*, i (1756), 349.
61. Ibid. 184: canto I, 280–8. *Shepheardes Calender*: 'October', lines 37–9.
62. *OET Liberty*, 200, 214: canto II, 27, 461.
63. Johnson, 289. H. S. Hughes, *The Gentle Hertford* (New York, 1940), 164, *Letters*, 209. *Works of Shelley*, ed. R. Ingpen and W. E. Peck (reprinted 1965), x. 21. Grant, 256. Earl R. Wasserman, *Elizabethan Poetry in the Eighteenth Century* (Urbana, Ill., 1947), 111, 116.
64. See Geoffrey Grigson, *The Harp of Aeolus* (1947), 24–46; James Thomson, *The Castle of Indolence and Other Poems*, ed. A. D. McKillop, (Lawrence, Kan., 1961) 206–9; *OET Liberty*, 437–8.
65. Numbers 17, 43, and 44 in *OET Liberty*, 291–2, 308–9.
66. Quoted in Roger Lonsdale, *Dr Charles Burney* (Oxford, 1965), 29. William Shenstone, *Letters*, ed. M. Williams (1939), 175.

67. Probably Andrew Reid, see Ch. 3 above.
68. Murdoch, p. xv. Shenstone, *Letters*, ed. Williams, 204. *Bee*, 6 (1791), 285. *Weekly Entertainer*. William Hone, *The Table Book* (1828), ii. 591.
69. *Culloden Papers* (1815), 306–7. *Letters*, 204–7.
70. *Letters*, 210. Shenstone, *Letters*, ed. Williams, 163, 175, Phillimore (ed.), *Memoirs and Correspondence of Lyttelton*, i. 406, 409.
71. R. P. Maccubbin and P. Martin (eds.), *British and American Gardens in the Eighteenth Century*, (Williamsburg, 1984), 58–9 and plate 29; Shenstone, *Letters*, ed. Williams, 163–4, 170, 172, 174; William Shenstone, *Letters*, ed. Duncan Mallam (Minneapolis, 1939), 283.
72. *Scots Magazine*, September, October, 1748; *London Magazine*, September, November, 1748.
73. Murdoch, p. xvi; *Bee*, 6 (1791), 285; *Culloden Papers* (1815), 309; Grant, 277, 280–1.
74. Smollett, *Continuation of the Complete History of England*, iv. 129; *London Chronicle*, 11 May 1762, quoted in Grant, 278.
75. *Letters*, 210. For Thomson's other siblings see above, p. 141 and 304, n. 29, p. 172 and 307, n. 37.
76. A. N. L. Munby (ed.), *Sale Catalogues of the Libraries of Eminent Persons*, (1971), 47.
77. *Letters*, 208.
78. Ibid. 211–12. *Irene* opened in February and *Merope* in April 1749, both at Drury Lane.
79. *Letters*, 213–14; Murdoch, p. xvi. Millar bought the copyrights of *Coriolanus, Alfred* (which he evidently regarded as Thomson's), and the fifteen 'Poems on Several Occasions' printed in Lyttelton's edition of Thomson's *Works* (1750); see *OET Liberty*, 273. In the case of *Coriolanus* and *Alfred*, already entered to Millar in the Stationers' Register, he may generously have bought the copyright twice.
80. Shiels, 216.
81. A print in the Raymond Mander and Joe Mitchinson Theatre Collection is reproduced in *The Revels History of Drama in English*, ed. Clifford Leech and T. W. Craik, v: *1660–1750* (1979), plate 28, and is described on p. 146.
82. Smollett ridiculed Quin in *Roderick Random*, ch. 63, also, but made amends at last in *Humphry Clinker* (letters of 30 April and 5 May).
83. George Anne Bellamy, *An Apology for the Life of George Anne Bellamy*, (1785), ii, 24. Bellamy's *Apology* contains several references to her taking supper at Quin's lodgings with Thomson and other guests. On one occasion it was Lyttelton, Mallet, and Smollett; on another, Lord Orford (Sir Robert Walpole's eldest son) and Shenstone. There is a story too of her entertaining Quin and Thomson to supper after they had foiled an unwanted admirer's plot to abduct her (*Apology*, i, 200–1, 205, 208–11). She links all these references, though, with specific stage appearances of her own, all of which, we know, were after Thomson's death. It is of course possible that, in her recollections forty years after the event, she was conflating her stage appearances in the 1748–9 season with her actual meetings with Thomson in her one earlier London season, 1744–5; even so, the abduction story is inherently improbable, whether Thomson was involved or not.
84. Shiels, 215–16; see also Murdoch, p. xvi.
85. Murdoch, p. xvi.

Bibliography

(Unless otherwise indicated, the place of publication is London.)

ADDISON, JOSEPH, *Miscellaneous Works*, ed. A. C. Guthkelch (2 vols., 1914).

ALLARDYCE, ALEXANDER (ed.), *Scotland and Scotsmen in the Eighteenth Century* (2 vols., Edinburgh and London, 1888).

ANDERSON, JAMES, *Constitutions of Masons*, new edn. by John Noorthouck (1784).

—— (ed.), *The Bee, or Literary Weekly Intelligence*, vols. 6 and 7 (Edinburgh, 1791–2).

ANON., *The Life of Mr James Quin, Comedian* (1766).

ANON., *The Tell-Tale* (1756).

ARTHOS, JOHN, *The Language of Natural Description in Eighteenth-Century Poetry* (Ann Arbor, Mich., 1949).

ATTO, CLAYTON, 'The Society for the Encouragement of Learning', *The Library*, 4th s. 19 (1938–9), 263–88.

BAKER, DAVID ERSKINE, *Biographia Dramatica*, with additions by I. Reed and S. Jones (2 vols., 1812).

BARRELL, JOHN, *The Idea of Landscape and the Sense of Place, 1730–1840* (Cambridge, 1972).

——, *English Literature in History, 1730–1780: An Equal Wide Survey* (1983).

BAYNE, WILLIAM, *James Thomson* (Edinburgh, 1898).

BELL, A. S., 'Three New Letters of James Thomson', *Notes and Queries* 217 (1972), 367–9.

BELLAMY, GEORGE ANN, *An Apology for the Life of George Anne Bellamy*, vol. ii (1785).

BISSETT, ANDREW, *Memoirs and Papers of Sir Andrew Mitchell*, (2 vols., 1850).

BLACK, JEREMY, *The British and the Grand Tour* (1985).

BOSWELL, JAMES, *Private Papers of James Boswell*, ed. Geoffrey Scott, vol. iii (1928).

——, *Boswell's Life of Johnson*, ed. G. B. Hill, rev. L. F. Powell (6 vols., Oxford, 1934–50).

BOWER, ALEXANDER, *The History of the University of Edinburgh*, vol. ii (Edinburgh, 1817).

BROWNSMITH, JOHN, *The Dramatic Time-Piece* (1767).

BUCHAN, DAVID STEUART ERSKINE, EARL OF, *Essays on the Lives and Writings of Fletcher of Saltoun and the Poet Thomson* (1792).

CAMPBELL, HILBERT H., 'Thomson and the Countess of Hertford yet again', *Modern Philology*, 67 (1970), 367–9.

——, *James Thomson (1700–1748): An Annotated Bibliography of Selected Editions and the Important Criticism* (New York and London, 1976).

——, *James Thomson* (Boston, 1979).

CARLYLE, ALEXANDER, *Anecdotes and Characters of the Times*, ed. James Kinsley (London, New York, and Toronto 1973).

CARSWELL, JOHN, *The Old Cause* (1954).

CARTER, ELIZABETH, *Letters between Elizabeth Carter and Catherine Talbot* (2 vols., 1809).

CHALKER, JOHN, *The English Georgic* (London and Baltimore, 1969).

CHAMBERS, ROBERT, *A Biographical Dictionary of Eminent Scotsmen*, vol. iv (1835).

——, *Traditions of Edinburgh* (Edinburgh, 1868).

CHESTERFIELD, PHILIP DORMER STANHOPE, EARL OF, *The Letters of Lord Chesterfield*, ed. Bonamy Dobrée (6 vols., 1932).

CHETWOOD, WILLIAM RUFUS, *A General History of the Stage* (1749).

CIBBER, THEOPHILUS: *see Shiels.*

COHEN, RALPH, *The Art of Discrimination* (1964).

——, *The Unfolding of* The Seasons (1970).

CONNOLLY, L. W., *The Censorship of English Drama 1737–1827* (San Marino, Calif., 1976).

CRISP, RICHARD, *Richmond and its Inhabitants from the Olden Time* (1866).

CRUIKSHANKS, EVELYN, and JEREMY BLACK (eds.), *The Jacobite Challenge* (Edinburgh, 1988).

CULLODEN PAPERS, ed. H. R. Duff (1815).

CUMBERLAND, RICHARD, *Memoirs of Richard Cumberland, written by himself* (1806).

CUNDALL, H. M., *Bygone Richmond* (1925).

DAVIES, THOMAS, *Memoirs of the Life of David Garrick* (2 vols., new edn. 1780).

——, *Dramatic Miscellanies* (3 vols., 1784).

DEFOE, DANIEL, *A Tour thro' the Whole Island of Great Britain*, ed. G. D. H. Cole (2 vols., 1927).

DOBRÉE, BONAMY, *English Literature in the Early Eighteenth Century, 1700–1740* (Oxford, 1959).

EVANS, JOHN, *Richmond and its Vicinity* (Richmond, 1825).

FAIRCHILD, HOXIE NEALE, *Religous Trends in English Poetry*, vol. i: *1700–1740* (New York, 1939).

FAULKNER, THOMAS, *Historical and Topographical Account of Fulham* (1813).

FERGUSON, WILLIAM, *Scotland: 1689 to the Present* (Edinburgh, 1978).

FIELDING, HENRY, *Tom Thumb and the Tragedy of Tragedies*, ed. L. J. Morrisey (Edinburgh, 1970).

——, *The Jacobite's Journal and Related Writings*, ed. W. B. Coley (Oxford, 1974).

——, *The True Patriot and Related Writings*, ed. W. B. Coley (Oxford, 1987).

FOXON, DAVID, *English Verse 1701–1750: A Catalogue*, (2 vols., Cambridge, 1975).

——, *Pope and the Early Eighteenth-Century Book Trade*, rev. and ed. James McLaverty (Oxford, 1991).

GARRICK, DAVID, *Private Correspondence of Garrick with Celebrated Persons*, (2 vols., 1831).

——, *Letters of David Garrick*, ed. D. M. Little and E. M. Kahrl (3 vols., Cambridge, Mass., 1963).

GENTLEMAN, FRANCIS, *The Dramatic Censor* (1770).

GERRARD, CHRISTINE, '*The Castle of Indolence* and the Opposition to Walpole', *Review of English Studies*, N. S. 41 (1990), 45–64.

GOLDGAR, B. A., *Walpole and the Wits* (Lincoln, Nebr., 1976).

GRANT, ALEXANDER, *The Story of the University of Edinburgh during its first Three Hundred Years*, (2 vols., 1884).

GRANT, DOUGLAS, *James Thomson, Poet of 'The Seasons'* (1951).

GRANVILLE, MARY, *The Autobiography and Correspondence of Mary Granville, Mrs Delaney*, 1st s. (3 vols., 1861).

GRAVES, RICHARD, *Recollections of William Shenstone* (1788).

GREENE, DONALD, 'From Accidie to Neurosis: The Castle of Indolence Revisited', in M. E. Novak (ed.), *English Literature in the Age of Disguise* (Los Angeles, 1978), 131–56.

GRIFFIN, DUSTIN, *Regaining Paradise: Milton and the Eighteenth Century* (Cambridge, 1986).

HAGSTRUM, JEAN, *The Sister Arts* (Chicago, 1958).

HERTFORD, FRANCES SEYMOUR, COUNTESS OF, *Correspondence between the Countess of Hertford and the Countess of Pomfret* (2 vols., 1805).

HERVEY, JOHN, LORD, *Memoirs of the Reign of George II*, ed. Rommey Sedgwick (3 vols., 1931).

HIGHFILL, PHILIP H. *et al.*, *Biographical Dictionary of Actors, Actresses, etc.* (Carbondale, Ill., 1973 — in progress)

HILL, AARON, *A Collection of Letters to the Late Aaron Hill* (1751).

——, *Works of the Late Aaron Hill* (4 vols., 1753).

HOARE, RICHARD COLT, *Recollections Abroad, during the Years 1785, 1786, 1787* (Bath, 1815).

HOLDSWORTH, WILLIAM, *A History of English Law*, 7th edn. (1956).

HOLLOWAY, JAMES, *William Aikman, 1682–1731* (Edinburgh, 1988).

HONE, WILLIAM, *The Table Book* (2 vols., 1828).

HUGHES, HELEN SARD, *The Gentle Hertford* (New York, 1940).

JOHNSON, SAMUEL, *Lives of the English Poets*, ed. Peter Cunningham (3 vols., 1854).

——, *Lives of the English Poets*, ed. G. B. Hill (3 vols., Oxford, 1905).

KERSLAKE, JOHN, *Early Georgian Portraits* (2 vols., 1977).

LANE, JOHN, *Masonic Records, 1717–1886* (1886).

LANGFORD, PAUL, *The Excise Crisis* (Oxford, 1975).

LENMAN, BRUCE, *The Jacobite Risings in Britain, 1689–1746* (1980).

LILLYWHITE, BRYANT, *London Coffee-House* (1963).

LOFTIS, JOHN, *The Politics of Drama in Augustan England* (Oxford, 1963).

——, 'Thomson's *Tancred and Sigismunda* and the Demise of the Drama of Political Opposition', in G. W. Stone (ed.) *The Stage and the Page* (Berkeley, Los Angeles, and London, 1981).

LONSDALE, ROGER, *Dr Charles Burney* (Oxford, 1965).

LYTTELTON, GEORGE, LORD, *The Works of George, Lord Lyttelton*, ed. G. E. Ayscough, 2nd edn. (1775).

MACAULAY, G. C., *James Thomson* (1908).

MACKENZIE, HENRY, *Anecdotes and Egotisms of Henry Mackenzie*, ed. H. W. Thomson (1927).

MCKILLOP, ALAN DUGALD, *The Background of Thomson's* Seasons (Minneapolis, 1942).

——, *The Background of Thomson's* Liberty, Rice Institute Pamphlet 38 no. 2, (July 1951).

——, 'Thomson and the Licensers of the Stage', *Philological Quarterly* 37 (1958), 448–53.

____, 'The Early History of *Alfred*', *Philological Quarterly* 41 (1962), 311–24.

____, 'Two more Thomson Letters', *Modern Philology* 60 (1962), 128–30.

MACQUEEN, JOHN, *The Enlightenment and Scottish Literature*, vol. i: *Progress and Poetry* (Edinburgh, 1982).

MALLET, DAVID, *The Works of Mr Mallet* (3 vols., 1759).

MENARY, GEORGE, *The Life and Letters of Duncan Forbes of Culloden* (1936).

MORE, JOHN, *Strictures, Critical and Sentimental, on Thomson's Seasons* (1777).

MOREL, LÉON, *James Thomson: sa vie et ses oeuvres* (Paris, 1895).

MUNBY, A. N. L. (ed.), *Sale Catalogues of the Libraries of Eminent Persons*, vol. i (1971).

NICHOLS, JOHN, *Literary Anecdotes of the Eighteenth Century*, (9 vols., 1812–15).

____, AND JOHN BOWYER NICHOLS, *Illustrations of the Literary History of the Eighteenth Century* (8 vols., 1817–58).

NICOLSON, MARJORIE HOPE, *Newton demands the Muse* (Princeton, NJ, 1946).

OSGOOD, C. G., 'Lady Philippina Knight and her Boswell', *Princeton University Library Chronicle* 4 (1943), 48–9.

PHILLIMORE, ROBERT (ed.), *Memoirs and Correspondence of George, Lord Lyttelton* (2 vols., 1845).

PIOZZI, HESTER LYNCH, *Observations and Reflections made in the Course of a Journey through France, Italy, and Germany* (2 vols., 1789).

____, *Autobiography, Letters, and Literary Remains*, ed. A. Hayward, 2nd edn. (1861).

____, *Thraliana: The Diary of . . . Mrs Piozzi*, ed. K. C. Balderson (2 vols. Oxford, 1942).

POPE, ALEXANDER, *Works*, ed. Joseph Warton (9 vols., 1797).

____, *The Twickenham Edition of the Poems of Alexander Pope*, general ed. John Butt (11 vols., London and New Haven, Conn., 1939–69).

____, *The Correspondence of Alexander Pope*, ed. George Sherburn (5 vols., Oxford, 1956).

RAMSAY, ALLAN, *Works*, ed. Burns Martin *et al.* Scottish Text Society (6 vols., Edinburgh, 1945–74).

REID, ANDREW, *The Present State of the Republick of Letters*, May 1728.

RICHARDSON, SAMUEL, *Correspondence*, ed. A. L. Barbauld (6 vols., 1804).

____, *Selected Letters*, ed. J. Carroll (Oxford, 1964).

RICHMOND, JOHN, *To the Memory of Thomson, in the Temple of the Muses at Dryburgh Abbey* (1818).

ROBERTSON, JAMES LOGIE ('Hugh Haliburton'), *Furth in Field* (1895).

RUNDLE, THOMAS, *Letters of the late Thomas Rundle . . . to Mrs Barbara Sandys* (2 vols., Gloucester, 1789).

RYAN, RICHARD, *Dramatic Table-Talk* (3 vols., 1825).

SAVAGE, RICHARD, *Poetical Works*, ed. C. Tracy (Cambridge, 1962).

SCOTT, HEW, *Fasti Ecclesiae Scoticanae*, rev. edn. (7 vols., Edinburgh, 1917).

SCOTT, MARY JANE W., *James Thomson, Anglo-Scot* (Athens, Ga., 1988).

SCOUTEN, ARTHUR H. (ed.), *The London Stage, 1660–1800, Part 3, 1729–1747* (2 vols., Carbondale, Ill., 1961).

SEWARD, WILLIAM, *Supplement to the Anecdotes of some Distinguished Persons* (1797).

SHIELS, ROBERT, *Lives of the Poets of Great-Britain and Ireland*, 'by Theophilus Cibber', (5 vols. 1753).

SHENSTONE, WILLIAM, *Letters*, ed. Duncan Mallam (Minneapolis, 1939).

SHENSTONE, WILLIAM, *Letters*, ed. Marjorie Williams (Oxford, 1939).

SMITH, J. E., *Bygone Briefs* (1896).

SMOLLETT, TOBIAS, *Continuation of the Complete History of England* (4 vols., 1760–1).

——, *Letters*, ed. L. M. Knapp (Oxford, 1970).

SOMERVILLE, THOMAS, *My Own Life and Times, 1741–1804* (Edinburgh, 1861).

SPACKS, PATRICIA MEYER, *The Varied God* (Berkeley and Los Angeles, 1959).

——, *The Poetry of Vision* (Cambridge, Mass., 1967).

SPENCE, JOSEPH, *Observations, Anecdotes, and Characters of Books and Men*, ed. J. M. Osborn (2 vols., Oxford, 1966).

——, *Letters from the Grand Tour*, ed. Slava Klima (1975).

SPENCER, JEFFRY, B., *Heroic Nature* (Evanston, Ill., 1973).

STOW, JOHN, *Survey of the Cities of London and Westminster*, brought down to the present time by John Strype (1720).

TAYLOR, E. G. R., *The Mathematical Practitioners of Hanoverian England, 1714–1840* (Cambridge, 1966).

THOMSON, JAMES, *The Works of James Thomson*, with 'Life' by Patrick Murdoch (2 vols., 1762).

——, *Poetical Works*, ed. Robert Bell (2 vols., 1855).

——, *Poetical Works*, with 'Memoir' by Sir Harris Nicolas (Aldine edn., 2 vols., 1830, rev. 1847, rev. by Peter Cunningham, 1860).

——, *Poetical Works*, ed. D. C. Tovey (2 vols., 1897).

——, *James Thomson (1700–1748): Letters and Documents*, ed. A. D. McKillop (Lawrence, Kan., 1958).

——, *The Castle of Indolence and Other Poems*, ed. A. D. McKillop (Lawrence, Kan., 1961).

——, *The Seasons*, ed. James Sambrook (Oxford, 1981).

——, *Liberty, The Castle of Indolence, and Other Poems*, ed. James Sambrook (Oxford, 1986).

——, *Plays*, ed. John C. Greene (2 vols., New York and London, 1987).

TRACY, CLARENCE, *The Artificial Bastard, a Biography of Richard Savage* (Toronto, 1953).

VICTOR, BENJAMIN, *Original Letters, Dramatic Pieces, and Poems* (3 vols., 1776).

VOLTAIRE, *Correspondence*, ed. Theodore Besterman (51 vols., Geneva, 1968–77).

WALPOLE, HORACE, *Correspondence*, ed. W. S. Lewis *et al.* (48 vols., London and New Haven, Conn., 1937–83).

WARTON, JOSEPH, *An Essay on the Genius and Writings of Pope* (2 vols., 1756–82).

WATSON, G., *The History of Jedburgh Grammar School* (1909).

Weekly Entertainer (Sherborne, 1800).

WILLIAMS, RALPH M., *Poet, Painter, and Parson: the Life of John Dyer* (New York, 1956).

WODROW, ROBERT, *Analecta or Materials for a History of Remarkable Providences, mostly relating to Scotch Ministers and Christians* (4 vols., Edinburgh, 1842–3).

WYNDHAM, MAUD, *Chronicles of the Eighteenth Century* (1924).

YOUNG, EDWARD, *Correspondence*, ed. E. C. Pettit (Oxford, 1971).

Index

Adam, Robert 279, 287
Addison, Joseph 15, 60, 116, 222; *Cato* 28,
  82–5, 90, 169; *Letter from Italy,*
  A 143; *Remarks on Several Parts of*
  Italy 106; *Spectator, The* 57–8, 266
Aeolian Harp 275
Aeschylus 212; *Agamemnon* 179, 181–2;
Aikman, William 31, 48, 61, 65–7, 72, 86,
  118; portrait of T 285, 287; 'On the Death
  of Aikman' 123
Ainslie, Sgt. 11
Akenside, Mark: *Voice of Liberty, The* 174
Alfred the Great 139, 146, 173, 213, 234; *see*
  also Thomson, James, writings: *Alfred*
Algarotti, Francesco 169, 307 n. 33
Amanda 148, 218, 227–8, 260; *see also*
  Young, Elizabeth
Amelia, Princess Royal 91, 98, 158
Ancrum 6, 20, 33
Anderson,—— 137–8
Anson, George, Baron Anson 250–1
Appian of Alexandria 82
Arabian Nights 265
Arbuthnot, John 31, 66
Argyll, Duke of, *see* Campbell, John
Armstrong, John 147, 154, 167–8, 235, 253,
  262, 276–7; *Art of Preserving Health,*
  The 154, 157, 235, 266; stanzas in *The*
  Castle of Indolence 154, 266–7
Arne, Cecilia 202, 248
Arne, Thomas Augustine 178, 201, 205, 208,
  248
Ashdown Park 122
Athenian Society 19
Augusta, Princess of Wales 168–9, 178, 186,
  190, 196, 199, 200–1, 242
Augusta, Princess (daughter of the
  above) 168–9, 200–1
Avignon 110, 112

Baillie, George 29–30, 34, 56
Baillie, Lady Grizel 1, 22, 29–30, 34, 97, 113
Baillie, Robert 1, 97
Baker, Sir Richard: *Chronicles* 192
Bandello, Matteo 82
Barbadoes 236, 252, 263
Barbarini, Signora 200
Barrell, John 162, 269
Barrington, Anne, Dowager Viscountess 248

Barrington, William, Viscount Barrington 210,
  242–3, 248
Basire, Isaac *or* James 285–6
Bath 107, 214, 225, 263
Beckingham, Charles 50
Bedingfield, Edward 265
Bell, Elizabeth, *see* Thomson, Elizabeth
Bell, Robert 206
Bellamy, George Ann 280–1, 317 n. 83
Bennet, Elizabeth 8, 10
Bennet, Sir William 7–9, 26–7, 29, 30, 77
Benson, Martin, Bishop 130
Benson, William 20
Berry, Miss 214
Bible: Job 35, 72; Psalms 19; Song of
  Solomon 215, 218; Matthew 34
Binning, Lord, *see* Hamilton, Charles
Birch, Thomas 155, 174, 176, 186, 188, 256,
  279, 315 n. 9
Birch, Tim 92–3; the second 185
Black Prince, *see* Edward
Blair, Robert 18
Bland, John 46
Blythe, Francis 148, 305 n. 47
Boccaccio, Giovanni 82, 238
Bolingbroke, Viscount, *see* St John
Bond, William 40
Booth, Barton 28, 86, 177, 244, 246
Booth, Hester 28
Boscawen Frances 199
Boswell, James 179–80, 208–9, 292 n. 98
Bounce (Pope's dog) 139, 214–15
Bower, Archibald 258–9
Boyle, Richard, Earl of Burlington 31, 96,
  123; his garden at Chiswick 188, 208, 254
Boyse, Samuel 94
Bramston, James: *Man of Taste, The* 121–2
Brentford 210, 268
Britannia 45, 48, 53, 101, 151, 205, 269; *see*
  also Thomson, James, writings: *Britannia* and
  'Rule Britannia'
British Journal 40, 49
Broad Bottom ministry 236, 239, 248–9,
  252
Brockes, Barthold Heinrich 252
Brooke, Francis, Baron Brooke 136
Brooke, Henry 171; *Gustavus Vasa* 190–1,
  193–4, 196, 203
Brown, Iain G. 285

Browne, Isaac Hawkins: *Pipe of Tobacco, A* 95, 147

Brownlow, John, Viscount Tyrconnel 156

Buchan, Earl of, *see* Erskine, David Steuart

Budgell, Ann 244

Buff (T's dog) 214–15

Burlington, Earl of, *see* Boyle

Burnet, Thomas 70

Burney, Charles 208, 275

Campbell, Alexander, Earl of Marchmont 121

Campbell, Archibald, Earl of Islay 6, 9, 14

Campbell, John, Admiral 250–1

Campbell, John, Duke of Argyll 6, 8–9, 14, 30–1, 98, 121, 158, 160

Carlyle, Alexander 252–3, 256

Caroline, Queen 57, 65, 74–6, 91–2, 96, 98, 119, 121, 125, 128–9, 134, 152, 158–60, 167, 175, 183, 187–8, 212

Carstares, William 12

Carswell, John 111, 119–20

Carter, Elizabeth 188, 244

Carteret, John, Earl Granville 184

Castelli, Valerio 144

Cave, Edward 132, 188

Cavendish, Margaret, Duchess of Portland 163

Chalons 112

Champion, The 200, 204

Chancery, Court of 125–7, 137–8, 161–2

Charles I 165–6

Charles Edward Stuart, Young Pretender 57, 252, 256

Charmer, The 201

Chatham, Earl of, *see* Pitt, William

Chaucer, Geoffrey 212, 234, 264

Chesterfield, Earl of, *see* Stanhope, Philip Dormer

Chetwood, William Rufus 89

Cheyne, George 107, 109

Chiswick 136, 188, 208, 254

Churchill, Charles: *The Duellist* 126, 163

Cibber, Colley 28–9, 33, 86–9, 122, 124

Cibber, Jane 90

Cibber, Susannah Maria 178, 180, 192, 243–4, 247, 256

Cibber, Theophilus 28, 177–8, 190–1

Clare, Frank 258

Clare, John 68

Claremont 188

Clarinda 136

Clarke, Alured 130, 132, 139

Clerk, Sir John, of Penicuik 61, 65–7, 72, 79, 86

Clive, Kitty 202

Clivedon 200–2

Cobham, Viscount, *see* Temple

Colden, Alexander 21

Collins, William 55, 253, 282

Common Sense 160–1, 169, 174

Compton, Sir Spencer, Earl of Wilmington 41–3, 56–7, 60–1, 65, 103

Congreve, William 201

Cooke, Thomas 49

Cooper, Anthony Ashley, Earl of Shaftesbury 20, 71, 97, 266

Copyright Act 149–50, 222, 270

Corneille, Pierre 82, 87, 94, 112

Cowper, William: *Charity* 126–7

Craftsman, The 59, 139, 146, 168–9, 174

Craig, James 24, 286, 307 n. 37

Craig, Mary, *see* Thomson, Mary

Craig, William 172, 307 n. 37

Cranstoun, John, the elder 6, 292 n. 9

Cranstoun, John, the younger 6, 11, 27

Cranstoun, William 6, 20–2, 26–30, 32–3, 137–8, 140–1

Critical Review 134, 138, 161–2

Criticism on the New Sophonisba, A 92–3

Cumberland, Richard: *Memoirs* 64, 176, 178, 243–4

Curll, Edmund 40, 122, 138

Daily Advertiser 124, 202

Daily Gazetteer 160, 167–9, 186, 196–7

Daily Journal 75, 90, 124

Daily Post 90, 187, 239–40, 249, 256

Dalacourt, James 132

Dalrymple, Sir David, Lord Hailes 56

Dalrymple, John, Earl, of Stair 121

Dalton, John: *Comus* 75–6, 201

Dante Alighieri: *Paradiso* 238

David (T's manservant) 199

Davies, Thomas: *Dramatic Miscellanies* 88–9, 174, 176, 182; *Memoirs of Garrick* 88, 165–6, 178–9, 185, 190, 192, 237, 243

Defence of the New Tragedy of Sophonsiba 93

Defoe, Daniel 24, 53; *Tour* 3, 9, 24, 157

Delane, Dennis 192, 244, 280

Dennis, John 44, 49, 61, 84, 88, 95–6, 124–5, 255, 292 n. 103

Desaguliers, John Theophilus 201

Dick, Sir Alexander 155

Dickson, Thomas 253

Diodorus Siculus 82

Dionysius of Halicarnassus 255

Dodington, George Bubb, Lord Melcombe 56, 60, 64–5, 72–3, 76, 78–9, 86, 92, 96, 98, 103, 108–13, 116–17, 119–21, 123, 128–9, 134, 136, 140, 208, 221, 252

Dodsley, Robert 213; *Collection of Poems* 261, 265, 275

Doran, John 240

Druids 267, 268, 269, 282–3
Drummond, Colin 12–13
Dryden, John 93, 238, 255
Duck, Stephen 158, 209
Dutton, Sir John 130
Dyer, John 39–40, 43, 62, 65, 144

East Barnet 29, 33–4
Eastbury 64–5, 72–3, 78–9, 113, 136, 140
Edinburgh 6, 8–12, 14, 17, 19–22, 24, 35, 40, 66, 151, 166, 172, 235; College 5–6, 8, 10, 12–19, 43, 57, 105, 136, 154–5
Edinburgh Miscellany, The 17–19
Ednam 1, 278
Edward I 159, 192–3
Edward III 146, 159, 201, 204
Edward, Black Prince 139, 159, 204, 213
Edwards, Thomas 197–8
Egerton, Park 38
Elizabeth I 94, 146, 201, 203
Elliot, family 6–7, 26, 292 n. 9
Erskine, David Steuart, Earl of Buchan 5, 7, 31, 33, 262, 278, 286
Erskine, John, Earl of Mar 8–9
Euripides 212; Alcestis 193

Farquhar, George: Constant Couple, The 28
Fermor, Henrietta Louisa, Countess of Pomfret 193
Fielding, Henry 60, 79, 132, 192, 222, 225, 252; Champion, The 161, 200, 204; Jacobite's Journal, The 270, 277; Tom Thumb, a Tragedy 93–4
Fleetwood, Charles 175, 190–2, 204, 236
Florence 110, 113–16
Fog's Weekly Journal 75
Forbes, Ann 285
Forbes, Duncan 30–1, 76, 96, 98, 112, 153, 160, 172, 262
Forbes, John 31, 112, 152–4, 172, 176, 210, 235, 262, 276–7
Fourdrinier, Pierre 96
Foxon, David 104
France 106, 110–12, 115, 168–9, 193, 234, 256
Frederick the Great 154
Frederick Louis, Prince of Wales 3, 74, 76, 87, 91, 103, 119–21, 124, 128–9, 133–4, 139–40, 150, 154–6, 158–61, 167–72, 178, 183, 190, 195–6, 200–1, 203–5, 213, 222, 234–6, 240, 242, 245, 248, 261, 271, 280
Free-Briton, The 60, 75
Frowde, Philip 132

Garrick, David 88, 165, 176, 178, 236, 243–4, 246–7, 256–7, 263, 279–80
Gay, John 19, 24, 31, 60, 204, 225

Gentleman, Francis 181
Gentleman's and London Magazine 196
Gentleman's Magazine 33, 132, 147–8, 188, 218, 227, 251, 286
George I 6, 30, 65, 200
George II 9, 41, 61, 65, 74, 76, 79, 87, 120, 125, 128, 139, 152, 159–60, 168–9, 183, 187–8, 195, 200, 204, 239
George III 154, 163, 201, 278
Gerrard, Christine 269–70
Gibson, Edmund, Bishop 129–30, 156
Glover, Richard 171, 213; Leonidas 161, 244
Golden Rump, The 160
Goldgar, Bernard 169
Goldsmith, Oliver: Traveller, The 111
Gothic Constitution 145, 173, 193, 196, 205
Graham, Lord George 16, 78, 237
Graham, James, Duke of Montrose 16, 24–5, 33–4, 66, 78, 121
Grainger, James: Sugar-Cane, The 224
Grant, Douglas: James Thomson 2, 93, 158, 242, 250, 275
Grant, Lady Jane 286
Granville, Ann 163
Granville, Earl, see Carteret
Graves, Richard 254, 258
Gray, John 57, 67, 155, 210
Greece 133, 144–5, 161, 173, 231
Greene, Donald 270
Gregory, David 13
Gregory, James 14
Grenville, George 258, 315 n. 9
Grotesque Club 16, 20
Grub-Street Journal 87–8, 92–5, 124, 131–2
Gusthart, William 5–6, 11, 151, 259–60, 276

Haddington, Earl of, see Hamilton, Thomas
Hagley Hall and Park 221–5, 229–30, 253, 258–9, 267, 277–8, 287
Hailes, Lord, see Dalrymple, Sir David
Hales, Stephen: Vegetable Staticks 70
Hallam, Ann 192
Hamilton, Charles, Lord Binning 22, 29–30, 33–4, 44, 56, 113
Hamilton, Gavin 172
Hamilton, Thomas, Earl of Haddington 30
Hamilton, William 14–15, 19, 61
Hammond, James 171, 204, 210, 234
Hardwicke, Earl of, see Yorke, Philip
Harrington, Earl of, see Stanhope, William
Harrington, James: Oceana 186
Havard, William 160, 178, 244
Hawke, Edward, Lord Hawke 251
Hay, John, Marquis of Tweeddale 154, 252
Hazlitt, William 35
Henley, John: Hyp-Doctor, The 197
Henry V 146, 159

Hertford, Countess of, *see* Seymour, Frances
Hertford, Earl of, *see* Seymour, Algernon
Hervey, John, Lord Hervey 85, 119, 121, 125, 128–9, 169–70
Hill, Aaron 16, 20, 38–44, 50, 57, 61, 71, 81, 107, 123–4, 134–5, 139–40, 148–50, 155–7, 168, 171–2, 187, 189–92, 204–5, 212, 235, 280; 'Caesar' 189–92, 205; *Plain Dealer, The* 16, 38–9; *Prompter, The* 135, 139–40, 176; *Tears of the Muses, The* 171–2; verses in *Winter* 41–3; *Zara* 123–4, 150, 192
History of Prince Edward, 194
Hive, The 119
Hoadly, Benjamin, Bishop 94, 138, 252
Hoadly, John 94, 236
Hoare, Richard Colt 111–12
Hobart, Mrs 165, 199
Hogarth, William 155, 212
Holloway, James 285
Holmes, John: *Art of Rhetoric, The* 187
Homer 53, 62, 135, 161, 183; *see also* Pope: Homer translation
Horton, Christiana 192–202
Hosier, Francis 74
Hudson, Thomas 286
Hull, Thomas 198
Hume, David 155
Hume, Patrick, Earl of Marchmont 1

Islay, Earl of, *see* Campbell, Archibald
Italy 53, 106, 110, 112–18, 132–3, 143–4, 150

Jail Committee 97, 235
James II 120, 141–2
James Francis Edward Stuart, Old Pretender 8–9, 59, 255
James, Robert: *Medicinal Dictionary* 236
Jedburgh 1–2, 4–6, 141
Johnson, Samuel 25, 73, 85, 100, 103, 106, 155, 170, 181, 209, 256, 260, 280, 294 n. 53, 299 n. 19; *Dictionary* 16, 37, 51, 294 n. 53; *Life of Savage* 28, 65, 156, 177, 189; *Life of Thomson* 28, 35–8, 41, 56, 62, 68, 84–6, 100, 102, 107, 114, 127, 147, 170, 178–9, 194, 197, 209, 274–5, 300 n. 45

Keats, John 69
Kelso 1, 7–8, 30
Kemble, John Philip 198, 280
Kent, William 96, 151
Kerslake, John 285, 287
Kew, *see* Richmond (Surrey)
King and Titi, The 160–1
King, William 173–4
Kircher, Athanasius 275

Knight, Henrietta, Lady Luxborough 254, 275, 277
Knight, Lady Philippina 217–18, 250–1

Lacy, James 236–7
Law, William 82
Leasowes, The 253–4, 258, 278
Lee, Nathaniel 82, 93–4, 244
Leeward Islands 236, 252, 258, 279
Leghorn 112, 115–16
Lens, Bernard 46
Le Sage, Alain-René: *Gil Blas* 236, 238
Lessing, Gotthold Ephraim 184, 308 n. 65
Licensing Act 160, 173–6, 178, 191, 196, 199, 245; *see also* Lord Chamberlain
Lillo, George: *George Barnwell* 92, 197
Literary Courier of Grub Street 185
Livy 82, 255
Loftis, John 175, 240
London 22–6, 28–9, 98, 136–7, 179; Charing Cross 24–5, 45, 57, 65, 152, 167–8; Chelsea 251; City 25, 44–5; Clapton 166; coffee houses and taverns 25, 57, 65–6, 77, 152–3, 157, 190, 207–9, 252–3; Covent Garden 25, 153, 179, 190, 211; Covent Garden Theatre 175, 191–2, 202, 236–7, 243, 256, 263, 279; Drury Lane Theatre 33, 86–92, 175, 178, 185–6, 190–1, 200–1, 204–5, 236–7, 242–3, 245, 248, 263, 279; Hammersmith 136, 262, 275, 312 n. 37; Haymarket Theatre 94, 124, 160; Little Tower Street 44–7, 66, 98; St James's 24–5, 66, 129, 169; Strand 25, 37–8, 152, 157, 253; Westminster 24, 29, 31, 57, 120, 129, 167–8, 173
London Daily Post 200–1
London Journal 41–2
London Magazine 132, 204
Lord Chamberlain 173, 175–6, 180, 191, 194–6, 197, 200, 204
Lowth, Robert 265
Lucan: *Pharsalia* 53
Luxborough, Lady, *see* Knight, Henrietta
Lyons 110–12
Lyttelton, George, Baron Lyttelton 64, 108, 128, 139, 148, 152, 159–61, 170–1, 185–6, 190, 203, 205, 221–5, 229–30, 234, 236–7, 239, 245, 248–9, 252, 256–62, 264, 266–7, 271, 278–9, 280–2, 287, 311 n. 25, 315 n. 9, 317 n. 83; editor of Thomson 98, 146, 206, 224–5, 300 n. 61; *Epistle to Mr Pope, An* 144, 146; *History of Henry II, The* 205; *Letters from a Persian* 138–9, 146, 170; *Observations on the Conversion of St Paul* 257, 278
Lyttelton, Lucy 257, 278

Lyttelton, Sir Thomas 222–3
Lyttelton, William 253–4, 278

MacDonald, Flora 57
Mackenzie, Henry 10
McKillop, Alan Dugald 119, 142, 214, 221, 286
Macklin, Charles 251
Macky, John 10
MacQueen, John 269
Maffei, Scipione 150
Maimbourg, Louis 239, 312–13 n. 60
Mallet, David 5, 16–20, 22–3, 25, 27, 29, 31–4, 37–44, 47–50, 56–7, 61, 63–7, 78–81, 85–6, 107, 121, 124, 131, 152, 154–5, 171, 176, 188–92, 198, 200–5, 210–13, 217, 221, 237, 242, 248, 253, 257, 260–1, 291 n. 75, 292 n. 103 317 n. 83; *Alfred* 200–5, 248; dedication to and verses in *Winter* 41–3; *Eurydice* ('Periander') 78, 81, 86; *Excursion, The* 47–8, 61, 66; *Mustapha* 189–92; Prologue to *Agamemnon* 176; Prologue to *Sophonisba* 85; *William and Margaret* 20, 23, 38; 'Winter's Day' 5, 33, 38
Malloch, *see* Mallet
Mar, Earl of, *see* Erskine, John
Marchmont, Earls of, *see* Campell, Alexander *and* Hume, Patrick
Marlborough Castle 62–5
Marlfield 7–8
Marquis (a dog) 214–15
Marrow, Arabella 136
Marston, John 82
Martyn, Benjamin: *Timoleon* 87–90, 92, 94–5, 109
Martyn, John 88
Mason, William 265
Medina, John 287
Melcombe, Lord, *see* Dodington
Melinda 217, 260
Memoirs of the Society of Grub Street 88, 95
Mendez, Isaac 207
Mendez, Jacob 166–7
Mendez, Moses 168, 198, 307 n. 23
Mendez, Solomon 166–8, 207, 236
Millan, John 37, 43–4, 49, 56, 61, 65, 73, 78, 103–4, 150, 187, 222
Millar, Andrew 66, 68, 74, 78, 87, 91, 96, 104, 132, 135, 149–50, 155, 162, 164, 169, 172–4, 185–7, 204, 210, 214, 222, 235, 245, 248, 252–3, 262, 265, 271, 275, 278, 280, 286, 317 n. 79
Miller, James: *Harlequin-Horace* 122
Mills, John 28, 89, 202
Milton, John 36, 53, 62, 88, 122, 125, 161, 173, 231, 274; *Areopagitica* 173–4, 186; *Il Penseroso* 29, 33, 36, 101; *Manifesto, A* 174–5, 186; *Paradise Lost* 37, 51, 100–1, 107, 175, 215, 230–1
Milward William 177, 202
Mitchell, Sir Andrew 153–5, 179–80, 208, 210, 235, 253, 262, 276, 278–9, 307 n. 33
Mitchell, Joseph 17, 40, 43, 49–50, 60, 92–3, 95
Moir, John 4
Molyneux, Samuel 611
Monthly Review 222
Montrose, Duke of, *see* Graham, James
Morel, Léon 50
Morell, Thomas 211–12, 264
Moore-Smythe, James 95
Morrice, Bezaleel 49, 95
Munbee, Valentine 107
Murdoch, Patrick 17–18, 21, 29, 73, 112, 122–3, 153–5, 172–3, 176, 217, 235, 253, 262, 264, 276–7; *Life of Thomson* 1, 5, 7, 11, 15, 18–19, 21–2, 27, 40–1, 57, 90, 105, 109–10, 127, 134, 147, 161, 164, 170, 187, 194–5, 200, 236, 247, 253–4, 263–4, 268–9, 275–6, 282
Murray, Sir David 82
Murray, Lady 56
Myra 215, 227, 294 n. 68

Nabbes, Thomas 82
Newton, Sir Isaac 13–14, 46, 52–3, 57–9, 76–7, 96, 172
Nicolas, Sir Harris 6–7
Norris, John 18
North Hall, Herts. 152, 263

Oldfield, Anne 28–9, 86, 88–91, 181
Oliver, William 209
Onslow, Arthur 76, 103
Oswald, James 275
Otway, Thomas 97
Ovid 208
Oxford 77, 86, 95, 107, 258–9

Painter, William 82
Paris 106, 108, 110–12, 115–16, 118–19, 150, 269
Paterson, William 17, 152, 154, 165, 167–8, 208, 235, 252, 261–3, 279, 315 n. 9; *Arminius* 200, 203
Patoun, John 250, 286–7
Pelham, Henry 236, 239, 249, 256, 261–2, 315 n. 9
Pendarves, Mary 90
Percy, Thomas, Bishop 62
Peter the Great 231, 267
Petersham 249
Petrarch 82, 254
Philips, Ambrose 88, 181

Philips, John 98

Piozzi, Hester Lynch 114, 208

Pitt, Christopher 73, 77

Pitt, William, Earl of Chatham 159, 185, 234, 237, 239, 287

Plumb, Sir John 131

Plutarch: *Lives* 109, 255

Pomfret, Countess of, *see* Fermor

Pope, Alexander 7, 15, 17, 31, 41, 57, 59–60, 66, 88, 94–6, 108, 121, 131–2, 138–40, 144, 147, 150, 161, 168, 186, 198, 214, 229, 254, 269, 279; and Hill 123–4, 159, 171–2, 187, 189–92; and Lyttelton 144, 161, 171, 190; and Mallet 85–6, 107, 118, 121, 124, 131, 188–9, 202–3; 'Bounce to Fop' 139, 214; *Brutus* 146, 205, 229; *Dunciad, The* 24–5, 95, 107, 138, 269; *Epistle to Dr Arbuthnot, An* 107–8, 146–7; Homer translation 27, 60, 104; Prologue to *Sophonisba* 85

Porteous riot 160, 197

Porter, Mary 29, 176–7, 182

Portland, Duchess of, *see* Cavendish

Pretender, *see* Charles Edward Stuart *and* James Francis Edward Stuart

Price, Martin 69

Primrose, Ann, Viscountess Primrose 56–7

Public Advertiser 208

Pulteney, William 60, 159

Quin, James 164–6, 168–9, 175–8, 185, 190–1, 201–2, 208, 210, 228, 236, 243, 254, 256–7, 263–4, 276, 278–82, 317 n. 83

Rabelais, François 126, 265

Racine, Jean 82

Ralph, James 77, 88, 121, 151, 200

Ramsay, Allan 7, 18, 35, 61, 66

Ramsay, John 7, 16

Reid, Andrew 57, 67, 276

Reinhold, Thomas 202

Riccaltoun, Robert 5, 19, 33, 35, 289 n. 23

Rich, John 191, 194, 200–1, 237, 256, 263

Richardson, Samuel 96, 154, 181, 235, 261, 280

Richmond, John 33

Richmond (Surrey) 156–9, 165–6, 168, 188–9, 199, 210, 214, 220–1, 225, 234, 236, 253–4, 258, 275–6, 278, 282

Ridley, Gloster 265

Ritson, Joseph 119

Robbison, Miss 210

Robertson, Mary 214–15, 217, 225, 227–8

Robertson, William 38, 165, 171, 208–10, 214, 217, 250–1, 253, 262, 276, 278, 291 n. 75

Rogers, Pat 45

Rolli, Paolo Antonio 106–7

Rome 72, 110, 112–16, 118, 132, 134, 143–6, 255, 268

Rooke, John 49, 295 n. 9

Ross, George 31, 151, 172, 175, 191, 279

Rowe, Elizabeth 61–3, 77, 90, 119, 136

Rowe, Nicholas 88, 192, 278; *Fair Penitent, The* 88, 91, 178, 243–4

Rundle, Thomas, Bishop 40, 57, 76–7, 90–1, 105, 108, 111, 122, 129–31, 151–2, 155–6, 162, 221

Ryan, Lacy 280

Ryan, Richard 245–6

Rysbrack, Michael 203, 206

St John, Henry, Viscount Bolingbroke 59–60, 110, 123, 131, 146, 184, 188–9, 202–3, 252, 254, 269; *On the Idea of a Patriot King* 134, 154, 202–3; *see also Craftsman*

St Leonard's Hill 136, 140

Saintsbury, George 37

Salway, Thomas 202

Sandys, Barbara 76, 105, 108, 151–2

Sansom, Martha Fowke 38–40, 43

Sargent, John 155, 167–8, 235

Satirists, The 210–11

Savage, Richard 27–8, 39–40, 49–50, 60, 64–5, 81, 85, 95, 125, 155–7, 161, 166–8, 170, 177, 188–9, 198–9, 209, 294 n. 64; *Of Public Spirit* 155–6, 167; *Savage's Miscellany* 33, 38

Scotland 1–4, 9–10, 35, 50, 98–9, 105, 172

Scott, George Lewis 154

Scott, Mary Jane W. 269

Scott, Sir Walter 157, 160, 192

Scott, William 12–13

Seneca: *Agamemnon* 181–3

Seraphina 136

Sewell, George 199

Seymour, Algernon, Earl of Hertford 62, 135–6, 209

Seymour, Frances, Countess of Herford 57, 61–5, 77, 79, 91, 103, 107, 112, 116–19, 122, 128, 134–6, 140, 191, 193, 198, 204, 209, 211, 214, 217, 254, 268, 275

Shaftesbury, Earl of, *see* Cooper

Shakespeare, William 28, 52, 89, 97, 174, 176–7, 190, 255–6, 278, 280

Shawford 33–4, 42, 65, 78

Shelley, Percy Bysshe 275

Shenstone, William 202, 224, 253–4, 258, 264–5, 275, 278, 317 n. 83; *see also* Leasowes

Sherburn, George 86, 108, 188

Sheridan, Richard Brinsley 198, 244

Sheridan, Thomas 244–5, 280

Shiels, Robert 103, 264; *Life of Thomson* 4–5,

17, 19–20, 25–6, 38, 50, 90, 92–3, 100, 110, 161, 164, 175, 177, 179, 194; *Musidorus* 264, 278
Siddons, Sarah 198
Sidney, Algernon 1, 97, 146
Sidney, Sir Philip 40, 97
Slaughter, Stephen 148, 286
Sloane, Sir Hans 57, 206, 236
Smollett, Tobias 224–5, 236–7, 253, 256, 271, 311 n. 25, 315 n. 9, 317 n. 83; *Peregrine Pickle* 44, 224–5, 281, 311 n. 25
Society for the Encouragement of Learning 151, 154–5, 171
Somerville, Thomas 4, 11, 33
Sophocles 184
Southampton 206
Southdean 2–5, 8–9, 137
Southerne, Thomas: *Oroonoko* 28
Spain 56, 59, 74–5, 104–5, 115–16, 168–9, 174, 200, 202
Spang, Michael Henry 279, 287
Spectator, The 15, 24, 192; *see also* Addison
Spence, Joseph 77, 95–6, 110–13, 115–16, 205; *Anecdotes* 29, 32, 34, 38, 56, 105, 147, 302 n. 18
Spenser, Edmund 86, 161, 171, 234, 264, 274; *Faerie Queene* 257, 264–5, 267, 271–2
Stage Licenser, *see* Lord Chamberlain
Stair, Earl of, *see* Dalrymple, John
Stanhope, Philip Dormer, Earl of Chesterfield 121, 128, 160, 170–1, 234, 252, 261
Stanhope, William, Earl of Harrington 249
Stanley, Elizabeth 206, 229
Stanley, Sarah 57, 206, 258
Steele, Sir Richard 25, 66, 97, 192–3
Stewart, Robert 12–14
Stewart, Walter 61
Stirling, James 46
Strahan, George 66, 68
Stubbes, George 79
Swift, Jonathan 31, 57, 59, 66, 94, 204, 279
Switzerland 106, 112, 116
Symmer, Robert 17, 18, 29, 136, 154, 262, 278

Talbot, Catherine 244
Talbot, Charles, first Baron Talbot 57, 75–6, 105, 121–2, 125, 128–31, 134, 138, 140, 150, 161–3
Talbot, Charles Richard 75, 105, 108–9, 111–13, 115–16, 122–3, 136–7, 141, 147
Talbot, George 304 n. 14
Talbot, William, second Baron Talbot 122, 130–1, 134, 140, 155, 160, 162–3
Talbot, William, Bishop 57

Tardieu, Nicolas Henri 96
Tasso, Torquato 265
Tate, Nahum 255
Tatler, The 15, 24, 66
Taylor, William 165, 171, 179, 199, 207–8, 262, 276
Tell-Tale, The 164–5
Temple, Richard, Viscount Cobham 121, 128, 148, 161, 230, 234
Thompson, William 265
Thomson, Alexander (brother) 2, 304 n. 29
Thomson, Andrew (brother) 2, 304 n. 29
Thomson, Andrew (nephew?) 199, 262
Thomson, Beatrix (mother) 1–2, 6, 11–12, 30
Thomson, David (uncle?) 7
Thomson, Elizabeth, Mrs Bell (sister) 2, 6, 11–12, 151, 172, 206–7, 259
Thomson, Gilbert (nephew?) 199, 262
Thomson, Isobel (sister) 2, 307 n. 37
THOMSON, JAMES
Important events in his life:
  parentage and birth 1–2
  at Jedburgh school 4–5
  earliest poetry 5–8
  at Edinburgh College 8–21
  death of father 11
  first published verse 18–20
  goes to London 21–7
  death of mother 30
  Winter 32–8, 40–4
  at Watts's Academy 44–6
  Summer 47–9, 51–6
  Poem to Newton 57–61
  Spring 63–4, 68–72
  subscription *Seasons*, including *Autumn* and 'Hymn' 65–7, 76–9, 96–103
  Britannia 73–5
  Sophonisba 81–94
  grand tour 106–19
  Secretaryship of the Briefs 125–7, 137–8
  Liberty 132–5, 141–7
  Castle of Indolence 152–3, 211–12, 263–75
  move to Richmond 157–9
  Poem to Talbot 161–3
  pension from the Prince of Wales 170, 261
  Agamemnon 175–85
  Edward and Eleonora 192–8
  Alfred 200–4
  courtship of Elizabeth Young 214–29, 249–50
  revision of *Seasons* 222–4, 229–35, 252
  Surveyor-Generalship of the Leeward Islands 236, 261
  Tancred and Sigismunda 237–47
  Coriolanus 254–7, 279–82
  death 275–8

Thomson, J., (*cont.*):
Characteristics, interests, and art:
allegory and personification 29, 54–5, 64,
74, 101–2, 132–3
ascent of mind 55–6, 58, 99, 141, 268
awkwardness 4, 21, 171, 179, 250, 253
coarseness 11, 18, 28, 63, 167, 209–11,
215, 254
complaisance 26, 207–8, 224, 262
conviviality 62–3, 107, 112, 122, 152–3,
165–6, 168, 188–9, 199, 207–11, 218,
228, 258–9, 302 n. 18; *see also*
freemasonry, *below*
debt, *see* finances, *below*
diction, *see* style, *below*
drinking and eating 62–3, 73, 152–3, 164–
5, 188–9, 208–11, 228, 231, 236, 250,
258–9, 276, 302 n. 18
education 4–5, 8–19
family affection 11–12, 30, 137, 151, 172,
206–7
finances 28–9, 37, 42, 44, 56, 60–1, 65, 68,
76, 78, 91, 104, 108, 126–7, 132, 138,
164–5, 170, 172, 187, 196, 207–8, 211,
222, 235, 250, 252, 261, 279–80
flattery 7–8, 38–9, 50, 111, 117, 149, 225,
271, 316 n. 56
freemasonry 167–8, 235
friends, *see* Aikman, William; Armstrong,
John; Collins, William; Cranstoun, John
and William; Dyer, John; Forbes,
John; Hill, Aaron; Mallet,
David; Mendez, Isaac, Jacob, *and*
Solomon; Millar, Andrew; Mitchell, Sir
Andrew; Murdoch, Patrick; Paterson,
William; Pope, Alexander; Quin,
James; Riccaltoun, Robert; Robertson,
William; Ross, George; Savage,
Richard; Shenstone, William; Smollett,
Tobias; Spence, Joseph; Symmer,
Robert; Warrender, Hugh
Gothic liberty 145–6, 192–3, 196, 203
Greece, ancient 12–13, 15, 82, 133, 144–5,
161, 173, 193, 231
history 2–3, 75, 101, 132–4, 141–3, 238–
9
nature description 2–4, 6, 11, 19, 30, 32–5,
43, 47–8, 54–5, 63, 68–71, 99, 102–3,
114–16, 145, 223, 229–30, 232–3, 261–
2, 272–3
Newtonianism 13–14, 46, 52, 57–9, 76–7
opposition politics 141–2, 160, 168–9,
173–6, 184–5, 188, 195–6, 204, 234–5,
269–70
painting 54, 106, 114, 117, 272
patriotism 31, 48, 53, 59, 71–2, 74–5, 91–
2, 99, 101, 103, 111, 146, 201–3, 255–6

patrons, *see* Baillie, Lady Grizel; Barrington,
Ann, Vicountess; Bennet, Sir
William; Clerk, Sir John; Compton, Sir
Spencer, Earl of Wilmington; Dodington,
George Bubb; Forbes,
Duncan; Frederick Louis, Prince of
Wales; Hamilton, Charles, Lord
Binning; Lyttelton, George,
Baron; Onslow, Arthur; Primrose, Ann,
Viscountess; Rundle, Thomas; Seymour,
Frances, Countess of Hertford; Stanley,
Sarah; Talbot, Charles, Baron *and*
William, Baron
personification, *see* allegory, *above*
philosophic melancholy 32–3, 36, 62, 99,
102, 273
playgoing 28–9, 33, 90, 179
poetic diction, *see* style, *below*
politics, *see* opposition politics, *above, and*
Whiggism, *below*
portraits of 31, 148, 250, 285–7, 305 n. 50
Presbyterian ministry, preparation for 8–9,
14, 19, 22, 26–7, 29
public virtue 49, 53, 84–5, 99, 131, 133,
139, 143, 145, 162, 268, 274
punctuation, *see* style, *below*
religion 1–3, 8–9, 13–15, 18, 20, 35–6,
52, 55–6, 58, 70, 76–7, 101, 118, 123,
141, 194, 197, 229, 255, 257, 278
Rome, ancient 53, 71–2, 82–5, 108, 117–
18, 132–4, 139, 142–3, 145, 231
science 13–14, 46, 51–2, 69–70, 101,
230–1; *see also* Newtonianism, *above*
Scots speech 16, 51, 176, 250, 259–60
sculpture 54, 114–15, 144, 278–9
sentimentality 52, 62–3, 148, 183–4, 191,
193, 203–4; *see also* Young, Elizabeth
solitude 3–4, 29–30, 32–3, 102, 152, 273
style 12, 16, 36–7, 50–1, 86, 88, 98, 103,
134, 147, 180, 265, 271–2
sublimity 2, 19–20, 35, 44, 47–9, 70, 76,
90, 125, 183, 230–1
travel literature 35, 43, 53–4, 75, 97, 101,
231–4, 236
tutorships 26–7, 29, 33–4, 44–6, 65
versification, *see* style, *above*
Whiggism 1, 9, 31, 60, 98, 130, 142, 239–
40, 252
women 8, 10–11, 21, 28, 50, 62–3, 79–80,
136, 148, 173, 182, 206–7, 209–11, 214,
217, 259, 294 n. 68, 298 n. 99; *see also*
Young, Elizabeth
Writings:
Agamemnon 152, 159, 164, 173, 175–87,
191, 196, 202, 213, 236–7, 239, 241,
242–4, 246, 252, 307–8 nn. 46 & 51
Alfred, a Masque 200–6, 213, 237, 248, 264,

317 n. 79

Antient and Modern Italy Compared 132–4, 139, 143, 187; see also *Liberty, a Poem*, below

Autumn 9, 31, 45, 72–3, 76, 78, 84, 96–103, 217, 224, 226, 229–31, 233, 260, 257

Britain 135, 141–2, 146; see also *Liberty, a Poem*, below

Britannia, a Poem 60, 73–6, 78, 87, 91, 103–4, 116, 119–20, 174–5, 196, 205, 234

Castle of Indolence, an Allegorical Poem, The 31, 98, 102, 118, 152–5, 163, 209, 211–12, 221, 231, 241–2, 263–75

'Come, dear Eliza' 218, 227

'Come, gentle God [Power]' 148, 227

Coriolanus 213, 221, 229, 248–50, 252, 254–7, 263, 279–82, 317 n. 79

'Description of ten a-clock' 10–11

Edward and Eleanora 181, 189, 191–200, 213, 228, 236–7, 239, 241, 244, 268, 280

Epilogue to *Tancred and Sigismunda* 244–5

Epitaph on Jacob Mendez 166–7

Epitaph on Miss Stanley 206, 229

'For ever, Fortune' 119, 148, 227–8

'Go, little Book' 257

Greece 132–5, 144, 187; see also *Liberty, a Poem*, below

'Hail to the Day' 225–7

'Happy Man, The' 73, 77, 261

'Happy the Man, who pisses' 95

'Hard is the Fate' 62, 227

'How long Eliza' 219–20

'Hymn on the Seasons, A' 65, 72, 78, 100–1, 103

'Hymn on Solitude' 29–30, 39, 63, 77, 261, 265, 274

'Incomparable Soporifick Doctor, The' 73, 77

Liberty, a Poem 57, 75, 85, 109–11, 114–16, 118, 123, 128, 130, 132–5, 138–9, 141–50, 152, 156–7, 161–2, 168–70, 173, 187, 194, 197, 205, 232, 252, 264–9, 274–5, 279, 286

'Morning in the Country, The' 18

'Nuptial Song, A' 86

'O thou! for whom these Letters speak' 249

'O thou, whose tender serious Eyes' 215–16, 227

'Ode on Aeolus's Harp' 275

'Ode, on the Winter Solstice, An' 260–1, 275

'Of a Country Life' 19, 229

'On the Death of . . . Aikman' 118, 123

'On J. M. S. *Gent*' 95

'On a Lady's . . . feeling his Pulse' 135–6

'On his Mother's Death' 30

'On the Report of a Wooden Bridge' 167, 275

'Paraphrase on . . . St Matthew' 34, 77

Poem to the Memory of . . . Newton, A 57–61, 65, 67, 72, 75–6, 78, 87, 103–4, 155, 169, 187, 268

Poem to the Memory of . . . Talbot, A 129, 162–3, 185, 264

Poems on Several Occasions 206, 317 n. 79

'Poetical Epistle to Sir William Bennet, A' 7–8

Preface to Milton's *Areopagitica* 173–4

Preface to *Winter* 43–4, 49, 72, 82, 125

Prologue to Mallet's *Mustapha* 191

Prologue to *Tancred and Sigismunda* 244

Prospect, The 135, 141–2; see also *Liberty, a Poem*, above

'Psalm 104 Paraphrazed' 19–20

Rome 132–3, 135, 139; see also *Liberty, a Poem*, above

'Rule, Britannia [An Ode]' 53, 99, 101, 201–2, 205, 248

Seasons, The 14, 16, 30, 34, 44, 53–4, 57, 71, 87, 94, 116, 141, 144–6, 148–9, 156–7, 162, 167, 169, 175, 187, 194, 197, 236, 244, 253, 266, 268, 272–3, 279

Seasons, The (1730) 7, 30–1, 57, 65–6, 68, 76–8, 87, 96–105, 119, 163–4, 187

Seasons, The (1744) 144, 206, 213, 221–2, 224, 227, 229–35, 249, 252, 264, 271

Seasons, The (1746) 257

'Smoaker Smoak'd, The' 147

'Snatch me some God' 143

Sophonisba 28, 68, 75–6, 80–95, 109, 128, 143, 163–4, 170, 175, 179, 181–2, 185, 196, 202, 237, 241, 266

Spring 3, 9, 57, 63–72, 76, 78, 81, 96–7, 99, 101, 107, 141, 217–19, 223, 225–7, 229–31, 234, 266–8, 272

Summer 11, 45–8, 51–6, 58, 60, 64, 67, 70, 72, 78, 83, 87, 96–7, 99–103, 144, 157, 206, 224, 227, 231–4, 249

'Sweet Tyrant Love' 136

Tancred and Sigismunda 181, 229, 236–48, 256, 267, 280–1, 313 n. 63

'To Miss Young' 227

'To . . . Mr Murdoch' 172–3

'To . . . the Prince of Wales, an Ode' 168–9

'To Retirement, an Ode' 135

'Unless with my Amanda' 148, 227

'Upon Beauty' 10

'Upon Elizabeth Bennet' 8, 10

'Upon Happiness' 18

'Upon the Hoop' 10–11

'Upon Marle-feild' 8

'Why not all faults' 50

Winter 3–6, 14, 17, 23, 32–8, 40–4, 47,

Thomson J., Writings (*cont.*):
  49–54, 56, 60–2, 67–8, 70, 72, 77–8, 82,
  84, 87–8, 96–7, 99–102, 104, 109, 141,
  206, 224, 231–2, 235, 266–7, 277
  Works (1738) 187, 224
  Works (1750) 64, 98, 317 n. 79
  Works (1762) 278, 285–6
  'Works and Wonders of Almighty
    Power' 20, 38
  'Yeilding Maid, The' 18
projected, unwritten works:
  'Blenheim' 77
  'Essay on Descriptive Poetry' 65, 78
  'Socrates' 62, 152, 221–2
  'Timoleon' 109

Thomson, Jean, Mrs Robert Thomson
  (sister) 2, 6, 11–12, 151, 172, 207, 259,
  279–80, 292 n. 98, 304 n. 29
Thomson, John (brother) 2, 11–12, 22, 30,
  137–8, 140–1, 304 nn. 21 & 29
Thomson, Margaret (sister) 2, 307 n. 37
Thomson, Mary, Mrs Craig (sister) 2, 6, 11–
  12, 172, 277–80, 307 n. 37
Thomson, Mary (supposed wife) 298 n. 99
Thomson, Robert (brother in law) 279
Thomson, Thomas (father) 1–2, 6, 11
Tickell, Thomas 64, 222
Tillotson, Geoffrey 36–7
Tindal, Matthew 197
Tompson, John 252
Trissino, Gian Giorgio 82, 150
Turnbull, George 155, 306 n. 67
Turner, J.M.W. 234
Tweeddale, Marquis of, *see* Hay
Twickenham 122–3, 139, 150, 158–9
Tyrconnel, Viscount, *see* Brownlow

Union of England and Scotland 3, 7, 9, 15, 53,
  71, 99, 101, 160, 269
Upton, John 86, 107, 265

Vanbrugh, Sir John 64, 124
Vanderbank, John 31, 285
Vaucluse, 110, 112, 254
Venice 110, 113
Vernon, Edward, Admiral 200, 262
Vernon, James 172
Victor, Benjamin 37–8, 86, 179–80, 191,

  239–40, 245–6, 249, 256, 313 n. 63
Virgil 36, 62, 161; *Eclogues* 282; *Georgics* 53,
  72, 98, 142, 261, 268
Voltaire 64–5, 110–11, 124, 150,
  166; *Socrate* 65, 221–2, 303
  n. 50; *Zaire* 110, 123–4, 150, 192

Wales, Prince of, *see* Frederick Louis
Wales, Princess of, *see* Augusta
Walpole, Horace 155, 163, 176, 213, 244
Walpole, Sir Robert 17, 31, 41, 49, 56–7,
  59–60, 65, 74–6, 96, 103, 105, 116, 119–
  21, 125, 128–32, 152, 158–60, 162, 168,
  170, 173, 183–4, 186, 191, 200, 204, 213,
  239, 269
Warburton, William, Bishop 252, 307 n. 22
Ward, Edward 24
Warner, Thomas 73
Warrender, Sir George 8
Warrender, Hugh 8, 154–5, 210, 262
Warton, Joseph 54, 56, 68, 77, 85, 107, 146,
  183, 209, 253, 269, 273
Warton, Thomas 253, 305 n. 56
Wasserman, Earl 275
Watts's Academy 44–6, 57, 65
Welsted, Leonard 95, 132
Wesley, John 198
West, Gilbert 148, 171, 229, 257, 261, 265,
  286
West Indies 174, 253, 261
White, Gilbert 68
Whitehall Evening-Post 67, 81
Wideopen [Widehope] 1, 7, 11, 33
Wilks, Robert 28, 86, 89, 92
William III 1, 12, 109, 120, 146, 201
Wilmington, Earl of, *see* Compton
Wodrow, Robert: *Analecta* 13–15, 61
Woffington, Margaret 242, 280–1
Wordsworth, William 69, 71, 102–3, 234

Yorke, Phillip, Earl of Hardwicke 125, 161–2,
  279
Young, Edward 38, 56, 60–1, 64, 73, 77, 94,
  125, 132, 204, 229
Young, Elizabeth 136, 148, 214–29, 234, 242,
  249–51, 260, 270, 276
Young, Mary, *see* Robertson, Mary
Young, Mrs (Elizabeth Y's mother) 217, 234,
  242, 250